Autodesk Official Training Guide

Essentials

Autodesk® Revit®

Architecture 2010

Learning Autodesk® Revit® Architecture 2010

Hands-on exercises guide new users through the concepts of building information modeling and tools for parametric building design and documentation.

Autodesk Certification Preparation

Autodesk®

Autodesk®

Published by: Autodesk, Inc.
111 McInnis Parkway
San Rafael, CA 94903, USA

Acknowledgements

The Autodesk Learning team wishes to thank everyone who participated in the development of this project, with special acknowledgement to the authoring contributions and subject matter expertise of Lay Christopher (Chris) Fox.

Chris has been using Autodesk projects since 1989. He has worked in architectural and engineering drafting and design since that time. He has written about AutoCAD and Architectural Desktop, and began writing about Autodesk Revit in 2001. He has written or co-written a number of books on Revit Architecture, **including Introducing and Implementing Revit Architecture**, published by Autodesk Press. He has authored Autodesk Official Training Courseware for Revit Architecture and Revit Structure. He currently leads Revit training courses and implementation efforts in Australia.

Cover Image
Cover courtesy of ONL [Oosterhuis_Lénárd]

Sr. Graphic Designer
Luke Pauw

Sr. Graphic/Production Designer
Diane Erlich

Special thanks go out to:

Willem Knibbe, Paul Mailhot, Jamie Morin, Sara Tolchin, and Barbara Vezos.

Table of Contents

Chapter 04

Chapter 05

Chapter 06

Chapter 07

Chapter 08

Chapter 09

Chapter 10

Chapter 11

Introduction

Welcome to the *Learning Autodesk Revit Architecture 2010* Autodesk Official Training Guide, a training guide for use in Authorized Training Center (ATC®) locations, corporate training settings, and other classroom settings.

Although this guide is designed for instructor-led courses, you can also use it for self-paced learning. The guide encourages self-learning through the use of the Autodesk® Revit® Architecture 2010 Help system.

This introduction covers the following topics:

- Course objectives
- Prerequisites
- Using this guide
- Completing the Exercises
- Installing the Excersise Data Files
- Imperial and metric datasets
- Notes, tips, and warnings
- Feedback

This guide is complementary to the software documentation. For detailed explanations of features and functionality, refer to the Help in the software.

Course Objectives

After completing this course, you will be able to:

- Describe building information modeling, bidirectional associativity, and parametric relationships in Revit.

- Understand the user interface, parametric objects, and families, and start projects using templates.

- Create and modify levels and grids.

- Create a basic floor plan, add and modify walls and compound walls, use editing tools, and work with doors and windows.

- Work with component families.

- Duplicate and manage views, control object visibility in views, and create elevation, section, and 3D views.

- Learn how to use dimensions and constraints.

- Create floors and ceilings, add roofs and curtain walls, and work with stairs and railings in a building model.

- Learn how to create callout views and work with text and tags, detail views, and drafting views.

- Create schedules, rooms and room schedules, and legends and keynotes.

- Work with drawing sheets and titleblocks, manage revisions, and present the building model using rendering, walkthroughs, and sun and shadow settings.

Prerequisites

This guide is designed for new users of Revit Architecture. No previous CAD experience is necessary.

It is recommended that you have:

- Architectural design, drafting, or engineering experience.

- Microsoft® Windows® 2000, Microsoft® Windows® XP, or Microsoft® Windows® Vista.

Using This Guide

The lessons are independent of each other. However, it is recommended that you complete these lessons in the order that they are presented unless you are familiar with the concepts and functionality described in those lessons.

Each chapter contains:

- **Lessons**
  Usually two or more lessons in each chapter.

- **Exercises**
  Practical, real-world examples for you to practice using the functionality you have just learned. Each exercise contains step-by-step procedures and graphics to help you complete the exercise successfully.

Completing the Exercises

You can complete the exercise in two ways, using the book or on screen.

- **Using the book**
  Follow the step-by-step exercises in the book.

- **On screen**
  Click the Learning Autodesk Revit Architecture 2010 icon on your desktop, and follow the step-by-step exercises on screen. The onscreen exercises are the same as those in the book. The onscreen version has the advantage that you can concentrate on the screen without having to glance down at your book.

After launching the onscreen exercises, you might need to alter the size of your application window to align both windows.

Installing the Exercise Data Files

To complete the exercises in this guide, you must download the data files from the following location and install them on your system.

1. Download the zip file from *www.sybex.com/go/learningrevitarchitecture2010*.
2. Unzip the file *Setup.exe*.
3. Double-click *Setup.exe* and follow the onscreen instructions to install the files.
4. After the install is complete, you can delete *Setup.exe* from your system (optional).

Unless you specify a different folder, the exercise files are installed in the following folder:

C:\Autodesk Learning\Autodesk Revit Architecture 2010\Learning.

After you install the data, this folder contains all the files necessary to complete each exercise in this guide.

Imperial and Metric Datasets

In exercises that specify units of measurement, alternative files are provided as shown in the following example:

- Open *i_export_ifc.rvt* (imperial) or *m_export_ifc.rvt* (metric).

In the exercise steps, the imperial value is followed by the metric value in parentheses as shown in the following example:

- For Length, enter **13'2"** (**4038** mm).

For exercises with no specific units of measurement, files are provided as shown in the following example:

- Open *c_boundary_conditions.rvt* (common).

In the exercise steps, the unitless value is specified as shown in the following example:

- For Length, enter **400**.

Notes, Tips, and Warnings

Throughout this guide, notes, tips, and warnings are called out for special attention.

 Notes contain guidelines, constraints, and other explanatory information.

 Tips provide information to enhance your productivity.

 Warnings provide information about actions that might result in the loss of data, system failures, or other serious consequences.

Feedback

We always welcome feedback on Autodesk Official Training Guides. After completing this course, if you have suggestions for improvements or if you want to report an error in the book or with the downloaded files, please send your comments to *learningtools@autodesk.com*.

Chapter 01
Building Information Modeling for Architectural Design

Building information modeling (BIM) is an integrated workflow built on coordinated, reliable information about a project from design through construction and into operations. The Revit® platform is purpose-built software for building information modeling.

Building information modeling (BIM) makes sustainable design practices easier by enabling architects and engineers to more accurately visualize, simulate, and analyze building performance earlier in the design process. Revit Architecture is interoperable with Autodesk Ecotect™ Analysis.

Objectives

After completing this chapter, you will be able to:

- Describe building information modeling methodology.

Lesson 01 | Building Information Modeling for Architectural Design

This lesson describes building information modeling (BIM) for architectural design.

Applying building information modeling helps in designing and delivering innovative projects faster and more economically.

BIM enables architects and engineers to use digital design information to visualize, simulate, and analyze their projects' real-world appearance, performance, and cost. BIM also enables architects and engineers to document the design more accurately. The consistent, coordinated information inherent in the BIM process helps in developing and evaluating multiple alternatives at the same time and enables easy comparison and better decisions related to sustainable design.

Image Courtesy of DDB Architectural International Ltd.

Objectives

After completing this lesson, you will be able to:

- Describe building information modeling.

- Describe bidirectional associativity.

About Building Information Modeling

Building information modeling is a building design and documentation process. It enables you to create and manage information about a building project, using the information about the building project which is stored in a 3D model. More importantly, the intelligent data inherent in the building model allows you to experience your design before it is real, simulate and visualize design alternatives, analyze performance, and make better informed design decisions earlier in the process.

The building industry has traditionally illustrated building projects with manually created drawings. Information was added to these drawings by using notes and specifications. With the advent of CAD technology, this process was made faster and easier; however, the output of manual drafting, graphics CAD systems, and object-oriented CAD systems remained the same: a graphic abstraction of an intended building design.

The development of the building information modeling methodology has turned this relationship around. Building information modeling software captures information about a building and then presents that information as 2D and 3D views, schedules, or in other required formats.

Architects and engineers can use digital design information to analyze and understand how their projects will perform before they are built. Developing and evaluating multiple alternatives simultaneously enables easy comparison and informs better sustainable design decisions. Building information modeling is core to Autodesk's sustainable design approach for building performance analysis and simulation.

Definition of Building Information Modeling

Building information modeling is an integrated process for exploring a project's key physical and functional characteristics digitally—before it is built. Autodesk® provides a comprehensive portfolio of BIM solutions, which assist customers in delivering projects faster and more economically, while minimizing environmental impact.

Coordinated, consistent information is used throughout the BIM process to:

- Design innovative projects and conduct analysis from the earliest stages

- Better visualize and simulate real-world appearance, performance, and cost

- Document more accurately

The Autodesk BIM solution is based on coordinated, data-rich models created with Autodesk® Revit®- based products and AutoCAD® Civil 3D® software. Complementing these core BIM products is a broad portfolio of applications further delivering on the power of BIM, including AutoCAD® software for documentation and conceptual 3D design and AutoCAD LT® software for professional drafting.

Revit and Building Information Modeling

Revit Architecture is purpose-built software for building information modeling.

Traditional drafting and CAD software represent the geometry of a design by using stylized symbols from designated illustrations. Some examples of these illustrations may be a series of plans, elevations, and sections. These illustrations are essentially independent of one another.

Building information modeling software represents the design as a series of intelligent objects and elements such as walls, windows, and views. These objects and elements have parametric attributes. The information about these objects and elements is stored in a single building model. You can extract any number of different views of the data from the model.

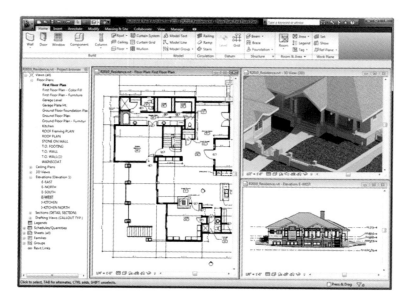

The Revit platform is a building design and documentation system that supports the design, documentation, and even construction efforts required for a building project. Because of its parametric change technology, any change you make is automatically coordinated everywhere in your project, including model views, drawing sheets, schedules, sections, and plans.

Building Information Tailored to the User

In building information modeling software, the building information is stored in a single building model instead of in a format predicated on a presentation format, such as a drawing file or a spreadsheet. The building information model presents information for editing and review in views and formats that are appropriate for and familiar to the user. Some examples of these formats are a 2D elevation, a 3D perspective, or a schedule.

Architects, for example, work on the information in the building model by using the conventions of the highly stylized, symbolic, and graphic language of building design. They may enter and review information in a format similar to architectural drawings, such as plans, sections, and elevations. Structural engineers work with the same data presented graphically in the form of framing and bracing diagrams. Therefore, the structural engineers' interface to data or the MEP engineers' is quite different from the architects' interface to data; however, the data is the same.

Managing Change with Building Information Modeling

Building information modeling solutions manage iterative changes in a building model throughout the design, construction, and operation phases. A change to any part of the building model is replicated in all other associated parts.

Maintaining a single, internally consistent representation of the building can improve drawing coordination and reduce the number of errors in documents. You can invest the time that you would otherwise spend manually checking and coordinating documents in improving the building designs. As a result, construction documents can be of better quality and the costs of changes and coordination can be reduced. Building information modeling tools can enable the design, construction, and occupancy of the building to proceed with less friction and fewer difficulties than conventional tools.

Capturing and Reusing Information

Building information modeling solutions capture and preserve information for reuse by third party industry-specific applications. Data is captured once as close as possible to its point of origin and stored so that it is available and can be presented whenever required.

For example, consider a personal financial management software application that captures information from your checkbook register as you write checks and make deposits. It stores and manages that information for a variety of purposes, such as to prepare your income tax return and to create a statement of your net worth. Building information modeling leverages data in a similar manner.

Characteristics of Revit Architecture for Building Information Modeling

Work the way architects and designers think about buildings:

- Enjoy a more intuitive process with software that mirrors the real world.

- The building information model contains essential information about a project, so as you design, Revit software automatically creates accurate floor plans, elevations, sections, and 3D views, as well as area calculations, schedules, and quantity takeoffs.

- Gain better design insight through in-process visualization and analysis.

Capture early design thinking to better support design, documentation, and construction:

- Enhance conceptual building design efforts to gain better design insight earlier in the process.

- Support smarter, more sustainable design through the analysis of materials, quantities, sun position, and solar effects. Exchange building information with partner applications to perform energy analysis and better predict building performance.

- Provide essential BIM data for use in clash detection, construction analysis, and fabrication.

Improve your business through better-coordinated, higher-quality project work:

- Accelerate decision making and shorten production time.

- Minimize coordination mistakes and rework with fully parametric change management.

- Gain a competitive advantage with increased client satisfaction and greater profitability through more efficient project delivery.

Analyzing a Design in the Context of BIM

Revit-based design models can be exported using the gbXML schema and imported directly into Autodesk Ecotect Analysis for simulation and analysis during the early conceptual design phase. At the onset of the design process, Autodesk Revit Architecture massing models can be used in combination with site analysis functionality in Autodesk Ecotect Analysis to determine the optimal location, shape, and orientation of a building design. This is based on fundamental environmental factors, such as daylight, overshadowing, solar access, and visual impact.

As the conceptual design evolves, energy, water, and carbon analysis can be conducted using integrated access to Autodesk® Green Building Studio® web-based technology in order to benchmark its energy use and recommend areas of potential savings. After these fundamental design parameters have been established, Autodesk Ecotect Analysis can be used again to rearrange rooms and zones, size and shape apertures, design custom shading devices, or choose specific materials—based on environmental factors such as daylight availability, glare protection, outside views, and acoustic comfort.

Autodesk Ecotect Analysis can also be used for detailed design analysis. For example, the visibility analysis displayed in the following illustration shows the amount and quality of views to the outside mapped over the floor area of an office.

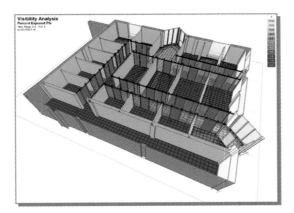

The consistent, computable data obtained from Autodesk Revit Architecture or Autodesk Revit MEP, combined with the breadth of performance analysis and meaningful feedback of Autodesk Ecotect Analysis, help reduce the cost and time required to perform energy modeling and analysis. The feedback from these analyses helps architects and other users to optimize the energy efficiency of their designs and work toward carbon neutrality early in the design process. The analyses are a key ingredient not only for incorporating energy efficiency into standard building design practices but also for mitigating the carbon footprint of the current built environment.

Example of Building Information Modeling

During the design of a building, if there is any change in the load conditions on the floor area, you may need to modify the design parameters of the structural system. Modifications could include an increase in the depth of beams or a change in beam profiles. A change in beam profiles may result in a change in the geometric parameters of these members in a 3D view. This change would also be reflected in plan and section views. Therefore, building information modeling ensures an effective interaction between the design and its representation.

About Bidirectional Associativity

A key feature of Revit is bidirectional associativity, which ensures that changes to any part of the design are immediately reflected in all associated parts.

Definition of Bidirectional Associativity

Bidirectional associativity is the ability of the building information model to coordinate changes made in any view and propagate these changes out to all other views. Bidirectional associativity is applied automatically to every component, view, and annotation. For example, a change in the position of a wall is reflected in all elements such as windows, doors, ceilings, and electrical outlets; all of which are associated with the wall and influenced by the change in the location of the wall. These elements are also affected by the constraints and alignments that have been established for the wall. Revit helps ensure that building sections and elevations are immediately available, up-to-date, and accurate.

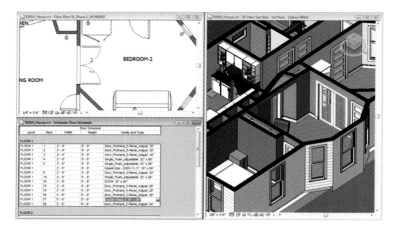

Parametric Relationships

The term parametric refers to the relationships among the elements of a building model. These relationships enable the software to coordinate and manage the changes made to the building model. The relationships are created either automatically by the software or by you. In mathematics and mechanical CAD, the numbers or characteristics that define these relationships are called parameters; therefore, the operation of the software is called parametric. It is these parametric relationships that deliver fundamental coordination and productivity benefits provided by the building information modeling methodology.

Updating the Building Model

A fundamental characteristic of building information modeling software is the ability to coordinate changes and maintain consistency. You do not have to intervene to update drawings or links. When you change something, the bidirectional associativity feature of the software determines the elements that are affected by the change and propagates that change to any affected elements.

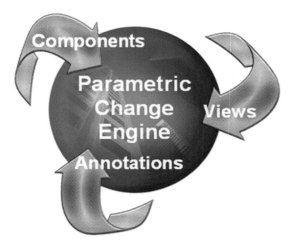

Examples of Bidirectional Associativity

- Flip a section line and all views update.

- Draw a wall in plan and it appears in all other views including material takeoffs.

- Change a door or a window type in a schedule and the change propagates throughout the graphical and nongraphical views.

Examples of Parametric Relationships

- A floor is attached to the enclosing walls. When a wall moves, the floor updates to remain connected to the walls.

- A series of equidistant windows have been placed along a wall. When the length of the wall changes, the windows redistribute to remain equidistant across the length of the wall.

- A relationship has been established between a column and a HVAC duct system to ensure that a design requirement or code requirement is maintained. When the column is moved, the duct system moves with it.

Chapter 02
Revit Architecture Basics

Before you begin to use Revit Architecture, you need to become familiar with the interface, the types of objects you will be using to create your designs, and basic project templates.

Objectives

After completing this chapter, you will be able to:

- Describe the Revit Architecture user interface.

- Work with different types of Revit elements and families.

- Start a new project with different templates.

Lesson 02 | Exploring the User Interface

This lesson describes how to use the different parts of the Autodesk® Revit® Architecture user interface. You begin the lesson by learning about the main user interface. Then, you learn about the ribbon tabs and some recommended practices for using the user interface. The lesson concludes with an exercise on exploring the user interface.

Revit Architecture provides a friendly user interface where tools and options are available on the ribbon. In addition, context menus provide quick access to commonly used tools. The status bar provides information and tips that assist you while you work. Familiarity with the user interface helps you work with the software more efficiently.

Revit Architecture user interface with a project file open

Objectives

After completing this lesson, you will be able to:

- Identify the different parts of the Revit Architecture user interface.

- Describe the Revit Architecture ribbon framework.

- State the recommended practices for using the user interface.

- Explore the Revit Architecture user interface.

The Revit Architecture User Interface

Revit Architecture is a powerful application that uses the building information modeling methodology and runs on the Microsoft Windows operating system. Like most Windows applications, the user interface of Revit Architecture features a ribbon with tabs and panels, toolbars, and dialog boxes that you can use to perform various tasks. You use the mouse to select buttons from the panels or toolbars to perform operations.

Recent Files Window

Every time you launch Revit Architecture, a startup window named Recent Files is displayed. This window provides links to recently opened project or family files.

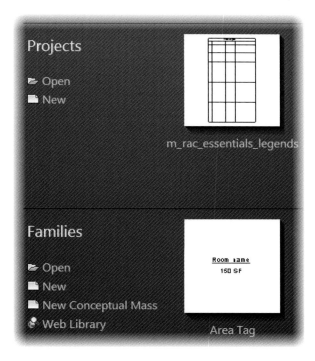

Recent Files window

Identifying the Primary User Interface Elements

The following illustration shows the ribbon in Revit with different tabs, panels, and buttons.

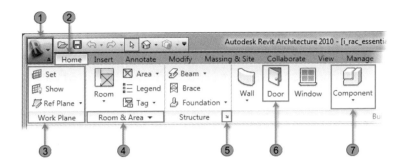

Application Button	Opens the application menu that provides access to common tools, such as Save, Print, and Publish.
Tab	Contains tools, settings, and standard functions. Only one tab can be active at a time and the active tab is on top.
Panel	Groups buttons for similar functions and tools.
Expanded Panel	Expands a panel to display available actions and is indicated by an arrow next to the panel name. You can temporarily pin an open expanded panel.
Dialog Launcher	Opens a dialog box.
Button	Starts a tool or operation.
Split Button	Opens a drop-down with actions for the particular tool.

The following illustration shows the Project Browser, status bar, View Control Bar, and other elements of the Revit Architecture user interface.

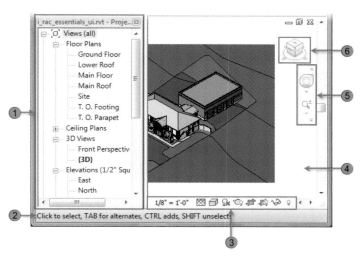

①	**Project Browser**	Displays a tree view of a logical hierarchy for all views, schedules, sheets, and families in the current project.
②	**Status Bar**	Displays the name of the family and element type when you position the cursor over an object. Displays tips or hints when you use a comment.
③	**View Control Bar**	Provides shortcuts to commonly used view commands, such as View Scale and Model Graphics Style.
④	**View Window**	Displays the view that you have selected in the Project Browser. Views can be tiled or maximized to fill the entire view window.
⑤	**Navigation Bar**	Displays Zoom controls and opens the Steering Wheels.
⑤	**View Cube**	Works as an orientation control for 3D views.

Application Menu

The application menu provides access to many common file actions. You can also access advanced options, such as Export and Publish, to manage files.

Application menu

Quick Access Toolbar

The Quick Access toolbar displays the commonly-used actions, such as undo and redo changes, which you can use on files. You can customize the default Quick Access toolbar by adding tools from the ribbon.

Quick Access toolbar

InfoCenter Toolbar

You use the InfoCenter toolbar to search for information through keywords and access subscription services and product-related updates. You can also access topics in Help.

InfoCenter toolbar

Context Menus

Context menus are displayed when you right-click an object or an area of the user interface. They list common options, such as Zoom, and other options related to the current task. For example, if you place a door in a drawing, select it, and then right-click it, the context menu displays options such as Flip Hand or Flip Facing.

The Ribbon Framework

The ribbon is displayed at the top of the application window. You use the ribbon to access tools and options that help you design a building project.

You can customize the ribbon by changing its view state and by rearranging the panels that contain the tools. You can toggle between the ribbon view states by using the control to the right of the Manage tab.

The following illustrations show the various ribbon view states.

Full ribbon

Ribbon minimized to tab and panel labels

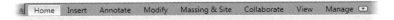

Ribbon minimized to tab labels

Ribbon Tabs

The ribbon displays eight tabs and all tools in Revit are available on these tabs. You make a tab active by clicking its name. Each tab consists of panels of grouped tools.

The following illustration shows the various ribbon tabs.

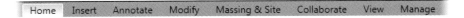

The following table lists the tools and options that you can access on the eight ribbon tabs in Revit Architecture.

Tab	Tools and Options
Home	Includes commonly used tools for placing building elements such as wall, door, window, stair, ramp, beam, and brace. This tab also includes tools grouped by Room and Area, Datum, Work Plane, and Model.
Insert	Includes tools for linking and importing files, loading family files, and seeking content online.
Annotate	Includes tools for placing dimensions, detailing, drafting, text, tags, and keynotes.
Modify	Includes tools for editing objects, geometry, linework, and faces. This tab also includes copy and paste tools using the clipboard, inquiry tools, and phasing tools.
Massing & Site	Includes tools for creating conceptual massing studies and creating and modifying landforms.
Collaborate	Includes tools for collaboration with internal and external team members. This tab also includes tools for workset creation, workset management, and coordination.

Tab	Tools and Options
View	Includes tools for controlling graphic appearance of objects, creating views, and adding sheets. This tab also includes options for toggling between views and displaying user interface toolbars.
Manage	Includes tools grouped by Project Settings, Project Location, and Macros. This tab also includes options for managing projects and design.

Contextual Tabs

When you start a tool or select elements, a contextual tab opens on the ribbon displaying a set of tools that relate only to the context of that tool or element.

The Type Selector drop-down and the Element Properties drop-down are available on the contextual tabs. Additional tools are also displayed on the contextual tab for working with the element that you are placing or modifying. The Options Bar appears under the contextual tab.

The following illustration shows the Place Wall contextual tab that opens when you activate the Wall tool.

① **Element Properties drop-down**

Provides the options to open either the Instance Properties or the Type Properties dialog box. Using these dialog boxes, you can change the properties of either an individual instance of a family type or all the instances of a family type.

② **Type Selector drop-down**

Allows you to change from one type of element to another. The contents of the drop-down change depending on the current tool or selected elements.

③ **Options Bar**

Displays options for configuring elements you create or modify. The options change depending on the current tool or selected elements.

Guidelines for Using the User Interface

User interface elements such as the ribbon, Options Bar, and Project Browser help you to work efficiently. The following guidelines help you to work with the user interface.

Guidelines

- Use the cursor tooltip to view keyboard shortcut commands for tools. The cursor tooltip displays when you hold it over a button on the ribbon. Instead of a command line in Revit, you can enter keyboard shortcut commands to access tools. For example, enter **VG** to open the Visibility/Graphics dialog box.

- Control tooltip appearance by using the Options dialog box. This helps you view the appropriate information for your experience level.

- While working with a tool, when no other action is active, the Modify action is active by default. To end a tool or operation quickly, press ESC twice to revert to the Modify status.

- Use the Options Bar to select command-specific tools such as setting wall height while you are placing walls. This is quicker than selecting and changing walls later.

- Use the Project Browser to create, delete, change, or switch between views. This helps you quickly manage the views in a project.

- Read the hints and tips displayed on the status bar while working. These provide valuable information about using the tools.

- Hide the Project Browser while working on big drawings so as to expand the view window and display a larger part of the drawing. You can also toggle the ribbon display to enlarge your view on small screens.

Exercise | Explore the Revit Architecture User Interface

In this exercise, you explore the different parts of the user interface.

Your firm is standardizing on Revit Architecture. You need to learn the user interface before you start work on a project.

You do the following:

- Explore views of a model.

- Explore model properties using the interface.

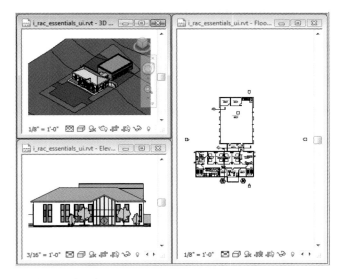

The completed exercise

Completing the Exercise: *To complete the exercise, follow the steps in this book or in the onscreen exercise. In the onscreen list of chapters and exercises, click Chapter 2: Revit Architecture Basics. Click Exercise: Explore the Revit Architecture User Interface.*

Explore Views of a Model

1   Open *i_rac_essentials_ui.rvt* or *m_rac_essentials_ui.rvt*. The file opens in the default 3D view of a completed project.

Note: *The illustrations in the exercise may vary depending on how you navigate in the project. In addition, the illustrations for the metric dataset will be slightly different from those shown here.*

2   Examine the tab names on the ribbon.

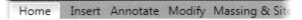

Home   Insert   Annotate   Modify   Massing & Site

3   Click each tab and examine the panels that they contain. Notice the organization of these tabs and where different tools and options are found.

4   On the InfoCenter toolbar at the upper-right corner of the screen, expand the drop-down for Help, as shown below.

Help   F1

User Interface Overview
Tutorials
Skill Builders
Families Guide
Documents on the Web
Where Is My Command?
New Features Workshop

Additional Resources

Customer Involvement Program

About

5   Press F1 to open the Revit Architecture User's Guide window. Ensure that the Contents tab is active.

Become familiar with this help system. You can continually utilize this system throughout your learning process and beyond.

6   Close the Revit Architecture User's Guide window.

7   Examine the Project Browser. It lists all the views associated with the building model. Notice that the default 3D view is bold, indicating it is the active view.

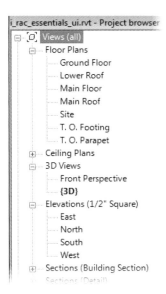

The Project Browser always contains all the views of a model and is used to navigate between the views. You can easily create and name new views as required in your design process.

8   To examine the different views available in this model, in the Project Browser:

- Under Views (All), Floor Plans, double-click Ground Floor. This activates the view.
- Activate other floor plan views.
- Activate the elevation views.

9   In the Project Browser:

- Expand the Sections (Building Sections) and Sections (Detail) branches.
- Ensure that the Schedules/Quantities branch is expanded.
- Activate the Door Schedule and Room Schedule views.
  Note: *You will not be working with the Families or Groups views in this exercise.*

10   Return to the default 3D view.

11   Right-click anywhere in the view window. Notice the context menu for this 3D view and click View Properties.

12 In the Instance Properties dialog box, for Visibility/Graphics Overrides, click Edit in the Value field.

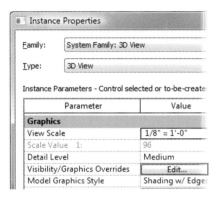

13 In the Visibility/Graphic Overrides dialog box, notice the visibility settings for this view.

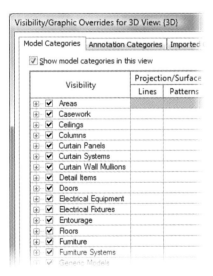

14 Click Cancel in both the dialog boxes.

15 In the view window, place the cursor over the large pitched roof. The edges will highlight and a tooltip and the status bar display information about the roof.

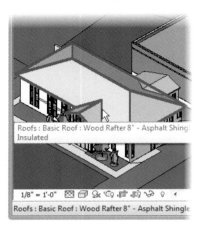

16 Click to select the pitched roof. The selected roof displays in blue. A contextual tab named Modify Roofs opens on the ribbon. Notice the tools available on this tab.

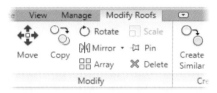

17 Right-click the selected roof. Click Elements Properties to open the Instance Properties dialog box.

18 In the Instance Properties dialog box:

- Notice the properties of the roof.

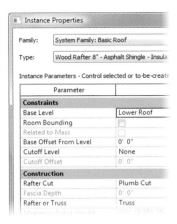

- Click Cancel to close the dialog box.

19 Examine the View Control Bar at the bottom of the application window. Move the cursor over the tools on the View Control Bar and view the tooltips.

20 Click View tab > Windows panel > Close Hidden. This closes the different views you opened while exploring the model using the Project Browser.

Explore Model Properties Using the Interface

1 In the Project Browser, under Views (All), Floor Plans, double-click Main Floor to open the view.

2   To zoom in to examine a portion of the view at close range:

- On the Navigation Bar at the right of the view window, click the drop-down arrow under the Zoom tool.
- Ensure that Zoom in Region is selected.

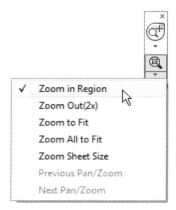

3   Click and drag a selection box around the lower half of the building to zoom in to that area.

Note: *If your mouse is equipped with a scroll wheel, you can scroll in and out in any view. Hold down the scroll wheel and you can pan side to side.*

4   In the lower-left room, move the cursor over a chair to highlight it. The chair type is displayed in the tooltip and on the status bar.

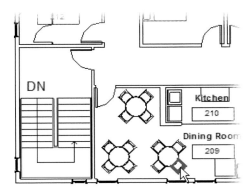

5   In the lower-left room:

- Move the cursor over the wall below the chair to highlight the wall.
- Click to select the wall. The color of the wall changes to blue indicating the selection. The wall type is displayed in the Type Selector drop-down on the Modify Walls tab.

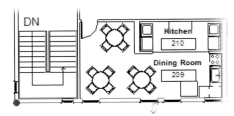

6   Click Modify Walls tab > Element panel > Element Properties drop-down > Instance Properties
to open the Instance Properties dialog box for the selected wall.

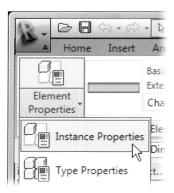

7   In the Instance Properties dialog box:

- Notice the wall properties. If you change these properties, only the selected wall
properties change.

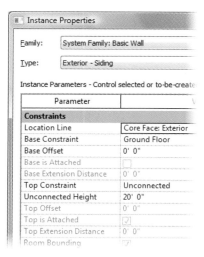

- Click Cancel to close the dialog box.

8   Examine the panels on the Modify Walls tab. Notice that the tab displays tools for modifying the selected wall.

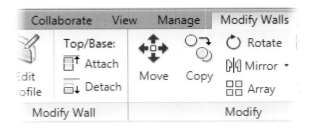

9   Click Home tab > Build panel > Wall. A contextual tab named Place Wall opens. Notice that the Options Bar below the ribbon displays options such as Location Line, Chain, and Offset for sketching or placing new walls.

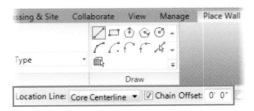

10 Click Place Wall tab > Selection panel > Modify to exit the Wall tool.

11 Click the Annotate tab. Notice the tools that are available on this tab.

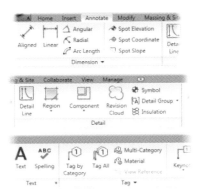

12   In the view window, select the southern exterior wall as selected previously.

13   Open the South elevation view. Notice that the wall remains selected.

Note: *Do not clear the wall selection. Reselect it in this view if you cleared it accidentally.*

14   Open the default 3D view.

15   In the view window:
   • Zoom in to the view and notice that the wall is still selected.
   • Clear the selection by clicking away from the wall.

16   On the View Control Bar:
   • Click Model Graphics Style to open the associated list.
   • Click Wireframe to change the view to wireframe.

   • Apply the other model graphic styles.

17   Return to the Shading with Edges style.

18   Click View tab > Windows panel > Tile to display all the views that you have opened.

19 On the Navigation Bar in the active view:

- Click the Zoom drop-down.
- Click Zoom All to Fit. Notice that each view is zoomed to fit within its tiled window.

20 Close the file without saving changes.

Lesson 03 | Working with Revit Elements and Families

This lesson describes how to work with different types of Revit elements and families. You begin the lesson by learning about building elements and families. Then, you learn about the recommended practices for working with elements and families. The lesson concludes with an exercise on Revit elements and families.

You create a building model by adding elements to it. These elements represent the different parts of a building, such as windows and doors. Revit provides collections of similar types of elements, called families. For example, a building model has different types of windows, such as fixed and opening, which can be of different sizes. The fixed windows of different sizes can form a single family. You can create custom building element families and modify them without additional programming.

In the following illustration, the highlighted windows are of two different types but belong to a single family. Similarly, the highlighted table and chair belong to different furniture families.

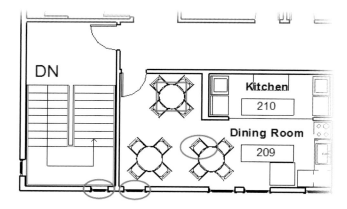

Objectives

After completing this lesson, you will be able to:

- Describe the different types of building elements.

- Describe families.

- State the recommended practices for working with Revit elements and families.

- Work with Revit elements and families.

About Building Elements

You use building elements, such as walls, doors, roofs, and windows, to create a building design. You can place, create, and modify building elements.

Definition of Building Elements

Revit building elements are the building blocks of a project and you add them when you are developing the project. When you place an element in a model, the individual element is called an instance of that element type. Elements can be broadly classified into three classes: Model, Annotation, and View.

The following table briefly describes each element class.

Element Class	Description
Model	Elements such as walls, windows, doors, and roofs that are used for the 3D representation of building design. Model elements have a specific location in the building.
Annotation	Elements such as dimensions, tags, and elevation symbols that add supplementary information required to document building design. Annotation elements have a specific location on a view. Annotations also include datum elements such as levels, grids, and reference planes that establish a context for project objects.
View	Elements such as plans, elevations, sections, 3D perspectives, and schedules that dynamically represent the parts of a building model. Changes made to part of the model in one view are automatically updated in all views that contain this part. Views have their own properties that can be modified or deleted. View elements also control the annotation elements placed in a view. If you delete a view, the annotations placed on the view are also deleted. View elements do not control model elements but determine how model and annotation elements are displayed.

Building Model Element Types

Building model elements are categorized as host and component. The following table describes these categories briefly.

Element Type	Description
Host	Elements such as walls, windows, doors, and roofs that are used for the 3D representation of building design. Model elements have a specific location in the building.
Component	Elements such as windows, doors, and furniture that fill out the details of building design. Components can be hosted, such as doors and windows that are hosted by walls, or can be freestanding, such as columns or furniture.

The following illustration categorizes building model elements.

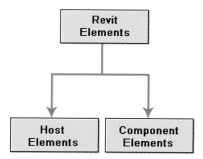

Revit Elements as Objects

Elements such as walls, doors, and windows are recognized as actual objects. The properties of these objects, such as structure and behavior, are called parameters. These properties simplify the process of creating a building model.

For example, when you draw a wall element, you do not need to ensure that the wall layer is active as in a conventional CAD application. You also do not need to separately draw the faces and internal structural details of the wall element. The wall element is part of the wall category and has all the visual attributes of a wall, such as the required lineweight and color. The wall element also behaves as a wall. You can join it to other walls; connect it structurally to floors and ceilings, and place windows and doors in it. Intelligence is programmed into elements so that their behavior is affected by the relationships they share with other elements.

Example of Building Elements

The following illustration shows various building elements.

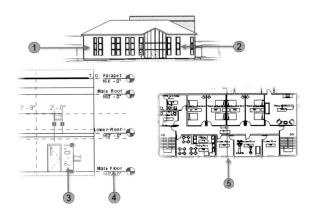

1	Host	wall attached to a roof
2	Component	window placed in the wall
3	Annotation	dimensions of the door
4	Datum	levels
5	View	plan view

About Families

Families are groups of similar elements. You will use a large number of predefined families in your projects. You can modify predefined families to suit project requirements. You can also create families for your projects by using specific templates for doors, windows, furniture, electrical fixtures, tags, and other components or annotation elements.

Definition of Families

A family integrates elements that have the same construction, use, and graphical representation. For example, doors of different construction and use, such as double glass, overhead-sectional, and single-flush, are generally found in different families. Within the double-glass door family, there may be variations in door size, glass size and placement, or frame style; these variations are called types within the family. Model families are divided into component families and system families.

The following illustration shows different door families in the Revit library.

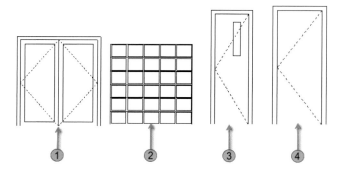

①   Double glass door

②   Overhead-sectional glass door

③   Single-flush vision door

④   Single-flush door

Family Types

Every family can contain multiple types. For example, families of tables might be created based on usage or shape, such as conference table, coffee table, or dining table. Each family has types for various sizes, such as round tables of different diameters.

Revit provides controls for how elements are constructed and located in a project using the Family, Type, and Instance Properties dialog boxes. The family properties control the geometry, the type properties control the size, and the instance properties control the location in space.

The following illustration shows table families in a project file, each with different types of tables listed by size.

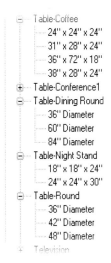

```
⊟   Table-Coffee
    ──── 24" x 24" x 24"
    ──── 31" x 28" x 24"
    ──── 36" x 72" x 18"
    ──── 38" x 28" x 24"
⊞   Table-Conference1
⊟   Table-Dining Round
    ──── 36" Diameter
    ──── 60" Diameter
    ──── 84" Diameter
⊟   Table-Night Stand
    ──── 18" x 18" x 24"
    ──── 24" x 24" x 30"
⊟   Table-Round
    ──── 36" Diameter
    ──── 42" Diameter
    ──── 48" Diameter
⊞   Television
```

Component and System Families

Component families are families of common components and symbols used in the building design that have standard sizes, configurations, and parameters. You can load component family files into a project or create them using family templates. You can also define properties and graphical representations for component families. Most families are component families, such as doors, windows, and furniture, which can exist outside a project.

System families have predefined parameters and graphical representations. They include walls, dimensions, ceilings, roofs, and levels. System families are not available as external files for loading into a project, nor can you create them.

You can modify the existing system families to suit project requirements or company standards. You can use a predefined system family to generate new types in that family in a project. For example, the structure of an exterior brick wall is predefined in the Basic Wall system family. You can create different types of brick walls with different compositions. You can transfer system families between projects, if required.

An in-place family is a special type of component family. It is specific to the project in which it is created and edited. A roof cornice is an example of an in-place family.

Example of Families

The following table gives an example of family, type, and instance for a wall object.

Family	Example
Family/System Family	Walls: Basic Wall
Type	Exterior - Brick on CMU
Instance	Actual user-drawn wall in a project

The following illustration shows Annotation Symbols, Doors, and Furniture families from the Project Browser. You can load these component families from the libraries.

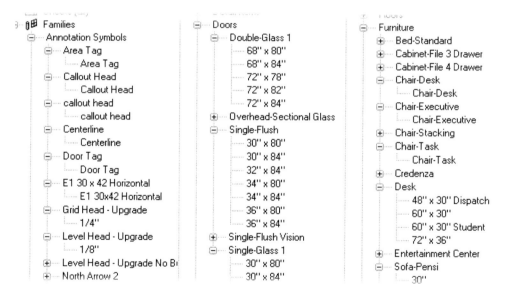

Guidelines for Working with Revit Elements and Families

Revit elements and families readily provide the building elements for your project. The following guidelines help you to work efficiently with these Revit elements and families.

Guidelines

- Familiarize yourself with the default content libraries that Revit installs and those created by other users in your organization. Then, you will be able to reuse existing elements, instead of creating content from scratch. You can also access Revit content online.

- Save a family back to the library folder after creating new types or modifying a type within it. This makes the new family type available across projects and to other users as well.

- Understand the structure of system families, such as walls, floors, and roof, and component families, such as doors and windows. This enables you to design buildings that can pass or exceed energy conservation requirements.

- Move the cursor over an element to view the tooltip information about its family and type while you are working in the view window. Be careful not to click elements, thereby modifying them accidentally.

Exercise | Work with Revit Elements and Families

In this exercise, you work with different types of building elements, families, and views. You want to explore and identify the elements and families in a project.

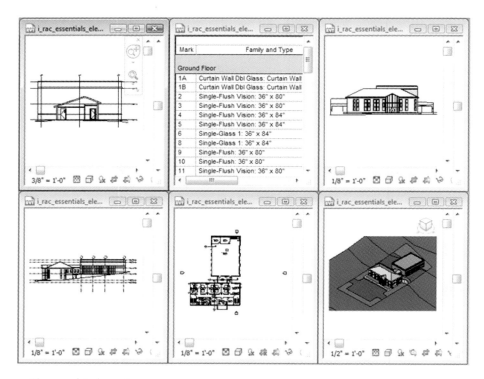

The completed exercise

Completing the Exercise: *To complete the exercise, follow the steps in this book or in the onscreen exercise. In the onscreen list of chapters and exercises, click Chapter 2: Revit Architecture Basics. Click Exercise: Work with Revit Elements and Families.*

1   Open *i_rac_essentials_elements_and_families.rvt* or *m_rac_essentials_elements_and_families.rvt*.
    The file opens in the 3D view showing a completed building project on a site.
    Note: The illustrations for the metric dataset will be slightly different from those shown here.
    The completed exercise illustration may also vary.

2   In the 3D view:

    • Move the cursor over host building elements, such as walls and roofs, to highlight
      them. Notice the information displayed in the tooltip and the status bar.
    • Move the cursor over component elements, such as doors and windows, placed in
      host elements to highlight them. Notice the information displayed in the tooltip and
      the status bar.
      Note: You can enable or disable tooltips in the Options dialog box, which you access
      by clicking Options on the application menu.

3   In the Project Browser, under Views (All), Elevations (Building), double-click South to open
    the south elevation view.

4   In the view window, move the cursor over the windows to highlight them. Notice that the
    windows are from the same family but have different sizes.

5   Select the second window from the left.

    Notice that the Modify Windows tab is activated.

6   Click Modify Windows tab > Element panel > Type Selector drop-down > Window : 30" W (m_Window : 760mm W). This changes only the type of the window instance, not its family.

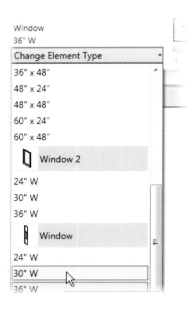

7   In the view window, notice the change in the width of the window.

8   In the Project Browser, under Floor Plans, double-click Main Floor to open the plan view. Notice that the window you changed is still selected.

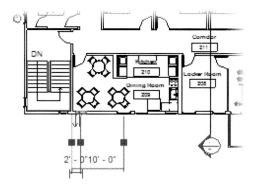

9   On the Quick Access toolbar, click Modify to clear the selection.

10   In the view window, move the cursor over various furniture components and view the information displayed.

11   In the Project Browser, under Views (All), Schedules/Quantities, double-click Door Schedule to display the schedule in the view window. The door schedule displays details such as Mark, Family and Type, and Width.

Door Schedule		
Mark	Family and Type	Width
Ground Floor		
1A	Curtain Wall Dbl Glass: Curtain Wall Dbl Gl	6' - 5 1/8
1B	Curtain Wall Dbl Glass: Curtain Wall Dbl Gl	6' - 5 1/8
2	Single-Flush Vision: 36" x 80"	3' - 0"
3	Single-Flush Vision: 36" x 80"	3' - 0"
4	Single-Flush Vision: 36" x 84"	3' - 0"
5	Single-Flush Vision: 36" x 84"	3' - 0"
6	Single-Glass 1: 36" x 84"	3' - 0"
7	Single-Glass 1: 36" x 84"	3' - 0"
8	Single-Glass 1: 36" x 84"	3' - 0"
9	Single-Flush: 36" x 80"	3' - 0"
10	Single-Flush: 36" x 80"	3' - 0"

Note: The schedule view itself is a view element, and each row displays certain properties of a door. A door is a component element.

12   Open the East elevation view.

13   In the view window, select the Single Glass door.

14   Click Modify Doors tab > Modify panel > Delete.

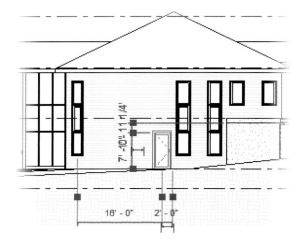

The component is deleted from all other views, including the Door Schedule view.

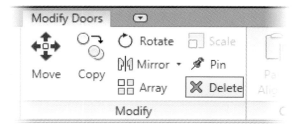

15   Open the Section 3 view.

16   In the view window, move the cursor over various datum elements such as levels and column grids and view the information displayed.

17   Click View tab > Windows panel > Tile.

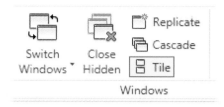

All the open views are displayed.

18   Click in any view except the Door Schedule view to make it active.

19   On the Navigation Bar of the active view, click Zoom All to Fit from the Zoom options drop-down.

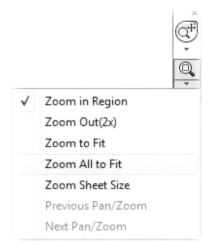

Notice that each view is zoomed to fit its tiled window.

20   Close the file without saving changes.

Lesson 04 | Starting a Project

This lesson describes how to start a new project with different templates. You begin the lesson by learning about projects and project templates. Then, you learn about the default project template, Revit file types, vector and raster data, toposurfaces, and some recommended practices for starting a new project. The lesson concludes with exercises on creating a new project template and using imported CAD data to start a project.

The basic template files hold predefined information and settings for a project. When you create a new project using any template, the project automatically takes the template settings. Every organization has its own standards that can be applied to blank project setups for efficiency, customization, and consistency. Useful modifications to standard content and settings can be captured in template files or transferred between active projects for reuse.

The following illustration shows a building model created using a project template.

Objectives

After completing this lesson, you will be able to:

- Describe a project.

- Describe project templates.

- Describe the default project template.

- Describe Revit file types.

- Describe vector and raster data.

- Describe toposurfaces.

- State the recommended practices for starting a new project.

- Create a new project template.

- Use imported CAD data to start a project. (Optional)

About Projects

A project provides all the essential information about a building model, such as the size and location of components, materials used, and annotations. The display settings in a project file define the appearance of the model in project views. Based on requirements, you can customize the default settings of a project. The project file is based on a template that provides initial settings such as material and display settings. You can customize templates. You can also start a project without using a template.

Definition of a Project

A project is the entire building design and the associated documentation. It provides complete information about various parametric building components required to represent a building model in standard dimensional views and schedules.

Recent Files Window

Every time you launch the software, a startup window named Recent Files is displayed. The window provides links to the recently opened project files or family files with thumbnail images. Under Projects, you can click the New link to open a new project using the default template. To create a new project using templates other than the default, click the application button in the upper-left corner to open the application menu and then click New > Project.

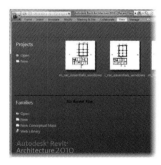

Recent Files window

You can open a recent project or family file by selecting its link in the Recent Files window. You can click Open on the Quick Access toolbar in the upper-left corner of the window to open a file browser. You can access the help and resource options using the Help drop-down on the InfoCenter toolbar in the upper-right corner of the window. The Recent Files window also contains a link to the web content.

Creating a Building Model

You add parametric building components such as windows, doors, and walls to a project while creating a building model. You can create plan, section, elevation, and 3D views and make the required changes to complete the building model. Revit and BIM then ensure that the changes that you make in one view propagate throughout the project, and all associated views automatically update to reflect the change.

Specifying the Project Environment

You define the environment of a project while creating a building model. The project environment includes the display and material settings such as colors, fill patterns, and line styles of various components. Defining the environment imparts a standard appearance to the building model. You can customize the environment settings at any point during the design process because they are saved with the project.

Saving Project Files

When you begin a project or work on existing project files, you may want to save your work frequently. Revit does not auto-save the project file. By default, Revit displays the Project Not Saved Recently dialog box every 30 minutes. You can change the reminder interval setting using the Options dialog box to suit your work style.

The following illustrations show the Project Not Saved Recently dialog box, and the Save Reminder Interval settings in the Options dialog box.

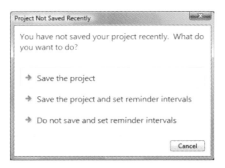

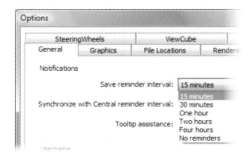

Project Files Backup

Each time you save a project file, Revit creates a backup copy of the file. Backup copies of a file are numbered incrementally, such as *MyNewDesign.0001.rvt* and *MyNewDesign.0002.rvt*. By default, Revit maintains three backup copies of each project. You can change the number of backup copies using the File Save Options dialog box accessed from the Save As dialog box.

Examples of a Project

The following illustration shows a project file in plan, elevation, and 3D views.

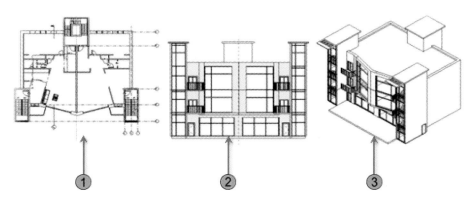

(1) Plan view

(2) Elevation view

(3) 3D view

About Project Templates

A project file is based on a template that provides the initial settings, such as the material and display settings. You can customize this template any time during the project. You can also start a project without using a template.

Definition of a Project Template

A project template enables you to start a project by providing initial conditions such as the default project units and settings, the default building levels and standard views, system families such as walls, floors, and others, and preloaded component families. You can either select a template from the template library, or you can save a project and use it as a new project template. New projects inherit all the families, settings, and geometry from the starting template.

Types of Project Templates

You can use the following standard project templates to start a project.

Template	Description
Default	For new projects, unless you specify otherwise.
Commercial	For designing commercial structures; includes additional levels and views. This template is available in imperial installations only.
Residential	For designing residential structures; includes additional levels and views. This template is available in imperial installations only.
Construction	For using views and preloaded schedules specific to the construction industry.

Project Template Settings

You can modify the settings for views, levels, materials, and annotations using project templates. Templates contain family content so that you can begin work quickly. You can provide wall types, windows, and doors to your templates to suit the types of buildings your company designs. You can specify building type in the template for generating energy calculations early in a project.

Additional Elements for Templates

You can create elements within project templates such as sheets, drafting views and details, schedules, additional families, cameras, groups, detail groups, links, and import/export settings.

View Templates

Views and their controls are very important for working effectively in Revit. You can create templates for view types to hold settings and then apply these templates to views. For example, furniture plans, floor finish plans, or electrical plans may all show the same area of a model, but they look very different.

Starting Without a Template

You can start a project without using a template; in this case, the project contains only one level with a plan view and a reflected ceiling plan view. You need to specify whether you want to use imperial or metric units. The only wall types that load are basic, curtain, and stacked; no windows, doors, or other components load; and no elevation view is created in the project.

Template File Type

Project template files have an *.rte* extension. By default, they are stored in the Imperial and Metric Templates folders at the same level as the Imperial and Metric Library folders.

Example of Using the Standard Template

The following illustration shows the location of the standard imperial templates.

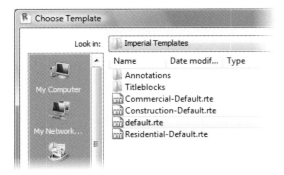

Note: *File locations are different on Microsoft Windows XP and Microsoft Windows Vista operating systems.*

About the Default Project Template

You can start a new project by using the default project template. This template provides default settings for colors, line styles, and line weights, and the standard views of the building model.

Definition of the Default Project Template

The default project template, the *default.rte* (*DefaultMetric.rte*) file, is a standard template that creates a new project with two levels, Level 1 and Level 2. It sets the default project units, imperial or metric, and loads a subset of component families that you can use to create the building design.

Default Project Template Views

The default project template creates standard views of the building model. They are north, south, east, and west elevations, two floor plans, two reflected ceiling plans, and a site plan. The floor plan view at Level 1 is the default view. You can use this view to start creating the walls of the building model. If you add more levels to the project, a plan view and a reflected ceiling plan view are automatically created for each new level.

The following illustration shows the default project template views.

Default Project Template Settings

The following settings define the appearance of the default project template.

Setting	Description
Colors	Define colors for line styles and families.
Titleblocks	Load titleblock families for the sheets in your project.
Families	Load the families you often use.
Line styles	Define line styles for model components and detail lines in a project.
Line weights	Define line weight for model and annotation components.
Fill patterns	Define fill or hatch patterns. Fill patterns are commonly used in materials and detailing.
Materials	Define material appearance for model components, including fill patterns, shading, and rendered images.
Units	Specify the unit of measurement for lengths, angles, and slopes.
Snaps	Set snapping increments for model views such as plan and 3D views.
Dimensions	Define the look and size of dimensions for a project.
Temporary dimensions	Set the display and placement of temporary dimensions.
Object styles	Define the display of components in various views.

Example of Default Project Template

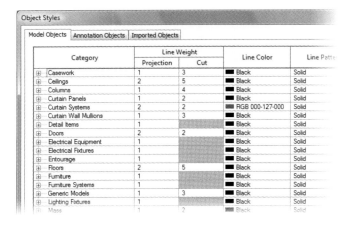

Object styles in the default template

About Revit File Types

Revit uses three types of files: project files, template files, and family files. Each one has a different file extension.

Definition of Revit File Types

You can save the project in three file formats. Revit project files, in which you work to create building models, have an *.rvt* extension. Revit family files, in which you create objects such as doors, windows, annotations, symbols, and titleblocks that are loaded into the project files, have an *.rfa* extension. Template files that are used to create project and family files have an *.rte* extension.

Saving Project Files

You can save and access template files on the local hard drive or on a network, depending on your setup. You save project files on a network at a location that everybody in the design team can access. You can also save a project file as a template file.

Example

The following illustrations show project and template file extensions and the default locations of template files.

Project and template file extensions   *Default locations of template files*

About Vector and Raster Data

You can use vector data from collaborators using CAD programs or from existing CAD files to create a building model, a detail, or a toposurface. You can use raster data or image files as background for a view, as sketch information to trace over when starting a building model, or as logos in titleblocks.

Definition of Vector and Raster Data

Vector data has both magnitude and direction. Vector graphics structure is used as a means of coding line and area information in the form of units of data expressing magnitude, direction, and connectivity.

Import Symbol

Elements such as lines, text, and blocks in imported vector data files become a single object called an import symbol. You can change the appearance of elements within import symbols. You can dimension individual parts in an import symbol and align objects with them. For example, you can snap walls to the lines representing walls in an imported drawing.

2D Data

You can import all 2D objects in CAD files, except for rays and construction lines, as import symbols in a drawing. You can explode an import symbol into text, curves, lines, and filled regions. You can also import a DWG™ or DXF™ file that contains rendering data.

3D Data

You can import 3D data from other CAD software as import symbols. Surfaces, regions, faces, and 3D solids are imported as 3D import symbols that have limited snapping. You can disassemble or explode the import symbol. However, it is not possible to explode all 3D objects.

The following illustration shows imported 3D solid objects such as a box, a cone, and a cylinder in hidden-lines view.

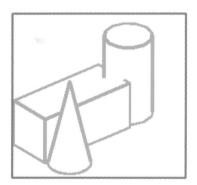

ACIS Objects

You can import ACIS objects from DWG, DXF, and SAT files. You can also import most DGN surfaces and solids, except B-spline surfaces, from MicroStation software.

Note: *To use ACIS imports for face-based host commands, you import geometry into an in-place family of the Mass or Generic Model category.*

Line Weights

You can import pen numbers from a DWG or DXF file and map them to a line weight. Each layer in the file is assigned a line weight based on pen number and line weight settings. Standard pen and line weight mappings that follow predefined national standards are provided in the default project template. You can also create your own mappings. When you save these mappings to a text file, they become the set mappings for the project. These settings are retained within the project template.

Scaling

You can determine the scale factor of imported DWG or DXF files in your project from the import units and scale factor properties of the import symbol. If you change the import units, the scale factor is automatically updated. You can also specify a different scale factor.

Example

The following illustrations show an example of vector and raster data.

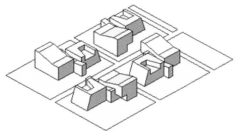

Imported 3D objects as vector data   *Imported raster image used as a logo in a titleblock*

About Toposurfaces

For some projects, you may want to create toposurfaces to represent site conditions. Toposurfaces hold different material definitions and heights and show contour lines. They can be modified to show an existing site or proposed site grading. You create a toposurface by placing points individually or by using points from an imported object or file.

Definition of Toposurfaces

A toposurface is a three-dimensional site object defined by points that can have different heights. It also has a defined bottom level that is given a different height from the top. This bottom level appears to have depth when viewed in an elevation or a section view.

Example

The following illustration shows a toposurface with contour lines. The surface is subdivided into different portions with each showing different materials such as asphalt, grass, and concrete.

Guidelines for Starting a New Project

When you start a new project, you select either the default project template or a standard template from the template library. Based on your requirements, you can customize the default template settings and save the new settings as a template file. The following best practices help when starting a project.

- When you use a template provided by your organization, familiarize yourself with the levels, views, and wall types before you create building model content. This helps you progress smoothly in the building design and prevents inconsistencies in the design.

- When you start a project using a standard template file, use the site view to create toposurfaces and the lowest floor plan view to create walls at the lowest level of the building. This is because in a project that uses the standard template, the lowest floor plan view and site view are at the same elevation and show the same level, but they have different settings and purposes. Floor plan views do not show toposurfaces by default. This helps you easily identify the site and floor plan views.

- When you work on a multistory project, define additional levels for the floors, roofs, and tops of exterior walls. This helps you create walls and other building elements with relevant constraints that you can adjust quickly.

- When you start your first project, begin with a standard template and then develop organization-specific graphic standards, such as line weights, line styles, symbols, and annotations. You can then use your first project file to create project templates for the organization. Building template development time into the budget for the first few projects helps you standardize, and saves considerable time in later projects.

Exercise | Create a New Project Template

In this exercise, you start a new project using a default template, make changes to specific settings, and save the file as a project template.

You want to create a template file for your organization.

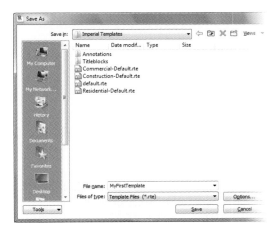

The completed exercise

Completing the Exercise:	To complete the exercise, follow the steps in this book or in the onscreen exercise. In the onscreen list of chapters and exercises, click Chapter 2: Revit Architecture Basics. Click Exercise: Create a New Project Template.

1   Click the application button to open the application menu.

2   Click New > Project.

3   In the New Project dialog box, under Template File, click Browse.

4   In the Choose Template dialog box:
   - Ensure that you access the Imperial Templates (*Metric Templates*) folder.
   - Ensure that *default.rte* (*DefaultMetric.rte*) project template is selected.
   - Click Open.

5   In the New Project dialog box:

- Under Create New, verify that Project is selected.
- Click OK to open a new project.
  Note: You are beginning a new project using the default project template. The default project template provides an easy and uncluttered way to begin a project.

6   In the Project Browser:

- Notice that Level 1 is bold, indicating that this view is active. Also, notice the other default views.
- Expand Families to view the list of families that are loaded in the default template.

7   Open the South elevation view. Notice that two levels, Level 1 and Level 2, are defined by default.

Chapter 02 | Revit Architecture Basics

8   On the application menu, click New > Project to open another concurrent project.

9   In the New Project dialog box, under Template File, click Browse.

10   In the Choose Template dialog box:

- Ensure that you access the *Imperial Templates (Metric Templates)* folder.
- Select the *Construction-Default.rte (Construction-DefaultMetric.rte)* project template.
- Click Open.

11   In the New Project dialog box, click OK. The new project file opens.

12   In the Project Browser, examine the list of views in the new project file, including views under Schedules/Quantities. Notice the difference in this project template. It contains more views and schedules than the default project template.

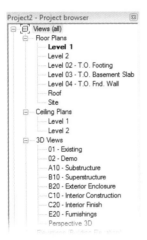

The default project template can be modified easily to look similar to the construction template, or you can create a custom project template based on your own criteria for new projects.

13   Click Manage tab > Project Settings panel > Project Units to change the measurement settings.

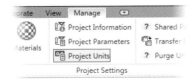

14 In the Project Units dialog box, for Length, click the Format field.

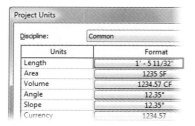

15 In the Format dialog box:

- Select To the Nearest 1/4" (To the Nearest 10) from the Rounding list.

- Click OK.

16 Click OK to close the Project Units dialog box.

17 On the Quick Access toolbar, click Save to save the new project file as a template.

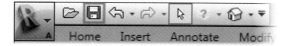

18 In the Save As dialog box:

- Select Template Files (*.rte) from the Files of Type list.
- For File Name, enter **MyFirstTemplate**.
- Click Save. This template file is now available in your template folder.

19 On the application menu, click Close to close the new template file.

20 Close all open files without saving changes.

Optional Exercise | Use Imported CAD Data to
Start a Project

In this exercise, you start a new project, import a CAD file, and use the file to create a toposurface.

You import site data from an AutoCAD® drawing file and use this data to generate a topographic surface in a new project file.

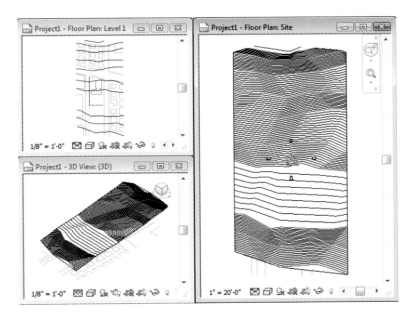

The completed exercise

Completing the Exercise: *To complete the exercise, follow the steps in this book or in the onscreen exercise. In the onscreen list of chapters and exercises, click Chapter 2: Revit Architecture Basics. Click Optional Exercise: Use Imported CAD Data to Start a Project.*

1   In the Recent Files window, under Projects, click New to open a new project using the default template.

2   Open the Site plan view.

3   Click Insert tab > Import panel > Import CAD to import a CAD file for use inside the new project.

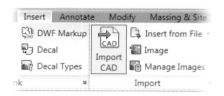

4   In the Import CAD Formats dialog box:
   • Browse to the folder where you saved the courseware datasets.
   • Select *site_model.dwg*.
   • Click Open.

5   Enter **ZF** to zoom out and view the complete imported CAD file. Notice the DWG file displaying the site and the outline of the proposed building footprint.

6   Click Massing & Site tab > Model Site panel > Toposurface to create a toposurface object using the imported CAD file.

7   Click Edit Surface tab > Tools panel > Create from Import drop-down > Select Import Instance.

8   In the view window:
    - Place the cursor over the imported toposurface to highlight it.
    - Click to select the toposurface.

9   In the Add Points from Selected Layers dialog box:
    - Clear all check boxes except C-TOPO-MAJR.
    - Click OK to generate points that define the toposurface.

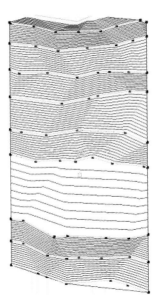

10 Right-click any one of the black points. Click Element Properties to study the points that Revit has created.

11 In the Instance Properties dialog box:
    - Notice the elevation associated with that point.
    - Click OK.

12 Notice the elevation associated with another point in the toposurface.

13 Click Modify Interior Point tab > Surface panel > Finish Surface.

14   On the Quick Access toolbar, click 3D view to open the default 3D view.

15   Notice that both the toposurface and the CAD file you imported are visible.

16   Open the Level 1 floor plan view. Notice that in this view, the CAD file is visible but not the toposurface.
      Tip: Enter **ZF** to zoom out and view the complete imported CAD file.

17   Tile the open views.

18   Click in any view to activate it.

19   Zoom to fit each view in its tiled window.

20   Close the project without saving changes.

Chapter Summary

You have now been introduced to the Revit Architecture user interface. You understand that elements are the parametric building blocks, and template files expedite project setup, and you can begin to create designs in Revit Architecture.

In this chapter, you learned to:

- Describe the Revit Architecture user interface.
- Work with different types of Revit elements and families.
- Start a new project with different templates.

Chapter 03
Starting a Design

When you start a design project in Revit Architecture, you first need to learn how to organize your content on levels and how to control the spacing and placement of structural elements for your building design using grids. In this chapter, you learn how to work with levels and grids.

▶ Objectives

After completing this chapter, you will be able to:

- Create and modify levels in a building model.

- Create and modify grids.

Lesson 05 | Creating and Modifying Levels

This lesson describes how to create and modify levels in a building model. You begin the lesson by learning about levels and their uses. Then, you learn the steps and some recommended practices for creating and modifying levels. The lesson concludes with an exercise on creating and modifying levels.

You use levels to define a vertical height or a story within a building. In Revit Architecture, levels act as horizontal reference planes to host building elements such as walls, roofs, and floors. With levels, you determine and control the placement of elements vertically in a building model.

The following illustration shows the various levels in a section view of a building model.

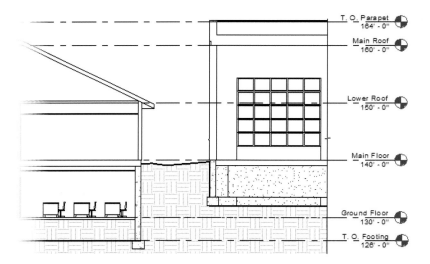

Objectives

After completing this lesson, you will be able to:

- Describe levels and their uses.

- Identify the steps to create and modify levels.

- State the recommended practices for creating and modifying levels.

- Create and modify levels.

About Levels

Levels define the vertical position and extent of building elements. Levels also form the work planes for plan views and reflected ceiling views.

Definition of Levels

Levels are finite horizontal planes that act as references in a building model for level-hosted elements, such as walls, roofs, floors, stairs, ramps, and ceilings. You use levels to define the vertical extents of walls and the vertical placement of elements, such as furniture. There are two types of levels, story and non story.

Using Levels for Vertical Positioning

You create a level for each known story or floor platform, in a building model. Each plan view of the model is at a level, and all elements placed in a plan view are based on the associated level for that view. You can add new levels or modify existing levels at any time during the design process. All elements set to a level move with the level.

Constraining Elements

When you create a wall, you place its base constraint on a level. You can set the top constraint for the wall either to a level or to a specified height. If you set the top constraint to a height, you can later modify it to a level. The advantage of constraining the tops of walls to a level is that if you change the placement of the level, the height of all the walls constrained to that level changes accordingly.

Views Associated with Levels

A story level has a floor plan view and reflected ceiling plan view associated with it. Both views have the same name as the level. If you change the name of the level, you are prompted to change the names of the corresponding plan and reflected ceiling plan views.

When you create a new level, the option to make plan views for that level is activated by default. You can create nonstory levels that do not have associated views by clearing the Make Plan View check box on the Options Bar. You can use nonstory levels as top or bottom constraints for walls and other level-based elements.

In Revit, a story level is represented by a blue level head, and a nonstory level is represented by a black level head.

Changing Level Extents

You can change the extents of a level in the views in which the level is visible. If you resize a level in the Model Extent mode, the extents of that level change in all parallel views that have the Model Extent control. If the level is in the View Specific Extent mode, any change in the extents of a level applies only to the view in which the change is made.

Example of Levels

The following illustrations show various levels.

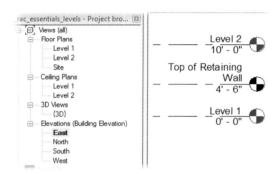

Levels 1 and 2 are story levels with associated floor and ceiling plans. The Top of Retaining Wall level is a nonstory level with no floor or ceiling plan.

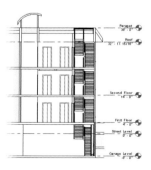

Section view with levels.

Creating and Modifying Levels

When you use the default template to create projects, Level 1 and Level 2 are available as predefined levels. These levels are displayed in the Project Browser under Floor Plan Views. Based on your requirements, you can create new levels or modify the existing levels in a project.

You use the Level command to create levels. This command is active in the section or elevation views. You sketch the required level lines. When you create a level, the Make Plan View check box on the Options Bar is selected by default. You can choose to create a floor plan, a ceiling plan, or both. However, if you clear the Make Plan View check box, the level is a reference but there is no view associated with and named for the level and the level head is black.

Procedure: Creating a Level

The following steps describe how to create a new level.

1   Change the active view to a section or an elevation view.

2   Click Home tab > Datum panel > Level.

3   On the Options Bar:
     - Verify that the Make Plan View check box is selected if you want to create a story level.
     - Clear the Make Plan View check box if you want to create a nonstory level.

4   Click Place Level tab > Draw panel > Pick Lines.

5   On the Options Bar, specify the offset value.

6   Place the cursor over the level line you want to offset to create the new level. Click to create the new level line.

Procedure: Modifying a Level

The following steps describe how to modify a level.

1   Click a level to display the controls for the level line.

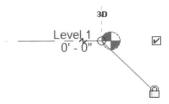

2   To rename the level, click the level name and enter a new name.

3   To change the level height, select the level line and do one of the following:
     • Drag the level to the new height. The height value field updates.
     • Click the level height field and enter a new height.

4   To change the control from Model Extents to View Specific Extents, click the 3D control. The value changes to 2D and the unfilled circle changes to a filled circle.

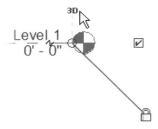

5   To change the control from View Specific Extents to Model Extents, click the 2D control. The value changes to 3D and the filled circle changes to an open circle.

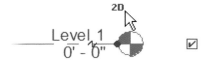

6   To offset the head from the level line, click the split-line symbol. The level head is offset and the split-line symbol changes to a filled blue circle. You can drag this circle to reposition the head.

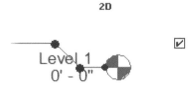

7   To turn off the display of the level symbol and fields, clear the check box next to the level head.

Guidelines for Creating and Modifying Levels

The following practices are recommended for working effectively when creating and modifying the levels in a building project.

- Create levels in project template files that are appropriate for your projects so that you can use these levels immediately when you start new projects. This helps you save time and eliminate the possibility of errors.

- Create levels without plan views during the concept design phase of a multistory project. This ensures that the Project Browser list of views is simple. During project development, as you determine the actual number of floors and start placing walls, you can create floor and ceiling plan views as required.

- Align the left and right ends of level lines so that they align with other levels. This helps you simultaneously resize all aligned levels, which saves time and keeps the view window tidy. To align a level line correctly, drag the level end so that it snaps and locks to the alignment line, which appears when this level end is in line with the other level ends. You can unlock a level line at any time if you need to adjust its position independently.

- Ensure that you zoom in close enough on the level head while dragging it to select the correct control point. This prevents you from picking the level line head offset control accidentally at certain zoom scales.

Exercise | Create and Modify Levels

In this exercise, you create and modify levels to control the vertical extents of the foundation, walls, and the roof.

You need to create levels such as T.O. Footing, Ground Floor, and First Floor before you add elements to a new building model. When you create levels at the start of the project, you can easily control the height of walls or the vertical placement of roofs, floors, doors, windows, and other building elements.

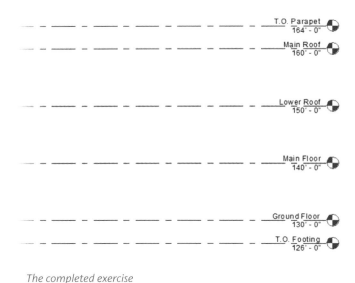

T.O. Parapet
164' - 0"

Main Roof
160' - 0"

Lower Roof
150' - 0"

Main Floor
140' - 0"

Ground Floor
130' - 0"

T.O. Footing
126' - 0"

The completed exercise

Completing the Exercise: *To complete the exercise, follow the steps in this book or in the onscreen exercise. In the onscreen list of chapters and exercises, click Chapter 3: Starting a Design. Click Exercise: Create and Modify Levels.*

1   Open *i_rac_essentials_levels.rvt* or *m_rac_essentials_levels.rvt*. The file opens in the Site
    plan view. This is a new project created using the default project template.
    Note: The illustrations for the metric dataset will be slightly different from those shown here.
    The completed exercise illustration may also vary.

2   In the Project Browser, change the view to the East elevation.
    Tip: Double-click the view name.

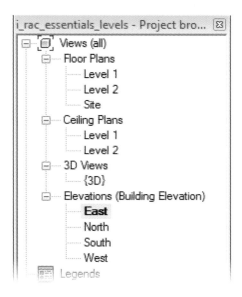

3   On the Navigation Bar, click Zoom In Region.

4   Drag a box around the level heads at the right end of the level lines.

    Notice the default levels in the project. Next, you will change the name and location of the
    existing levels and create other levels to define elevations for footings, floors, and roofs.

5   To change the Level 2 name:
    • Select the Level 2 line.
    • Select the level name to make it editable.
    • For level name, enter **T.O. Footing**. Press ENTER.

6   When you are prompted to change the names of the corresponding views, click Yes.
    Notice that the corresponding floor and ceiling plan views change their names in the
    Project Browser.

7 The Ceiling Plan view for the top of underground footings is not required. To remove this view from the project:

- In the Project Browser, under Ceiling Plans, click the T.O. Footing view to select it.
- Press DELETE.

8 To change the height of the T.O. Footing level:

- Under the level line, double-click the height field to make it editable.
- Enter **126** (**38400** mm).
  Note: The default imperial unit is the foot and the default metric unit is the millimeter. Imperial users do not need to enter the foot symbol if inches are not involved and metric users do not need to enter mm.

- Press ENTER.

The level line moves to the specified height and you no longer see it in the view window at the current zoom resolution.

9 In the view window:

- Rename Level 1 and its corresponding views to **Ground Floor**.
- Set the height of the Ground Floor level to 130' (39600 mm).

10 Click in the view window to clear the selection.

11 Right-click in the view window. Click Zoom To Fit.

12 Click Home tab > Datum panel > Level.

13   In the view window:

   - Place the cursor over the upper-level line on the left so that the alignment plane appears.
   - Move the cursor up **10' - 0"** (**4000 mm**).

   - Click to place the tail of the new level line.

14   Drag the level line to the right until it is aligned with the head of the Ground Floor level and a green dashed line appears. Click to place the head of the new level line.

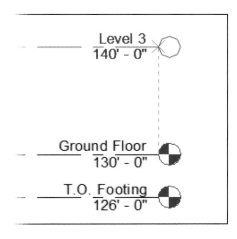

15   In the view window, change the level name to Main Floor.

16 Add three more levels with the following names at the indicated heights:

- **Lower Roof, 150' (47600** mm)
- **Main Roof, 160' (51600** mm)
- **T.O. Parapet, 164' (52800** mm)
  Tip: When you locate the tail of a level line, directly enter its offset distance from the level above or below it. This saves time. Then press ESC once to clear the screen of temporary dimensions after you have placed a level. The Level tool remains available and you can place the next level.

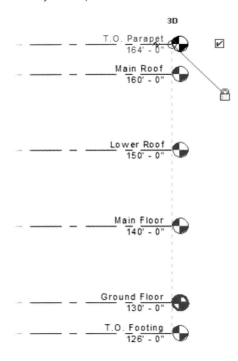

17 Click anywhere in the view window to clear the selection.

18 Right-click in the view window. Click Zoom To Fit to zoom out to the full extents of the model.

19 To make adjustments to the level line lengths:

- Select any level line that is not aligned with other level ends.
- Click and drag the model end grip as necessary to align it with the other levels.

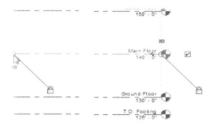

A padlock symbol will appear when level ends align.

20 Close the file without saving changes.

Lesson 06 | Creating and Modifying Grids

This lesson describes how to create and modify grids. You begin the lesson by learning about grids and the process of creating and modifying grid lines. Then, you learn some recommended practices for creating and modifying grids. The lesson concludes with an exercise on creating column grids.

Grids are used for spacing, aligning, and placing elements in a building. Most often, these elements are columns. You can use column grids to accurately reference the position of building elements in the plan, elevation, or section view.

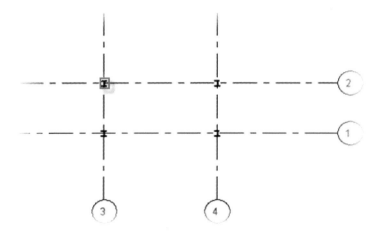

Column added to a grid

Objectives

After completing this lesson, you will be able to:

• Describe grids.

• Identify the steps in the process of creating and modifying column grids.

• State the recommended practices for creating and modifying column grids.

• Create column grids.

About Grids

Grids are usually created early in the design process. Using the Grid tool, you can create a grid system to manage the placement of columns and other elements.

Definition of Grids

Grids are finite vertical planes represented as lines in the plan, elevation, and section views. In the plan view, you can create grid lines as straight lines or arcs. In the elevation and section views, you can create grid lines only as straight lines. Both straight and arc grid lines are displayed in all plan views, but only straight grid lines are visible in the elevation and section views.

Note: *Grids do not appear in 3D views.*

Column Grids

When you place columns at grid intersections, the grid is called a column grid. In a column grid, columns automatically snap to grid lines and intersections. As a result, when there is a change in the design criteria in a project, you can simply move a grid line and all building elements aligned with it also move.

Placing Beams on Grid Lines

You generally add beams after creating a column grid. By using the grid placement option, you can quickly add multiple beams to selected grid lines when columns are present at the working level.

Example of a Column Grid

The following illustration shows a building plan with square columns on a grid. Walls and footings are also present.

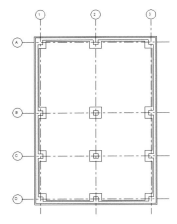

Process of Creating and Modifying Column Grids

You create grid lines using the Grid tool. You can then place columns on grid lines and grid intersections to create column grids. To modify a grid, you need to modify the grid line placement or properties.

Process: Creating and Modifying Column Grids

The process of creating and modifying column grids is shown in the following illustration.

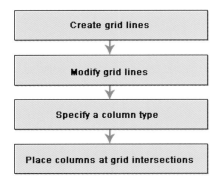

The following steps describe the process of creating and modifying column grids.

1   **Create grid lines.**
    Create grid lines with the Grid tool on the Datum panel of the Home tab. To specify the starting point of a grid line or arc, you use the Draw option. You create a grid line by clicking in the drawing to specify the starting point and then moving the cursor in the required direction. You then click to finish drawing the grid line. You use the Pick Lines option to place a grid line according to a pre-existing element such as a wall or a line.

2   **Modify grid lines.**
    Modify grid line properties by selecting a grid line. You can modify the grid type, name, size, or position. After you have drawn some grid lines, you can use editing tools such as Copy, Rotate, Mirror, or Array to create additional grid lines.

3   **Specify a column type.**
    Place columns by using the Column tool on the Build panel. Specify architectural or structural column. Architectural columns are decorative placeholders, and structural columns are actual engineered structural elements. Based on the requirement of your project, you can place either of these two columns. The columns can be changed or modified later. To specify the column type, you select a column type from the Type Selector drop-down.

4   **Place columns at grid intersections.**
    Place columns by clicking in the plan view. When you place columns, they snap to grid lines and intersections. Use the On Grids tool on the Multiple panel of the Place Structural Columns tab to place structural column instances. You can do this by selecting multiple grid lines that cross. The columns are automatically placed at the grid intersections.

Guidelines for Creating and Modifying Grids

The following best practices for creating and modifying grids help you work with grids effectively.

Guidelines

- After creating a grid, you can pin its location to prevent it from being moved accidentally. To pin the location of a grid, select the grid line and use the Pin tool on the Modify panel of the Modify Grids tab.

- Columns that are placed at grid intersections or on grid lines move with the grids. Columns that are placed off grids can be constrained to move with grids by placing and locking column dimensions. Carefully constraining building elements to grids saves considerable time later in the project if grid spacing changes.

- You will quite often work with imported data. If you import a CAD file, you can select grid lines in that file and create grids of the same length as the CAD lines. Creating grids of the same length saves time and eliminates errors from tracing.

- If you have many grid lines to place equidistant from each other, you can select a grid line and use the Copy tool with the Multiple option or use the Array tool. The use of these editing tools saves time and helps you accurately place grid lines individually or in groups.

Example of Pinning the Location of Grids

The following illustration shows an example of pinning the location of grids to prevent them from being moved accidentally.

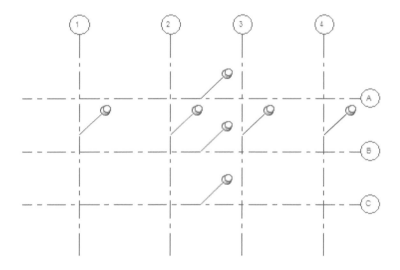

Exercise | Create Column Grids

In this exercise, you create a grid to control the placement of columns. You then add structural columns to the grid intersections.

You are designing the floor of an equipment bay, which is supported by square concrete columns. To create the support structure, you first create a grid and then add dimensions. By adding dimensions, you move the grid lines and position the grids precisely. You then add columns to the grid intersections to begin creating the foundation plan.

You do the following:

- Create a grid.

- Add dimensions and position the grid.

- Add structural columns to the grid intersections.

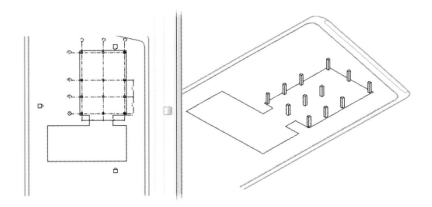

The completed exercise

Completing the Exercise: *To complete the exercise, follow the steps in this book or in the onscreen exercise. In the onscreen list of chapters and exercises, click Chapter 3: Starting a Design. Click Exercise: Create Column Grids.*

Create a Grid

1   Open *i_rac_essentials_grids.rvt* or *m_rac_essentials_grids.rvt*. The file opens in the Ground
    Floor view.
    Note: The illustrations for the metric dataset will be slightly different from those shown here.
    The completed exercise illustration may also vary.

    This view displays model lines derived from an imported CAD site plan file. The green lines
    represent concrete sidewalks, and the black lines represent the footprint of the building you
    will create in this project.

2   Zoom in to the upper rectangular outline, which will be the equipment bay of a municipal
    fire station.

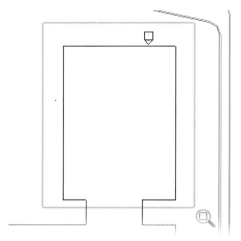

3   Click Home tab > Datum panel > Grid.

4   Click Place Grid tab > Draw panel > Pick Lines.

5   On the Options Bar, for Offset, enter **2'** (**600** mm). Notice that 1/4" Bubble (6.5mm Bubble) is
    displayed in the Type Selector drop-down. You can create customized grid bubbles.

6   In the view window:
    • Place the cursor inside the rectangle toward the left edge.
    • Click to place a vertical grid line when a dashed line displays to the right of the
      highlighted line.

7   Add three more grid lines inside the rectangular outline, as shown, to create grid lines for the building shell.

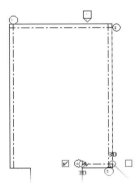

Note: The grid lines number consecutively as you add them.

8   Click Place Grid tab > Selection panel > Modify to exit the Grid tool. You can also press ESC two times.

9   To place grid lines inside the equipment bay footprint, you can copy these grid lines. Select the top horizontal grid line, grid line 2.

10 Click Modify Grids tab > Modify panel > Copy.

11 On the Options Bar, select the Multiple check box to make copies of the grid line.

12   To place the copied grid lines, in the view window:

- Click near grid line 2. The exact location is not critical.
- Drag the cursor below grid line 2.
- Click to place a copy of the grid line. The exact location of the new grid line is not important because you will move it later.

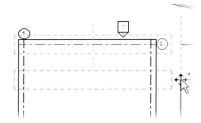

13   Place another copy of the grid line below the grid line you just placed.

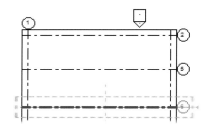

14   End the Copy tool.
Tip: Press ESC or click Modify.

15   Create a copy of vertical grid line 1 to its right anywhere in the equipment bay.
Note: Before clicking to place the copy of the grid line, ensure that the Multiple check box on the Options Bar is cleared.

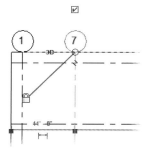

16 To reposition and align the heads of the grid lines so they do not obscure the model:

- Select grid line 3.
- Clear the check box below the grid line to toggle the bubble off.
- Select the check box above the grid line to toggle the bubble on.

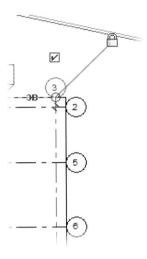

17 To reposition the heads of the vertical grid lines:

- With grid line 3 still selected, on the head of grid line 3, click the model end grip.
- Drag the grid bubble above the elevation symbol using the model end grip (the smaller circle).

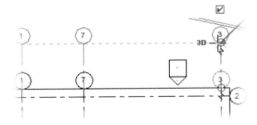

Note: When you move grid line 3, grid lines 1 and 7 move in alignment. If they do not move, you can align them manually.

18   Reposition each horizontal grid line bubble to the left end using the grid toggle for each grid line.

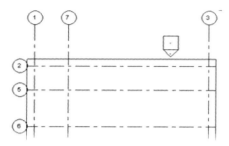

19   Select any of the horizontal grid lines and drag the head to the left of the equipment bay outline so that all three grid heads move, as shown.

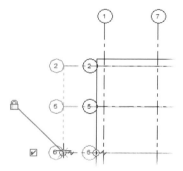

Similarly, select grid line 4 and drag its head to the left so that it snaps in alignment with the other grid lines.

20   To change the names of the horizontal grid lines:
   • Select grid line 2.
   • Click the number in the head of the grid line.
   • Enter **A** and press ENTER.
   • Rename the other three horizontal grid lines **B**, **C**, and **D**.

21 Rename vertical grid line 7 as **2**.

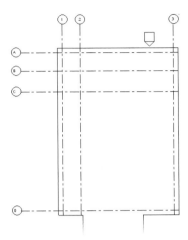

Add Dimensions and Position the Grids

1 Click Annotate tab > Dimension panel > Aligned.

2 To place dimensions between vertical grid lines:
   - Select vertical grid lines 1, 2, and 3.
   - Click below grid line D to place the dimension.

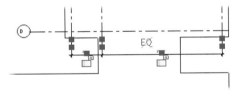

3 Click the EQ label with the slash through it to set equal dimensions between the vertical grid lines.

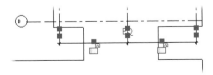

The slash disappears, and the center line moves into a position that is halfway between the outer lines.

4　Click the two padlocks below the dimension line to lock the dimensions.

5　The Dimension tool is still active. To place dimensions between horizontal grid lines:
- Select the lower-right end of the building footprint as shown.
- Select the horizontal grid lines D, C, and B in succession.
- Click anywhere to the right of grid line 3 to place the dimension.

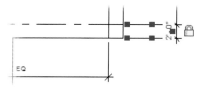

6　Click the lower padlock to lock the dimension value between the black line and grid line D.

7　Click Place Dimensions tab > Selection panel > Modify.

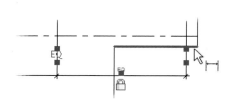

8　To reposition grid line C, in the view window:
- Click grid line C to select it.
- In its lower dimension, enter **19' 0"** (**5500** mm).
- Press ENTER.

9　Reposition grid line B to **19' 0"** (**5500** mm) north of grid line C. You may have to drag the square grip on the temporary dimension line to grid line C first, then enter the value.

Note: Remember that you can input just 19 for 19' 0".

Add Structural Columns to Grid Intersections

1   Click Home tab > Build panel > Column drop-down > Structural Column.

2   Select Concrete-Square-Column 24 x 24 (M_Concrete-Square-Column 600 x 600mm) from the Type Selector drop-down.

3   Click Place Structural Column tab > Multiple panel > On Grids. This locks the new columns to the grid intersections.

4   In the view window, press CTRL and select grid lines 3, A, B, C , and D to add columns to each grid intersection.

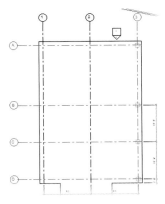

   Note: If you accidentally select one or more elements you did not want to include in the selection, press the SHIFT key and select that element to remove it from the selection.

5   Click Place Structural Column > At Grid Intersection tab > Multiple Selection panel > Finish Selection. The columns update on grid line 3.

6   Click Modify.

7   Select the new columns either by using a left to right window selection or by pressing CTRL and selecting each column.

8   Click Copy.

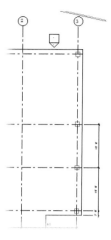

9   On the Options Bar, ensure that the following check boxes are selected.
- The Multiple check box
- The Copy check box
- The Constrain check box

10   Select grid line 3 to establish a start point, then select grid line 2 and grid line 1. The columns copy to the left to fill the column grid.

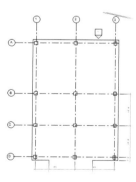

11   Exit the Copy tool and then view the columns in the default 3D view.

12   Tile the view windows.

13   Close the file without saving changes.

Chapter 03 | Starting a Design

Chapter Summary

Now that you have learned how to work with levels and grids, you can effectively set up and start working on your design.

In this chapter, you learned to:

- Create and modify levels in a building model.
- Create and modify grids.

Chapter 04
The Basics of the Building Model

With Revit Architecture, you usually start with a basic floor plan and place elements in them. You can then create many different types of walls. In this chapter, you learn about basic floor plans and walls, and then you learn how to create, modify, and place walls. You also learn how to use editing tools to add walls and components to a model quickly. After you have created walls, you can add doors and windows to the building model.

A computable Autodesk Revit Architecture design model is devised for sustainability analyses—even during early conceptual design. As soon as the layout of a building's walls, windows, roofs, floors, and interior partitions (elements that define a building's thermal zones) are established, the information employed to create a Revit model can be used to perform sustainability analyses.

Objectives

After completing this chapter, you will be able to:

- Create a basic floor plan and place building elements in it.

- Add and modify walls.

- Create and modify compound walls.

- Use editing tools to add and modify walls.

- Add and modify doors in a building model.

- Add and modify windows in a building model.

Lesson 07 | Creating a Basic Floor Plan

This lesson describes how to create a basic floor plan and place building elements in it to start creating a building design. You begin the lesson by learning the steps to create walls in a floor plan. Then, you learn about temporary dimensions and drawing aids. Next, you learn about some recommended practices for placing walls. The lesson concludes with an exercise on adding walls in a floor plan view.

Revit Architecture provides floor plan views in which you develop a building layout by placing elements such as walls, doors, windows, floors, and standalone components. You use dimensions and constraints to control and document the placement of building elements.

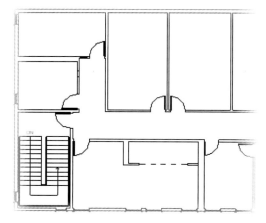

Floor plan view with walls, doors, windows, and stairs

Objectives

After completing this lesson, you will be able to:

- Create walls in a floor plan.

- Describe temporary dimensions.

- Describe drawing aids.

- State the recommended practices for placing walls.

- Add walls in a floor plan view.

Creating Walls in a Floor Plan

In Revit, you can either draw objects or place them—the process is the same. The objects can be either model objects, such as walls and doors, or annotation objects, such as dimensions and spot elevations. You begin by selecting the necessary tool on the Home or Annotate tab. Next, you specify Draw options, such as straight or arc lines, for sketched objects and set variables using the Options Bar. Finally, draw or place the object.

> **Note:** *You can place objects without setting options beforehand. You can change object properties at any time.*

Walls are the basic building elements that constitute a building model. They host elements such as doors and windows, and define rooms. You create walls for a building design in the floor plan views.

In Revit, walls are elements that represent physical walls. Walls automatically set their base to a level. When walls meet or intersect, they automatically join and combine with their internal structures. Walls do not attach automatically to other building elements such as roofs and ceilings. You must attach walls manually by selecting them and using the Attach and Detach options.

You can use the following wall types in a building model. You can modify wall types for specific purposes.

Wall Type	Description
Generic	Generic walls are types of the basic wall system family. They have a simple structure and are differentiated by the thickness of the walls. Generic walls are designed to be used as placeholders that you replace with more complex wall structures later in the design process.
Complex	Complex walls are also types of the basic wall family. They are composed of parallel layers of materials as actual walls. These layers consist of planes of material such as gypsum board, studs, insulation, air spaces, bricks, and sheathing.

Wall Type	Description
Curtain	Curtain walls are in the curtain wall system family. They consist of panels divided by grid lines. You can specify the material of each panel and place mullions of specific shape, size, and material on the grid lines to represent actual mullions.
Stacked	Stacked walls belong to the stacked wall system family. They consist of basic wall types placed one over the other.

Procedure: Creating Walls

The following steps describe how to create architectural walls.

1   Click Home tab > Build panel > Wall drop-down > Wall.

2   On the Place Wall tab, Element panel, select the required wall type from the Type Selector drop-down.

3   Set the Draw or Pick option, as necessary.

Note: *You can pick lines to place walls along their length.*

4   On the Options Bar, select the position of the location line from the Location Line list.

5   On the Options Bar, select a top constraint level from the Height list to control the height of the wall.

Note: *If you select Unconnected from the Height list, enter a dimension value for Height.*

6   On the Options Bar, select the Chain check box to draw walls sequentially.

Chapter 04 | The Basics of the Building Model

7   Click in the view window to specify the starting point of the wall. Drag the cursor from the starting point to draw the wall. Click to place the wall segment endpoint. Notice that the temporary dimensions and angle orientations are displayed.

Note: *If you use the Pick Lines tool, select a line in the drawing area.*

8   Click Place Wall tab > Select panel > Modify to finish drawing the wall.

About Temporary Dimensions

Temporary dimensions indicate the element size and relative position of an object that you select or want to place. These dimensions help you find elements accurately in a building model.

Definition of Temporary Dimensions

Temporary dimensions appear when you create or select elements, such as a wall. These dimensions are displayed in reference to the nearest element that is perpendicular or parallel to the one you select. A temporary length dimension for a wall is also displayed from the starting point to the endpoint of the wall.

Listening Dimensions

Listening dimensions are the temporary dimensions for which you can specify values during placement. Listening dimensions appear in bold and change when you drag the cursor to create an element, such as a wall.

Viewing Temporary Dimensions

When you select an element, temporary dimensions display in reference to the nearest element. Therefore, they might differ from the listening dimensions originally displayed during creation. You can move the witness lines of temporary dimensions to reference-specific elements. To do this, select the Move Witness Line grip on the witness line and drag the grip to a different element. Changes made to witness lines are not saved.

Modifying Temporary Dimensions to Modify Elements

You can resize or move elements by modifying their temporary dimensions. For example, you can move the wall between two rooms by modifying the temporary dimensions associated with the wall.

Tip: *Modifying temporary dimensions is a basic skill in Revit, and understanding how to do this will speed your design work considerably.*

In the following illustration, the drawing on the left shows the temporary dimensions for a selected wall. After you modify the temporary dimension on the left of this wall element from 8 feet to 6 feet (2.4 m to 1.8 m), the wall moves 2 feet to the left. This is shown in the illustration on the right.

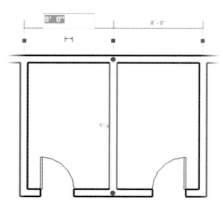

Before modification

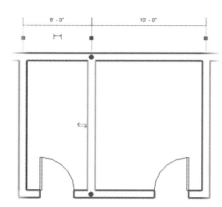

After modification

Example of Temporary Dimensions

The following illustrations show listening and temporary dimensions.

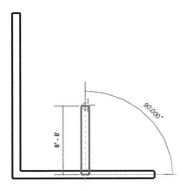

Listening dimensions

Temporary dimensions

About Drawing Aids

Revit provides dimensions and other indicators that help in building the design model accurately. These aids include listening dimensions, alignment lines, and snaps.

Definition of Drawing Aids

Drawing aids appear as you create or place objects while sketching a design. For example, when you place a wall in a building, listening dimensions and alignment lines appear to show its position with reference to nearby walls. A snap appears when you join a wall to an existing wall.

Alignment Lines

Alignment lines appear when you move the cursor horizontally or vertically, or when you cross the extension of a line or wall while placing an element.

Snaps

Snaps appear when you move the cursor over geometric points in a sketch such as endpoints and midpoints. Snaps display individual icons for recognition.

Example of Drawing Aids

The following illustrations show horizontal and vertical alignment lines, and endpoint and midpoint snaps.

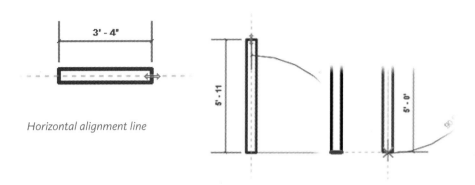

Horizontal alignment line

Vertical alignment lines

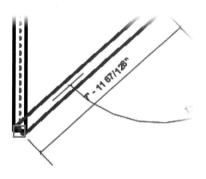

Endpoint snap

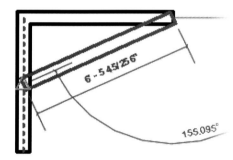

Midpoint snap

Guidelines for Placing Walls

Walls are host elements in Revit. You can create a variety of walls in a building design. The following best practices help you create walls effectively.

Guidelines

- Choose to draw walls of a specific height or constrain their tops to levels. Setting wall heights to the appropriate level helps you create an accurate model more quickly.

- Create exterior walls from the lowest to the highest level and interior walls from floor to floor. This ensures that the building exterior is consistent in all plan views and allows you to change the interior layouts as required.

- Place walls quickly and accurately by entering distance values using the keyboard to save time.

- If you are placing walls with the Draw option, you do not need to be too accurate with the cursor because snaps help you to place the walls accurately. If the snap increment is not precise enough, increase the view zoom level. You can set snap preferences by clicking Snaps in the Settings drop-down on the Project Settings panel of the Manage tab.

- Use the Chain option when placing a series of connected walls to save time.

- Use the Edit tools to locate walls precisely after they have been placed. Edit tools, such as Align and Trim, save time once you get used to them.

- Reuse previously drafted information whenever possible by importing and referring to CAD plans. You can trace over or pick lines in the CAD files to create Revit elements accurately. Then, you can model existing conditions quickly.

- Combine the Pick option with TAB+select to create walls around building outlines and save multiple picks. The Pick option saves the effort of tracing.

- Hold down the SHIFT key while drawing to force walls to be orthogonal, either vertical or horizontal, and eliminate the possibility of errors when drawing long walls.

Example

The following illustration shows a chain of lines selected using the Pick option while working with the Wall tool.

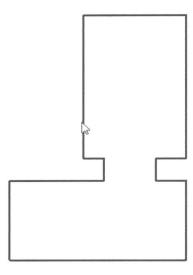

Chapter 04 | The Basics of the Building Model

Exercise | Add Walls in a Floor Plan View

In this exercise, you open a project file and add walls in a floor plan view.

You are working on a project and you need to add walls to start developing one wing of the building. You use temporary dimensions to modify the location of walls.

You do the following:

- Add walls to a building model.
- Modify the temporary dimensions and type of a wall.

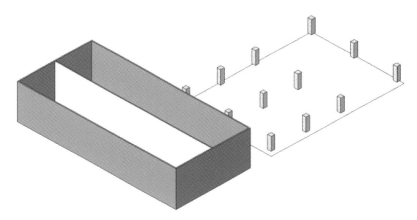

The completed exercise

Completing the Exercise:	*To complete the exercise, follow the steps in this book or in the onscreen exercise. In the onscreen list of chapters and exercises, click Chapter 4: The Basics of the Building Model. Click Exercise: Add Walls in a Floor Plan View.*

Add Walls to a Building Model

1   Open *i_rac_essentials_basic_plan.rvt* or *m_rac_essentials_basic_plan.rvt*. The file opens in the Ground Floor view. Notice columns and grids in the upper half of the view. The lines in the lower portion of the view provide an outline for the new building footprint.
Note: The illustrations for the metric dataset will be slightly different from those shown here.

2   Zoom in to the lower half of the view.

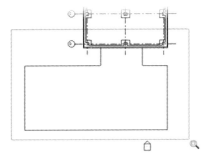

3   Click Home tab > Build panel > Wall.

4   On the Place Wall tab, Element panel, ensure that Basic Wall : Generic - 6" (Basic Wall : Generic - 150mm) is selected in the Type Selector drop-down.

5   Click Place Wall tab > Draw Panel > Rectangle to create four walls by clicking two corner points.

6   On the Options Bar, ensure that Core Face: Exterior is selected in the Location Line list.

7   In the view window:
     • Position the cursor on the upper-left corner of the rectangle.
     • When a square endpoint snap displays, click to start drawing the walls.

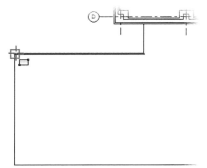

8   Move the cursor to the lower-right corner of the rectangle. When the endpoint snap displays, click to draw four walls.

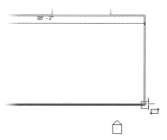

9   Click Modify.

10   Open the default 3D view.

11   On the View Control Bar, click Model Graphics Style > Shading with Edges.

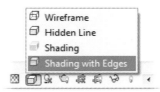

12   The walls in the 3D view appear as shown. Zoom in as necessary to view the walls clearly.

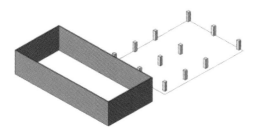

Modify the Temporary Dimensions and Type of a Wall

1   Open the Ground Floor view.

2   Select the Wall tool again to place a wall inside the building.

3   On the Draw panel, ensure that Line is selected.

4   On the Options Bar, select Wall Centerline from the Location Line list.

5   In the view window:
     • Place the cursor over the left wall so that the triangular midpoint snap displays.

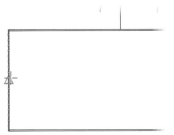

     • Click to start drawing the new wall.
     • Drag the cursor to the right wall.

6   When the triangular midpoint snap displays, click to finish drawing the new wall segment.

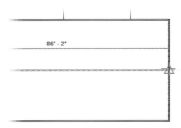

7   Notice that the Wall tool is still active. The wall you just placed shows temporary dimensions.

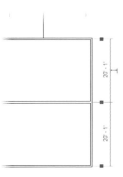

8   To move the wall slightly:

- Click the value field of the lower temporary dimension.
- Enter **20** (**6000** mm).

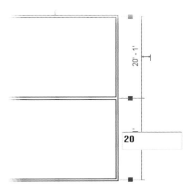

- Press ENTER. The wall moves down slightly and the dimensions are updated.

9   Click Modify. The dimensions disappear.

10   In the view window, select the new wall to assign a specific type to the wall.

11   Select Basic Wall : Interior - 5" Partition (2-hr) or Basic Wall : Interior - 135mm Partition (2-hr) from the Type Selector drop-down.

12   Click anywhere in the view window to clear the selection.

13   Open the default 3D view to check your work. Notice that the interior wall has gypsum wallboard on both the surfaces.

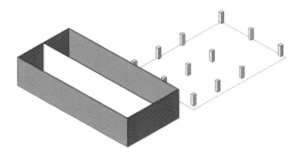

14   Close the file without saving changes.

Lesson 08 | Adding and Modifying Walls

This lesson describes how to add and modify walls. You begin the lesson by learning about walls and wall properties. Then, you learn the steps to modify walls. Next, you learn about joins, the steps to edit and prevent wall joins, and about structural walls and foundations. The lesson concludes with some recommended practices for working with walls and joins, followed by exercises on adding and modifying walls and adding structural walls and footings.

Walls in Revit are parametric elements that have height, thickness, materials, and other properties associated with them.

The following illustrations show various examples of adding and modifying walls in different views.

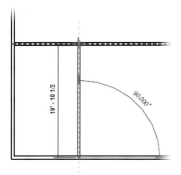

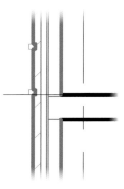

Wall being added in a plan view

Wall selected in a section view

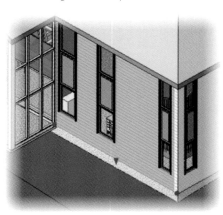

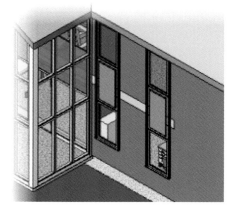

Wall selected in a 3D view

Same wall with a different wall type applied

Objectives

After completing this lesson, you will be able to:

- Describe walls.

- Describe wall properties.

- Modify walls.

- Describe joins.

- Edit and prevent wall joins.

- Describe structural walls and foundations.

- State the recommended practices for adding and modifying walls.

- Add and modify walls.

- Add structural walls and footings. (Optional)

About Walls

Walls are important elements that constitute the shell and internal partitions of a building model. In Revit, walls are 3D parametric elements that host elements such as doors and windows, and define rooms.

Definition of Walls

Walls in Revit are elements that represent the physical walls of a building. Like actual walls, they can be monolithic or composed of parallel layers of materials. These layers can consist of a single continuous plane of material such as Concrete Masonry Units (block) or multiple materials such as gypsum board, studs, insulation, air spaces, bricks, and sheathing.

Wall Layers

Each layer within a wall element has a definite thickness and physical composition and a specific purpose. For example, some layers provide structural support and some act as thermal barriers. Each layer has material, thickness, and function parameters.

The following illustration shows wall layers in a floor plan view with medium or fine detail level.

Location Line of a Wall

You create a wall and its layers by sketching its location line in a plan view or 3D view. The location line represents a vertical plane in the individual wall segment, which does not change with the wall type. For example, if you draw a block wall and set its location line to Core Centerline, the location line does not change when you change the structure of the wall to stud.

You can change the location line properties as an instance property of the wall. If you change the location line for a wall, the wall does not move to align itself with the new location line. If you change the wall type or orientation, the wall may change its position around the location line based on its internal structure.

In the following illustration, the location line, wall centerline, is represented by a dashed line.

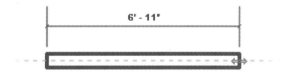

 Note: *The centerlines of two collinear walls of different widths are automatically aligned.*

Wall Function Type Parameter

You use the wall function type parameter for scheduling walls in a project. You can set the wall function type parameter to the following settings: Interior, Exterior, Retaining, Foundation, and Soffit. For example, you can use the Retaining parameter to create a retaining wall.

Example of a Wall

The following illustrations show a wall with different wall types applied.

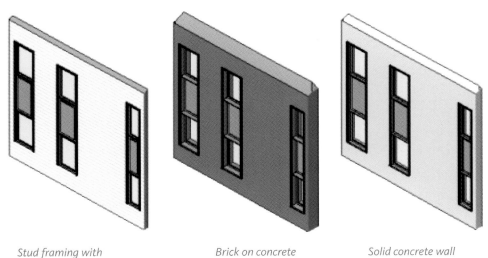

Stud framing with wood siding wall

Brick on concrete block wall

Solid concrete wall

About Wall Properties

You might face a situation, such as a change in level height, when you also need to modify the associated walls. Revit allows you to change the properties of wall instances and wall types at any stage of the design process.

Definition of Wall Properties

The properties of a wall define its appearance, structure, and size. The properties of a wall are categorized into type and instance parameters. Some wall properties are common to all wall types, and some are specific to only a few wall types.

Type Parameters

Type parameters are common to all the elements of a family type in a project. When you modify a family type, the change is reflected throughout the project. For example, if you increase the thickness of the stud layer in a wall type, all the walls with the same wall type update automatically in the project.

To modify type parameters, you create a new wall type, change the required type parameters, and then apply the new type to the selected walls. This prevents you from unintentionally modifying other walls of the original type. You can modify the type parameters that affect the structure of a wall, its layers and materials, behavior at inserts and ends, wall function, and display.

The following illustration shows wall type parameters in the Type Properties dialog box.

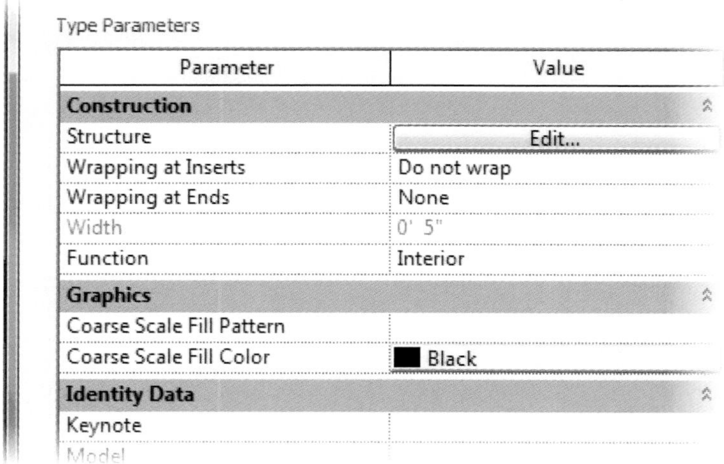

Type Parameters

Parameter	Value
Construction	⌄
Structure	Edit...
Wrapping at Inserts	Do not wrap
Wrapping at Ends	None
Width	0' 5"
Function	Interior
Graphics	⌄
Coarse Scale Fill Pattern	
Coarse Scale Fill Color	Black
Identity Data	⌄
Keynote	
Model	

Instance Parameters

When you change an instance parameter, the properties of only selected walls are altered. Some of the instance parameters that you can change are Location Line, Base Constraint, Top Constraint, Room Bounding, and Structural Usage.

The following illustration shows instance parameters of a particular wall element.

Instance Parameters - Control selected or to-be-created instance

Parameter	Value
Constraints	
Location Line	Finish Face: Exterior
Base Constraint	Ground Floor
Base Offset	0' 0"
Base is Attached	☐
Base Extension Distance	0' 0"
Top Constraint	Unconnected
Unconnected Height	20' 0"
Top Offset	0' 0"
Top is Attached	☐
Top Extension Distance	0' 0"
Room Bounding	☑
Related to Mass	☐
Structural	
Structural Usage	Non-bearing
Dimensions	
Length	40' 2"

Example of Wall Properties

The following illustrations show a wall before and after modifying the Top Constraint parameter.

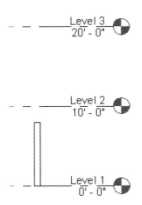

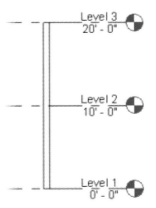

Top Constraint parameter set to an unconnected height

Top Constraint parameter set to Level 3

Modifying Walls

You can modify wall properties, such as length, height, and alignment, by changing the wall structure. You can also modify wall profiles and add openings or cuts on walls.

Procedure: Modifying Wall Properties

The following steps describe how to modify wall properties.

1   In the view window, select the wall that you want to modify.

2   To resize the wall, do one of the following:
    • Drag the end grip to a new length.
    • Select the temporary dimension for the wall and enter a new value.

3   To flip the orientation of the wall between the exterior and the interior, click the flip arrows.

 Note: *The flip arrows are always displayed on the exterior.*

4   To change the wall type:
    • Click Modify Walls tab > Element panel > Element Properties drop-down > Instance Properties.
    • In the Instance Properties dialog box, select a new wall type from the Type list.

5   To change the wall height or base and top constraints:
    • In the Instance Properties dialog box, change the Base Constraint parameter to move the lower end of the wall up or down to other levels.
    • Set the Unconnected Height parameter to another value, if required.
    • Set the Top Constraint parameter to the appropriate level.

6   Close the Instance Properties dialog box.

7   To modify all instances of a wall type:
    • Right-click one instance of a wall. Click Select All Instances.
    • Click Modify Walls tab > Element panel > Element Properties drop-down > Instance Properties.
    • Enter new values for the properties you want to change.

Note: *You can change all instances of a wall to a different type. The modified walls are located relative to the location lines. The position of the location lines is based on the value of the Location Line parameter for each wall segment.*

Procedure: Modifying Wall Profiles

The following steps describe how to modify wall profiles.

1   Open an elevation or section view from the Project Browser.

2   Select the wall that you want to modify.

3   Click Modify Walls tab > Modify Wall panel > Edit Profile.

4   Select an existing wall boundary line. You can resize, redraw, or drag the line to a new position.

   You can also draw new lines or arcs. The outline of the wall must be a closed series of lines or arcs. If you open the boundary profile, you must add new lines to close the boundary.

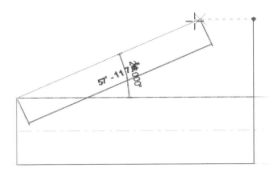

5   Click Finish Wall to complete the changes to the wall profile.

Procedure: Adding Openings to Walls

The following steps describe how to add openings to walls by editing the profile.

1   Open an elevation or section view from the Project Browser.

2   Select the wall that you want to modify.

3   Click Modify Walls tab > Modify Wall panel > Edit Profile.

4   On Modify Walls > Edit Profile tab, Draw panel, select the line type tool that you need to use.

5   Draw the openings. Each opening must have a closed, nonintersecting boundary.

6   Click Finish Wall to complete the changes to the wall profile.

About Joins

Joins help connect walls and show corners in a building design. Typically, walls join automatically to form corners. When they do not join automatically, you specify a join to show the design intent.

Definition of Joins

Joins represent the display of the intersection of two walls in a plan view at the medium or fine detail level. You use joins to clean up the intersection of wall layers. Based on the situation and the components, you can specify joins using the Wall Joins option on the Edit Geometry panel of the Modify tab. You can also use the Trim option on the Edit panel of the Modify tab.

Wall Joins

Revit automatically joins the intersection of walls. You can classify wall joins as Butt, Miter, and Square Off. All wall joins are butt joins by default. Joins with angles less than 20 degrees are miter joins, and joins with wall ends squared off to 90 degrees are square off joins.

Radius Joins

You use radius joins to create rounded corners at wall intersections. You create radius joins by drawing a wall using the Fillet Arc draw option and then picking two walls to create a fillet between them. You can specify the radius or drag the radius wall to create the join. Revit does not allow you to specify multiple radius joins at one location. The following illustration shows a radius join.

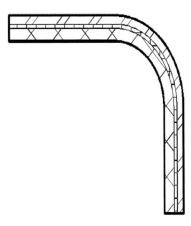

Example of Joins

The following illustration shows different types of wall joins.

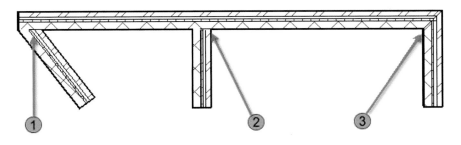

1. Square Off join

2. Butt join

3. Miter join

Editing and Preventing Wall Joins

The internal structure and layers of walls meet and join at corners. You can edit wall joins to suit design requirements.

You can prevent walls from automatically joining with other walls when you want to display control joins or expansion spaces in masonry walls. You may need to show an expansion joint of a few millimeters between two walls while designing a building or you may be unable to show a particular condition you need at a corner by joining the walls. You facilitate this expansion by preventing the ends of walls from joining.

Procedure: Editing a Wall Join

The following steps describe how to edit a wall join.

1   Change the view to a plan view.

2   Set the detail level of the view to medium or fine.

3   Click Modify tab > Edit Geometry panel > Wall Joins.

4   Position the cursor over a wall join until a large square is displayed around the join. Click to select the join.

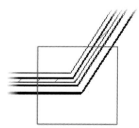

5   On the Options Bar, select Clean Join from the Display list to clean up the join.

 Tip: *Select Don't Clean Join if you do not want the internal wall layers to join. The default display setting is Use View Setting, which is Clean Join by default.*

6   Click a Configuration option to change the type of wall join to Butt, Miter, or Square Off.

7   Click Next or Previous to toggle through the possible configurations.

8   End the Wall Joins tool.

Procedure: Preventing a Wall Join

The following steps describe how to prevent a wall end from joining with another wall end.

1   Click Modify tab > Edit Geometry panel > Wall Joins.

2   Position the cursor over a free end of a wall until a large square is displayed.

3   Click to select the end of the wall.

4   On the Options Bar, click Disallow Join.

Note: *You can also select a wall in a plan view and right-click over a wall end grip. Click Disallow Join.*

About Structural Walls and Foundations

Structural walls and foundations form an integral part of building design. You designate walls as structural when you need to track their structural properties. You place foundations after adding structural walls and columns.

Definition of Structural Walls and Foundations

Structural walls resist gravity and seismic forces. They are designed and scheduled accordingly. Structural walls hold up walls and floors that are placed on top of them.

A structural wall in Revit differs from nonstructural walls by the value of an instance parameter named Structural Usage. This parameter classifies walls as Non-bearing, Bearing, Shear, and Structural Combined. For all walls placed using the Partition Wall option on the Build panel of the Home tab, this property is set to Non-bearing by default. To create structural walls, use the Structural Wall option on the Build panel of the Home tab.

Foundations are added to the base of a wall or column to provide support to it. Foundations in Revit can be walls or foundation objects. You place foundation walls with the Wall tool. For foundation walls, the base of the wall instance is set down from the level by the distance set in the Depth value field, and the top of the wall is set to the current level. Foundation walls schedule as walls.

Structure Panel

To place foundations, either isolated or as wall footings, use the Foundation option on the Structure panel of the Home tab.

Foundations placed under wall segments are different from foundation walls placed by using the Wall or Structural Wall tools. A Foundation object snaps to the base of a wall or column and moves with the wall when the base of the wall is moved up or down. Foundation objects schedule as foundations.

Example of Structural Walls and Foundations

The following illustrations show structural walls with various foundations.

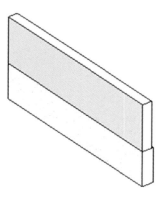

Structural wall with a foundation wall at the base

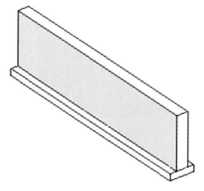

Structural wall with a foundation object attached to the base

Guidelines for Adding and Modifying Walls

You add different types of walls while creating a building design. You can modify the properties of the walls at any stage while creating a design and specify various joins between walls based on your requirements. The following best practices help you work with walls and joins efficiently.

Guidelines for Working with Walls

- Constrain the tops of walls to levels rather than to specific heights so that you can change the height of the walls by changing the height of levels and have the walls, floors, and rooms adjust automatically. This saves a significant amount of time and minimizes errors.

- Specify the length of the wall by entering a value while drawing the wall so that the wall is automatically drawn to size. This saves time and provides greater accuracy than specifying the length while drawing.

- Use the flip orientation double arrow controls while drawing or modifying walls to ensure that the exterior faces of the exterior walls are properly set. By using these controls correctly, you can display the compound walls properly at medium or fine detail level in the plan, elevation, section, and 3D views. The wall flip control ensures an accurate display of wall layers.

- Offset a wall from the cursor as you sketch it by specifying a value for Offset on the Options Bar. You can also specify whether the offset is measured to the near edge, centerline, or far edge of the wall. You save time when you specify a precise offset while placing walls.

- Use generic wall types early in a project and replace them as the design develops with more specific wall types. This allows you to populate a design quickly and make changes later.

Guidelines for Working with Wall Joins

- Display wall joins in plan views set to medium detail level and an appropriate view scale so that you can clearly observe the wall joins. Revit manages line weights automatically according to view scale.

- You can use the Thin Lines display toggle from the Graphics panel on the View tab to observe wall join intersections more clearly while joining complex wall types. Note that this is only a display toggle and it affects all views.

- Set wall join priorities in the Wall Properties dialog box. Wall layers with lower bracket numbers in the Function field will cut layers with higher numbers. Setting priorities correctly allows you to display most standard join conditions without additional view detailing.

- Use detail lines and fill patterns to illustrate complex wall join specifications instead of using the Edit Wall Joins option. Complex wall joins can produce a large number of configurations, and you may have to try various configurations to find the desired one. Using detail lines and fill patterns may be quicker and easier than trying to make the software calculate the join.

Example of Guidelines for Working with Walls

The following illustrations show a wall in a plan view and the use of flip orientation controls.

Flip orientation controls on the exterior side

Flip orientation controls with wall exterior reversed

Example of Guidelines for Working with Wall Joins

The following illustrations show a wall join with and without the Thin Lines option selected.

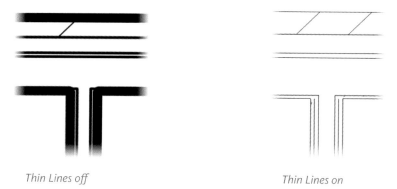

Thin Lines off

Thin Lines on

Chapter 04 | The Basics of the Building Model

The following illustration shows stud walls meeting a block wall when Thin Lines is selected. The stud wall type on the right has different join priorities from the wall on the left, so the layers join differently.

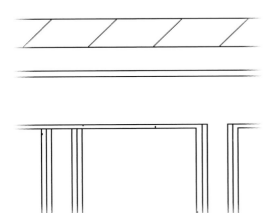

Exercise | Add and Modify Walls

In this exercise, you add and modify walls in a building model.

You want to add new interior and exterior walls to a building project. You need to place and modify walls using a combination of techniques.

You do the following:

- Add foundation walls to the model.

- Create a new wall type from an existing wall type.

- Modify existing walls.

- Add and modify interior walls.

- Create a new interior wall type.

- Place and modify a new wall.

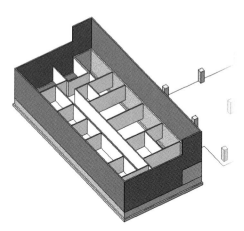

The completed exercise

Completing the Exercise: *To complete the exercise, follow the steps in this book or in the onscreen exercise. In the onscreen list of chapters and exercises, click Chapter 4: The Basics of the Building Model. Click Exercise: Add and Modify Walls.*

Add Foundation Walls to the Model

1 Open *i_rac_essentials_adding_walls.rvt* or *m_rac_essentials_adding_walls.rvt*. The file opens in the default 3D view. The walls and columns are visible in the view.
Note: The illustrations for the metric dataset will be slightly different from those shown here.

2 Select the interior partition wall. You need to first adjust the height of the interior partition wall to make it one story.

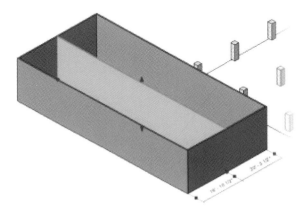

3 Click Modify Walls tab > Element panel > Element Properties drop-down > Instance Properties.

4 In the Instance Properties dialog box:
   - Set the Top Constraint parameter to Up to Level: Main Floor.
   - Click OK.

5 Open the Ground Floor view.

6 Zoom in around the walls in the lower half of the view.

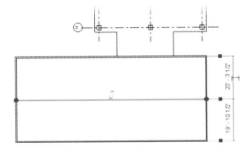

7   Press ESC to clear the wall selection.

8   Activate the Wall tool to place foundation walls under all the exterior walls that you see in the view.

9   Select Basic Wall : Foundation - 12" Concrete (Basic Wall : Foundation - 300mm Concrete) from the Type Selector drop-down.

10   On the Options Bar:
     - Select T.O. Footing from the Depth list.
     - Select Core Face: Exterior from the Location Line list.
       Note: When creating foundation walls, the top of the wall is set to the current level by default and the walls are created downward. Therefore, you set the depth of the foundation walls, not the height.

11   On the Draw panel, select Rectangle to place four walls.

12   In the view window:
     - Position the cursor over the exterior upper-left corner of the walls.
     - When the square endpoint snap is displayed, click to start drawing the foundation walls.
     - Move the cursor to the lower-right corner of the existing walls and click at the square endpoint to finish drawing the foundation walls.

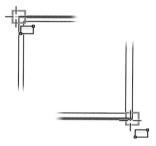

13   Close the warning message box that states that none of the created elements are visible in the Floor Plan: Ground Floor view. This is because the foundation walls are below the view range.

14   Click Modify.

15   Open the default 3D view to check the placement of walls.

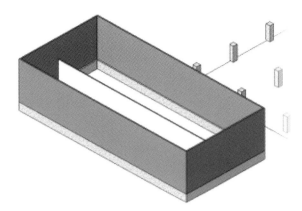

Create a New Wall Type from an Existing Wall Type

1   Open the T.O. Footing view. The new foundation walls are visible.

2   Activate the Wall tool. You will now create a new wall type and create footings as walls for the foundation walls.

3   Ensure that Basic Wall : Foundation - 12" Concrete (Basic Wall : Foundation - 300mm Concrete) is selected in the Type Selector drop-down.

4   Click Place Wall tab > Element panel > Element Properties drop-down > Type Properties to view the properties of this wall type.

5   In the Type Properties dialog box, click Duplicate.

6   In the Name dialog box:
     • For Name, enter **Footing**.
     • Click OK.

     This creates a duplicate of the Basic Wall : Foundation - 12" Concrete (Basic Wall : Foundation - 300 mm Concrete) foundation wall type, named Footing.

7   In the Type Properties dialog box:
     • Notice that Footing is selected in the Type list.
     • Under Construction, for Structure, click Edit.

8   In the Edit Assembly dialog box, under Layers:
- For Structure [1] layer, click the Thickness field.
- Enter **2' 0"** (**600** mm).

9   Click OK to close all dialog boxes.

10   Notice that Basic Wall : Footing is displayed in the Type Selector drop-down.

11   On the Options Bar:
- For Depth, enter **1' 6"** (**450** mm).
- Select Wall Centerline from the Location Line list.

12   On the Draw panel, click Rectangle.

13   Right-click anywhere in the view window. Click View Properties.

14   In the Instance Properties dialog box, under Extents, for View Range, click Edit to set the view range so that you can see the footing in the view when you place the footing.

15   In the View Range dialog box:
- Notice the current settings.
- Under View Depth, select Unlimited from the Level list.
- Click OK.

16   Click OK to close the Instance Properties dialog box.

17 In the view window:
- Zoom in to the corners of the foundation to pick the wall centerline.
- Sketch the footing by snapping the rectangle to the centerline at the upper-left and lower-right corners of the foundation. The new footing walls appear below the foundation walls.

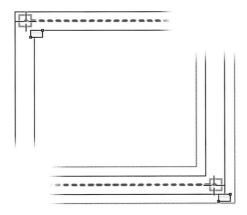

Tip: You can use the scroll wheel on the mouse to zoom in and zoom out.

18 Click Modify.

19 Click View tab > Create panel > Section to check the wall placement.

20 In the view window:
- Click below the lower wall, approximately near the center, and extend the section line upwards.

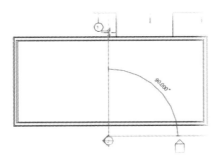

- Click above the upper wall to create the section across the middle of the building.

21 Right-click the section line. Click Go To View to change the active view to the new section.

22 In the Section 1 view, notice the three types of walls that align vertically, face to face, and face to centerline.

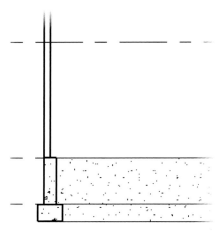

Modify Existing Walls

1 Return to the Ground Floor view.

The building you are designing is on a site that slopes down from north to south. You need to now create stepped foundation walls to account for the fall in grade.

2 In the view window, select the upper horizontal wall.

3 Open the Instance Properties dialog box.

4 In the Instance Properties dialog box:
- Under Constraints, change the value of Base Constraint to Main Floor to raise the base of this wall to the main floor level.
- Click OK. The upper horizontal wall is no longer displayed in the Ground Floor plan view.

5 Click Modify tab > Edit panel > Split to split the side walls and raise a portion of the walls to the main floor level, rather than draw new walls.

6 Zoom in to the upper part of the left wall. Click at 10' 0" (3000 mm) from the top to split the wall.

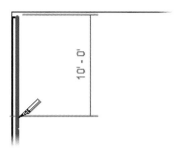

7 Split the upper part of the right wall also at 10' 0" (3000 mm) from the top.

8 Exit the Split tool.

9 In the view window, CTRL+select both the 10' 0" (3000 mm) wall segments.

10 Open the Instance Properties dialog box.

11 In the Instance Properties dialog box:
- Under Constraints, change the value of Base Constraint to Main Floor to raise the base of the wall segments to the main floor level.
- Click OK. The wall segments are no longer displayed in the Ground Floor plan view.

12 Open the default 3D view. Notice that the foundation walls do not meet the exterior wall segments that you moved to the main floor.

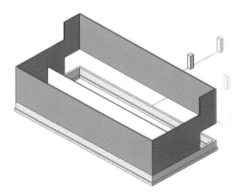

13 Select the long (north) foundation wall.

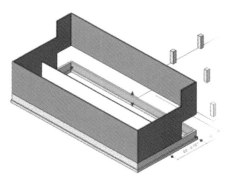

Note: Depending on the zoom level, you may have difficulty highlighting the wall. While selecting objects, pressing TAB multiple times cycles the selection options. You can then click the required object when it highlights.

14 Open the Instance Properties dialog box.

15 In the Instance Properties dialog box:
- Under Constraints, change the value for Top Constraint to Up to Level: Main Floor.
- Click OK to update the wall.

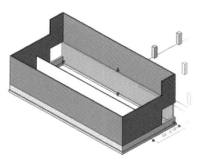

16 In the view window, select the west foundation wall. You need to raise the top of this wall without splitting it.
Tip: Press TAB+select to highlight the correct wall.

17 Click Modify Walls tab > Modify Wall panel > Attach.

18 On the Options Bar, ensure that Top is selected.

Chapter 04 | The Basics of the Building Model

19   Select the wall segment that is raised above the foundation wall to join the walls.
The lower wall updates to meet the upper one.

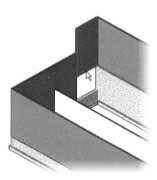

20   Attach the east foundation wall to the wall above it.

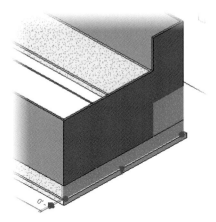

Add and Modify Interior Walls

1   Open the Ground Floor view. You need to place interior walls at the Ground Floor level.

2   Activate the Wall tool.

3   Select Basic Wall : Interior - 4 7/8" Partition (1- hr) or Basic Wall : Interior - 123mm Partition
(1- hr) from the Type Selector drop-down.

You get an error message stating that the top of the wall is lower than the base of the wall. This is because the previously selected footing wall measures down rather than up for its second constraint. Notice that the settings are grayed out on the Options Bar.

4   In the error message box, click Reset Constraints to set the wall constraints back to the default conditions. Notice that the Options Bar is now active.

5   Select Basic Wall : Interior - 4 7/8" Partition (1- hr) or Basic Wall : Interior - 123mm Partition (1-hr) again from the Type Selector drop-down.

6   On the Options Bar:
    - Select Main Floor from the Height list.
    - Ensure that the Chain check box is selected.
    - Ensure that Wall Centerline is selected in the Location Line list.

7   On the Draw panel, ensure that Line is selected.

8   Open the Instance Properties dialog box.

9   In the Instance Properties dialog box:
    - Under Constraints, set the Base Offset value to 0.
    - Click OK.

10 In the view window:
    - Place the cursor over the left end of the lower wall and drag the cursor to the right along the wall. The temporary dimensions appear.
    - Enter **10 9** (**3200** mm).

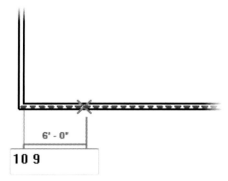

    - Press ENTER to begin the interior wall at the specified distance from the left end of the lower wall.

Note: Imperial users can enter feet and inch values using SPACEBAR rather than by using the foot and inch symbols.

11 Drag the cursor up to the horizontal interior wall and click to place a vertical wall.

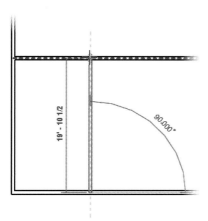

12 Add another interior wall on the far right that is perpendicular to the central horizontal wall and extends to the south wall. To place the wall precisely:

   • Click the dimension field of the temporary dimension.
   • Enter **10 9** (**3200** mm).

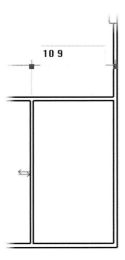

   • Press ENTER.

13 Press ESC to clear the dimensions but keep the Wall tool active.

14 Draw a horizontal wall that is 6' 0" (1800 mm) below the central horizontal wall and between the two vertical walls as shown.

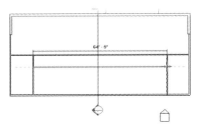

15 Place four more interior walls in the lower portion of the building model as shown. The exact location is not critical.

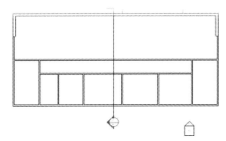

16 Exit the Wall tool.

17 In the lower-left section of the drawing:
   • Select the first vertical wall you just drew.
   • Specify its distance from the wall to the left as **14** (**4300** mm).

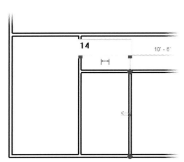

- Set the center-to-center distances between the subsequent walls from the left to the right as **11' 0"**, **11' 0"**, and **17' 8"** (**3400** mm, **3400** mm, and **5400** mm).

Note: You are editing the left temporary dimensions for each wall. If you click the permanent dimension control accidentally, the temporary dimensions become permanent. You can use the Undo option to make the dimension temporary again.

18 Activate the Wall tool.

19 In the upper portion of the building model, place five vertical walls above the central horizontal wall and extending to the north horizontal wall as shown. The exact position of the walls is not critical.

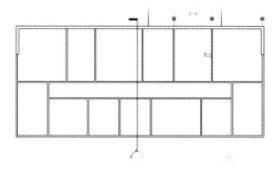

Note: If the Chain check box is selected, use the ESC key to end one placement and begin another.

20 Place two horizontal walls as shown. The position of the walls is not important.

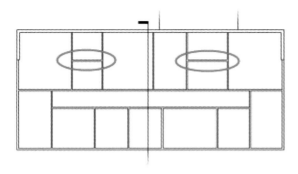

Note: The view you get may differ depending on the placement of the walls.

21 Click Modify.

22 In the upper section of the drawing:
   - From left to right, select the first vertical wall.
   - Specify its distance from the exterior left wall as **17' 6"** (**5300** mm) by modifying the left dimension.

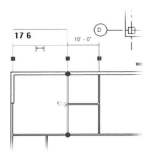

   - Set the center-to-center distances between the subsequent walls moving left to right as **10' 0", 14' 0", 15' 0",** and **14' 0"** (**3000** mm, **4300** mm, **4600** mm, and **4300** mm).

Note: You may have to adjust the Move Witness Line grips on the temporary dimension line depending on how you sketched the walls. Select and drag the grip to the center of the exterior wall, if necessary.

23 In the upper section of the drawing:
   - Select the small horizontal wall on the left.
   - Specify **6' 5"** (**2000** mm) as the distance from the central horizontal wall.
   - Select the small horizontal wall on the right.
   - Specify **10' 6"** (**3200** mm) as the distance from the central horizontal wall.

24 On the Quick Access toolbar, click Modify.

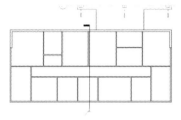

Note: At any time, you can view your design by opening the default 3D view.

Create a New Interior Wall Type

1   Ensure that the Ground Floor view is active. You need to create a new interior wall type for a plumbing wall.

2   Activate the Wall tool.

3   Ensure that Basic Wall : Interior - 4 7/8" Partition (1-hr) or Basic Wall : Interior - 123mm Partition (1-hr) is selected in the Type Selector drop-down.

4   Open the Type Properties dialog box.

5   In the Type Properties dialog box, click Duplicate.

6   In the Name dialog box:
   • For Name, enter **Interior - Plumbing Chase.**
   • Click OK.

7   In the Type Properties dialog box, under Construction, for Structure, click Edit to open the Edit Assembly dialog box.

8   In the Edit Assembly dialog box:
   • Under Layers, select the row for Layer 3. The function is Structure [1].
   • Click Insert two times to create two additional wall layers above the one you selected.
   • Starting with row 3, set the thickness values for the three Structure [1] layers to **0' 2 1/2"**, **0' 4"**, and **0' 2 1/2"** (**90** mm, **120** mm, and **90** mm).

   Note: Imperial users need to use the inch symbol to specify the inch, fractional inch, or decimal inch values.

   • Click OK.

9   Click OK to close the Type Properties dialog box.

   Note: You have just created a new interior wall type. This Interior - Plumbing Chase wall type will now be available to you for use in your design work whenever required.

Place and Modify a New Wall

1   Verify that Basic Wall : Interior - Plumbing Chase is selected in the Type Selector drop-down.

2   In the view window, in the upper-left corner of the building model, sketch a horizontal wall starting from the foundation wall to the interior wall. The exact placement of the wall is not important.

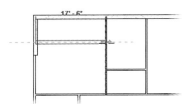

3   Click Modify tab > Edit panel > Align.

4   On the Options Bar, verify that Wall Faces is selected in the Prefer list.

5   In the view window, select the lower end of the vertical foundation wall on the left.

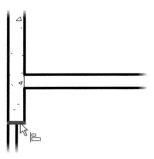

6   Select the lower face of the horizontal plumbing chase wall that you just sketched. The plumbing chase wall moves down and aligns with the lower end of the foundation wall.

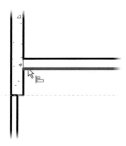

7   Exit the Align tool.

8   Select any of the interior walls other than the plumbing chase. You need to place another interior wall to make a hallway.

9   Click Modify Walls tab > Create panel > Create Similar.

10   In the view window, in the upper section of the drawing, sketch a vertical wall starting from the central horizontal wall and extending to the horizontal plumbing chase wall. The placement of the wall is not critical.

11   Click the right temporary dimension of the vertical wall and specify **5' 6"** (**1680** mm) as the distance from the first vertical wall in the upper section.

12   Click Modify tab > Edit panel > Split to remove a segment of the wall to define the hallway.

13   On the Options Bar, select the Delete Inner Segment check box. This option removes the segment between the two locations being split.

14   In the view window:
     • Zoom in and place the cursor along the upper hallway horizontal wall at the lower end of the vertical wall you just placed.

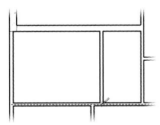

     • When both centerlines appear, click to split the central horizontal wall.
     • Move the cursor along the horizontal wall until it meets the right vertical wall.

15 When both the centerlines appear, click to complete the split. The segment is deleted from between the two splits.

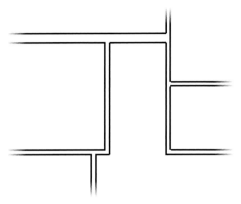

Note: Use the Align or Trim tool to clean up these walls, if necessary. Remember that when you use the Align tool, the wall face you select first holds still and the other wall face moves.

16 With the Split tool still active, move the cursor to the upper end of the left vertical wall and click to split the horizontal plumbing chase wall. Make only one split, so that no wall segment is deleted.

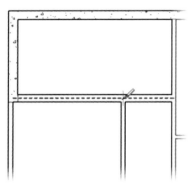

17 Exit the Split tool.

18 In the view window, select the right segment of the plumbing chase wall you just split.

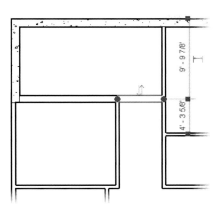

19 Select Basic Wall : Interior - 4 7/8" Partition (1- hr) or Basic Wall : Interior - 123 mm Partition (1-hr) from the Type Selector drop-down. The wall segment changes to this type and the modified wall segment width reduces.

20 Click Modify tab > Edit panel > Align.

21 In the view window, click the upper horizontal part of the plumbing chase wall segment as shown.

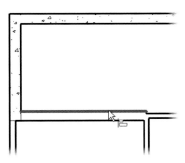

22 Click the upper horizontal part of the new wall segment to align the two segments of the plumbing chase wall.

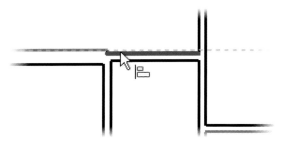

23 Exit the Align tool.

24 Open the default 3D view.

25 Use the view cube to spin the view and display the interior walls that you created.

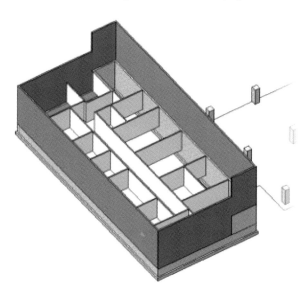

26 Close the file without saving changes.

Optional Exercise | Add Structural Walls and Footings

In this exercise, you add structural walls and footings to a building model.

You need to place load-bearing walls in a wing of the building model. You also need to place foundations under walls and columns.

You do the following:

- Place structural foundation walls.

- Place continuous wall footings and isolated footings.

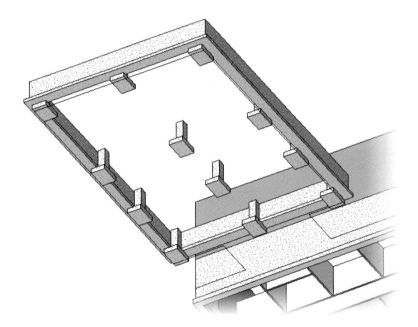

The completed exercise

Completing the Exercise: *To complete the exercise, follow the steps in this book or in the onscreen exercise. In the onscreen list of chapters and exercises, click Chapter 4: The Basics of the Building Model. Click Optional Exercise: Add Structural Walls and Footings.*

Place Structural Foundation Walls

1   Open *i_rac_essentials_structural_walls.rvt* or *m_rac_essentials_structural_walls.rvt*. The file
    opens in the default 3D view.
    Note: The illustrations for the metric dataset will be slightly different from those
    shown here.

2   Open the Main Floor view.

3   Zoom in to the upper part of the view.

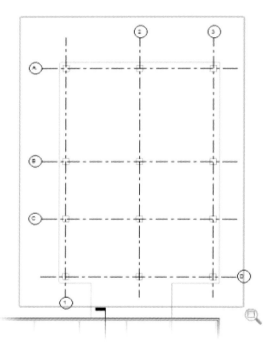

4   Click Home tab > Build panel > Wall drop-down > Structural Wall.

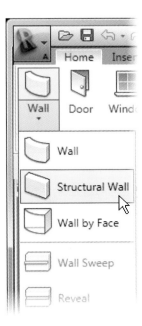

5   Select Basic Wall : Foundation - 12" Concrete (Basic Wall : Foundation - 300mm Concrete)
    from the Type Selector drop-down.

6   On the Options Bar:
    • For Depth, enter **6' 6"** (**3100** mm).
    • Select Core Face: Interior from the Location Line list.

7   On the Draw panel, click Rectangle.

8   In the view window, to draw the structural walls:

  • Select the upper-left corner of the gray outline as the first point.
  • Select the lower-right corner of the outline as the second point.

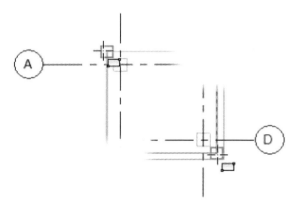

9   Click Modify.

10   In the view window, select one of the structural walls that you just placed.

11   Open the Instance Properties dialog box.

12   In the Instance Properties dialog box:

  • Under Structural, notice that the Structural Usage parameter is set to Bearing.
  • Click Cancel to close the dialog box.

13   Press ESC to clear the wall selection.

Place Continuous Wall Footings and Isolated Footings

1   Click Home tab > Structure panel > Foundation drop-down > Wall Foundation to place footing objects. These objects are different from walls that are placed as footings.

2   In the view window:
   - Place the cursor over one of the structural walls.
   - Press TAB to highlight all four walls.
   - Click to place continuous wall footings under the walls.

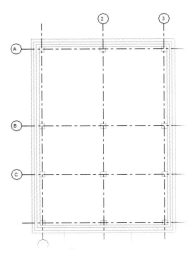

3   Click Modify.

4   Click Home tab > Structure panel > Foundation drop-down > Isolated Foundation to place footings for columns.

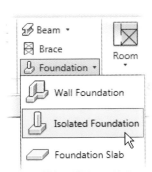

5   Click Place Isolated Foundation tab > Multiple panel > At Columns to place footings under all
    the columns simultaneously.

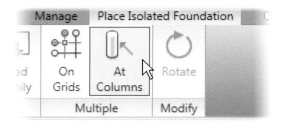

6   In the view window, draw a selection box around the upper rectangle to select all
    the columns.

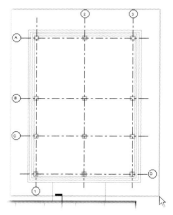

7   On the Multiple Selection panel, click Finish Selection.
    Note: A warning appears stating that the attached structural foundation will be moved to the
    bottom of the column. Close the warning.

8   Click Modify.

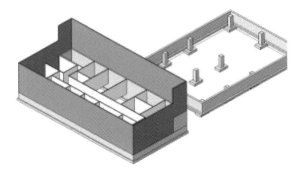

9   Open the default 3D view.

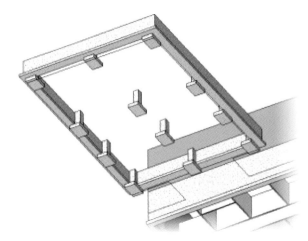

10 Use the view cube to spin the view to notice the underside of the columns, pad footings, and
    wall footings.

    Note: The view may differ depending on the spin.

11 Close the file without saving changes.

Lesson 09 | Working with Compound Walls

This lesson describes how to create and modify compound walls. You begin the lesson by learning about compound walls and how to modify them. Next, you learn the steps to set layer wrapping in compound walls. Then, you learn about the structure of vertically compound walls and the recommended practices for working with compound walls. The lesson concludes with an exercise on creating and modifying compound walls.

You can create compound walls that consist of different layers of material. The wall layers can be of different types of material. You can add sweeps and reveals to wall layers.

The following illustration shows a compound wall with block and brick material in its exterior finish layer, sweeps, and reveals.

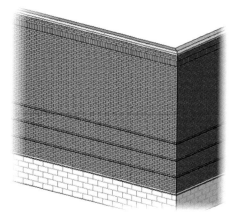

Objectives

After completing this lesson, you will be able to:

- Describe compound walls.

- Describe how to modify compound walls.

- Set layer wrapping in compound walls.

- Describe the structure of vertically compound walls.

- State the recommended practices for working with compound walls.

- Create and modify compound walls.

About Compound Walls

Compound walls are composed of multiple layers that provide space for structural components, underlayment, insulation, air space, membranes or moisture barriers, and finish surfaces.

Definition of Compound Walls

Compound walls are made of parallel layers that consist of a single continuous plane of material, such as plywood, gypsum board, stud, insulation, air space, brick, and sheathing.

Layers in Compound Walls

Each layer within a compound wall has a definite purpose. For example, some layers provide structural support whereas others act as thermal barriers. Each layer in a compound wall has its own material, thickness, and function. Layers in compound walls are visible in plan and section views when the detail level of the view is set to Medium or Fine. Wall layers are not visible when the detail level of the view is set to Coarse. Layers are visible in all four model graphics styles: Hidden Line, Wireframe, Shading, and Shading with Edges.

Layer Join Cleanup in Compound Walls

When two layers are joined, the join is cleaned up if the layers have the same material. For example, a drywall surface layer of one wall type can automatically join a drywall surface layer of another wall type. If the two layers are made of different materials, they do not clean up and a solid line is displayed between them.

The following illustration shows two intersecting walls of a compound wall type consisting of air, masonry brick, and insulation layers.

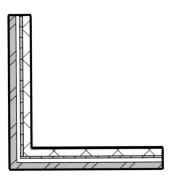

Materials Used in Compound Walls

You can assign a different material to each layer in a compound wall. You distinguish materials assigned to different layers by fill patterns that follow certain recognized graphic standards. Fill patterns are assigned to a cut or a projection display. Walls are cut in floor plans and sections. They are projected in elevation views so that their surfaces and edges are displayed. Compound walls display fill patterns at medium and fine levels, which are appropriate for close-up or detail views. You can specify a fill pattern at the coarse level of detail to distinguish between walls of different types or phases. The coarse detail level generally shows walls as two lines.

The following illustration shows a section view of a compound wall with gypsum board and metal stud layers.

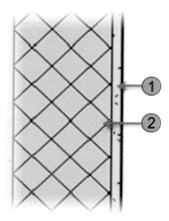

1 Gypsum board

2 Metal stud

Functions of Compound Wall Layers

You can assign a specific function to each layer of a compound wall to ensure that each layer is joined to its corresponding functional layer when two compound walls are joined. Layer functions follow an order of precedence. High-priority layers are connected before low-priority layers. For example, when you join two compound walls, a priority 1 layer in the first wall is joined to a priority 1 layer in the second wall.

A priority 1 layer has the highest priority and can pass through low priority layers before it is joined. A layer with a lower priority cannot pass through a layer of equal or higher priority.

The following table describes various layers with their priorities.

Function/Priority	Description
Structure (priority 1)	Supports the remainder of the wall, floor, or roof.
Substrate (priority 2)	Consists of materials such as plywood or gypsum board, which act as a foundation for another layer.
Thermal/Air Layer (priority 3)	Provides insulation and prevents air penetration.
Membrane Layer	Prevents water vapor penetration. The membrane layer should have zero thickness.
Finish 1 (priority 4)	Used as the exterior layer.
Finish 2 (priority 5)	Used as the interior layer.

The following illustration shows a compound wall with joined layers based on their priority.

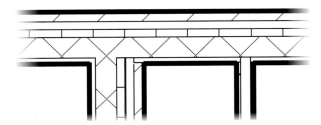

Layer Wrapping in Compound Walls

Compound wall layers can wrap or blend at end caps of the walls and at inserts such as doors and windows. Layers can also wrap with nonrectangular shapes.

Layer wrapping displays only in plan views. You modify layer wrapping characteristics or edit the layer structure in the Type Properties dialog box.

The following illustrations show different types of layer wrappings in a compound wall.

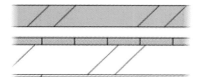

Compound wall with no end cap wrapping

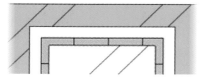

Exterior surface of wall wrapping at end caps

Layers as References

You can select a wall layer as a reference point for dimensioning or alignment while placing building components such as windows and doors. By default, every basic wall type has two layers called core boundary. The core boundary layers do not have any thickness, but they can be used as references. You cannot modify the core boundary layers.

Example of Compound Walls

The following illustrations show compound walls in different views.

Compound exterior wall in a 3D view

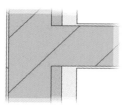

Compound walls joining in a plan view

Segment of a compound wall in a 3D view

About Modifying Compound Walls

You can modify compound walls and their properties in several ways before or after placing them in a building model. For example, you can modify one instance of a compound wall or you can modify a family type and apply the change to all the walls of that type.

Definition of Modifying Compound Walls

You modify compound walls to specify changes during the course of the design process. For example, based on project requirements, you can change a brick wall to a wood wall. You can modify the type, appearance, and properties of compound walls. You can also change the orientation and modify the layer pattern display of a compound wall.

Modifying the Wall Type

You modify a wall type by selecting a new wall type from the Type Selector drop-down. For example, to create a curtain wall, you can select a Basic wall and change its type to Curtain wall.

Modifying Wall Properties

Every wall has a set of properties that define its appearance, structure, and size. Properties that apply only to a selected wall in a view are called instance parameters. If you change an instance parameter, only the selected walls are affected.

You can also modify the family type parameters. If you modify a family type, the change is reflected in all the components of that family type. For example, if you increase the width of the concrete masonry layer for the Exterior - Brick on CMU wall type, all walls in the project that have the same wall type are also modified.

Modifying the Layer Pattern Display

The material of a layer is represented with fill patterns. You specify the fill pattern and fill color properties of the materials in a compound structure based on the project requirements. You can view fill patterns in the Coarse, Medium, and Fine levels of display. To view the fill pattern in the desired detail level, change the detail level of the view.

Note: *To modify the family type properties for a particular set of walls, you create a new family type. You can then make the required modifications and apply the new type to the walls requiring change. This prevents you from unintentionally modifying other walls that belong to the same family type.*

Flipping the Orientation

When you select a compound wall in a plan view, control arrows are displayed. If you click the control arrows, the layers of the wall reverse position. You can also flip the orientation of a compound wall in plan view by pressing SPACEBAR.

The following illustration shows the flip controls of a wall.

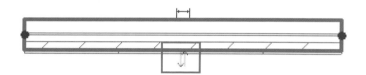

Note: *If you do not keep walls in proper orientation, they will not join correctly and elevation views will not display surface patterns correctly.*

Example of Modifying Compound Walls

The following illustrations show various modifications on compound walls.

Before and after flipping the orientation control

Before and after changing coarse scale fill pattern

Before and after changing wall type

Setting Layer Wrapping in Compound Walls

You can insert additional layers in a compound wall according to your requirements. You can set the properties of each layer individually. Using the Type Properties and Edit Assembly dialog boxes, you can also set layer wrapping that determines how the layers of the wall wrap at inserts such as doors and windows.

Procedure: Setting Layer Wrapping in the Type Properties Dialog Box

The following steps describe how to set layer wrapping in the Type Properties dialog box.

1   Select a wall.

2   Click Modify Walls tab > Element panel > Element Properties drop-down > Type Properties.

3   In the Type Properties dialog box, set layer wrapping at wall ends and inserts. You do this by selecting appropriate options from the Wrapping at Inserts and Wrapping at Ends lists under Construction in the Type Properties dialog box.

Procedure: Setting Layer Wrapping in the Edit Assembly Dialog Box

The following steps describe how to set layer wrapping in the Edit Assembly dialog box.

1   Select a wall.

2   Open the Type Properties dialog box.

3   In the Type Properties dialog box, for Structure, click Edit to open the Edit Assembly dialog box.

4   In the Edit Assembly dialog box, under Layers, select the check box in the Wraps column to set the wrap capability for individual layers.

Note: *Windows and doors have a type property called Wall Closure. This property overrides the wrap settings that you set in the Edit Assembly dialog box.*

About Vertically Compound Walls

You can create a vertically compound wall consisting of different materials along its height. For example, you can create a wall layer with a stone facing lower part and a brick facing upper part.

Definition of Vertically Compound Walls

A wall with non-uniform structure throughout its height is known as a vertically compound wall. You can divide the layers of a vertically compound wall into vertical parts. Each part can be composed of a different material. You can define the structure of vertically compound walls by using either layers or regions.

You can also create vertically compound walls with sweeps or reveals. A sweep is a profile that is added to a wall layer at a certain elevation, such as a row of brick that stands out from the rest of the wall surface. A reveal is a profile that is removed from a wall layer, such as a row of brick that is indented from the rest of the wall surface.

Structure

You specify the structure for vertically compound walls by defining the location of sweeps, reveals, and splits in layers.

The following illustration shows a vertically compound wall with a sweep and multiple reveals. This is an exterior wall that combines structure with decoration. The exterior layer has been divided with a different material assigned to each new layer. Layer 1, which is white in the illustration, is made of concrete block and appears on row 1 of the structure table. Layer 2 is made of bricks and appears on row 2 of the table.

Row

A row is a horizontal unit in the Layers group of the Edit Assembly dialog box. You assign a function, material, and thickness to each row. You can also specify wrapping in the row. You add a row to specify a function and material definition. Then, you can assign this function to a region that you create when you split a vertical layer.

Layer

A layer is a rectangular part of a wall that has a constant thickness and spans the height of the wall. It usually does not span the full width of a compound wall. You can change the thickness of a layer in the row assigned to the layer in the Edit Assembly dialog box.

The following illustration shows a vertically compound wall with a sweep and layers.

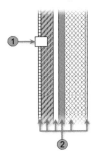

1️⃣ Sweep

2️⃣ Layers

Region

A region is any shape that does not extend throughout the wall. Regions can have constant or variable thickness, in which case a numeric or variable value, respectively, is assigned to the row. You cannot change the thickness of the region in the row assigned to the region in the Edit Assembly dialog box. The thickness value appears shaded and cannot be modified. You can only change the thickness and height of a region graphically in the preview pane.

Example of a Vertically Compound Wall

The following illustration shows vertically compound walls of block and brick on the exterior face. The walls have a protruding ledge at the top of the block, three rows of brick inset from the main face of the wall, a row of brick standing vertically, and a cap. All these conditions are defined in the wall type.

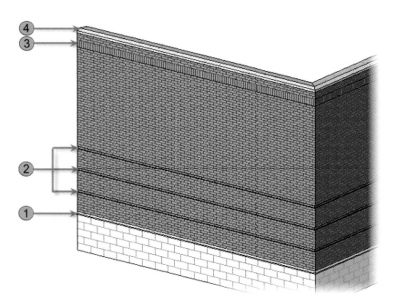

(1) Protruding ledge at the top of the block

(2) Three rows of brick inset from the main face of the wall

(3) Row of brick standing vertically

(4) Cap

Guidelines for Working with Compound Walls

You create and modify compound walls in a building according to your design requirements. You also assign different functions to the layers in a compound wall. The following best practices aid you in working with compound walls.

Guidelines

- Define a wall with variable thickness by using the stacked wall type instead of a vertically compound basic wall type. This results in greater accuracy in section views and provides better control over the model. The wall defined with variable thickness varies with the material you specify for the wall. For example, the wall changes in thickness when you change a stone facing wall to brick facing or a concrete wall to metal structure.

- Duplicate an existing wall type before changing it instead of editing it directly because that can cause standard wall types to deviate from one project to another. You can delete duplicate, unwanted wall types later.

- Ensure that rows outside core boundaries follow a priority order, moving in towards the boundaries. While setting the priority, a high number represents low priority and a low number represents high priority. Error messages are displayed if you place a finish layer inside core boundaries and a structure layer outside.

- Schedule sweeps, such as cornices or rails, separately from walls rather than creating them in a vertically compound wall type. You do this by applying sweeps using the Wall Sweep tool. This is recommended because wall sweeps that are part of a vertically compound wall do not appear as separate items on schedules. As a result, the Wall Sweep tool provides greater flexibility and accuracy in your schedules.

- Create additional layers or rows in the assembly table to place different materials. This saves time and effort and is more accurate than splitting a wall layer horizontally to place different materials.

Exercise | Create and Modify Compound Walls

In this exercise, you create and modify a compound wall with different layers.

You quickly created the walls in your building project using generic wall types. Now you want to change the wall types to suit the design requirements.

You do the following:

- Create and modify a compound wall.

- Create a copy of a wall type.

- Assign material to a layer.

- Add wall sweeps.

- Add wall reveals.

- Place the new wall.

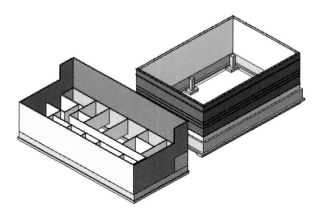

The completed exercise

Completing the Exercise: *To complete the exercise, follow the steps in this book or in the onscreen exercise. In the onscreen list of chapters and exercises, click Chapter 4: The Basics of the Building Model. Click Exercise: Create and Modify Compound Walls.*

Create and Modify a Compound Wall

1   Open *i_rac_essentials_compoundwalls.rvt* or *m_rac_essentials_compoundwalls.rvt*. Ensure that
    the Ground Floor view is displayed.
    Note: The illustrations for the metric dataset will be slightly different from those shown here.

2   Zoom in around the lower portion of the building model.

3   In the view window, select the south exterior wall.

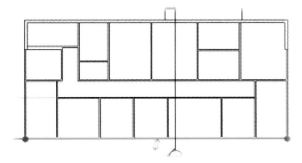

4   Open the Type Properties dialog box.

5   In the Type Properties dialog box, click Duplicate.
    Note: As a best practice, you create a new wall type by duplicating an existing wall type.
    Then, you can use this new type you are creating for projects as well as the original type.

6   In the Name dialog box:
    • For Name, enter **Exterior-Siding**.
    • Click OK to create a new wall type with the specified name.

7   In the Type Properties dialog box, under Construction, for Structure, click Edit to open the
    Edit Assembly dialog box.

8   In the Edit Assembly dialog box:
    • For Layer 2, click the Material field.
    • Click [...] to open the Materials dialog box.

9   In the left pane of the Materials dialog box:
    • Select Wood - Stud Layer from the list.
    • Click OK.

10 In the Edit Assembly dialog box, under Layers:

- For Layer 2, Thickness column, enter **0' 5 1/2" (140** mm**)**.
- Select row 1 and click Insert to add a new layer to the wall type.
- For the new layer 1, click the Function field and select Substrate [2] from the list.
- For the Substrate [2] row, open the Materials dialog box.

11 In the left pane of the Materials dialog box:

- Select Wood - Sheathing - Plywood from the list.
- Click OK.

12 In the Edit Assembly dialog box, under Layers:

- For the Substrate [2] row, Thickness column, enter **0' 0 3/4" (20** mm).
- Select row 1 and click Insert three times to create three new layers.

13 Set the following values for the three new layers that you just inserted:

Layer 1:

- Function: Finish 1 [4].
- Material: Finishes - Exterior - Siding / Clapboard.
- Thickness: **0' 0 5/8" (18** mm).

Layer 2:

- Function: Membrane Layer.
- Material: Vapor / Moisture Barriers - Vapor Retarder (Vapour / Moisture Barriers - Vapour Retarder).
- Thickness: **0" (0** mm).

Layer 3:

- Function: Finish 2 [5].
- Material: Finishes - Interior - Gypsum Wall Board.
- Thickness: **0' 0 3/8" (10** mm).

14 In the Edit Assembly dialog box:

- Select row 3 with the Finish 2 [5] function.
- Click Down four times to move the layer to row 7.
- Move other layers as shown.

Layers

	Function	EXTERIOR SIDE Material
1	Finish 1 [4]	Finishes - Exterior - Siding
2	Substrate [2]	Wood - Sheathing - plywo
3	Membrane Layer	Vapor / Moisture Barriers
4	**Core Boundary**	**Layers Above Wrap**
5	Structure [1]	Wood - Stud Layer
6	**Core Boundary**	**Layers Below Wrap**
7	Finish 2 [5]	Finishes - Interior - Gypsu

15   Click OK to close all the dialog boxes.
      Note: Close the Revit Architecture warning box stating that the highlighted walls overlap.
      Tip: You have just created a new wall type. You can copy or transfer this type to your project
      template so that it is available in other projects.

16   In the Project Browser, expand Families > Walls > Basic Wall.

17   Notice that the new Exterior-Siding wall type is in the list. You will now replace all the generic
      walls with the new wall type.

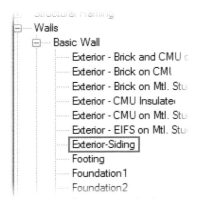

      Right-click the Generic - 6" (Generic - 150mm) wall type. Click Select All Instances to change
      all instances of that wall type.

      Note: You can also select Generic - 6" (Generic - 150mm) directly in the view window and
      right- click to select the Select All Instances option from the shortcut menu.

18   Select Basic Wall : Exterior-Siding from the Type Selector drop-down.

19   Open the Section 1 view.

20   In the view window, press ESC to clear the selection.

21   Zoom in to the area shown below. Notice that the exterior face of the wall now extends past the face of the wall below because you have added thickness outside the core boundary.

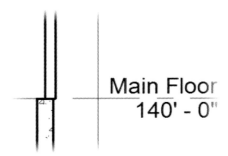

22   On the View Control Bar, toggle the detail level from Coarse to Medium to display the layers you have created.

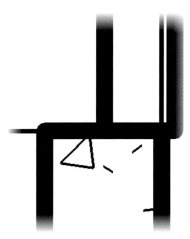

Note: The view scale controls the line weight display. You have zoomed in closer than the view scale is designed for. In closeup detail views, you use an appropriate view scale. You can change the view scale from the View Control Bar. You can also use the Thin Lines toggle on the Graphics panel of the View tab to turn off the line weight display temporarily.

23 Open the default 3D view.

24 Zoom in to examine the new wall finish material. Notice the fill pattern. You can change the fill pattern to show wider boards.

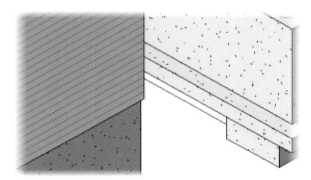

Create a Copy of a Wall Type

1 You will now create and place compound walls on the other wing of the building. These walls will have a complex vertical structure. Open the Main Floor view.

2 Click the Wall tool.

3 Ensure that Basic Wall : Exterior - Brick on Mtl. Stud is selected in the Type Selector drop-down.

4 Open the Type Properties dialog box.

5 In the Type Properties dialog box, click Duplicate and create a new wall type named **Exterior - Brick and Block on Mtl Stud**.

6 Open the Edit Assembly dialog box.

7 In the Edit Assembly dialog box, click Preview to display the preview pane.

8 In the left pane of the Edit Assembly dialog box, select Section: Modify Type Attributes from the View list to change the preview to a section view.

9 Right-click anywhere in the preview pane. Click Zoom In Region.

10 Zoom in on the lower part of the wall.

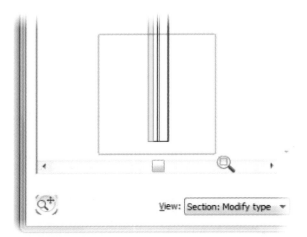

11   In the right pane of the Edit Assembly dialog box, under Modify Vertical Structure (Section Preview Only), click Split Region.

12   In the preview pane, place the cursor along the left edge of the wall so that a line and its associated dimension appear.

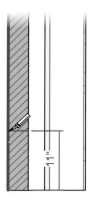

13   Click the left and right edges of the brick layer to split it into two parts. The exact position is not critical.
     When you split the layer into regions, dimensions are displayed, showing the location of the split. Notice that both regions have the same material as the original layer and the Thickness setting for Layer 1 is now set to Variable. After a layer is split, the thickness is no longer recorded as a fixed value.

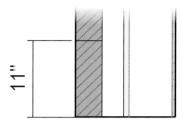

14 You will now locate the split line correctly. In the right pane of the Edit Assembly dialog box, under Modify Vertical Structure (Section Preview Only), click Modify to exit the Split tool.

15 Place the cursor over the split. When the border between the split regions in Layer 1 is highlighted, click to select the border.

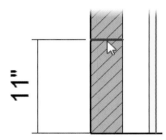

16 Click the temporary dimension. Change the value to **3' 6"** (**1050** mm) and press ENTER. You may now need to scroll in the preview pane to view the temporary dimension.

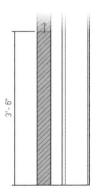

Note: The split line has an arrow flip control so that you can specify it from the bottom or the top of the wall.

Assign Material to a Layer

1   The two regions you have created from a single layer can display different materials. You need to create a layer in the assembly to define the additional material you will use. In the right pane of the Edit Assembly dialog box, under Layers:

- Select row 1.
- Click Insert to add a new wall layer at the top of the list.
- From the Function list of the new layer, select Finish 1 [4].
- For row 1, open the Materials dialog box.

2   In the left pane of the Materials dialog box:

- Select Masonry - Concrete Masonry Units (Masonry - Concrete Blocks) from the list.
- Click OK. Notice that the thickness for the function is set to 0' 0" (0.0 mm) in the Edit Assembly dialog box.

3   In the right pane of the Edit Assembly dialog box:

- Select row 1 again.
- Under Modify Vertical Structure (Section Preview Only), click Assign Layers.

4   In the preview pane, place the cursor over the layer that you have split. Click the left edge of the lower region to assign the layer to this region. This region has the same thickness value as the other Finish 1 [4] layer and the material hatch pattern updates. Depending on the zoom level, the change may not be visible in the preview pane.

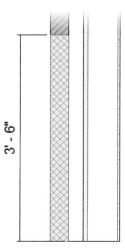

Note: You may have to click the lower region more than once to assign the layer to this region. The assignment of the layer becomes apparent by the change in the material hatch pattern.

Add Wall Sweeps

1   You will now add decorative sweeps to the exterior face of the wall. The first sweep will be a cap at the top of the block section to shed water.

In the right pane of the Edit Assembly dialog box, under Modify Vertical Structure (Section Preview Only), click Sweeps.

2   In the Wall Sweeps dialog box, click Add to add a wall sweep.

3   In the Profile column, click Default and select Sill-Precast : 5" Wide (M_Sill-Precast : 125mm Wide) from the list.

4   Open the Materials dialog box.

5   In the left pane of the Materials dialog box:
   - Select Concrete - Precast Concrete (Concrete - Cast-in-Place Concrete) from the list.
   - Click OK.

6   In the Wall Sweeps dialog box:
   - For Distance, enter **3' 6"** (**1050** mm).
   - Verify that Base is selected in the From list.
   - Verify that Exterior is selected in the Side list.
   - Verify that 0' 0" (0 mm) is set for Offset.
   - Verify that the Flip check box is clear.

7   Click Apply. In the preview pane, notice the wall sweep.

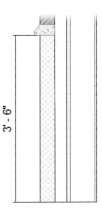

Note: You may have to move the Wall Sweeps dialog box to view the change in the preview pane.

8   In the Wall Sweeps dialog box, click Add to add another wall sweep.

9   For the newly added wall sweep, in the Profile column:
   - Click Default.
   - Select Wall Sweep-Brick Soldier Course : 1 Brick (M_Wall Sweep-Brick Soldier Course : 1 Brick) from the list.

10   Open the Materials dialog box for the newly added wall sweep.

11   In the left pane of the Materials dialog box:
   - Select Masonry - Brick Soldier Course from the list.
   - Click OK.

12   In row 1 of the Wall Sweeps dialog box:
   - For Distance, enter -**4' 0"** (-**1200** mm).
   - Select Top from the From list.
   - For Offset, enter -**0' 3"** (-**75** mm).
   - Click OK.

13   To view the new sweep, in the preview pane of the Edit Assembly dialog box:
   - Scroll up to view the wall sweep.
   - Adjust the zoom to view the top of the wall as well.

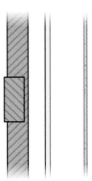

14   You will now place a cap on the wall in such a way that it extends above the roof, making a parapet, which makes the wall weather-proof.

     Under Modify Vertical Structure (Section Preview Only), click Sweeps.

15   In the Wall Sweeps dialog box, click Add to add another wall sweep.

16   For the newly added row:

   - Select Parapet Cap-Precast : 16" Wide (M_Parapet Cap-Precast : 350mm Wide) from the Profile list.
   - For Material, select Concrete - Precast Concrete (Concrete - Cast-in-Place Concrete).
   - For Distance, ensure that 0' 0" (0 mm) is specified.
   - Select Top from the From list.
   - Click Apply.

17   Click OK to close the Wall Sweeps dialog box. View the parapet cap in the preview pane.

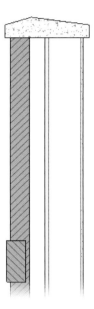

   Note: Adjust the zoom to view the changes.

Add Wall Reveals

1   You will now complete the wall structure by adding decorative reveals or recessed brick lines. In the right pane of the Edit Assembly dialog box, under Modify Vertical Structure (Section Preview Only), click Reveals.

2   In the Reveals dialog box, click Add three times to add three reveals.

3   Select Reveal-Brick Course : 1 Brick (M_Reveal- Brick Course : 1 Brick) for all the reveals from the Profile list.

4   For Distance, enter **9' 0"** (**2700** mm) for the first reveal, **11' 0"** (**3300** mm) for the second reveal, and **13' 0"** (**3900** mm) for the third reveal.

5   Verify that Base is selected in the From list for all three reveals.

6   Verify that Exterior is selected in the Side list for all three reveals.

7   Click OK to close the Reveals dialog box. Notice the reveals in the preview pane.

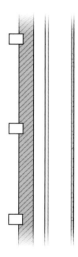

8   Click OK to close all dialog boxes.

Place the New Wall

1   The Wall placement tool is still active and you are now ready to place instances of the new wall type.

Verify that Basic Wall : Exterior - Brick and Block on Mtl Stud is selected in the Type Selector drop-down.

2   On the Options Bar:

- Select T.O. Parapet from the Height list to set the wall height to the level T.O. Parapet.
- Select Wall Centerline from the Location Line list.

3   Click Place Wall tab > Draw panel > Rectangle.

4   On the Options Bar, for Offset, enter **1' 6"** (**450** mm).

5   In the view window:

- In the upper part of the building plan, place the cursor at the grid intersection A1.

Note: Adjust the zoom to view the upper part of the building plan.

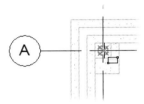

- Click to begin sketching the wall.
- Move the cursor to the grid intersection D3. Click to complete sketching the wall.

6   Click Modify to exit the Wall tool.

7   On the View Control Bar, toggle the Detail Level from Coarse to Fine to examine the new wall structure in the model.

8   Open the default 3D view.

Tip: Adjust the zoom to view the new walls in the model.

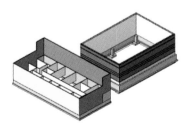

9   Close the file without saving changes.

Lesson 10 | Using Editing Tools

This lesson describes how to use editing tools in Revit. You begin the lesson by learning about the various tools on the Create, Modify, Edit, and Clipboard panels. Then, you learn some recommended practices for using editing tools. The lesson concludes with an exercise on adding and modifying walls using editing tools.

Most building designs repeatedly use similar areas or sections. You can speed up the process and accuracy of adding building components by using editing tools to capitalize on the symmetry and repetition in the design. The following illustration shows copying a wall six times by using the Array tool.

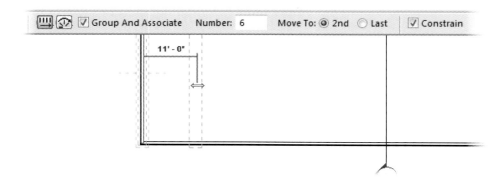

Objectives

After completing this lesson, you will be able to:

- Describe the Create and Modify tools.

- Describe the Edit tools.

- Identify the Clipboard tools.

- State the recommended practices for using editing tools.

- Add and modify walls using editing tools.

Create and Modify Tools

When you select elements in a drawing, a context-sensitive tab opens. The tab contains the Modify and Create panels that hold various tools used to create designs quickly. The tools on the Modify panel are Move, Copy, Rotate, Array, Mirror, Scale, Pin, and Delete. The Create panel provides the Create Similar and Create Group tools. You can use these tools during the design and development phase.

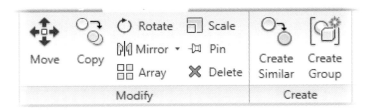

Tools on the Create and Modify panels

Create Group

You use the Create Group tool on a selection set to create a new group object with a different name. Groups can include model and annotation objects. Groups have a center point for placing copies that you can edit. Groups appear in the Project Browser.

Groups allow you to make many copies of the same arrangement of items. If you edit one instance of a group, all others update. You can also ungroup items and modify them separately.

Create Similar

The Create Similar tool helps you place an object by copying the way you placed an existing object. You can use this tool to place walls, doors, windows, and other components without having to know in advance the type of object you are placing.

Move

The Move tool allows you to change the location of selected objects. You can constrain the motion of objects, disjoin them, and copy them. You move objects by first selecting a reference point and then specifying another point to establish distance and direction. You can edit the distance value directly from the keyboard.

Copy

You use the Copy tools to create one or multiple copies of the selected objects. Copy is a two-click operation. You select an object in the view window, select Copy, and then select two points in the view window to establish distance and direction.

Rotate

The Rotate tool allows you to rotate an object about a central point. The central point is displayed graphically, and you can select and drag it to another point. Rotate is a two-click operation. You first click to establish the location of a rotation start vector, then drag to establish the vector angle. You can type the angle value directly.

The following illustrations depict various steps of Rotate.

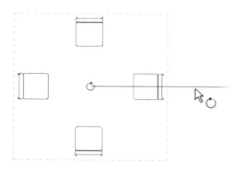

Rotation center appears at the middle of a selection

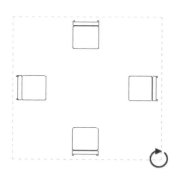

Relocation of the central point

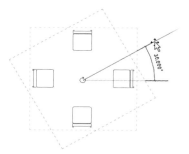

Vector start and vector angle

Mirror

The Mirror tool allows you to relocate or copy objects across a mirror axis. You can draw or pick the axis. You use the Pick option to find walls, edges, lines, and reference planes. Using the Draw option, you pick two points to establish a mirror axis, which can be at any angle. The following illustration shows an object being mirrored along a drawn axis that does not appear as a line after the mirror operation is complete.

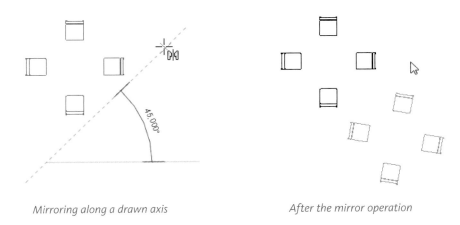

Mirroring along a drawn axis   After the mirror operation

Array

The Array tool places copies of objects in a linear or radial pattern. To create a linear array, you specify the number of objects and the Move To option. Move to 2nd means that the distance and angle you define are between every two objects in the array. Move to Last means that the distance and angle cover the entire array.

To create a radial array, you set the center point (as for the Rotate Tool) the number, and the angle. The Move To option works the same as the linear array. You can specify the angle value in a field on the Options Bar.

Note: *By default, Array makes a parametric group of the arrayed components. After you create an array, you can edit the number of objects in the array. Clear the Group and Associate check box if you want to edit arrayed objects independently of one another.*

Scale

The Scale tool works on walls and lines, which can be scaled in size. Scale options include Graphical, in which you pick two points to establish a relative size factor, or Numerical, in which you specify a size. For example, to double the length of a wall in both directions along its centerline, select the wall, select Scale, check Numerical, and enter **2**. The wall doubles in size.

Pin

The Pin tool helps you lock the location of objects so that you do not move the items accidentally. For example, once a floor plan has been finalized, you pin the walls so that you can experiment with furniture arrangements without unintentionally moving a wall over a short distance.

Delete

The Delete tool removes the selected elements from a project database. The tool does not remove the families or types, only the selected instances. You can delete instances, families, and family types by right-clicking the elements and then selecting the appropriate option. The Delete tool does not place items on the Clipboard.

Edit Tools

The Edit panel on the Modify tab contains many frequently used tools. The ones you will use most often for editing objects are Align, Trim, Extend, Split, and Offset.

Tools

The following illustration shows the tools available on the Edit panel of the Modify tab.

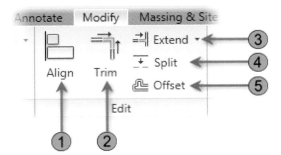

| 1 | **Align** | The Align tool is a two-click operation that aligns elements such as walls. To align one object with another or with a line or reference plane, first select the item that holds its position. Then, select another object that moves so that its selected edge lines up with the selected edge or face of the first object. When you align two objects, a padlock option appears so that you can lock the alignment relationship. |

| 2 | **Trim** | Trim operates on walls or lines. You trim to form a corner. |

| 3 | **Extend** | You can trim or extend walls or lines to form a T-junction or terminate multiple lines on another line to make multiple T-joins. Revit displays lines to indicate how the new intersection appears. In all Trim/Extend operations, the wall segment or line that you select is retained after the operation. |

| 4 | **Split** | The Split tool breaks walls or lines at a specified location. You split walls to apply different conditions to two wall segments. For example, you can specify a different type, height, or base elevation to each section. The Delete Inner Segment check box on the Options Bar removes a segment of the wall or the line between two split pick points. |

| 5 | **Offset** | The Offset tool moves or copies walls or lines at a distance that you define either numerically or graphically. Revit displays a dashed line at the offset location. This tool repeats the operation until you click Modify or press ESC. |

Clipboard Tools

The Clipboard panel on a context-sensitive tab contains standard Windows-based commands. Using the tools on the Clipboard panel can help you save time while working in Revit.

Tools

The Cut, Copy, and Paste tools in Revit work just as they work in any Windows-based application. The following illustration shows the tools on the Clipboard panel.

Note: *The Paste and Paste Aligned tools are also available on the Clipboard panel of the Modify tab.*

Paste Aligned

The Paste Aligned tool is useful when copying items to or from one level to another in a multistory building project. You can select level names from a list, pick level lines when in a section or an elevation view, and select views by name when appropriate.

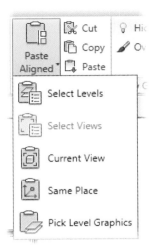

Paste Aligned tool drop-down

Example of Using Paste Aligned

Consider a scenario where you have designed restroom layouts for the first floor as part of a multistory project. You can draw a selection window around the restroom layout and copy it to the clipboard. Then, using Select Level from the Paste Aligned drop-down, you can paste the elements vertically to any other level in the project.

The following illustration shows the Select Levels dialog box that opens when you choose Select Levels from the Paste Aligned drop-down.

Guidelines for Using Editing Tools

You can use various editing tools that aid you in placing objects in a building design. The following best practices help you use the editing tools effectively.

Guidelines

- Editing tools can make the process of filling in a design more precise than locating individual items by using the cursor. Determining in advance where you can capitalize on symmetry and repetition in a layout makes editing more efficient.

- When using the Array tool, verify the state of the Group and Associate check box. If you want to edit or locate the arrayed items later, ensure that the Group and Associate check box is not selected. If you want to change the placement of the arrayed objects within the span of the array, ensure that you select the Group and Associate check box. This creates one group that you can edit with a single click. The different behaviors of the Array tool save time in placing objects in a building design.

- The Trim and Extend tools create corners and join walls more quickly and efficiently than if you select each wall and drag its ends. For example, you can use the Trim and Extend tools, particularly combined with Split, to make rooms down a hallway.

- The Create Group tool makes placing standard layouts, such as toilet areas or furniture plans for office groupings, quick and precise. Locate the group origin point to make placement easy.

- Offset quickly places linear arrangements of walls. You can change the distance during placement as often as required. This tool saves considerable effort when you are placing objects.

- The Align tool removes the necessity of drawing every wall in its exact final position. You do not need to know distances or offsets when using this tool. You will often find it quicker to place walls in an interim location and move them precisely after placement.

Exercise | Add and Modify Walls Using Editing Tools

In this exercise, you add interior walls to the floor plan of a building model using Editing tools.

You are working on a building project and you need to add interior walls. You create and locate copies of walls by using editing tools rather than by drawing the walls.

You do the following:

- Add interior walls.

- Use the Array and Mirror tools to add walls.

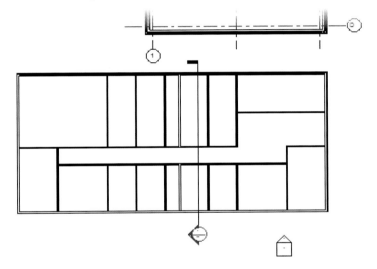

The completed exercise

Completing the Exercise: *To complete the exercise, follow the steps in this book or in the onscreen exercise. In the onscreen list of chapters and exercises, click Chapter 4: The Basics of the Building Model. Click Exercise: Add and Modify Walls Using Editing Tools.*

Add Interior Walls

1   Open *i_rac_essentials_editing.rvt* or *m_rac_essentials_editing.rvt*. The file opens in the default 3D view.
    Note: The illustrations for the metric dataset will be slightly different from those shown here. The completed exercise illustration may also vary.

2   Open the Main Floor view.

3   Zoom in to the lower rectangle of the building. This is the area where you add walls. Notice the light gray interior walls that extend from the Ground Floor level to the Main Floor level.

4   Click any stud partition wall.

5   Click Modify Walls tab > Create panel > Create Similar to create walls on this floor level.

6   Click Place Wall tab > Draw panel > Pick Lines.

7   On the Options Bar, select Finish Face: Interior from the Location Line list.

8   In the view window:

    • Place the cursor over the lower horizontal hallway wall so that the dashed line appears in the center of that wall, as shown.

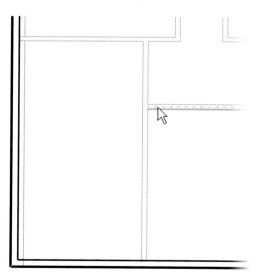

    • Click to place a wall.

9   Pick the lower-left vertical wall perpendicular to the one you just picked to place another wall.

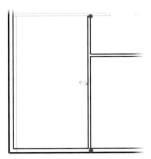

10 Click Modify to end wall placement. You will now use editing tools.

11 Right-click in the view window. Click View Properties.

12 In the Instance Properties dialog box:
    • Under Graphics, for Underlay, select None from the Value list.
    • Click OK.

13 Click Modify tab > Edit panel > Offset to begin copying the horizontal internal wall.

14 On the Options Bar:
    • Ensure that Numerical is selected.
    • For Offset, enter **5' (1500** mm).

15 In the view window:
    • Place the cursor over the horizontal internal wall so that the preview line appears
      above it.

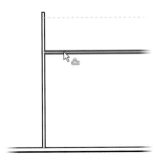

    • Click to place a new wall.

16   On the Options Bar, change the Offset value to **14'** (**4200** mm).

17   Place a copy of the vertical wall on the right. Notice that the walls overlap.

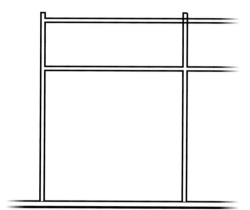

You will now trim and extend the walls to create room spaces.

18   Click Modify tab > Edit panel > Extend drop-down > Trim/Extend Single Element.

19   In the view window:
   • Click the left exterior wall.
   • Place the cursor over the upper horizontal wall. Notice the dashed indicator line.

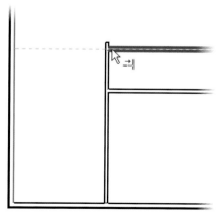

   • Click the wall to extend it.

20 Extend the upper horizontal wall to the right exterior wall.

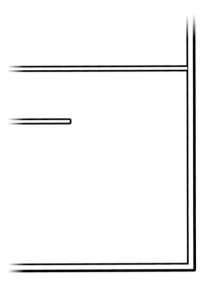

21 To shorten the interior left vertical wall:

- Click the upper horizontal wall.
- Place your cursor over the left vertical wall, below the horizontal wall. The highlight shows how the wall will trim.

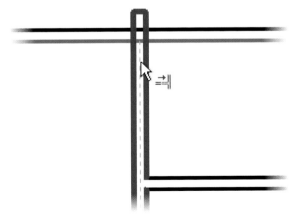

- Click to trim the wall.

22 To trim the interior right vertical wall:
- Click the lower horizontal wall.
- Click the right vertical wall below the horizontal wall.

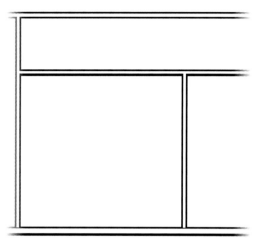

23 Click Modify to exit the Trim/Extend tool.

Use the Array and Mirror Tools to Add Walls

1 To copy walls using the Array tool:
- Select the right vertical wall.
- Click Modify Walls tab > Modify panel > Array.

2 On the Options Bar:
- Ensure that Linear is selected.
- Ensure that the Group and Associate check box is clear.
- For Number, enter **3**.
- For Move To, ensure that 2nd is selected.
- Select the Constrain check box.

3 In the view window:
- Click anywhere to establish a start reference and drag the cursor to the right.
- Enter **8' (2400** mm) and press ENTER. The arrayed walls are shown.

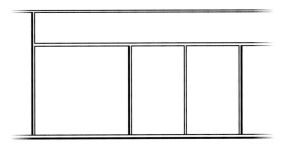

4   Click and drag the cursor from the right to the left across the vertical walls to select the walls
    Tip: You can also use CTRL+select to select each wall individually.

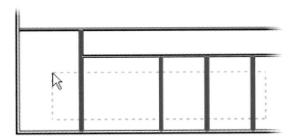

5   Click Modify Walls tab > Modify panel > Mirror drop-down > Draw Mirror Axis to mirror walls
    for making rooms.

6   In the view window:

   • Place the cursor over the midpoint of the lower horizontal exterior wall.

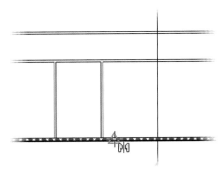

   • Click when the midpoint symbol displays and drag the cursor up.

7   Click to mirror the vertical walls.

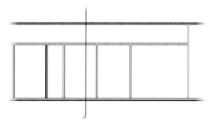

8   You now need to create walls in the upper half of the floor plan. In the view window, select the six vertical walls below the hallway.
     Note: Select only the vertical walls, not the horizontal walls or the section line.

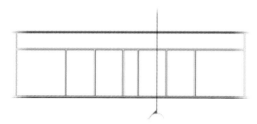

9   Click Modify Walls tab > Modify panel > Mirror drop-down > Pick Mirror Axis to use an existing wall as the axis.

10   Select the upper horizontal interior wall.

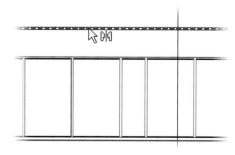

11   Click Modify tab > Edit panel > Extend drop-down > Trim/Extend Multiple Elements to edit the length of the walls.

12 In the view window:

- Select the upper horizontal exterior wall.
- Select the vertical walls to extend them to the exterior wall.

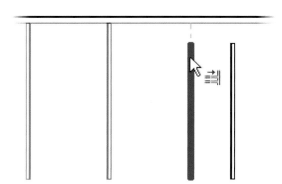

13 Click Modify tab > Edit panel > Extend drop-down > Trim/Extend Multiple Elements to reset the Extend tool.

14 Extend the vertical walls to the upper horizontal interior wall.

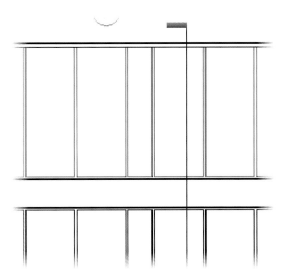

15 Click Modify tab > Edit panel > Split to split the horizontal wall and make a passageway.

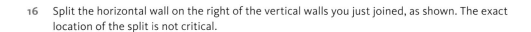

16   Split the horizontal wall on the right of the vertical walls you just joined, as shown. The exact location of the split is not critical.

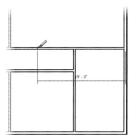

17   Click Modify tab > Edit panel > Trim to create corners for the passageway.

18   Click the vertical and horizontal walls to the left of the split, as shown.

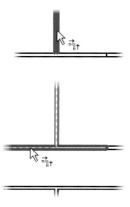

19   Using the Trim tool, make a corner to the right of the wall you split.

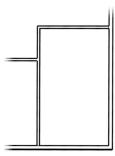

20   Click Modify or press ESC.

21   In the view window, select the horizontal wall to the right of the corner you just created.

22   Click Modify Walls tab > Modify panel > Copy.

23   On the Options Bar:
      • Ensure that the Constrain check box is selected.
      • Ensure that the Copy check box is selected.
      • Ensure that the Multiple check box is not selected.

24   In the view window:
      • Click anywhere to establish a start point.
      • Drag the cursor up and enter **10'** (**3000** mm).

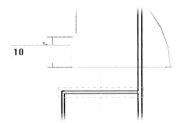

      • Press ENTER.

25   Click the dot on the left end of the new wall and drag it to the left to meet the closest
      vertical wall.

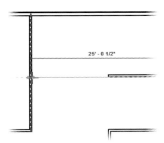

26   Click Modify.

27   Adjust the zoom level and examine the floor plan you created.

28   Close the file without saving changes.

Lesson 11 | Adding and Modifying Doors

This lesson describes how to add and modify doors in a building model. You begin the lesson by learning about doors and the steps in the process of adding and modifying them. Next, you learn the steps in the process of creating a new door type, followed by some recommended practices for working with doors. The lesson concludes with an exercise on adding doors to a building model.

Doors are wall-hosted component elements that you can place in any type of wall, including arc walls. You can place doors in plan, elevation, and 3D views.

Two doors placed in a wall

Objectives

After completing this lesson, you will be able to:

- Describe doors.

- Identify the steps in the process of adding and modifying doors.

- Create a new door type.

- State the recommended practices for working with doors.

- Add doors to a building model.

About Doors

You create doors in a project by placing instances of door families. You can place doors in different views and modify the door parameters. You can also modify the swing direction and the hinge location using the control arrows.

Definition of Doors

Doors are wall-hosted elements; you can place a door only in an existing wall. When you add a door to a wall in a plan, elevation, or 3D view, the software automatically cuts an opening in the wall and the door is placed in that opening.

Doors as Component Elements

Doors are component elements. Therefore, you can create a new door family and save it as a separate Revit family (RFA) file. You can then use this new door family in other projects.

Modifying Door Parameters

After you create a door, you can modify both the type parameters and instance parameters of the door. Type parameters include dimensions and materials, and instance parameters include swing direction and side, materials, and level. Changes that you make to the type parameters apply to all the instances of that type of door in your project. However, changes that you make to the instance parameters apply only to the selected instances of the door.

Placing a Door

You can place doors in the basic wall types in the plan, elevation, and 3D views using the Door tool. While placing the door in a plan view, the swing direction of the door is set to the side of the wall that you touch with the cursor. When the door is placed, you can change the swing direction and hinge placement of the door with control arrows without exiting the Door tool. By selecting the Tag on Placement check box on the Options Bar, you can tag doors as you place them. You can also tag doors later, if you prefer.

Example of Doors

The following illustration shows a door in a 3D view.

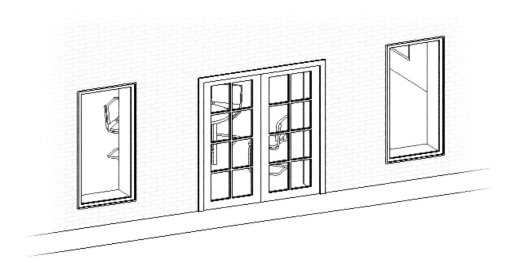

Process of Adding and Modifying Doors

After you add a door to a wall, you can modify its swing and direction. You use Instance Properties and Type Properties from the Element Properties drop-down on the Element panel of the Place Door tab to modify various properties of the door.

Process: Adding and Modifying Doors

The following illustration displays the process of adding and modifying doors.

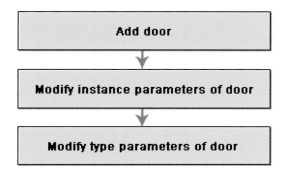

The following steps describe the process of adding and modifying doors.

1   **Add door.**
    You add a door in a basic wall by selecting the Door tool. You then select a door type from the Type Selector drop-down and a wall in which you want to place the door.

2   **Modify instance parameters of door.**
    You can modify the instance parameters, such as Level, Sill Height, and Phase, of a selected door.

3   **Modify type parameters of door.**
    You can modify the type parameters, such as Door Material, Thickness, and Height, of a selected door.

Creating a New Door Type

You can create new door types by modifying an existing door type to suit your requirements. The process of creating a new door type is similar to creating new wall types or any new element type. You use the Edit Type option in the Instance Properties dialog box and the Duplicate option in the Type Properties dialog box to create a new type within the door family.

Procedure: Creating a New Door Type

The following steps describe how to create a new door type.

1   Click Home tab > Build panel > Door.

2   Select a door type from the Type Selector drop-down.

3   Open the Type Properties dialog box.

4   In the Type Properties dialog box, click Duplicate.

5   In the Name dialog box, enter a name for the new door type.

6   Enter new values for the type parameters that you want to set for the new door type.

Guidelines for Working with Doors

The following recommended practices help you work with doors efficiently.

- Learn the difference between doors in basic walls and doors in curtain walls to prevent errors. You need to load specific door families for curtain walls from the library folder to place a door in a curtain wall panel. Then, select the curtain wall panel where you want the door to appear and change its Type property accordingly.

- Clear the Tag on Placement check box to place doors without the door tags appearing automatically. You can always tag doors later using specific commands. Placing doors without tags keeps the screen less cluttered, and you can move doors without moving the associated tags, which saves time.

- Select the tag along with its door if you want to move a door that has been tagged while keeping the tag in the same distance relationship with its host. You can select only the tag and move it separately from the door to make sure that annotations do not obscure model graphics.

- Use SPACEBAR to change the door swing while positioning the door for placement to save time.

Exercise | Add Doors

In this exercise, you add doors to exterior and interior walls. You then modify the instance parameters of these doors. You also load new door families and add instances of these doors into your project.

In your project, you need to add a door in the exterior wall and several doors in the interior walls of the first level. For this, you will load double-glass, single-flush, and single-glass door types from the Revit library, and place instances of these doors in your project.

You do the following:

- Add doors and modify their properties.

- Load new door types from the library.

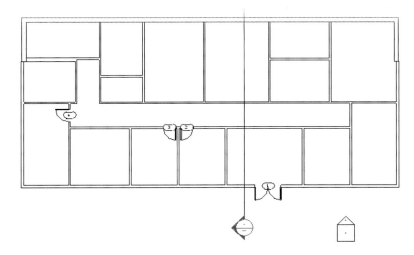

The completed exercise

Completing the Exercise: *To complete the exercise, follow the steps in this book or in the onscreen exercise. In the onscreen list of chapters and exercises, click Chapter 4: The Basics of the Building Model. Click Exercise: Add Doors.*

Add Doors and Modify their Properties

1   Open *i_rac_essentials_doors.rvt* or *m_rac_essentials_doors.rvt*. Ensure that the Ground Floor view is displayed.
    Note: The illustrations for the metric dataset will be slightly different from those shown here.

2   Zoom in to the lower part of the model.

3   Activate the Door tool.

4   Verify that Single-Flush : 34" x 80" (M_Single- Flush : 0860 x 2030mm) is selected in the Type Selector drop-down.
    Notice the Option Bar settings for tagging the door components as they are placed.

5   In the view window:
    - Position the cursor on the south exterior wall to the right of the section line. The exact location is not critical. The cursor snaps weakly to a point midway between the walls. The swing of the door depends on the position of the cursor on the wall.
    - Press SPACEBAR two times and see the change in the door swing.

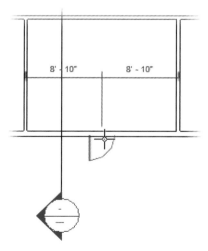

    - Click to add the door.

6   The Door tool is still active but you can modify the door position. To do this:
    - Click the temporary dimension value that is displayed between the door and either wall.
    - Change the left dimension value to **8' 0"** (**2400** mm).

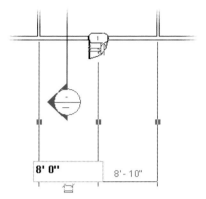

- Press ENTER. The door position updates.
  Note: If the door dimensions do not display, click Modify to exit the Door tool and then select the door.

7   Zoom in to the door.

8   Click the arrows that are parallel to the wall to flip the hand of the door from left to right and back again.

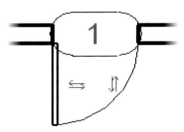

9   Click the arrows that are perpendicular to the wall to flip the face of the door so that it opens inwards. Then, return it to open to the exterior.

10   To place more doors, select Single-Flush 34" x 84" (M_Single-Flush 0860 x 2130mm) from the Type Selector drop-down.
     Note: If you have exited the Door tool, activate it first.

11   Use the Pan tool to display the main hallway. Zoom out if required.

12   In the view window, add two interior doors.

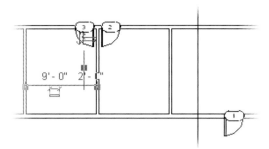

13   Exit the Door tool.

Load New Door Types from the Library

1   To load door types that are not in the project file, click Insert tab > Load From Library panel > Load Family to browse library files.

2   In the Load Family dialog box:
  • Verify that the Imperial Library (*Metric Library*) folder is displayed in the Look In list.
    Note: In XP, you can find the Imperial and Metric Libraries in the *C:\Documents and Settings\All Users\Application Data\Autodesk \RAC 2010* folder. In Vista, you can find the Imperial and Metric Libraries in the *C:\Program Data\Autodesk\RAC 2010* folder.
  • Double-click the *Doors* folder.
  • Select *Double-Glass 1.rfa (M_Double-Glass 1.rfa)*.
  • Click Open to load this family into the project file.
  • Notice that the view does not change.

3   To place instances of the family you have added, in the view window:
  • Select the exterior door.
  • Select Double-Glass 1 : 72" x 84" (M_Double-Glass 1 : 1830 x 2134mm) from the Type Selector drop-down. The door changes to an instance of the selected type from the family that you loaded.

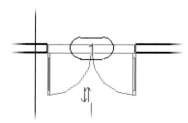

4   Load the *Single-Flush Vision.rfa* (*M_Single-Flush Vision.rfa*) and *Single-Glass 1.rfa* (*M_Single-Glass 1.rfa*) door types from the library into your project.
       Note: You can load families from the Place Door panel as well as the Insert panel. If the Reload family dialog box is displayed, click Yes.

5   Activate the Door tool.

6   Verify that Single-Flush Vision : 36" x 84" (M_Single-Flush Vision : 0915 x 2134mm) is selected in the Type Selector drop-down.

7   Pan to the left end of the hallway, if necessary.

8   Place the door on the left end of the hallway.

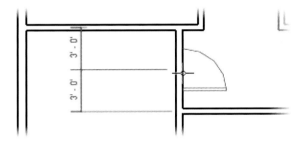

9   Adjust the swing and hinge so that the door opens into the room. If necessary, use the temporary dimensions to center the door in the wall.

10   Exit the Door tool.

11   Zoom to fit in the view.

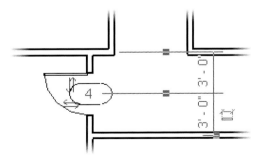

12   Close the file without saving changes.

Lesson 12 | Adding and Modifying Windows

This lesson describes how to add and modify windows in a building model. You begin the lesson by learning about windows. Then, you learn about the process and some recommended practices for adding and modifying windows. The lesson concludes with an exercise on adding windows to a building model.

Windows are wall-hosted elements in Revit. You can either use any of the varieties of windows provided in the software libraries or create custom windows for projects, as required.

The following illustration shows different types of windows: fixed single pane, casement, fixed multipane, and fixed pane over awning.

Objectives

After completing this lesson, you will be able to:

- Describe windows.

- Identify the stages in the process of adding and modifying windows.

- State the recommended practices for adding and modifying windows.

- Add windows to a building model.

About Windows

Windows are important components to consider for the energy usage of buildings. Placement and size of windows, their exposure to weather, and the materials used all contribute to the design of ventilation and heating and cooling systems. In the early design process, it is recommended to analyze your model using tools, such as Green Building Studio, and adjust window parameters to conform to the sustainable design requirements and regulations. This is the same for walls and for almost all building components you will model with Revit.

You can place window instances in any type of basic wall, such as brick and CMU, in various views. In addition, you can place windows in curtain walls. You can modify the type and instance parameters of a window. New window types from library files can be used in any project.

Definition of Windows

Windows are basic component elements that are hosted by walls in a building. You can only place windows in existing walls. When you add a window to a wall, Revit cuts an opening in the wall and places the window. You add windows to basic walls by using the Window tool on the Home tab. You add windows to curtain walls by selecting a panel and designating it as a window.

Windows as Component Elements

Windows are component elements. Therefore, you can create a new window type by modifying the properties of an existing type, and then use the new window type in other projects.

Modifying Window Parameters

You can modify window parameters using the Instance and Type Properties dialog boxes. There are two types of window parameter, instance and type. Type parameters are settings such as dimensions and materials that are common to all instances of the type. Instance parameters are settings such as facing direction, head height, level, and sill height that are specific to a particular instance.

When you change the type parameters of a window type, the change is applied to all instances of that type of window in the project. Changes that you make to the instance parameters modify only the selected instance of that window type.

Placing a Window in a View

You can place windows in plan, elevation, section, and 3D views. Like walls, windows have interior and exterior faces. You specify the window face direction when you place the window. For example, while placing the window in plan view, if you first click the exterior face of a vertical wall, the window faces the exterior wall. You can use the flip arrow controls to change the direction of the window face.

Setting the Default Sill Height

Sill height is the elevation above the level on which the bottom of a window frame is placed. In a plan view, the window family determines the default sill height for the windows. When you place windows in elevation, section, or 3D views, a green dashed line marks the default sill height.

Examples of Windows

The following illustrations show windows in various views.

Windows in a plan view

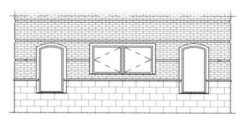

Windows in an elevation view

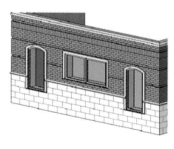

Windows in a 3D view

Process of Adding and Modifying Windows

You can add windows in a wall and then modify their properties in the Instance and Type Properties dialog boxes. You can also create new window types by modifying an existing window type.

Process: Adding and Modifying Windows

The following illustration shows the process of adding and modifying windows.

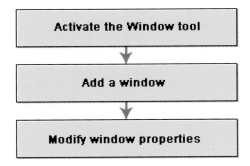

The following steps describe how to add and modify windows.

1   **Activate the Window tool.**
    You activate the Window tool on the Build panel of the Home tab and select the required window type.

2   **Add a window.**
    You add a window to a wall. You can tag the window instances automatically during placement or afterwards. After adding a window, you can change the window face direction, if necessary, and then continue to place more windows.

3   **Modify window properties.**
    You modify window properties of a selected window instance. You use the Instance Properties dialog box to change the required instance parameters for the window. You can also change the required type parameters using the Type Properties dialog box.

Guidelines for Adding and Modifying Windows

The following best practices help you in adding and modifying windows.

Guidelines

- Place windows quickly in their rough locations and constrain them precisely after placement. This helps you place windows faster and more accurately.

- Use a few basic window types as placeholders early in a project, and add or change to specific or custom window types as the design develops. This helps expedite the initial design phase in the project and preserves flexibility.

- Use the tools on the Modify and Clipboard panels of the Modify Window tab to take advantage of symmetry and precision in most floor plans. Proper use of editing tools saves time and prevents errors. For example, use Copy/Paste to copy and paste from one level to another or Copy to copy windows up or down in a wall in the elevation or section views. If you clear the Constrain check box on the Options Bar, you can copy windows from one wall in a plan view to another. Use Mirror to mirror existing windows with careful placement of the axis.

- Use Create Similar on the Create panel of the Modify Windows tab and Match Type on the Clipboard panel of the Modify tab if you have many window types in a project. This saves time while placing windows.

- Place windows without tags and tag them later. This expedites initial placement and keeps views less cluttered.

Example

The following illustrations show various instances of adding and modifying windows.

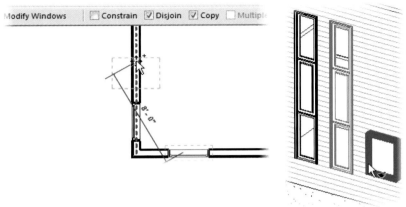

Copying a window from one wall to another

Using the Match Type tool to make the selected window type match the one on its left

Exercise | Add Windows to a Building Model

In this exercise, you add windows to a project. You also create a new window type, modify its properties, and then add windows of that type to the project.

You are designing a building project and need to place windows in a two-story wing. The building model requires several windows of different sizes.

You do the following:

- Add windows.

- Create and add new window types.

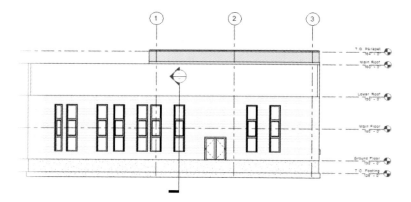

The completed exercise

Completing the Exercise: *To complete the exercise, follow the steps in this book or in the onscreen exercise. In the onscreen list of chapters and exercises, click Chapter 4: The Basics of the Building Model. Click Exercise: Add Windows to a Building Model.*

Add Windows

1   Open *i_rac_essentials_windows.rvt* or *m_rac_essentials_windows.rvt*. Ensure that the Ground
    Floor view is displayed.
    Note: The illustrations for the metric dataset will be slightly different from those shown here.

2   Zoom in to the lower-left corner of the administration building.

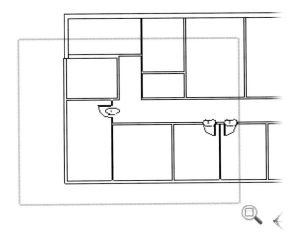

3   Click Home tab > Build panel > Window to activate the Window tool.

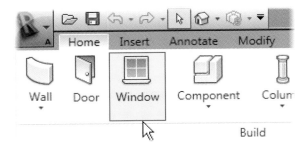

4   On the Options Bar, ensure that the Tag on Placement check box is selected.

5   Select Window : 24" W (m_Window : 610mm W) from the Type Selector drop-down.

6   In the view window, add one instance of the window on the exterior of the left end of the south wall. The exact location is not critical, but note that the side of the wall where you place the cursor to add the window determines the facing of the window.

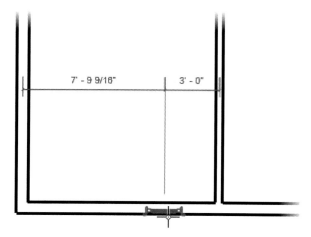

7   In the view window:

- Click the temporary dimension between the window and the centerline of the wall on the right. The value field opens for editing.
- Enter the distance as **2'** (**600** mm).

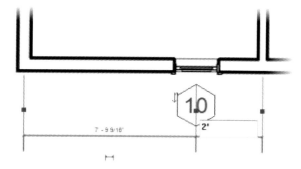

- Click anywhere in the view window away from the dimension or press ENTER to set the value.

8   With the Window tool still active, from the Type Selector drop-down, select Window 30" W (m_Window 762mm W).

9   Add one instance of this window to the right of the partition wall. Again, the exact location is not important.

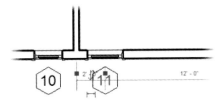

10   Use the temporary dimensions, if necessary, to position the window 2'-0" (600 mm) from the wall.

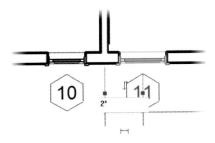

Create and Add New Window Types

1   You need a window type that is not in the project. You will create a new window type from an existing one. In the view window:
   - Ensure that the Window tool is not active.
   - Ensure that the window you just placed is selected.

2   Open the Type Properties dialog box.

3   In the Type Properties dialog box, click Duplicate.

4   In the Name dialog box:
   - For Name, enter **36" W** (**900** mm **W**).
   - Click OK.

5   In the Type Properties dialog box:
   - Under Type Parameters, Dimensions, for Width, enter **3' 0"** (**900** mm).
   - Click OK.

6   Notice the change in the width of the window and the updated tag number.

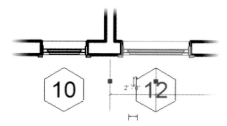

7   You will now add copies of the new window. To do this, on the Modify panel, click Copy.

8   On the Options Bar, ensure that the Multiple check box is not selected.

9   In the view window:
- Click near the selected window to establish a Move start point. The exact location of the start point is not important.
- Move the cursor to the right. Notice the window outline that moves along the south wall.

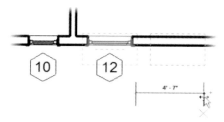

- Click to place a copy of the window in the same room.

10   The new window instance is highlighted, and temporary dimensions appear. Change the temporary dimension between the two windows to **9'** (**2700** mm).

Note: The tag does not copy unless selected.

11   With the new copied window still selected, click Copy to create copies of the window.

12   On the Options Bar, select the Multiple check box to create multiple copies of the window.

13   To place the copies of the selected window:
      • Click to establish a start point on the wall.
      • Add six additional 36" W (900 mm W) windows as shown. The exact location of the
         windows is not important.
      • Exit the Window tool.

14   Select each window instance in turn. Edit the temporary dimensions to position each window
      instance 2' (600 mm) from the closest wall.

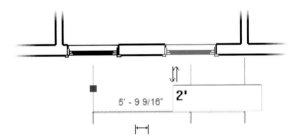

15   Press ESC to clear the selection.

16   Open the default 3D view.

17   In the view window:
      • Right-click any one of the new windows. Click Create Similar.
      • Place a new window on the east wall as shown.

Hint: A dashed line displays when the window is located at the default sill height. Use the View Cube to rotate the model, if necessary, so that you can move down the model and not place the window on a wall intersection.

18 Press ESC two times to clear the selection and exit the Window tool.

19 You will now examine the construction of this window in the section view. Return to the Ground Floor view.

20 In the view window:

• Select and drag the section line through one of the new windows.

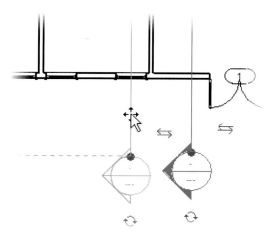

• Right-click the section line. Click Go To View.

21   On the View Control Bar:
- Set the view scale to 1" = 1'-0" (1:10).
- Set the Detail Level to Medium.
  Note: The view scale and line weights work together. This view scale is appropriate for a close-up detail view.

22   In the view window, zoom in to the window head to examine the window and wall.

23   You will now change a property of only this window. Select the window.

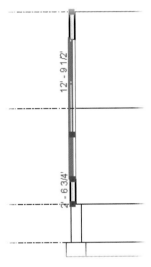

Note: The window dimensions displayed may vary depending on the placement of the window.

24   Open the Instance Properties dialog box to change the window property.

25   In the Instance Properties dialog box:
- Under Constraints, for Sill Height, enter **3'-0" (900** mm).
- Click OK.
  The window instance moves up.

26   In the view window, clear the window selection.

27   Open the South Elevation view. Notice the position of the windows.

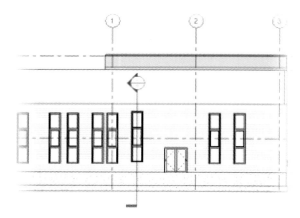

28 On the Quick Access toolbar, click Undo to move the window to its previous position.

29 Close the file without saving changes.

Chapter 04 | The Basics of the Building Model

Chapter Summary

Now that you have learned how to create and modify many different types of walls and how to insert doors and windows in those walls, you can model a building's exterior shell and interior layout.

In this chapter, you learned to:

- Create a basic floor plan and place building elements in it.
- Add and modify walls.
- Create and modify compound walls.
- Use editing tools to add and modify walls.
- Add and modify doors in a building model.
- Add and modify windows in a building model.

Chapter 05

Loading Additional Building Components

In Revit Architecture, you use components of many different types to complete a design. You can load components from external libraries, modify their properties, and create your own component types. In this chapter, you learn how to load and place components into your designs. You also learn how to use components from other designs and modify a family of components to suit your needs.

▶ **Objectives**

After completing this chapter, you will be able to work with component families in a project.

Lesson 13 | Working with Component Families

This lesson describes how to work with component families in a project. You begin the lesson by learning about component families and the steps in the process of adding components. Next, you learn about modifying component families and the steps to create and modify these families. The lesson concludes with some recommended practices to add and modify component families, followed by an exercise on loading component families and adding components in a project.

A component family groups elements with a common set of parameters, identical use, and similar graphical representation. Any modifications that you make to the parameters of a component family are automatically reflected in every element of that family type.

The following illustration shows domestic components, such as a washer/dryer and oven placed from domestic equipment families, and counters and cabinets from casework families.

Objectives

After completing this lesson, you will be able to:

- Describe component families.

- Identify the steps in the process of adding components.

- Describe how to modify component families.

- Work with component families.

- State the recommended practices for adding and modifying component families.

- Load component families and add components in a project.

About Component Families

You add elements such as windows and doors that represent the basic parts of a building model using component families. You can also use these families to add freestanding elements, such as tables and chairs, which do not require a host such as a wall or the floor. You can use predefined component families shipped with Revit®, create your own custom families, or download custom families from the Internet.

Definition of Component Families

A component can be any element of a building model that is placed and not drawn, such as a door, a window, a desk, and a tree. All components are family-based. A component family, also known as loadable family, is a grouping of components.

Each component family can have multiple components defined within it, each with a different size, shape, material set, or other parameter variables.

Component family files have the *.rfa* extension.

Component Tool

You use the Component tool on the Build panel of the Home tab to place freestanding components and component families, such as furniture and plumbing equipment, in a project. Windows, doors, and columns have their own placement tools.

Load Family from Library

You can load component families into projects from external files in folders called libraries. You can load families that you create or predefined families that are not currently in the project. Examples of families that can be loaded are doors, windows, annotation symbols, and title blocks.

Autodesk Seek

You can also load these families using Autodesk Seek within Revit. Autodesk Seek takes you to the Autodesk design content portal, where you can browse and download families. When you run the search on Autodesk Seek, the following Web page opens:

http://seek.autodesk.com/

The following illustration shows the Autodesk Seek panel.

Seek design content	🔍
Find product design files online	
Autodesk Seek	

After you download a family, you can load and save it in a project.

 Note: *You can access component libraries of other companies from the following sites:*

- *Using the http://www.revitcity.com and http://www.augi.com URLs, you can access the library of windows associated with the Anderson Corporation.*

- *You can also access the http://www.turbosquid.com/revitsite to purchase Family files from TurboSquid, an Autodesk partner for Revit content.*

Detail Components

Not every aspect of your project needs to be modeled in 3D. You can add detail components in views to place 2D drafted representations of elements rather than model objects. By doing this appropriately, you can save time. Detail components scale with the view so that they are always of the correct size even if the scale of the view changes. Detail components can include elements such as a two-by-four board, a metal stud, or a shim. Revit contains a large detail components library.

You can place detail components using the Detail Component tool in the Component drop-down on the Detail panel of the Annotate tab.

 Note: *Like dimensions and text notes, detail components are visible only in the view in which they are placed.*

The following illustration shows detail components being placed in a section.

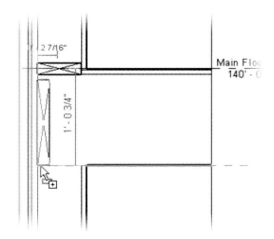

Locking Components

After placing a component, you can lock it to an element, such as a wall, so that the component moves with the associated element. For example, if you lock a bed to a wall and then move the wall, the bed moves with the wall. The software determines the element to which the component is locked. However, you do not lose the ability to move the component independent of the associated element.

Example of Component Families

The following illustration shows freestanding elements, tables and chairs, that belong to furniture component families.

Process of Adding Components

In addition to basic building components, you can add other components that represent actual parts of a building and its environment, such as trees and parking spaces.

Process: Adding Components

The process of adding components is shown in the following illustration:

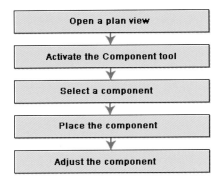

The following steps describe how to add components in a project.

1 **Open a plan view**.
   Open a plan view.

2 **Activate the Component tool**.
   Activate the Component tool by clicking Place a Component on the Component drop-down.

3 **Select a component**.
   Select the desired component from the Type Selector drop-down. If the component you want is not loaded into the project, you can load it from the library.

4 **Place the component**.
   Place the component by positioning the cursor in the plan view where you want the component to be displayed and then clicking to add the component.

5 **Adjust the component**.
   Adjust the component, if required, by using editing tools such as Move, Copy, or Rotate on the context tab. You can also change the component type.

About Modifying Component Families

You can modify different types of component families in a project. You can also create a single family and make many family types from it.

Definition of Modifying Component Families

Component family types are categorized by size and differ in the values of key dimensions. These dimensions are defined as type parameters when the component is created. If you modify type parameters, all instances of a component type are changed. You modify a component family in the Family Editor. You can also duplicate and modify the family types to create new types.

Dimension Parameters

You can use the Family Editor to label and change the already labeled dimensions.

Each new family type has a property set that includes labeled dimensions and their values. You can also add additional values for standard family parameters, such as material, model, manufacturer, and type mark. You can create different family types within the project after loading a family into a project.

Instance Parameters and Shape Handles

When you create families, you set certain labeled dimensions as instance parameters that can be modified when placed in a project. Labeled dimensions set as instance parameters can also have shape handles. Shape handles are points that are displayed when the family is loaded into a project. Shape handles allow you to drag and resize individual components in the project.

Standard Component Families

Standard component families are standard sizes and configurations of common components and symbols used in the building design. You define the geometry and size of the family by modifying the appropriate standard family template. You then save the family as a separate RFA file and can load the family in any project.

Editing Standard Component Families

You can edit a loaded family and reload it into the same project or family or any new project. You can save the family to a library with the same name or rename it before or after reloading the family in a project. You cannot load or save system families.

In-Place Families

An in-place family is created within the context of the current project. By creating in-place families, you create custom components unique to a project or components that reference geometry within the project. For example, if you need to create a reception desk that must fit between several other items in a room, you can design the reception desk as an in-place furniture family.

You cannot save an in-place family to a file and load it in other projects. In-place family creation is an advanced topic and is not covered in depth in this lesson.

When you edit an in-place family, you first select the entire family. Then, in the Family Editor, you select the individual element and edit it in the sketch mode.

Copying Family Types Between Projects

You can copy family types from one project into another. The copied family type must have a unique name. If the family type already exists in the target project, rename one family and then paste the new family type into the project. You can copy in-place families from one project to another.

Family Templates

You create a family from a template that contains most of the information needed to place the family in the project. Templates can include reference planes, dimensions, and predefined geometry, such as window trim.

There are six kinds of generic model family templates.

Family Template	Description
Wall-based	For components inserted into walls, such as doors and windows.
Ceiling-based	For components inserted into ceilings, such as sprinklers and recessed lighting fixtures.
Face-based	For components placed on mass faces or faces of walls and roofs, such as equipment.
Floor-based	For components inserted into floors, such as a heating register
Roof-based	For components inserted into roofs, such as soffits and fans.
Stand-alone	For components that are not host-dependent, such as columns, furniture, and appliances.

Wall-based, ceiling-based, face-based, floor-based, and roof-based templates are called host-based templates. You can place a host-based family in a project only if an element of its host type is present. Host-based components can include openings. When you place a component with an opening on the host, it also cuts an opening in the host.

You can use stand-alone templates to place components anywhere in a project and you can dimension them to other stand-alone or host-based templates.

Example of Modifying Component Families

The following illustration shows two desk components. The lower one has been assigned different material properties. This component is a new type within the family, and it can be saved back to the library for reuse.

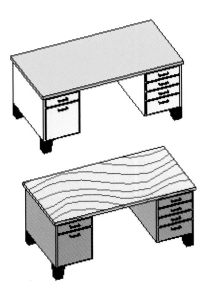

Working with Component Families

You can add a component family to a project and edit it within the project. You can create a new family type or copy an existing family type from one project to another using the Project Browser or the view window.

Procedure: Adding New Family Types in a Project

The following steps describe how to create new family types in a project.

1   In the drawing area, select an instance of the family.

2   Click Element Properties drop-down > Type Properties.

3   In the Type Properties dialog box, create a new family type by clicking Duplicate.

Procedure: Copying a Family Type from the Project Browser

The following steps describe how to copy family types from one project to another using the Project Browser.

1   Open the source project.

2   In the Project Browser, expand Families until you can see the family type that you want to copy.

3   Right-click the family type to be copied. Click Copy to Clipboard.

4   Open the target project.

5   Click Modify tab > Clipboard panel > Paste.

Procedure: Copying a Family Type from the View Window

The following steps describe how to copy family types directly from the view window.

1   Open the source project.

2   In the view window, select an instance of the family type you want to copy. To select multiple family types, such as a specific wall, window, and door, press CTRL and select each type.

3   On the Clipboard panel, click Copy.

4   Open the target project.

5   Open the target view. Click once in the view window.

6   On the Clipboard panel, click Paste.

7   In the view window, drag the object or objects to the position where you want to place them.

8   Click Modify Model Groups tab > Tools panel > Finish. The family type is displayed in the Project Browser under its designated family.

Procedure: Editing a Family in a Project

The following steps describe how to edit a family in a project.

1   Within a project, select the component family that you want to edit.

2   On the Family panel, click Edit-in-Place.
     Note: You can also right-click in the view window and click Edit Family.

3   Click Yes to open the family RFA file for editing.

4   In the Family Editor, make modifications to the family.

5   Save the family.

6   On the Family Editor panel, click Load into Projects.
     Note: If only one project or family is open in the background, the family is loaded into the
     project. Otherwise, a dialog box is displayed in which you can specify the projects or families
     into which the edited family is to be loaded.

7   If the modified family is used in the project, in the Reload Families dialog box, click Yes to
     overwrite the existing version.

8   Close the family file.

Guidelines for Adding and Modifying Component Families

You use component families to add new element types in a project. The following best practices
enable you to effectively add and modify component families.

Guidelines

- Load commonly used component families into your project templates. This saves time during
  the design development process.

- If you edit a component in the Family Editor by making substantial changes, such as adding
  types by size to the family, use the Save As > Family option on the application menu to save
  the family with an appropriate name in the library folders. This enables other project team
  members to use the customized family file right away.

- Save the family files in which you make significant changes, such as modifying standard family files or creating new families by using standard family templates. You should save these files in library folders separate from the default folders. This enables you to preserve the family files even if the library folders are overwritten during a product update.

- Use the Pick Host option on the context tabs to move selected components from the level or host they were originally placed on.

- Purge unused components from the project using Purge Unused on the Project Settings panel of the Manage tab, to keep the project file size small.

- Copy or paste the required in-place families from other projects to share or reuse these families.

Note: *You cannot save in-place families to standard family files.*

Exercise | Load Component Families and Add Components

In this exercise, you load a component family into your project. You then add components from the new family to your project and copy the components between levels.

You are working on a building project and you need to load and place plumbing components in the toilet rooms on the ground floor of the administration building. To save time, you will copy the component layout to the toilet rooms on the main floor. You will also create a new door type from an existing type by modifying dimensions and materials.

You do the following:

- Add toilets and sinks to the toilet rooms.

- Duplicate the layout of the ground floor toilet rooms one level up.

- Create a new door type.

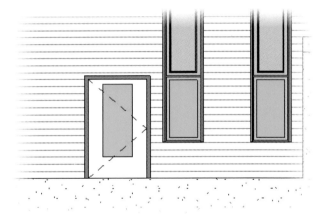

The completed exercise

Completing the Exercise:	*To complete the exercise, follow the steps in this book or in the onscreen exercise. In the onscreen list of chapters and exercises, click Chapter 5: Loading Additional Building Components. Click Exercise: Load Component Families and Add Components.*

Add Toilets and Sinks to the Toilet Rooms

1   Open *i_rac_essentials_components.rvt* or *m_rac_essentials_components.rvt*. The file opens in the Ground Floor Admin Wing plan view.
Note: The illustrations for the metric dataset will be slightly different from those shown here. The completed exercise illustration may also vary.

2   Load *Toilet-Commercial-Wall-3D.rfa* (*M_Toilet- Commercial-Wall-3D.rfa*) and *Urinal-Wall-3D.rfa* (*M_Urinal-Wall-3D.rfa*) from the Plumbing Fixtures folder in the Imperial (Metric) Library.

3   In the view window, zoom in to the upper-left corner of the administration building where the public toilets for men and women are located.

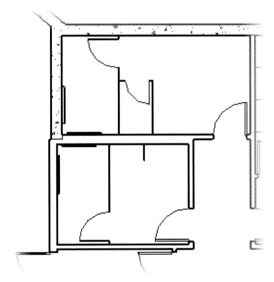

4   Click Home tab > Component drop-down > Place a Component.

5   Select Toilet-Commercial-Wall-3D : 19" Seat Height (M_Toilet-Commercial-Wall-3D : 480mm Seat Height) from the Type Selector drop- down.

6   In the view window:
- Place the cursor over the upper-left stall of the plumbing chase wall that separates the two rooms. The exact position is not critical.

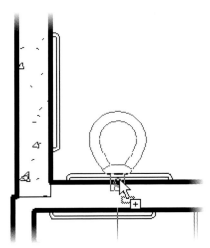

- Click to add the toilet to the women's public toilet room.

7   Exit the Place a Component tool.

8   Select the toilet you added.

9   In the view window, move the cursor over the square control of the temporary dimensions toward the left of the toilet. Notice that the tooltip displays Move Witness Line.

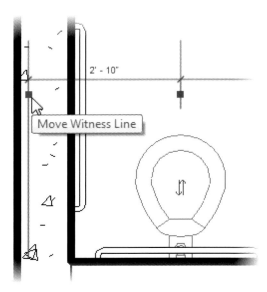

10   Drag the square control to the inner face of the concrete wall.

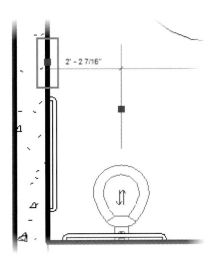

11   In the view window:
      - Click the left dimension between the wall face and the centerline of the toilet.
      - Enter **1' 6"** (**450** mm).

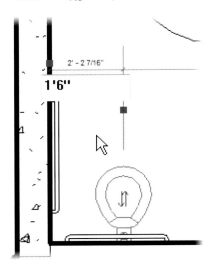

      - Press ENTER. The position of the toilet adjusts to the new dimension.

12 Add a Toilet-Commercial-Wall-3D 15" Seat Height (M_Toilet-Commercial-Wall-3D 380mm Seat Height) in the stall to the right of the first toilet.

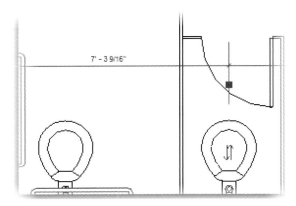

Note: Be careful with your component selection because toilets with different seat heights need to be placed in accessible and nonaccessible toilet stalls. The plan representations of different toilet types are the same but they schedule differently. You can always change a component type later, but careful work early prevents errors and time loss.

13 Move the temporary dimension's witness line and set the distance between the right face of the toilet partition and the centerline of the toilet to **1' 6"** (**450** mm).

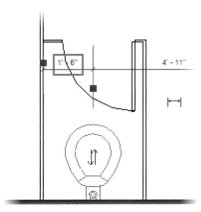

14   Add a Toilet-Commercial-Wall-3D 19" Seat Height (M_Toilet-Commercial-Wall-3D 480mm Seat Height) to the men's public toilet room. Move the winess line and place the toilet at a distance of 1' 6" (450 mm) from the inner face of the west wall.

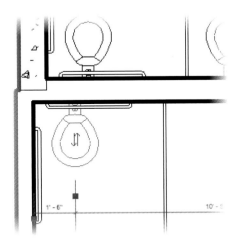

15   Add a Urinal-Wall-3D (M_Urinal-Wall-3D) in the right section at a distance of 1' 6" (450 mm) from the toilet partition.

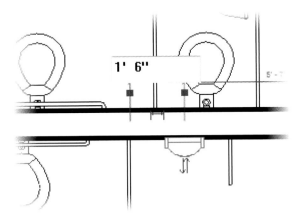

16   Add a Sink-Wall-Barrier Free-3D 22" x 27" (M_Sink-Wall-Barrier Free-3D 560 x 685mm) to each toilet room, as shown. Do not place the dimensions; they are for reference only.

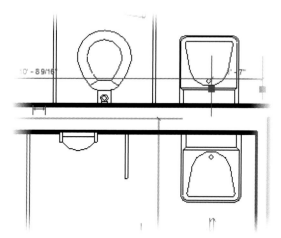

17   Click Modify to exit tools and clear selections.

Duplicate the Layout of the Ground Floor Toilet Rooms One Level Up

1   In the view window, draw a selection box around the components as shown. Notice that this selection box selects walls and grab bars as well as the components you placed.

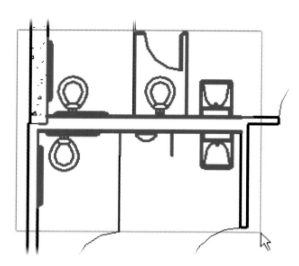

2 Click Multi-Select tab > Filter panel > Filter.

3 In the Filter dialog box:
   • Verify that all the objects in the selection box are listed by category.

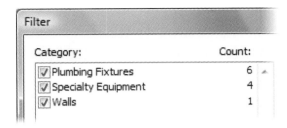

Note: The category list may vary depending on the objects that you have selected.

   • Clear the check boxes except for Plumbing Fixtures and Specialty Equipment.
   • Click OK.

4 Press SHIFT and select the toilet stall walls and urinal screen panels to remove them from the selection. Only the toilets, sinks, urinal, and grab bars should be selected.

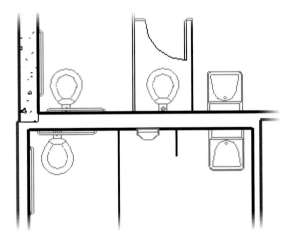

5 On the Clipboard panel, click Copy.
   Note: Be careful not to select the Copy tool on the Modify panel by mistake.

6   Open the Main Floor Admin Wing floor plan view.

7   Click Clipboard panel > Paste Aligned drop-down > Current View. The selected objects are
     copied to the main floor.
     Note: You need to align some of the components because the floors differ in wall thickness.
     If a warning box appears stating that there are identical instances of the components in the
     same place, resulting in double counting in schedules, close it.

8   Clear the selection set.

9   In the upper toilet room, CTRL+select the toilet and grab bars in the large stall or use a
     selection window. Zoom in if necessary to make the selection.

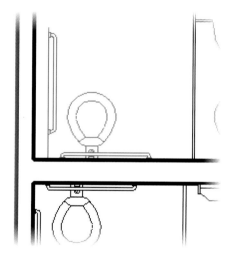

10   On the Modify panel, click Move.

11   Set the base point from where you want to move the component at the end of the grab bar.

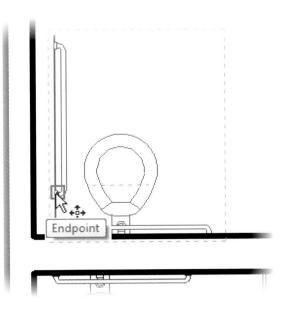

12 Move the cursor over the left of the interior face of the wall. When the interior face of the wall is highlighted, click to place the component at the selected location.

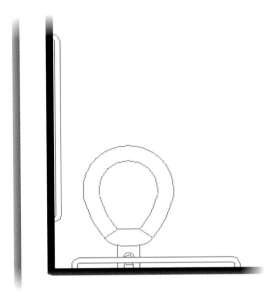

Create a New Door Type

1   The design requires a door type that does not exist in the library, so you create this door type. Click Home tab > Build panel > Door.

2   Verify that Single-Glass 1 : 36" x 84" (M_Single- Glass 1 : 0915 x 2134mm) is selected from the Type Selector drop-down.

3   Open the Type Properties dialog box.

4   In the Type Properties dialog box:
    - Duplicate the door type with the new name **48" x 84" Stainless** (**1200 x 2134**mm **Stainless**).
    - Click Preview to display the preview window.
    - Select Elevation: Exterior from the View list.
    - Under Type Parameters, Dimensions, for Width, enter **4' 0"** (**1200** mm) in the value field.

5   In the Type Properties dialog box, under Type Parameters, Other:
    - For Rail Width - Base, enter **1' 6"** (**450** mm) in the value field.
    - For Stile Width - Hinge, enter **1' 0"** (**300** mm) in the value field.
    - For Stile Width - Latch, enter **1' 0"** (**300** mm) in the value field.
    - Click Apply to see the changes in the preview window.

6   In the Type Properties dialog box, under Type Parameters, Other, open the Materials dialog box for Door Material.

7   In the Materials dialog box:
    - Under Materials, select Metal - Stainless from the list.
    - Click OK.

8   Set Metal - Paint Finish - Dark Gray, Matte as the material for Frame Material.

9   Click OK to close all the dialog boxes.

10 Exit the Door tool. You have created a new door type. You now replace an existing door with the new door type.

11 Open the Ground Floor Admin Wing floor plan view.

12 Zoom in to the door on the center of the east wall.

13 Click the door to select it. The temporary dimensions are displayed.

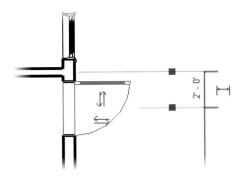

14 Select Single-Glass 1 : 48" x 84" Stainless (M_Single-Glass 1 : 1200 x 2134mm Stainless) from the Type Selector drop-down to change the selected door type.
    Note: A warning message displays stating that the insert conflicts with the joined wall. Close the warning.

15 In the view window:
    • Select the temporary dimension that displays the distance of the door from the wall.
    • Enter **2' 6"** (**750** mm).

16 Press ENTER. The door moves down, away from the conflicting wall.

17 Open the East elevation view.

18 Zoom in to the door.

19 On the View Control Bar, click Model Graphics Style > Shading with Edges.

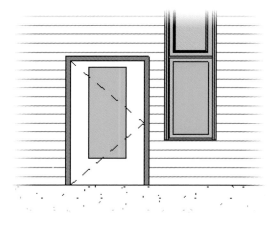

20 Close the file without saving changes.

Chapter Summary

Now that you have learned the basics of loading and placing components, and how to modify a family of components, you can begin to build an endless library of components for your designs.

In this chapter, you learned to work with component families in a project.

Chapter 06

Viewing the
Building Model

Lesson 14 | Managing Views

This lesson describes how to use the different views displayed in the Project Browser. You begin the lesson by learning about views and the steps to create and edit them. Then, you learn about view properties, view templates, and some recommended practices for working with views. The lesson concludes with an exercise on navigating different views displayed in the Project Browser and modifying view properties.

Views are essential elements of a project. They gather all the information related to a specific part of a building model and represent it as required. The changes made to the properties of one view do not affect the changes made to the properties of another view. However, if you change the model in a particular view, the changes are visible in all the associated views as well.

In the following illustration, the properties of plan view are shown, such as View Scale set to 1/8"=1'- 0", Detail Level set to Coarse, and Model Graphics Style set to Wireframe. The plan view properties are not reflected in the 3D view, which has a View Scale of 1"=1'-10", Detail Level set to Medium, and Model Graphics Style set to Shading with Edges. However, when the size of a window is changed in the plan view, the change is also reflected in the 3D view. Notice the selected window on the right of the staircase in both the plan and 3D views.

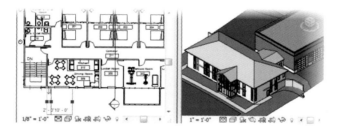

Objectives

After completing this lesson, you will be able to:

- Describe views.

- Create and edit views.

- Describe view properties.

- Describe view templates.

- State the recommended practices for working with views.

- Explore different views displayed in the Project Browser and modify view properties.

About Views

The Project Browser displays a list of all project views. You can create and browse the views to observe different representations of a building model. When you open a view, or create a new view, the views that were already open remain open and their settings do not change.

Definition of Views

Views provide a unique picture of a building model. You use views to display a building model from different directions and references. You create a variety of views, such as plan, elevation, section, and 3D views, for the building model. You can display a plan view as underlay in another plan view to highlight the relationship between components on different levels.

When you start a project, certain views are created by default based on the project template that you select. You can edit the properties of these views and create new views, as required. You can navigate within a view using the mouse wheel, Steering Wheels, or the ViewCube.

Only one view can be active at any given time. However, you can switch between views in the middle of an activity. For example, you can select a floor in the 3D view and edit it in the plan view. You can also duplicate existing plan and 3D views to create new views.

Bidirectional Associativity

Bidirectional associativity ensures that the changes made in one view are automatically reflected in all the associated views. It is applied to every component, view, and annotation of a building model. For example, a change made to the dimensions of a window in the plan view is reflected in all the associated views, such as elevations, the 3D view, and the window schedule view.

Navigating Building Model Views

You use the Project Browser to navigate between different views of a building model. The Project Browser displays views in a tree structure.

When you add a new level in a building model, a new floor plan view and a new ceiling plan view are automatically created by default. However, you can bypass this behavior, if required.

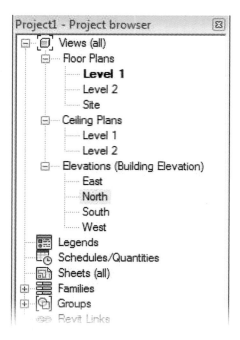

Views of a building model in the Project Browser

Options for Duplicating Views

You duplicate views to allow you to use different settings for views that display the same portion of a project model.

Following are the three options that you can use to duplicate views.

Option	Description
Duplicate	Creates a view that is a copy of the primary view. A duplicate view displays model elements but not annotation elements from the original view.
Duplicate with Detailing	Creates a view that inherits all details of the primary view. A duplicate with detailing view displays both model and annotation elements from the original view.
Duplicate as a Dependent	Creates a view that inherits view properties and view-specific elements from the primary view. In a dependent view, you show only a specific area of the view. You can insert Matchlines to indicate where the view is split, and view references to link views. This option helps to create views that show portions of a plan when the entire plan is too large to fit on a drawing sheet.

Underlay

You use the underlay property of a plan view to display another plan view of the model under the current plan view. Underlay can be above or below the current level and appears in halftone. You use underlay to understand the relationship between components on different floors. You can select and modify elements in the underlay or snap to the underlay elements for the purpose of the design layout.

In the following illustration, the halftone lines show a lower-level plan view as underlay in the current plan view.

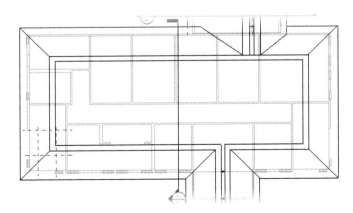

Example of Views

The following illustration shows the different views of a building model.

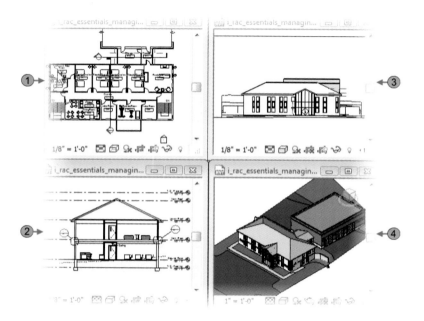

(1) Plan view

(2) Section view

(3) Elevation view

(4) 3D view

Creating and Editing Views

When you create a building model, you will need to work on different views such as floor plans and ceiling plans. You use the Create panel of the View tab to create new views. You can also duplicate existing views and change their properties using the Project Browser.

You use the horizontal and vertical scroll bars of the view window to pan horizontally or vertically. You can use the Steering Wheels control on the Navigation Bar to scroll or zoom in a flat view and spin the 3D view. You use ViewCube in 3D views to spin the model or reorient the view. You can use the mouse wheel to zoom and pan in any model view, and you can use the mouse wheel and the SHIFT key to spin the model.

You can see all the open views together by using the Tile or Cascade option on the Windows panel of the View tab.

You can also identify a split so that you can place portions of large views on small sheets correctly in a view by adding a Matchline. Matchlines are 3D objects in plan views. You can set their vertical extents so that they display only at certain levels. Matchlines coordinate views when they are placed on sheets.

While duplicating and cropping views that are too large to fit on your sheet, you can add a Matchline to indicate the appropriate crop location. You can customize the look of the Matchline by editing the line weight, color, and pattern.

Procedure: Creating a New View

The following steps describe how to create new views of various types.

1   To create a floor plan, click View tab > Create panel > Plan Views drop-down > Floor Plan.

2   In the New Plan dialog box:
   - Select the level at which you want to create the view.
   - Clear the Do Not Duplicate Existing Views check box to create a duplicate view.

3   To create an elevation view:
   - Make a plan view as the active view.
   - Click View tab > Create panel > Elevation drop-down > Elevation.
   - Set the elevation marker at the desired elevation location to create a new elevation view.

4   To create a section:
   - Click Create panel > Section.
   - Select two points to sketch a new location for the section line.

Note: You can place a section in a plan, section, or elevation view.

5   To create a new component schedule, click Create panel > Schedules drop-down > Schedule/
    Quantities. In Revit, Schedules are views as well.

6   In the New Schedule dialog box, select a Category for the new schedule.

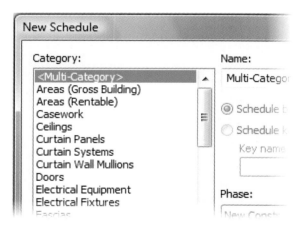

7   In the Schedule Properties dialog box, add the parameters you want to create in the view.

Procedure: Adding a Matchline

The following steps describe how to add a Matchline to a view.

1   Open the original view from which you created the duplicate or dependant view.

2   On the View Control Bar, click Show Crop Region to make the crop region visible.

3   Click View tab > Sheet Composition panel > Matchline.

4   Sketch a Matchline of the required length in the view window.

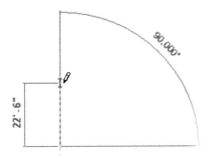

5   Select Finish Matchline to finish sketching the Matchline.

6   Crop the view to the Matchline from one direction.

7   Open the duplicated or dependant view and make the crop region of the view visible.

8   Crop the view to the Matchline from the other direction. When both views are placed on sheets, the Matchline indicates where they meet.

9   You can place view reference annotations near Matchlines to identify the connected views by their sheet and detail numbers.

View Properties

You use view properties to set and modify different parameters associated with the active view, such as scale, graphics style, and underlay. Certain view instance properties are available on the View Control Bar at the bottom of each view window. You can modify the properties of a view by using the Instance Properties dialog box for that view.

The following illustration shows the Instance Properties dialog box for a plan view.

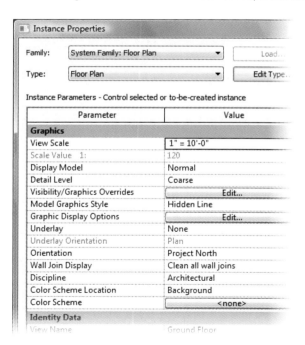

View Property Parameters

View property parameters affect the way a building model is displayed in the active view window. Various types of views have some properties that may differ. The following illustration shows parameters in the Instance Properties dialog box of a plan view.

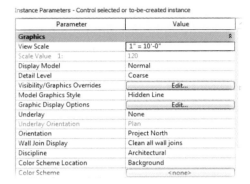

Instance Parameters - Control selected or to-be-created instance

Parameter	Value
Graphics	⌃
View Scale	1" = 10'-0"
Scale Value 1:	120
Display Model	Normal
Detail Level	Coarse
Visibility/Graphics Overrides	Edit...
Model Graphics Style	Hidden Line
Graphic Display Options	Edit...
Underlay	None
Underlay Orientation	Plan
Orientation	Project North
Wall Join Display	Clean all wall joins
Discipline	Architectural
Color Scheme Location	Background
Color Scheme	<none>

The following table describes the key parameters available in the Instance Properties dialog box of a view.

Parameter	Description
View Scale	Changes the scale of the view as it appears on the drawing sheet.
Scale Value	Defines a custom scale value. Scale Value is enabled when Custom is selected for View Scale.
Display Model	Comprises three settings. The Normal setting displays all elements normally. It is intended for all non-detail views. The Do Not Display setting hides the model and displays only detailed view-specific elements. These elements include lines, regions, dimensions, text, and symbols. The As Underlay setting displays all detail view-specific elements normally and model elements appear dimmed.
Detail Level	Applies a Coarse, Medium, or Fine detail level setting to the view scale.This setting overrides the automatic detail level setting for the view.
Visibility/ Graphics Overrides	Controls the visibility of objects by category in your view. You can specify visibility settings using the Visibility/Graphic Overrides dialog box. This is a powerful feature of Revit and you will learn more about it later.

Parameter	Description
Model Graphics Style	Specifies different graphic styles for a project view. The styles are Hidden Line, Wireframe, Shading, and Shading with Edges.
Graphic Display Options	Controls the shadows and silhouette lines in the view.
Discipline	Specifies the discipline of the project view and controls the display of model objects. You can select Architectural, Structural, Mechanical, Electrical, and Coordination disciplines for the project.
Color Scheme	Specifies a color pattern to be applied when rooms are visible in the view.
View Name	Displays the name of the active view. The view name also appears in the Project Browser and on the title bar of the view.
Title on Sheet	Shows the name of the view as it appears on the sheet; the name is separate from the value in the View Name property. This parameter is not available for sheet views.
View Range	Controls the specific geometric planes that define the boundaries of plan views. You can set these boundaries by defining the height of the Top Clip Plane, the Cut Plane, and the Bottom Clip Plane.
Phase Filter	Applies a specific phase filter to a view. This parameter controls the appearance of model objects based on their phase status.
Phase	Displays the specific phase of a view. View Phase, Phase Filter, and Object Phase work together to determine which model components are visible in the view and how they appear graphically.
Crop View and Crop Region Visible	Sets a boundary around the building model. You can select the boundary and resize it using the drag controls. The visibility of the model changes when you resize the boundary. To turn off cropping, clear the Crop Region check box. To turn off the boundary and maintain the cropping, clear the Crop Region Visible check box.

View Range

Plan views are three-dimensional. All plan views and reflected ceiling plan views have an instance property called View Range, which is a group of horizontal planes that affect object visibility and appearance in a view. View Range has four horizontal planes: Top, Cut plane, Bottom, and View Depth. The Top and Bottom planes represent the top and bottom extents of the view, respectively. The Cut plane determines the display of elements in a view. While model elements above the Cut plane are not displayed, model elements below the Cut plane are in Projected lineweight. Model elements that pass through the Cut plane are displayed in Cut lineweight, which is heavier than Projected. When the View Depth plane is set below the Bottom plane, the view displays the elements below the Bottom plane, down to the View Depth level, in Beyond lineweight, which is lighter than Projected.

The following illustration shows walls that are Cut in the view, Projected, which is below the Cut plane and above the Bottom plane, and Beyond, which is below the Bottom plane and above the View Depth plane.

Walls shown as Cut, Projected, and Beyond

View Control Bar

The View Control Bar located in the lower-left corner of the view window provides quick access to select view properties that affect the way a building model is displayed in the view window. You access the view properties using the buttons on the View Control Bar: Scale, Detail Level, Model Graphics Style, Shadows Off, Crop View, Show Crop Region, Temporary Hide/Isolate, and Reveal Hidden Elements.

Scale

You can change the view scale values in the drawing by using Scale on the View Control Bar. View scale determines how the view will fit on a sheet. You can select from a set of predefined scale values, or specify a custom scale value for the drawing. Annotations resize automatically when the view scale changes.

The following illustration shows various imperial scale options available on the View Control Bar.

```
1" = 20'-0"
3/64" = 1'-0"
1" = 30'-0"
1/32" = 1'-0"
1" = 40'-0"
1" = 50'-0"
1" = 60'-0"
1/64" = 1'-0"
1" = 80'-0"
1" = 100'-0"
1" = 160'-0"
1" = 200'-0"
1" = 300'-0"
1" = 400'-0"
1/8" = 1'-0"
```

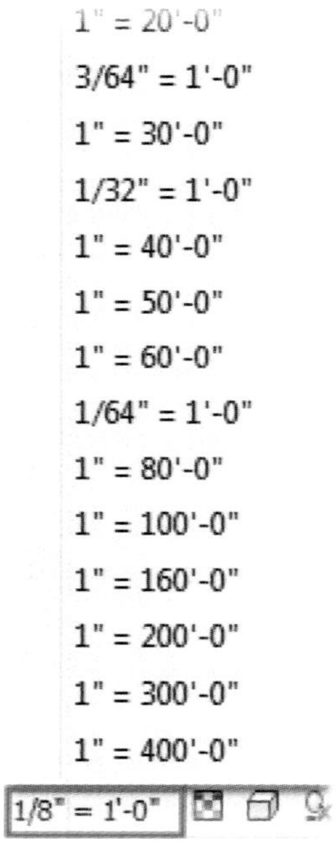

Detail Level

You use Detail Level to specify the extent of detail that you wish to display in a view. Detail level affects the display of component geometry, and is coordinated with view scale. You can change the detail level of a view to coarse, medium, and fine. Coarse displays only the outlines of walls, floors, roofs, and any applied coarse detail fill patterns. The medium and fine levels display the internal structures of compound components.

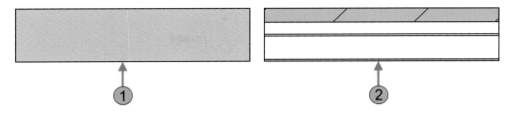

1 Coarse level display of a compound wall

2 Medium and Fine level display of the same wall

Model Graphics Style

You use Model Graphics Style to select graphic styles, such as Wireframe, Hidden Line, Shading, and Shading with Edges, for the building model.

The different types of Model Graphics Style options applied to a building model are shown.

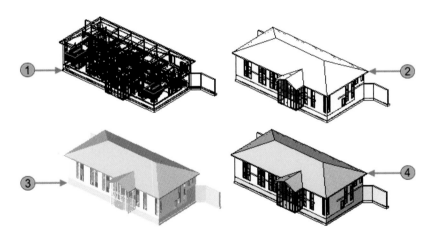

1 Wireframe

2 Hidden Line

3 Shading

4 Shading with Edges

Shadows

You use the Shadows property to turn the shadows on or off in a view. Some jurisdictions may require shadows to be visible as part of the planning and approval process. The Shadows parameter is useful in such scenarios.

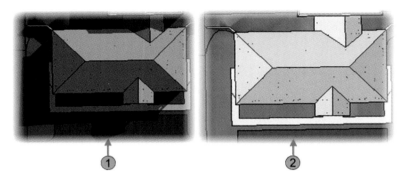

① Building model with shadows on

② Building model with shadows off

Crop View

You use Crop View to display and modify the boundaries of a view. You can hide or show a crop region in a view. When a crop region is visible, you can resize its edges by dragging the Far Clip Plane indicators. You create a cropped copy of a large view so that working in or displaying a portion of the original view becomes easy.

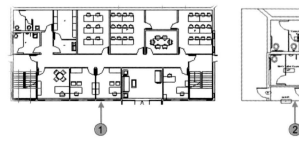

① Plan view without cropping

② Plan view with cropping

Chapter 06 | Viewing the Building Model

Temporary Hide/Isolate

You use the Temporary Hide/Isolate property to temporarily hide selected elements in the active view. This option is useful when you want to view or edit the elements of a certain category in a view because the options for an element are enabled only when it is selected in the active view. You can hide a particular element in a view with Hide, and you can isolate an element by hiding all other elements in a view with Isolate. Hide/Isolate does not affect printing of objects.

The following illustration shows instances of selecting, isolating, and hiding a wall category.

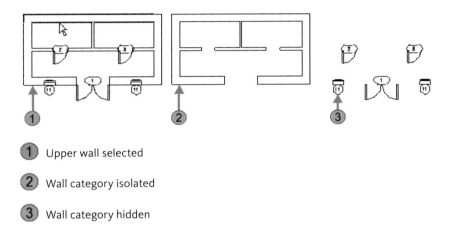

1 Upper wall selected

2 Wall category isolated

3 Wall category hidden

Thin Lines

You use thin lines to toggle the display of line widths on and off in a building model. Revit shows lines with applied widths by default, so that each view approximates how it will print according to drafting standards. With Thin Lines turned on, you can easily differentiate between closely spaced lines when you need to work in a busy part of a view. Thin Lines is available on the Graphics panel of the View tab. It affects all the views.

In the following illustration, when thin lines are turned on, you can view the exact intersection detail at the top of the wall, and when thin lines are turned off, the slanting roof hides the top of the wall.

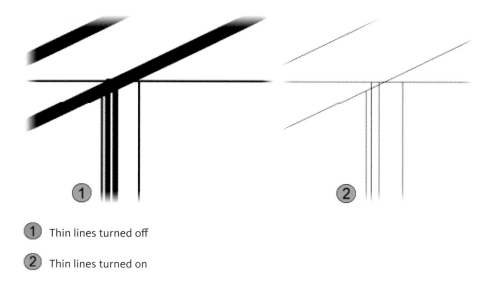

① Thin lines turned off

② Thin lines turned on

View Templates

View templates contain the standard settings of a view. Revit has default view templates that you can apply to views, and you can also create your own view templates for specific view conditions.

The following illustration shows the View Templates dialog box, which you access by clicking View Template Settings from the View Templates drop-down on the Graphics panel of the View tab.

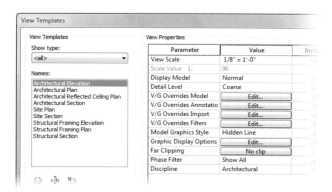

View Templates Options

After you set up a view, such as furniture plan, plumbing plan, or electrical plan, to display a model, you can create a named view template from that view. You can also apply a named template to any model view. You can do this in two ways, using the shortcut menu of the Project Browser or selecting View Templates on the Graphics panel of the View tab.

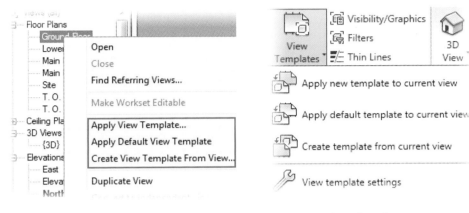

Shortcut menu of the Project Browser   *View Templates drop-down*

Guidelines for Working with Views

The following recommended practices help you to work effectively with views.

- When working in a view that you plan to develop further using drafting elements, you should adjust the crop region as required and then pin the view boundary in position. This prevents you from inadvertently moving the view boundary.

- You need to set up detail views and start drafting on the views after the model design is developed sufficiently to prevent unnecessary rework.

- You need to add 2D drafting and detail elements in the relevant views, not on sheets. This ensures that when you move the views on a sheet, the elements placed in the view automatically move with the view. This saves time when you compose sheets for printing.

- You can open a view by double-clicking the name of the view in the Project Browser. This is the quickest way to open a view.

- You can select Close Hidden Windows on the Windows panel of the View tab to close all open views except the active view in each project. Do this to keep your Switch Windows list manageable and conserve system resources.

- You should check your work often in 3D view. Observing the model in 3D view helps you discover shortcomings, discrepancies, or errors in the building model.

- The default 3D view reorients to its original position when you exit Revit and restart it. You can create 3D views of specific parts of the building model that you need to revisit and save the views with appropriate names. This saves time when you need to check a certain portion of the model during design development.

- In a 3D view, by default, the orbit function uses the center of the model as the pivot point. You can orbit about a particular element by selecting the element first and then orbiting the view. This helps maintain the orientation during orbit.

- You can dock, undock, and close the Project Browser to make the view window larger when required. This provides more working space and speeds up work, particularly if you plan to work in a single view for a while.

- You can use CTRL+ select to select multiple views from the Project Browser if you want to change the properties of a number of views simultaneously. This saves time and reduces the chance of errors.

Exercise | Explore Views and Modify View Properties

In this exercise, you explore the different views displayed in the Project Browser and modify their view properties.

You are designing a building project. You want to observe the different views of the model and change the view properties to get a clear idea of the project as it develops.

You do the following:

- Explore views displayed in the Project Browser.

- Change the view properties.

- Change element display in a view.

- Change wall display.

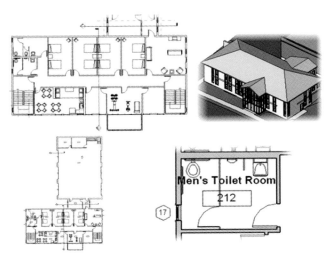

The completed exercise

Completing the Exercise:	*To complete the exercise, follow the steps in this book or in the onscreen exercise. In the onscreen list of chapters and exercises, click Chapter 6: Viewing the Building Model. Click Exercise: Explore Views and Modify View Properties.*

Explore Views Displayed in the Project Browser

1   Open *i_rac_essentials_managing_views.rvt* or *m_rac_essentials_managing_views.rvt*. The building model opens in the 3D view of the almost complete project.

2   On the Navigation Bar, click the Steering Wheel.

3   On the Steering Wheel, click Pan, Zoom, and Orbit to browse the 3D view.

4   Right-click Steering Wheel to view the options. Click Options.

5   In the Options dialog box:
    - Ensure that the SteeringWheels tab is displayed.
    - Notice the options available.

    - Click Cancel.

6   Close the Steering Wheel.

7   Place the cursor over the compass portion of the View Cube so that the direction indicator highlights.

8   Click the left mouse button and drag an orbit. This enables a flat orbit of the model in which the ground plane does not move in the view.
Note: You can also click a compass direction indicator to orient the view to that direction.

9   Place the cursor anywhere over the cube portion of the View Cube. You can orient the view to an angle by clicking the appropriate portion of the View Cube. Drag a 3D orbit, holding the left mouse button.

Note: You can click the Home icon to return to the original view.

10   Open the Main Floor plan view.

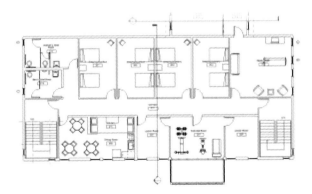

11   Zoom in to the lower building.

12   Open the Section 1 view.

13   Verify that the callout symbol on the right of the building is named Callout of Section 1.
      Tip: Notice the status bar in the lower-left corner of the application to view the callout
      symbol name.

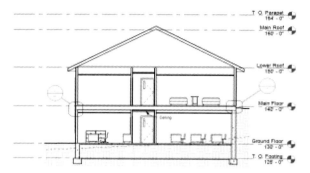

14   In the view window, right-click the callout. Click Go to View to make Callout of Section 1 the
      active view.

15   In the Project Browser, right-click Main Floor. Click Duplicate View > Duplicate to create a
      duplicate copy of the Main Floor view.

16   Duplicating a view will retain the original view settings for the new view. Notice that a new
      view named Copy of Main Floor is displayed in the Project Browser and is active in the view
      window.

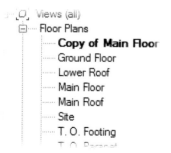

17   Rename the Copy of Main Floor view as **Main Floor - Furniture Plan**
      Tip: Right-click Copy of Main Floor to rename it.

18   Create a duplicate with detailing copy of the Main Floor view.

19 Rename the Copy of Main Floor view as **Main Floor - Annotated.**Compare Main Floor - Furniture Plan with Main Floor - Annotated. Notice that the door, window, and room tags are visible in Main Floor - Annotated but not in Main Floor - Furniture Plan.

20 Tile all the open views.
Note: You can click in a view window to make it active.

21 Maximize Main Floor - Furniture Plan.

22 Open the Instance Properties dialog box. Notice the parameters you can set for this view.

23 For the Visibility/Graphics Overrides parameter, click Edit to open the Visibility/Graphic

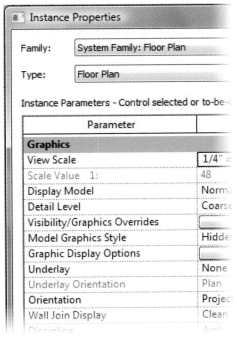

Overrides dialog box for this view.

- Notice the categories on each tab.
- On the Model Categories tab, clear the Furniture check box.
- Click OK to close the dialog boxes and return to the view.

24 To reset the display of furniture for the view:

• Enter **VG**. This is a shortcut to the Visibility/ Graphic Overrides dialog box.
• On the Model Categories tab, select the Furniture check box.
• Click OK.

The Visibility Graphics Overrides parameter is used to control the visibility of objects by category in your views. This is a powerful feature of Revit, and you will learn more about it later.

Change the View Properties

1 Activate the 3D view.

2 Zoom in to the building with the pitched roof.

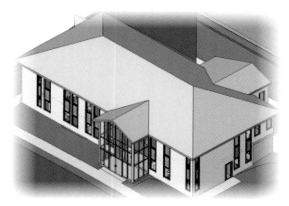

3 On the View Control Bar, click Model Graphics Style > Wireframe.

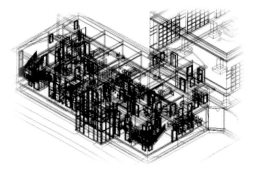

4   Apply the other Model Graphics Style options and observe the results.

5   On the View Control Bar, click Shadows > Shadows On to display the shadows.

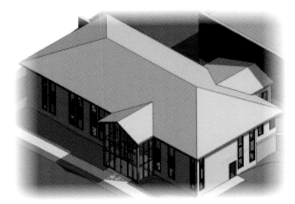

Note: The Shadows icon on the View Control Bar changes to reflect the new condition.

6   On the View Control Bar, click Shadows > Shadows Off to turn the shadow off in the view.

Change Element Display in a View

1   Open the Main Floor view.

2   Enter **ZF** to fit the view in the view window.

3   Select one of the exterior walls of the administrative building as shown.

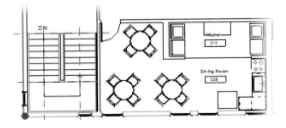

4   On the View Control Bar, click Temporary Hide/Isolate > Isolate Category to observe the changes.

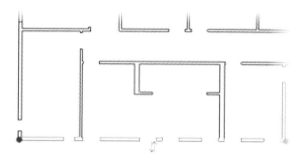

5   On the View Control Bar, click Temporary Hide/ Isolate > Reset Temporary Hide/Isolate to return to the previous state.

6   Select the exterior wall of the administrative building again.

7   On the View Control Bar, click Temporary Hide/ Isolate > Isolate Element to isolate the wall.

8   Reset the view.

Change Wall Display

1   Zoom in to the lavatory room in the upper-left corner of the lower building.

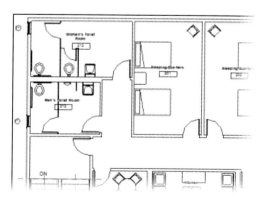

2 On the View Control Bar, click Model Graphics Style > Shading with Edges. The walls in the drawing appear shaded.

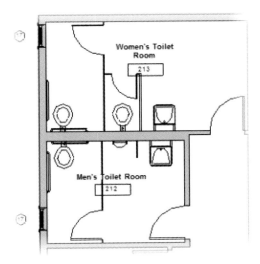

3 On the View Control Bar, click Scale > 1/8" = 1'-0" (1: 100). This drawing scale applies when the view is placed on a sheet.

4 Zoom in to the lavatories. Notice that the size of the labels and tags changed relative to the scale of the building model view.

5 Close the file without saving changes.

Lesson 15 | Controlling Object Visibility

This lesson describes how to control the visibility and appearance of elements in different views. You begin the lesson by learning about object visibility settings and the steps to modify line styles to control object visibility. Then, you learn about user-defined filters, the steps to use filters in a project, and some recommended practices for controlling object visibility. The lesson concludes with an exercise on controlling object visibility.

By controlling object visibility, you define which elements should be displayed in a selected view. This enables you to focus on specific elements and achieve a desired layout. For example, you can create a furniture layout view by hiding other elements such as room tags.

The following illustration shows floor plan views with and without the furniture details and door tags.

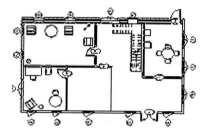 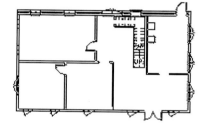

Objectives

After completing this lesson, you will be able to:

- Describe object visibility settings.

- Modify line styles to control object visibility.

- Describe user-defined filters.

- Create and use filters in a project.

- State the recommended practices for controlling object visibility.

- Control object visibility.

Object Visibility Settings

Revit controls the visibility of a building model by element, object category, and view. You can control the visibility of objects in a view to display objects in specific ways. You can either specify visibility settings or apply a view template to control the elements that are displayed in a view. You can manage the display of elements and line styles. You can also modify views by applying filters.

Visibility/Graphic Overrides Dialog Box

You use the Visibility/Graphic Overrides dialog box to control the visibility and appearance of model, annotation, imported or linked Revit, and workset elements for each view. Using this dialog box, you manage views for specific purposes such as furniture layout, equipment plan, and fire-safety plan.

You can also change visibility settings for the current view in the Visibility/Graphic Overrides dialog box, which has tabs for model categories, annotation categories, imported categories, and filters. Additional tabs for Revit links and worksets appear if the project has linked Revit models and the model is workset-enabled.

Visibility/Graphic Overrides dialog box

Visibility Overrides by Element, Category/Subcategory, and Filter

You can select an element in a view and use the controls on the shortcut menu to change its visibility or component category, or to filter it from the view with user-created filters.

Hide in View options   Override Graphics in View options

The Override Graphics in View options provide access to the Visibility Graphic Overrides and View-Specific Element Graphics dialog boxes. Using these dialog boxes, you can hide the element, make it visible in halftone, or make it transparent. You can also change its line weight, line color and pattern, and surface color and pattern.

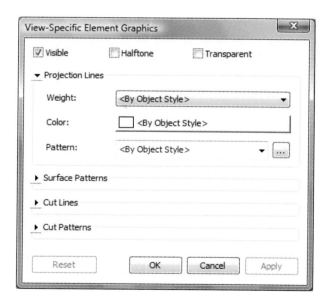

View-Specific Element Graphics dialog box

Transparency

You use transparency to display only lines for an element or a category. When elements are transparent, only their edges are visible in the view. The elements behind or beneath a transparent element are visible.

Overriding Host Layers

You can control the visibility of cut edges in host layers in the plan and section views. The hosts to which you can apply an override are walls, roofs, floors, and ceilings. These overrides are dependent on the detail level of the view. When you place overrides on wall layers, the overrides display at medium or fine detail level.

The following illustration shows a stud wall displayed in the plan view without and with host layer overrides.

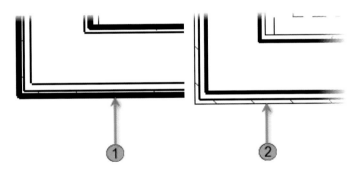

① Standard view showing the exterior and interior finish layer line weights.

② View with overrides to give finish layers a light line weight and structure a heavy line weight.

Object Styles

You use the Object Styles dialog box to specify the default line weights, line colors, line patterns, and materials for different categories and subcategories of model elements, annotation elements, and imported elements. The object style configurations control the display of elements in all views until overrides are placed in particular views.

Temporary Hide/Isolate

Temporary Hide/Isolate on the View Control Bar temporarily changes the visibility of selected elements in the view. You use this tool when you want to see or edit only a few elements of a certain category in a view. The tool affects only the active view in the view window.

When you exit Temporary Hide/Isolate, the selected elements remain hidden and the Temporary Hide/Isolate icon on the View Control Bar appears blue. You can reset the view to its original state or make the Hide/Isolate permanent for the view, in which case the icon appears white. Element visibility reverts to its original state when you close the project, unless you make the changes permanent. Changes made using the Temporary Hide/Isolate tool do not appear in print.

Reveal Hidden Elements

You can make hidden elements visible by using Reveal Hidden Elements on the View Control Bar. Reveal Hidden Elements is a toggle that shows the outlines of elements that are hidden by element or category. You can select these objects and reveal the element or category.

View Templates

A view template is a named collection of view properties such as view scale, discipline, detail level, and visibility settings that are common for a view type such as a plan or an elevation view. You use view templates to apply a defined set of view properties to a specific view. For example, you can create a view template with specific view properties for a plan view that shows furniture layout. If you create other plan views that require the same properties as the furniture plan, you apply that view template to the new views. You can standardize the display of the project views by defining a view template that you can apply to multiple views simultaneously.

Project views and view templates are not linked. When a view template changes, all the views created from that template do not update automatically. To update the views with changes, you need to reapply the template.

Applying and Creating View Templates

You can save a view template from one type of view and apply the same template to any other view. For example, if you save a template from a plan view, you can apply that same template to a 3D view. Although the view range property applies only to the plan and reflected ceiling plan (RCP) views, the template is still applied to the 3D view using properties applicable from the plan and RCP views.

The following illustration shows the Project Browser shortcut menu options you can use to create or apply a view template by using an existing view.

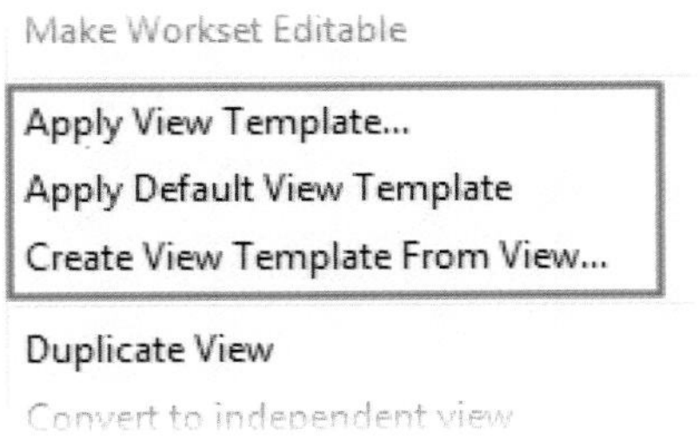

Make Workset Editable

Apply View Template...
Apply Default View Template
Create View Template From View...

Duplicate View
Convert to independent view

Modifying Line Styles

You can use the Visibility/Graphic Overrides dialog box to modify the line styles for an object category in a building model view. When you modify line style, you can change the weight, color, and pattern of lines.

You can change default line styles by using the Line Styles dialog box. Access this dialog box by selecting Line Styles from the Settings drop-down on the Project Settings panel of the Manage tab. You can also change line styles that are applied to objects by using the Object Styles dialog box on the Settings drop-down.

Procedure: Modifying Line Styles in a View

The following steps describe how to modify the projected line styles in a particular view.

1   Click View tab > Graphics panel > Visibility/Graphics.

2   In the Visibility/Graphic Overrides dialog box, Model Categories tab, under Projection/ Surface, Lines column, click Override for a model object category.

3   In the Line Graphics dialog box, click the Color tab.

4   Select a color for the line.

5   Select a pattern for the line from the Pattern drop-down menu.

About User-Defined Filters

User-defined filters enable users to group elements across categories. You can use user-defined filters to speed up the process of making visibility changes to views and create visibility controls for components that share common characteristics.

Definition of User-Defined Filters

A user-defined filter is a rule that you can apply to a view to control the display of various components. User-defined filters provide a way to override the graphic display and control the visibility of elements that share common properties in a view.

Creating Filters by Category

You use the Filters dialog box, accessible from the Graphics panel of the View tab, to create filters that can hold one or more object categories. The parameters for these categories are then available to set rules for the filter. For example, you can set a filter for fire walls that includes all walls with a fire rating value above a certain amount. After you have created filters, you apply them to views in the Visibility/Graphic Overrides dialog box. You can also open the Filters dialog box from within the Visibility/Graphic Overrides dialog box.

Setting Visibility for Filters

When filters are applied to views, you can set the visibility overrides for each filter. In the previous example, a fire wall filter could be set in a view to show all fire walls with a certain line weight and color.

Examples of User-Defined Filters

The following illustrations show examples of user-defined filters.

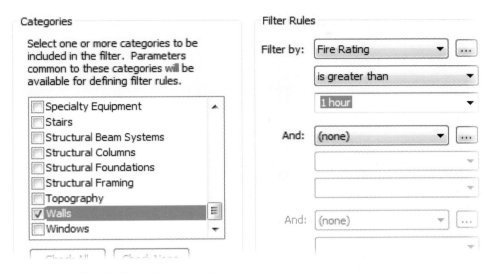

Filter for walls with Fire Rating greater than 1 hour

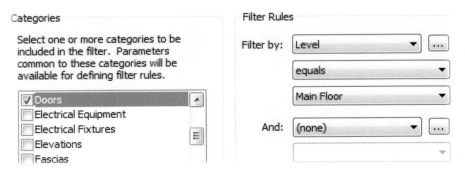

Filter for doors on a specific floor level

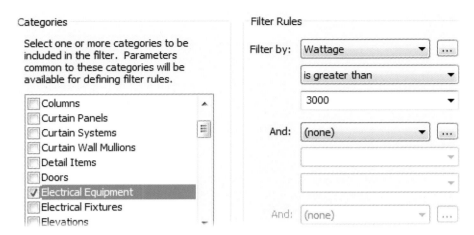

Filter for electrical equipment that draws more than 3,000 watts

Creating and Using Filters

You use filters to efficiently control the visibility of various elements in a view. You can use specific parameters that you apply to objects for defining their appearance in views.

Procedure: Creating and Using a New Filter

The following steps describe how to create and use filters.

1   Click View tab > Graphics panel > Filters.

2   In the Filters dialog box, click New.

3   In the Filter Name dialog box, enter a name for the filter.

4   In the Filters dialog box, under Categories, select one or more model object categories.

5   Under Filter Rules, specify the filter rules from the Filter By list. When you select a parameter, the rule-defining list is activated. You can create up to three levels of rules. All the rules must apply to an object for it to be filtered.

6   Open the Visibility/Graphic Overrides dialog box for the view you want to change.

7 On the Filters tab:
- Click Add.
- In the Add Filters dialog box, select one or more filters.
  Note: You can also create a new filter by clicking Edit/New.

8 In the Visibility/Graphic Overrides dialog box, select the line and pattern graphics to override the lines and patterns of the filtered objects.

Guidelines for Controlling Object Visibility

You modify the way lines are displayed to control the visibility of elements in a view. The following recommended practices can help you control object visibility.

Guidelines

- Create custom line styles or change default line styles using the Line Styles dialog box. The line styles you create using this dialog box are available for all objects in all views and give you alternatives when the default line styles do not match your requirements.

- Apply custom line styles or change the default line styles globally using the Object Styles dialog box. This creates default settings that appear in every view, which is quicker than changing the properties of individual views.

- Insert in project templates the custom line styles or object styles that you create to match your company graphic standards. By inserting them in project templates, you will make them available to all users.

- Create overrides to the global style to change a view on a category or element basis by using the Visibility/Graphic Overrides dialog box or the shortcut menu. This enables you to change a specific view according to your requirements.

- Learn how Revit defines complex objects, such as compound structure walls, to save time when you want to modify the appearance of plan and section views according to specific graphic standards. Knowledge of object definitions is important because the visibility of wall, floor, roof, and ceiling layers depends on lines that represent projected or cut edges, hidden lines, common edges, or sweeps.

- Overwrite line styles, halftones, transparency, and the detail level of the components in a view to customize the visibility of different components.

- Apply the changes in the Visibility/Graphic Overrides dialog box before closing it. This prevents you from reopening the dialog box multiple times while you are testing changes to a view.

Exercise | Control Object Visibility

In this exercise, you control the visibility of elements in a view.

You want to de-emphasize the building structure in a floor plan view and emphasize the furniture in this view. You do the following:

- Change the visibility settings.

- Create and apply a view template.

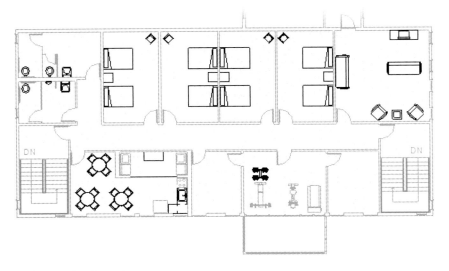

The completed exercise

Completing the Exercise: *To complete the exercise, follow the steps in this book or in the onscreen exercise. In the onscreen list of chapters and exercises, click Chapter 6: Viewing the Building Model. Click Exercise: Control Object Visibility.*

Change the VisibilitySettings

1 Open *i_rac_essentials_visibility.rvt* or *m_rac_essentials_visibility.rvt*. Ensure that the Ground Floor view is displayed.
Note: The illustrations for the metric dataset will be slightly different from those shown here. The completed exercise illustration may also vary.

2 Open the Visibility/Graphic Overrides dialog box.

3 On the Model Categories tab, under Visibility:
   - Clear the Furniture check box.
   - Click OK.

4 In the view window, verify that the furniture elements such as desk chairs, filing cabinets, and sofa sets are no longer visible in the Ground Floor view.

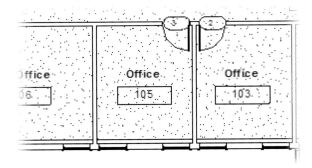

5 To create a plan view to emphasize the furniture, duplicate with detailing the Ground Floor view as **Ground Floor-Furniture Plan** and make it the active view.

6 Click anywhere inside the view window. Enter **VG**.

7 Make the furniture elements visible.

8   Under Halftone, select the check boxes for the following:

- Curtain Panels
- Curtain Systems
- Curtain Wall Mullions
- Doors
- Floors
- Railings
- Specialty Equipment
- Stairs
- Structural Columns
- Walls
- Windows

9   Click the Annotation Categories tab.

10   Clear the Show Annotation Categories in this View check box.

11   Click OK to close the Visibility/Graphic Overrides dialog box. The modified view shows the background architecture in halftone and the furniture in dark lines.

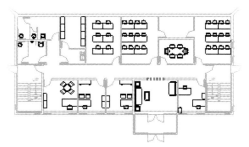

Create and Apply a View Template

1   Click View tab > Graphics panel > View Templates drop-down > Create Template from Current View.

2   In the New View Template dialog box:
- For name, enter **Furniture Layout**.
- Click OK.

3   In the View Templates dialog box, under View Properties, for V/G Overrides Model, click Edit in the value field.
    The Visibility/Graphic Overrides dialog box opens showing the halftone changes you made.

4   Close all the dialog boxes.

5   Duplicate with detailing the Main Floor view as Main Floor-Furniture Plan and make it the active view.

6   On the View Templates drop-down, click Apply New Template to Current View.

7   In the Apply View Template dialog box:
    • Select Furniture Layout to apply the view template to the view.

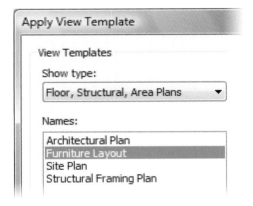

    • Click OK.

    The view is updated with furniture in dark lines, no annotations, and background in halftone.

8   Close the file without saving changes.

Lesson 16 | Working with Section and Elevation Views

This lesson describes how to create and modify section and elevation views. You begin the lesson by learning about section and elevation views. Then, you learn some recommended practices for creating these views. The lesson concludes with an exercise on creating and modifying section and elevation views.

You create a section view to represent a vertical cross section of a building model to display the structure. You create an elevation view to represent a side profile of a building model to show materials. You also use the section and elevation views to sketch levels and add design elements to your building model.

The following illustrations show a section and an elevation view of a building.

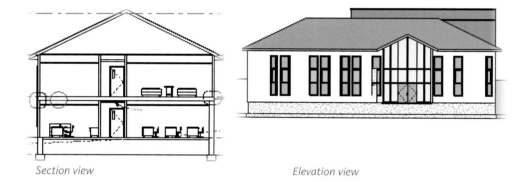

Section view

Elevation view

Objectives

After completing this lesson, you will be able to:

- Describe the characteristics of a section view.

- Describe the characteristics of an elevation view.

- State the recommended practices for creating section and elevation views.

- Create and modify section and elevation views.

About Section Views

You use section views to see the elevation of a building model along a specific vertical plane. You can split a section into segments. You can also create reference sections for existing views.

Definition of Section Views

A section is a cross section in a building model that you place by drawing a line. The view associated with this section is known as a section view.

A section cuts through a model so that the interiors of model components along the section line are visible. There are three default types of sections: building, wall, and detail. Each type of section appears in a separate listing in the Project Browser.

Segments in Section Views

You can split sections into segments that are at right angles to the view direction. You can then use these segments to show parts of a building model located at different distances. You do not need to create a separate section view for each segment. For example, to show a section that displays a portion of the exterior, a portion of a room, and a portion of another room, you split a section line into segments, as shown.

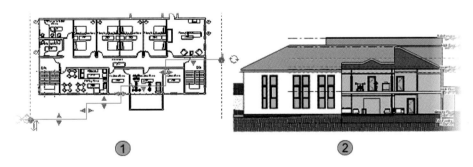

1   Segments in plan view

2   Section view

References in Section Views

Reference sections are sections that reference an existing view. You can place reference sections in plan, elevation, section, drafting, and callout views. Reference sections can reference section views, callouts of section views, and drafting views. When you add a reference section to a building model, a new view is not created.

There is no parametric relationship between the reference section and the referenced view. Therefore, when you resize the section line of a reference section, it does not affect the crop region of the referenced view.

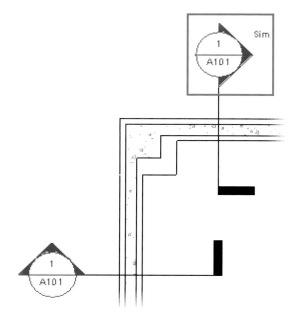

A reference section based on an existing section

Section Tag Visibility of Section Views

Section tags, which include section head, section tail, and break control, are symbols associated with section views. You see section tags in plan, elevation, or other section views, as long as the crop region of the section intersects the view range. For example, if you resize the crop region of a section view so that it does not intersect the view range of a plan view, the section symbol is not displayed in the plan view.

Chapter 06 | Viewing the Building Model

Section symbols are visible in elevation views even if the crop region is turned off. A section symbol is displayed in elevation view if the section line intersects the elevation clip plane. If you resize the clip plane so that it no longer intersects the section line, the section is not displayed in the elevation view.

You can set section tags so that they display only at certain view scales. For instance, site plan views in a large scale do not show section lines through walls, but floor plan views show the sections. By setting the section view scale display parameter, you do not need to hide or display the section line in each view.

Line Breaks in Section Views

If you do not want the section line to be displayed in the building model in a specific view, you can break it into disconnected segments. You use the break control to break section lines and to join broken section lines.

The following illustrations show breaking and rejoining a section line.

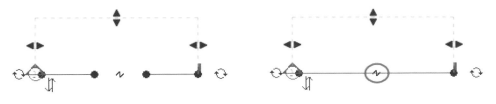

Section break in the middle of a section   *A rejoined section line*

Note: *A break in a section line is view specific and affects the display of the section only in the view in which the break was made.*

Type Properties of Section Views

Each section view has type parameters that control the section tags, callout tags, and reference labels. You set the properties of these type parameters in the Type Properties dialog box. You can define the appearance of section tags and callout tags by selecting Section Tags from the Settings drop-down on the Project Settings panel of the Manage tab.

The reference label parameter in the Type Properties dialog box sets the text displayed next to the section bubble of a reference section.

A section bubble is the symbol on a section line that is created at the end containing the section head. A section bubble contains the detail number for the section, which is automatically populated when the section view is placed on a sheet. A section bubble also displays a default arrow symbol that points in the direction of the section view. A section line also displays a symbol at the tail end. You can toggle the symbols displayed at the ends of a section line.

The Revit default templates contain predefined section types such as Building Sections, Wall Sections, and Detail Sections. You can also create various section types. The custom section types are listed separately in the Project Browser.

Instance Properties of Section Views

Section views have instance properties, such as scale, detail level, model graphics style, and shadows. Section views are 3D. You can control the depth of a section by dragging the Far Clip Plane indicator in a plan view or by adjusting the Far Clip Offset value in the View Properties dialog box.

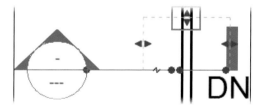

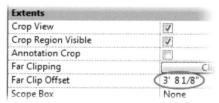

Far Clip Plane indicator in a plan view

Far Clip Offset in the View Properties dialog box

You can use the Far Clip property of a section view to specify how the view represents its clip depth on the faces of objects that are oblique to the view. The Far Clip property of a section view has three options: No Clip, Clip Without Line, and Clip With Line.

The following illustration shows the options of the Far Clip property of a section view.

Example of Section Views

The following illustrations show section views of a building.

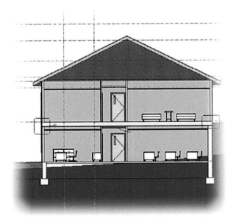

Section view

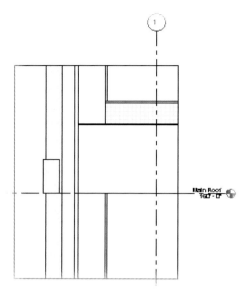

Detail section view

About Elevation Views

You use elevation views to show a horizontal view of a building model from a certain point. Elevation views show levels, grids, door and window placement, and materials. Interior elevation views show the detailed features and finishes of interior walls.

Definition of Elevation Views

Elevation views that are part of the default project template provide a snapshot of a building model from the specified direction. When you create a project using a project template, the north, south, east, and west elevation views are automatically created.

Elevation Tag Visibility in Plan Views

You designate elevation views with elevation tags in plan views. An elevation tag is an elevation symbol with an arrowhead that snaps to walls when you place it in a view.

The elevation view indicator specifies the crop region of the elevation view that intersects the view range of the plan view.

Type Properties in Elevation Views

Every elevation view has type parameters that control tags and labels. You set the properties of these type parameters in the Type Properties dialog box. You can define the appearance of elevation tags by selecting Section Tags in the Settings drop-down of the Project Settings panel of the Manage tab. The reference label parameter of reference elevations specifies the text that is displayed next to the tag of a reference elevation.

The software contains predefined elevation types such as Exterior and Interior elevations. You can also create various elevation types. The custom elevation types are listed separately in the Project Browser.

Instance Properties of Elevation Views

Elevation views have instance properties, such as scale, detail level, model graphics style, and shadows. Elevations are 3D. You can control the depth of an elevation view by dragging the Far Clip Plane indicator in a plan view or by adjusting the Far Clip Offset value in the View Properties dialog box.

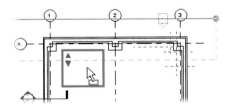

Far Clip Plane indicator in a plan view

Far Clip Offset in the View Properties dialog box

You can use the Far Clip property of an elevation view to specify how the view represents its clip depth on the faces of objects that are oblique to the view. The Far Clip property of an elevation view has three options—No Clip, Clip Without Line, and Clip With Line.

References in Elevation Views

Reference elevations are elevations that reference an existing view. You can place reference elevations in plan, drafting, and callout views. Reference elevations can reference elevation views, callouts of elevation views, and drafting views. When you add a reference elevation to a building model, a new view is not created.

Elevation View Symbols

Elevations in a plan view are specified by elevation tags. These tags are complex objects consisting of round or square symbols and arrow indicators for the four views that you can create for a tag.

The following illustrations show the elevation view symbols that appear when you activate the Elevation tool by clicking Elevation on the Create panel of the View tab. By convention, the round symbol denotes an interior elevation and the square symbol denotes an exterior elevation.

Interior elevation symbol

Exterior elevation symbol

Activating Elevation Views

You can activate up to four elevation views from an elevation tag. When you select an elevation tag, check boxes for each direction are displayed. You can select the check boxes for the required elevation views to appear in the Project Browser.

The following illustration shows an elevation symbol with check boxes for creating elevation views. The circular arrow enables you to rotate the elevation tag and the associated view.

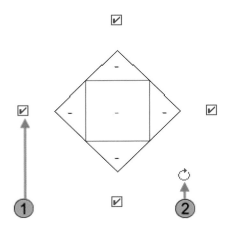

1   Check box for creating elevation view

2   Circular arrow for rotating tag

Framing Elevations

Framing elevations are useful for adding vertical bracing to a building model or for any task that requires quick work plane alignment to a grid or to a named reference plane. When you add a framing elevation, Revit sets the work plane and Far Clip Offset at the selected grid or reference plane. Framing elevations snap to grid lines and ignore walls.

You create a framing elevation by clicking Framing Elevation in the Elevation drop-down of the Create panel of the View tab. You can also select the Attach to Grid check box on the Options Bar while placing a standard elevation.

Example of Elevation Views

The following illustrations show various elevation views of a building model.

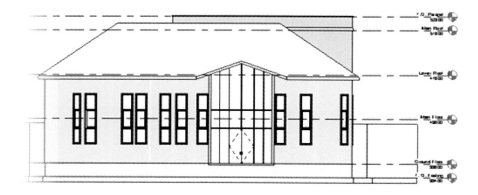

Exterior elevation view

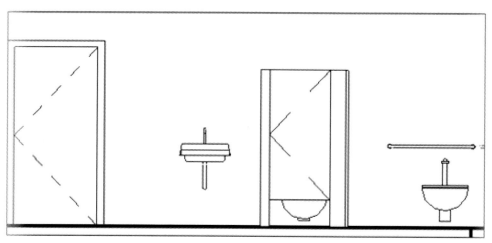

Interior elevation view

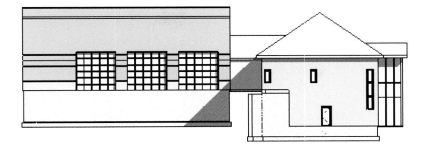

Exterior elevation view with shadows

Guidelines for Creating Section and Elevation Views

The following are recommended practices for creating elevation and section views.

Guidelines

- During the design development process, you can create section and elevation views to check specific design areas. You can create temporary section and elevation view types in the Project Browser to segregate temporary views. You can also customize the graphic appearance of the tags for such views.

- The view name in the Project Browser is different from the view name when you place it on a sheet, therefore, you can use a descriptive and meaningful name in the Project Browser and a standard name in the document set. This is to easily identify views and save time during the design development process.

- You do not have to spend time populating elevation and section bubbles with text and numbers because Revit automatically numbers them when you place the views on sheets.

- Annotate views only when the design development process is near completion, because the annotations may need to be updated if you change the building model during the process.

- You can pin section and elevation tags in place in plan views before adding text, detail components, and other annotations to the elevations and sections. Pinning prevents the view tag from being inadvertently moved.

- Elevation tags are separate from elevation view location lines. You can move elevation tags for clarity in plan views without changing the elevation location.

Exercise | Create and Modify Section and Elevation Views

In this exercise, you create and modify a section view to show the interior of a building model. You also create an interior elevation from which you activate the four elevation views. You then modify one of the elevation views.

You need to create section and elevation views of a building model to show the interior design of the building. You also want to create a segmented section to show the building structure at different locations.

You do the following:

- Create and modify a section view.

- Create and modify an elevation view.

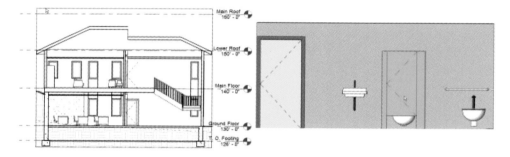

The completed exercise

Completing the Exercise: *To complete the exercise, follow the steps in this book or in the onscreen exercise. In the onscreen list of chapters and exercises, click Chapter 6: Viewing the Building Model. Click Exercise: Create and Modify Section and Elevation Views.*

Create and Modify a Section View

1   Open *i_rac_essentials_sections_elevations.rvt* or *m_rac_essentials_sections_elevations.rvt*. Ensure that the file is open in the Ground Floor view.
Note: The illustrations for the metric dataset may be slightly different from those shown here.

2   Click View tab > Create panel > Section. Notice the information on the Options Bar.

3   In the view window:

- Position the cursor to the left of the main entrance in the lower building.

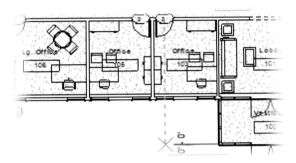

- Click to place the section head.
  Note: The building model looks slightly different in the metric dataset.

4   Drag the cursor straight up past the north wall of the building and click to place the section tail. The new section view named Section 4 is created in the Project Browser.

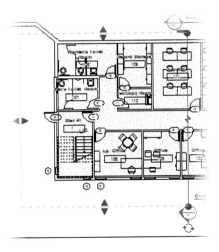

5   Open the Section 4 view. The crop boundary is selected.

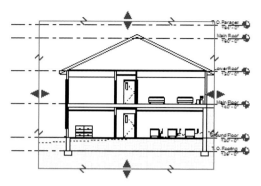

6   With the crop boundary selected, drag its control arrows closer to the building to resize the view area.Notice that the Parapet Level line disappears when it no longer intersects the section boundary.

7   Return to the Ground Floor view. The section line is still selected.

8   In the view window:
   • Place the cursor over the section line.
   • When the cursor changes to a double-headed arrow, drag the section line toward the right in the lower building to the room on the left of the right-side staircase.

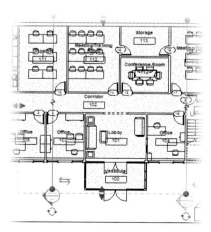

Note: The illustrations that follow may slightly differ from what you see in your building model based on where you placed the section line.

9   In the view window, click the flip control arrows that are displayed close to the section head to change the direction of the section symbol.

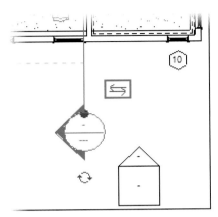

10   Click Modify Views tab > Section panel > Split Segment. The cursor changes to a knife.

11   In the view window:
     • Move the cursor to approximately where the section line intersects the northern wall of the interior corridor.

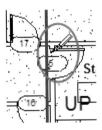

     • Click below the point of intersection to split the section.

12   In the view window:
     • Drag the lower part of the section line toward the staircase on the right.

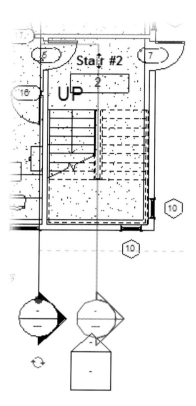

- Click to place the section line.

13 Exit the Split Segment tool.

14 In the view window:
- Select the section line.
- Drag the Far Clip boundary of the section closer to the building, keeping it to the right of the exterior wall.

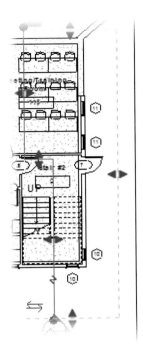

15 Right-click the view and click Go to View to activate the section view and see the changes made so far.

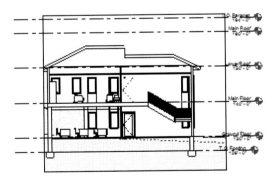

Create and Modify an Elevation View

1 Open the Main Floor view.

2 Zoom in to the toilet rooms in the upper-left corner of the lower building.

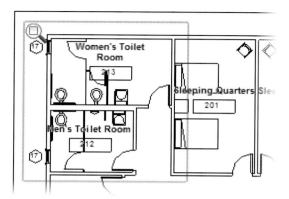

3   Click View tab > Create panel > Elevation. The cursor displays a square elevation tag. The point of the tag orients towards the nearest wall.

4   In the view window:
   • Position the cursor in the Women's Toilet Room so that the view arrow points to the southern wall to which the sink is attached.
   • Click to place the elevation.

5   Exit the Elevation tool.

6   Notice that the elevations are automatically listed in the Project Browser as Elevations 1 - a, 1 - b, 1 - c, and 1 - d.
     In the view window:
   • Select the elevation.
   • Select all check boxes around the elevation to create additional elevations.

7   Open the Elevation1 - a view.

8   On the View Control Bar:
    • Set the view scale to 1/4" = 1'-0" (1: 50).
    • Set Model Graphics Style to Shading with Edges.

9   In the view window:
    • Select the crop region of the view.
    • Drag the bottom edge up to the floor line.

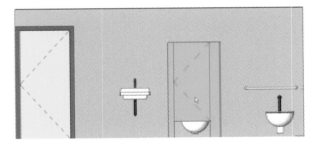

Note: The crop region snaps weakly to the floor. If you place the crop boundary edges just outside the wall, floor, and ceiling edges, the edges will display with a cut (heavy) lineweight to provide a dark border.

10 Close the file without saving changes.

Lesson 17 | Creating and Modifying 3D Views

This lesson describes how to create and modify 3D views. You begin the lesson by learning about 3D view types and cameras. Next, you learn the steps to create and modify camera views and some recommended practices for creating and modifying 3D views. The lesson concludes with exercises on creating the 3D perspective and 3D orthographic views and creating a section box 3D view.

You can create 3D views of a building model to help your design team or client visualize the model. You can also use 3D views to review alternative designs.

3D perspective view of a building model

Objectives

After completing this lesson, you will be able to:

- Describe 3D view types.

- Describe cameras.

- Create and modify camera views.

- State the recommended practices for creating and modifying 3D views.

- Create the 3D perspective and 3D orthographic views.

- Create a section box 3D view. (Optional)

About 3D Views

You can present a building model by using two types of 3D views, perspective and orthographic. These views represent your design vision and demonstrate the form and function of the building model.

Definition of 3D Views

A 3D view shows the building model from a point of view using the camera. You can position the camera anywhere and create a 3D view of the model. The direction of the camera is determined by positioning the view target. You can increase or decrease the angle of view of the camera by adjusting the side clipping boundaries of the view.

3D View Types

In the perspective view, objects that are far from the camera appear smaller than objects of similar size that are closer to the camera. In this view, the receding parallel lines appear to converge to vanishing points.

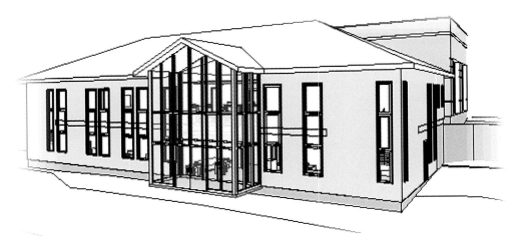

Perspective 3D view of a building

In the orthographic view, objects that are far from the camera are the same size as objects of similar size that are closer to the camera. In this view, the receding parallel lines remain parallel and do not appear to converge at a vanishing point.

Orthographic 3D view of a building

 Note: *You can orient 3D views to any direction and save them with different names.*

Section Box Views

A section box is a 3D crop boundary created in a 3D view. You create section box views to display a specific part of the 3D view, which helps isolate a part of a building model for the purpose of study or illustration.

To create a section box in a perspective or orthographic view, you enable the section box by selecting the Section Box check box in the Instance Properties dialog box. The section box provides triangular control grips that you can use to crop the required portion of the building model and limit the scope of visibility in the 3D view.

You can use the section box view to control lighting during the rendering process and save processor time. You can hide the section box in the view and retain its crop effect.

The following illustration shows the section box view.

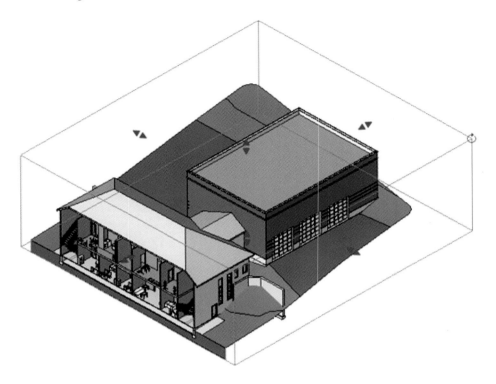

Mouse Navigation

A mouse wheel provides zoom, pan, and orbit controls in a 3D view. The pan and orbit controls allow you to orient a particular view to give you the view you want.

You move the mouse wheel to zoom in and zoom out a view. You can also use the CTRL key and the mouse wheel to zoom. To pan the view (side-to-side), you hold down the mouse wheel. To orbit in a view, you use the mouse wheel and the SHIFT key at the same time.

Steering Wheels Navigation

You open the Steering Wheels by clicking the Steering Wheel on the Navigation Bar or pressing F8. The Steering Wheel can display as the full navigation wheel, the view object wheel, or the tour building wheel. The three wheels provide controls that allow you to zoom, pan, orbit, place the view center, look around from the camera position, move the model up or down, walk around the view (in perspectives only), and rewind through recent actions. You can control the appearance of the Steering Wheel using the Options dialog box.

 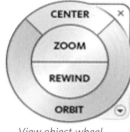 

| Full navigation wheel | View object wheel | Tour building wheel |

The following table describes the options on the three Steering Wheels.

Wheel	Button	Description
Full navigation wheel	Orbit	Rotates the camera eye about the entire model or selected objects.
	Zoom	Magnifies the view.
	Pan	Moves the view left, right, up, or down.
	Rewind	Steps back through recent actions.
	Center	Sets the center for Zoom or Orbit.
	Walk	Moves the camera toward the model in the direction the cursor is dragged.
	Look	Spins the camera while holding its position.
	Up/Down	Moves the camera up or down, holding the same target point.

Wheel	Button	Description
View object wheel	Center	Sets the center for Zoom or Orbit.
	Zoom	Magnifies the view.
	Rewind	Steps back through recent actions.
	Orbit	Rotates the camera eye about the entire model or selected objects.
Tour building wheel	Forward	Zooms in toward a selected target.
	Look	Spins the camera while holding its position.
	Rewind	Steps back through recent actions.
	Up/Down	Moves the camera up or down, holding the same target point.

Mini Wheels Navigation

You can also open mini versions of the three wheels: full navigation wheel, view object wheel, and tour building wheel. Mini wheels are designed for users who are experienced in 3D navigation and prefer to have more screen space and smaller controls.

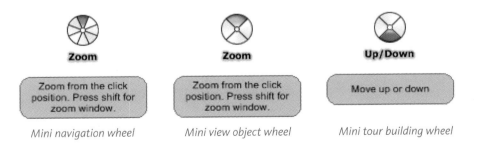

Zoom	Zoom	Up/Down
Zoom from the click position. Press shift for zoom window.	Zoom from the click position. Press shift for zoom window.	Move up or down
Mini navigation wheel	*Mini view object wheel*	*Mini tour building wheel*

You control the appearance of Steering Wheels using the Options dialog box.

The following illustration shows the SteeringWheels tab in the Options dialog box.

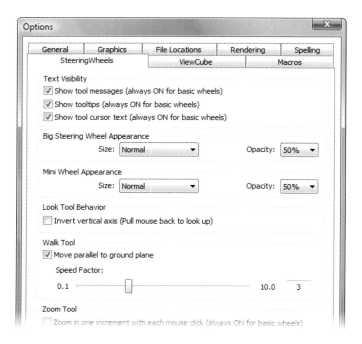

View Cube Navigation

In 3D views, the view cube is present in the upper-right corner of the view window by default. The view cube is composed of a compass and a cube.

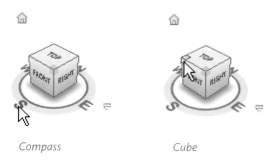

Compass   *Cube*

To orient the view in a specific direction, you select the appropriate compass direction indicator and drag. You can place your cursor over the compass and select and drag the model on the ground plane. You can also orbit the model by selecting any part of the cube and dragging it. To orient the view, you select any named face, edge, or corner of the cube. To return the view to its original position, you select the home icon.

You control the appearance of the view cube in the Options dialog box. The following illustration shows the ViewCube tab in the Options dialog box.

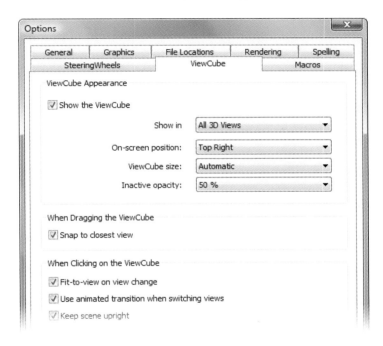

You can also toggle the display of the view cube by selecting or clearing the ViewCube check box that can be accessed from the User Interface drop-down on the Windows panel of the View tab.

The following illustration shows the selected ViewCube check box.

Example of 3D Views

The following illustrations show a camera positioned in a plan view and the corresponding perspective 3D view of the model created by the camera.

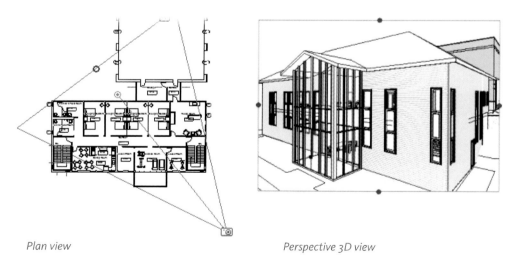

Plan view   *Perspective 3D view*

About Cameras

To create a 3D view, you add a camera to a project and focus the camera on the model in views such as floor plan and elevation. After you add a camera to a project, you can move either the camera or the view target to change the 3D view of the project. You can also set and modify the properties of 3D views and save the views.

Definition of Camera

A camera presents a scene from a particular point of view. Camera objects simulate still-image, motion picture, or video cameras in the real world.

Creating Additional 3D Views

You change a camera view by modifying the camera properties. You can add cameras to create new 3D views. For example, you can produce a view inside a building model by placing the camera inside the walls of the model. 3D views differ from each other on the basis of the actions you perform, such as changing the position of the camera or the target point. Additionally, you can modify the far clip plane associated with the camera to change what the 3D view displays.

Rotating 3D Views

The target point defines the axis of rotation for a 3D view. You can rotate a 3D view about this axis by modifying the camera level and its focal point. When you change the building model in a 3D view, the changes also occur in other views. You can tile all the open views in the view window to watch the changes simultaneously. In plan or elevations views, you can make the cameras of 3D views visible. You can also modify camera position and target points.

Naming and Saving Views

When you first place a camera, a 3D view of the current project is opened in the Project Browser, which is named 3D View 1. Additional camera view names increment in the Project Browser as they are created.

The default 3D view is an orthographic aerial view oriented to the southeast. It is named {3D} in the Project Browser. If this view is not present in a project, you can create it by selecting the Default 3D option from the 3D View drop-down on the Quick Access toolbar. You can also open the default 3D view by selecting 3D View from the 3D drop-down on the Create panel of the View tab. Once this view is created, you can use the Quick Access toolbar icon or the 3D View tool from the ribbon to open the view, not create a copy.

You open a 3D view by double-clicking the name of the view in the Project Browser. You can modify the orientation of the default 3D view but it will revert to the default orientation the next time you open the project. To save the changes to the default 3D view, rename the view in the Project Browser. You can then open another default 3D view. You can duplicate the default 3D view or any 3D view. You organize views by name so that you can manage projects with multiple 3D views.

Modifying 3D Views

You can modify 3D views by setting their properties, such as the model graphics style, view scale, far clip offset, and crop region.

You can change the crop region, which defines the boundaries for the 3D views, by moving the top, bottom, right, and left clip planes.

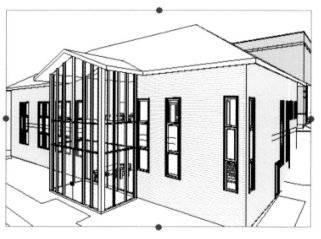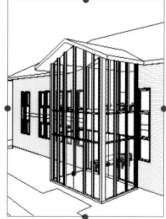

Crop region defining the boundaries for 3D perspective view

Additionally, you can modify the eye elevation and target elevation, which are also referred to as camera height and target point height, respectively, for 3D views.

Note: *Changes made to the orientation or position of the default 3D view are temporary until you save the view.*

Examples of Cameras and Camera Views

The following illustrations show a camera positioned in the plan and elevation views and how the camera creates a 3D view from the plan and elevation views.

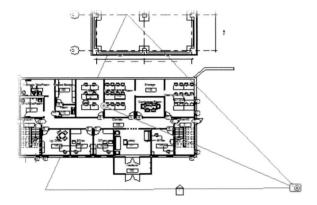

Camera positioned in the view

3D view created by the camera positioned in the plan view

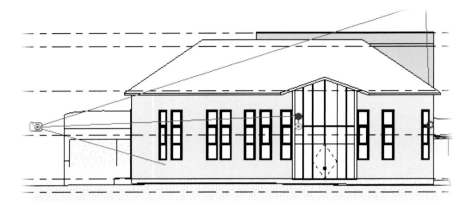

Camera positioned in the elevation view

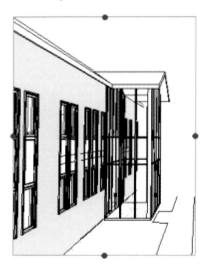

3D view created by the camera positioned in the elevation view

Creating and Modifying Camera Views

You create a 3D perspective or orthographic view of a building model by adding a camera. You modify the view by changing the camera position, target, or field of view.

Chapter 06 | Viewing the Building Model

Procedure: Creating 3D Perspective Views

The following steps describe how to create a 3D perspective view.

1   Open the plan, elevation, or section view in which you want to place the camera.

2   Click View tab > Create panel > 3D View drop-down > Camera.

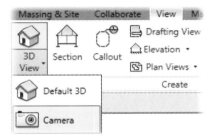

3   On the Options Bar, select the Perspective check box.

4   In a plan view, on the Options Bar, set the camera level and Offset, which is set by default to the height of the eye above the level of the view.
    Note: These options are not available in the section or elevation view.

5   Place the camera and drag the target point.

6   Set the camera target.

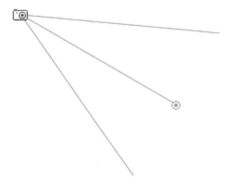

   Note: The Project Browser contains a default name, such as 3D View 1 or 3D View 2, for the newly created 3D perspective view. You can rename the view.

Procedure: Creating 3D Orthographic Views

The following steps describe how to create a 3D orthographic view.

1   Open the plan, elevation, or section view.

2   Click the Camera tool.

3   On the Options Bar:
   - Clear the Perspective check box.
   - Specify the view scale.

4   In the view window:
   - Place the camera.
   - Drag the camera to a location where you want to position the camera.
   - Place the target point.

   Note: The Project Browser displays the default name of the view under 3D Views. You can rename the view.

Procedure: Modifying Existing Camera Views

The following steps describe how to modify an existing camera view.

1   In the Project Browser, double-click the 3D view name.

2   On the Navigation Bar, click SteeringWheels.

3   On the selected Steering Wheel, use the buttons to perform the required actions.
   Note: You can also navigate using the mouse wheel.

4   If you are in the default 3D view, save the view to retain the modification. Changes to camera views persist.

Guidelines for Creating and Modifying 3D Views

The following are some best practices for creating and modifying 3D views.

Guidelines

- Place the camera far enough from the building model when placing a camera for a perspective view so that the field of view lines show what you want to see in the view. Placing the camera too close to the model provides severe angles that may be unrealistic or may not reveal the perspective view. If you place the camera farther away, it will be easier to adjust the view.

- Place a camera in a plan view carefully so that you are aware of the level you are working on because initially the level determines the height of the camera. Careful placement reduces the chance of unexpected results in the camera view. You can change the camera level later, if required.

- Use the View Control Bar tools at the bottom of the view window to edit the display properties of a 3D view. To save system resources, keep perspective views in Hidden Line display while adjusting them until you are ready to export images or display them to a client.

- Right-click the view name in the Project Browser and click Show Camera to make the camera visible in plan, elevation, and other 3D views. You can then drag the camera, target, or far clip plane to modify the view. This is a quick method to adjust the appearance and crop for a perspective view.

- Save or rename the default 3D view to retain the camera position changes. If you do not do this, your work could be lost when you close the file. Creating named orthographic views is a quick method to provide multiple views for a design review.

Example

The following illustration shows a camera placed in a plan view with field of view lines showing that the entire building is in the view.

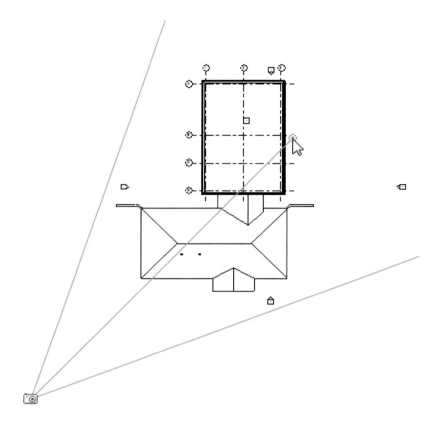

Field of view camera

Exercise | Create 3D Perspective and 3D Orthographic Views

In this exercise, you create 3D perspective and 3D orthographic views of a building model.

You are designing a building with two wings. You need to create the 3D perspective and aerial views of the building model to show to your client during the design phase.

You do the following:

- Create a 3D perspective view.

- Create 3D orthographic views.

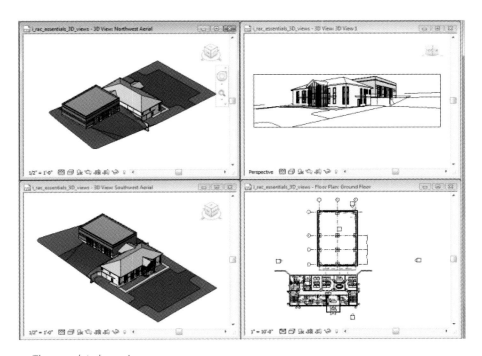

The completed exercise

Completing the Exercise: *To complete the exercise, follow the steps in this book or in the onscreen exercise. In the onscreen list of chapters and exercises, click Chapter 6: Viewing the Building Model. Click Exercise: Create 3D Perspective and 3D Orthographic Views.*

Create a 3D Perspective View

1   Open *i_rac_essentials_3D_views.rvt* or *m_rac_essentials_3D_views.rvt*. The file opens in the default 3D view.
     Note: The illustrations for the metric dataset will be slightly different from those shown here.

2   You will create a perspective view of the south face of the lower building. Open the Ground Floor view.

3   Zoom in to the lower part of the building model.

4   Click View tab > Create panel > 3D View drop-down > Camera.

5   In the view window:
     • Position the cursor to the left of the entrance below the south wall of the lower building.
     • Click to place the camera, as shown.

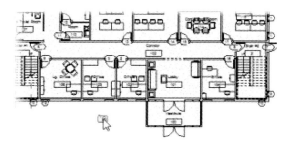

6   Move the cursor inside the entrance passage to place the camera target point, as shown.

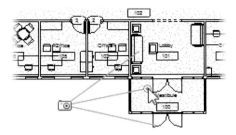

7   Click to place the target point. In the Project Browser, a new 3D perspective view with the default name 3D View 1 is created and it becomes the current view. However, this view is too zoomed in to be useful.

8   To adjust the new 3D view to show more of the building, click outside the crop region box to clear the selection.

9   Open the Ground Floor view.

10   Right-click in the view window. Select Zoom Out (2x).

11   In the Project Browser, right-click 3D View 1. Click Show Camera. Notice that the camera is selected.

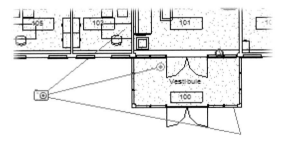

12   In the view window:
- Drag the camera to a new location to the right of the model.
- Drag the target point to the new location, as shown.

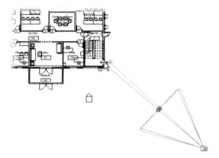

- Adjust the triangular camera field.

13 Drag the clip plane handle on the edge of the triangular camera view to move the clip plane away from the camera so that it extends past the model. This ensures that the walls and roof are displayed.

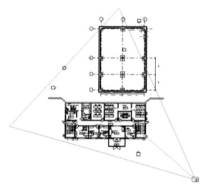

Note: The clip plane on your screen might look different depending on the camera position.

14 Open the 3D View 1 view to have a look at the model.
Note: Drag the top and bottom of the crop region, as necessary, to display the roof and walls.

15   Adjust the crop size for printing. Click Modify Cameras tab > Crop panel > Size Crop.

16   In the Crop Region Size dialog box:
   • For Width, enter **10"** (**250** mm).
   • Click OK.

   Note: The illustration might look different depending upon the placement of the camera.

17   In the view window, press ESC to clear the crop selection.

18   Right-click in the view window. Click Zoom To Fit.

Create 3D Orthographic Views

1   You will now create additional 3D aerial views. Open the default 3D view.

2   In the view window:
   • Right-click the view cube. Click Orient to a Direction > Southwest Isometric.

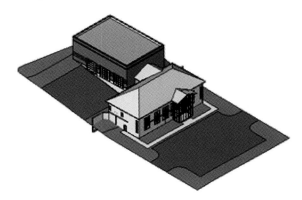

   • Right-click the view cube. Click Save View.

3   In the Enter Name for New 3D View dialog box:

    • For Name, enter **Southwest Aerial**.
    • Click OK.

4   In the Project Browser, right-click the Southwest Aerial view. Click Duplicate View > Duplicate.

    A view named Copy of Southwest Aerial appears in the Project Browser and opens as the active view.

5   On the view cube, click the corner between Top and Left, as shown, to orient the model to the northwest.

6   In the Project Browser, right-click the Copy of Southwest Aerial view and rename it **Northwest Aerial**.

7   Tile the open views.

8   Zoom to fit each view in its tiled window.

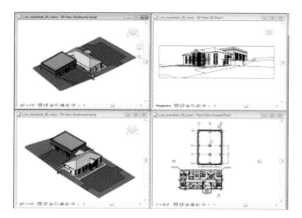

9   Close the file without saving changes. Alternatively, you can continue using this dataset to perform the optional exercise that follows.

Optional Exercise | Create a Section Box 3D View

In this exercise, you create a section box 3D view of a building model.

You want to provide a cutaway view of a building model for the client to verify possible furniture and equipment arrangements. To do this, you create a section box 3D view of the model.

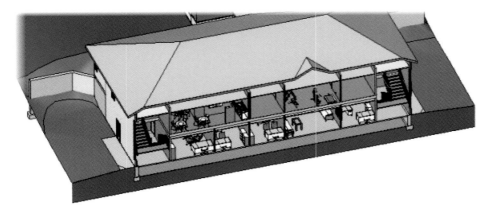

The completed exercise

Completing the Exercise: To complete the exercise, follow the steps in this book or in the onscreen exercise. In the onscreen list of chapters and exercises, click Chapter 6: Viewing the Building Model. Click Exercise: Create a Section Box 3D View.

1   You now make a section box in the Southwest Aerial view to make a cut-away view. In the view window:

   • Maximize the Southwest Aerial 3D view window.
   • Click Zoom to Fit in the view.

   Note: The illustrations for the metric dataset will be slightly different from those shown here.

2   In the Project Browser, right-click the Southwest Aerial view. Click Properties.

3   In the Instance Properties dialog box:
    • Under Extents, select the Section Box check box.
    • Click OK.

4   In the view window:
    • Select the section box.
    • Drag the blue control grip present on the south side to the left to create a cut-away view of the administration building.

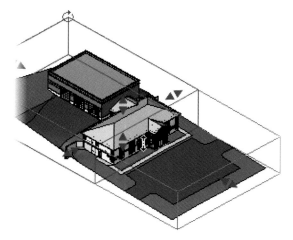

5   To hide the section box, right-click the section box. Click Hide in View > Elements.

6   Explore this view. You can rotate the view and zoom in. You can place this view on a drawing sheet to print it for the client, if required.
    Note: The completed exercise illustration may differ, depending on how you explored this view.

7   Close the file without saving changes.

Chapter Summary

Now that you have learned how to create and manage views of your building model, you can work in these views and present them in ways that best illustrate your design.

In this chapter, you learned to:

- Explore the different views displayed in the Project Browser and modify their properties.
- Control the visibility and appearance of elements in different views.
- Create and modify section and elevation views.
- Create and modify 3D views.

Image Gallery

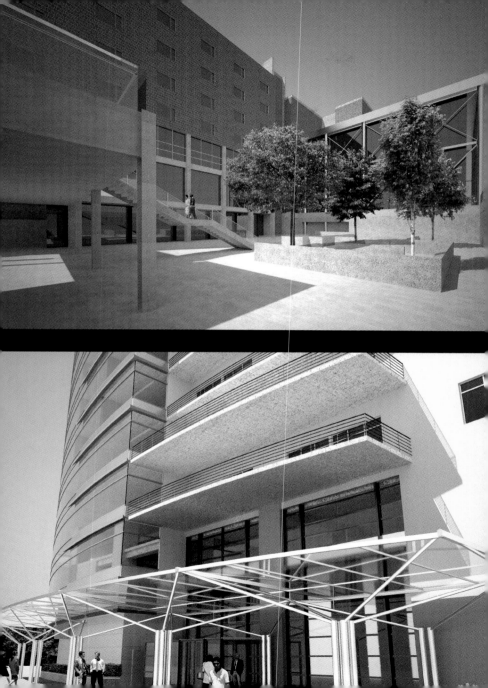

Chapter 07

Using Dimensions and Constraints

In Autodesk Revit Architecture, you use dimensions to show and control object positioning. You can also use constraints to lock two elements together at a fixed distance, keep a series of objects equally spaced, or lock two elements in an alignment. Both tools allow you to control and automate the location of objects in your design. In this chapter, you learn about using dimensions and constraints.

Objectives

After completing this chapter, you will be able to:

- Work with dimensions in a building model.

- Apply and remove constraints in a building model.

Lesson 18 | Working with Dimensions

This lesson describes how to work with dimensions in a building model. You begin the lesson by learning about temporary and permanent dimensions. Next, you learn about some recommended practices for working with dimensions. The lesson concludes with an exercise on working with dimensions in a building model.

You place dimensions to set and modify the distance between the elements in a building model. You use temporary dimensions to quickly and accurately populate a design, and permanent dimensions to annotate the design.

The following illustration shows a dimension associated with a wall element.

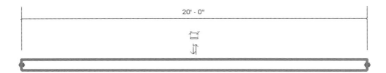

Objectives

After completing this lesson, you will be able to:

- Describe temporary dimensions.

- Describe permanent dimensions.

- State the recommended practices for working with dimensions.

- Work with dimensions in a building model.

About Temporary Dimensions

Dimensions are system families that have type and instance properties. You can customize these properties to create new dimension types that better suit your requirements. For example, you can change the tick mark, line weight, and color of dimensions. In addition, you can control the witness lines for dimensions. You can also set the font, height, and unit format for dimension text.

Dimensions can be of two types, temporary and permanent. Temporary dimensions are automatically displayed when you select an element in a building model. They enable you to place and move elements accurately in a building model.

Definition of Temporary Dimensions

Temporary dimensions are the dimensions displayed in reference to the nearest element that is perpendicular or parallel to the element that you are creating or have selected.

The following illustration shows the temporary dimensions of various objects.

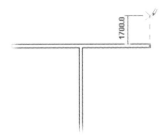

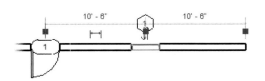

Temporary dimensions for a wall being created   *Temporary dimensions for a selected element*

Temporary dimensions disappear when you add another element to the building design, reducing dimension clutter. To edit a temporary dimension, you need to select the element and change the dimension value.

Listening Dimensions

Temporary dimensions that appear when you create elements are called listening dimensions. Listening dimensions appear in bold and change as you create an element, such as a wall. You use listening dimensions to adjust the length or placement of elements.

The following illustration shows the listening dimension that displays while you draw a wall. Notice that the listening dimension is displayed from the start to the end point of the wall.

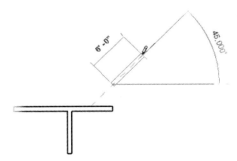

You can modify the listening dimension while creating or after placing an element in the drawing by typing the required dimension directly.

The following illustrations show the listening dimension of a wall modified by typing the new dimension.

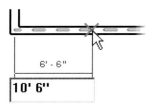

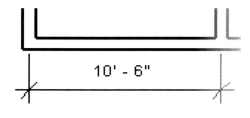

Start point of a wall offset from the left wall at 10' 6"

Wall drawn

> **Note:** *When you enter dimension values using imperial units, you can enter either the feet and inch symbols, such as 10' 6 3/4", or just the feet and inch numbers separated by a space, such as 10 6 3/4. If you enter a value without specifying a unit, such as 10, it is interpreted as 10 feet (10').*

Creating Elements with Temporary Dimensions

You can specify temporary dimension settings and dimension increment values.

Specifying Temporary Dimension Settings

You can specify settings such as snapping points for temporary dimensions. For example, you can specify that temporary dimensions snap to the centerlines or to the faces of a wall. To specify such preferences, you use the Temporary Dimension Properties dialog box, which can be accessed from the Settings drop-down on the Project Settings panel of the Manage tab. You can set separate preferences for walls, doors, and windows.

Dimension Increments

When you create an element, its temporary dimension value is incremented based on the amount you zoom in the view. The increment also depends on the dimension snap increment settings specified in the Snaps dialog box, which is also accessible from the Settings drop-down. You can set increment values for length and angular dimensions separately using the Snaps dialog box.

Viewing Temporary Dimensions

You view the temporary dimensions of an element by using the Modify option on the Quick Access toolbar or on contextual ribbon tabs that appear during specific operations. When you click Modify, other commands end and you can select the desired element.

The temporary dimensions for an element might differ from those that were originally displayed while creating the element. This is because when you are creating an element its temporary dimensions are displayed in reference to the nearest element, which might have changed.

Modifying Temporary Dimensions

You can resize or move elements by modifying their temporary dimensions and you can move the witness lines of temporary dimensions to reference specific elements. To do this, you use the blue square control on the witness line. Selecting the square enables you to cycle its position, such as from wall centerline to alternate faces. The changes made to the witness lines are not saved.

The following illustrations show a wall being repositioned by having its temporary dimensions modified.

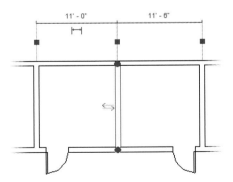

Before modifying the temporary dimensions

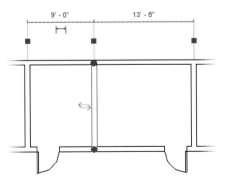

After modifying the temporary dimensions

Example of Temporary Dimensions

The following illustration shows the temporary dimensions of a selected wall. The temporary dimensions indicate the length of the wall and its position relative to the other walls in the drawing.

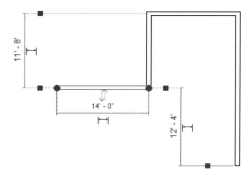

About Permanent Dimensions

You use permanent dimensions if you want to continuously display the dimensions of the elements in a building model view. Dimensions adjust to the scale of the view. You do not need to create dimension styles for standard view scales. There are two methods by which you can associate permanent dimensions with an element. You can make temporary dimensions permanent by using the dimension symbol, or you can add permanent dimensions using the Dimension tools on the Dimension panel of the Annotate tab.

Definition of Permanent Dimensions

Permanent dimensions are the dimensions that you add to elements after placing them in a building model. Unlike temporary dimensions, permanent dimensions are visible even if the elements are not selected.

Permanent dimensions occur in two states, modifiable and nonmodifiable. Permanent dimensions for an element can be modified individually only when the element is selected. In the nonmodifiable state, you cannot edit the values of permanent dimensions because the element with which they are associated is not selected. You can select dimensions and change their properties, lock or unlock them, and apply equality constraints.

The following illustrations show the two states of permanent dimensions.

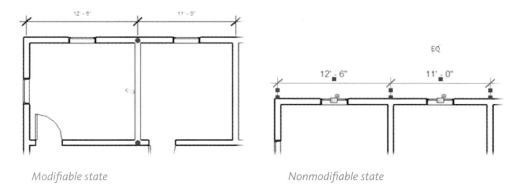

Modifiable state   *Nonmodifiable state*

Using the Dimension Symbol

A dimension symbol appears near the temporary dimension of an element. You need to select this symbol to change a temporary dimension to permanent.

The following illustrations show how to use a dimension symbol.

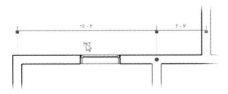
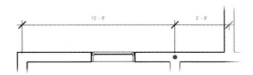

Before clicking the dimension symbol   *After clicking the dimension symbol*

Using Dimension Tools

You can add five types of permanent dimensions using the Dimension tools. You can add dimensions for chains and for an entire wall with one click.

The following table describes the permanent dimension types that you can use.

Types	Description
Aligned	Placed between selected references and aligned to the references.
Linear	Placed between selected references and aligned either to the horizontal or the vertical axis of the view.
Radial	Placed in the radial dimension of an arc.
Angular	Placed on multiple references that share a common intersection.
Arc Length	Placed on an arc object.

Specifying Wall Dimension Preferences

You can specify the way the pointer snaps when you assign permanent dimensions to a wall. For example, you can specify the reference line that should be highlighted first. You can also specify the place where the pointer snaps first when you move it over a wall. You can make these specifications by selecting appropriate options from the Place Dimensions list on the Options Bar.

The following illustration shows the Place Dimensions list on the Options Bar.

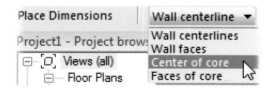

 Note: *The Place Dimensions list is activated for all dimension types except the linear dimension.*

Chapter 07 | Using Dimensions and Constraints

Wall Centerlines

Using this option, you can make the wall measurable from the centerline.

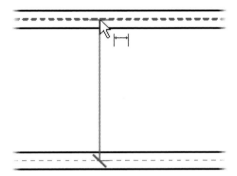

Wall Faces

Using this option, you can set the dimension of a wall based on the inner or outer faces of the wall.

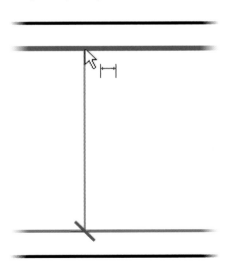

Center of Core

Using this option, you can make a wall measurable between the centerline of the core boundaries. This is applicable for walls with more than one layer, such as compound walls.

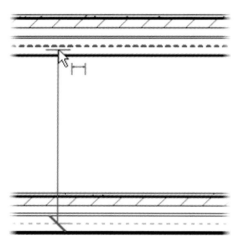

Faces of Core

Using this option, you can make the wall measurable between the inner or outer faces of the core boundaries.

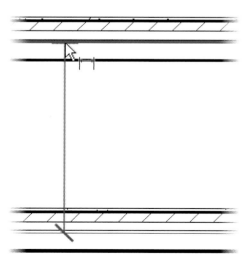

Chapter 07 | Using Dimensions and Constraints

Point Dimensions

When you add a permanent dimension to wall elements, you can create dimension references from corner points on walls. You can use TAB to cycle through available references to reach points and wall faces.

The following illustrations show aligned dimensions placed by corner points.

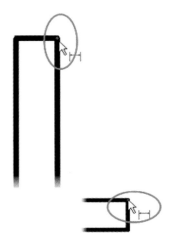

Placing an aligned dimension to exposed wall points

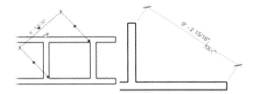

Aligned dimensions placed between two wall points

Locking Permanent Dimensions

When you add a permanent dimension to an element, an unlocked padlock appears near the dimension line. The padlock indicates that you can modify the length of a wall and the distance between walls. For example, you can drag the wall ends on either side to increase the wall length. You can also drag the wall upward or downward to adjust the distance between two walls. After making the required modifications, to prevent the dimensions of a wall from changing, you can lock the permanent dimensions by using the padlock. If required, you can unlock dimensions that you have locked.

The following illustrations show locked and unlocked permanent dimensions for a wall.

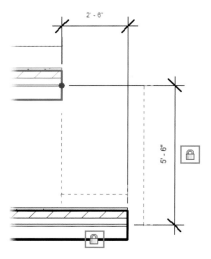

Locked permanent dimensions

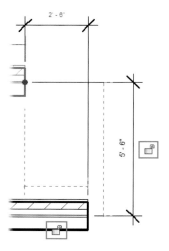

Unlocked permanent dimensions

Overriding Permanent Dimensions

You can change the text display of permanent dimensions by using the Dimension Text dialog box. You can replace the numeric value with text, and specify the text position above, before, after, or below the actual value.

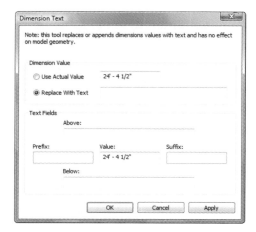

Dimension Text dialog box

Editing Witness Lines

You can add witness lines to a permanent dimension using the Edit Witness Lines tool. This tool is available on the Witness Lines panel of the Modify Dimensions contextual tab that appears when you select a dimension. You can also right-click a dimension and select Edit Witness Lines from the shortcut menu. Then, you click additional objects to include them in the dimension string. The resulting dimension string is a single object. You can remove witness lines from a dimension string using Edit Witness Lines with select+SHIFT.

The following illustrations show the use of the Edit Witness Lines tool to extend a dimension string to other objects.

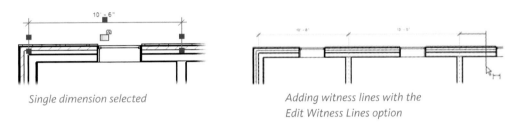

Single dimension selected   *Adding witness lines with the*
                                  Edit Witness Lines option

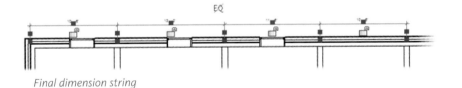

Final dimension string

Example of Permanent Dimensions

The following illustration shows a horizontal wall with permanent dimensions. The length of the horizontal wall is 11 feet, and the distance of the vertical wall from the left end of the horizontal wall is locked at 5 feet.

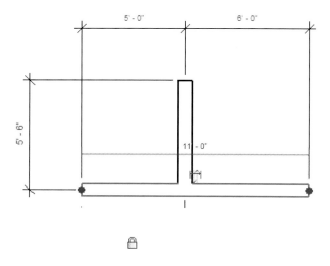

The following illustration shows the position of the two walls after the vertical wall is moved to the left. The length of the horizontal wall is now 13 feet, but the distance of the vertical wall from the left end of the horizontal wall remains fixed because it is locked.

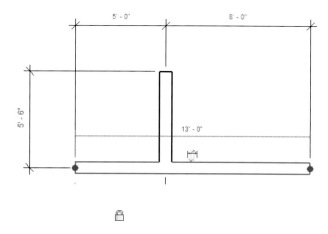

Guidelines for Working with Dimensions

The following best practices help you work efficiently with dimensions.

Guidelines

- Change temporary dimensions to permanent when you need to refer to the distance between various objects frequently while working. Using permanent dimensions is quicker than selecting the same object repeatedly to find out its distance from other objects. You can delete permanent dimensions at any time if they clutter a view; you can always re-create them later.

- Click the EQ symbol when creating a dimension string to quickly set objects at an equal distance.For example, you can create a series of equidistant rooms down a hallway in an efficient way.

- Add parallel reference planes or model lines at the corners of a room when you want to place dimensions across the corners quickly. This is recommended because Revit does not easily add dimensions to nonparallel objects. After adding parallel reference planes, you can place the dimensions between these parallel reference planes and then hide the reference planes. You can add dimensions to certain wall endpoints and corners by using select+TAB.
  Note: Alternatively, you can use the Tape Measure tool to determine the distance between corners.

- Add dimension styles to project templates to avoid having to create dimension styles for each project.

- Use the Duplicate View > Duplicate option to create a copy of a view that does not display the dimensions and notes you placed while working on a building model. This helps you show a neat view to the client without losing the details.
  Note: You can hide individual dimensions as well.

- Adjust view scale before placing dimensions and text. Dimensions and text automatically adjust size to the view scale of the view they are placed in, but if you change the scale of a view after placing dimensions and notes, you may need to check the placement of dimension text and notes to maintain clarity.

Exercise | Work with Dimensions

In this exercise, you place dimensions to modify the position of walls in a building. You also add a wall and place dimension strings around the exterior of the building.

You want to work with walls in your design. To do this, you place dimensions for walls and then change the dimensions to modify the position of walls.

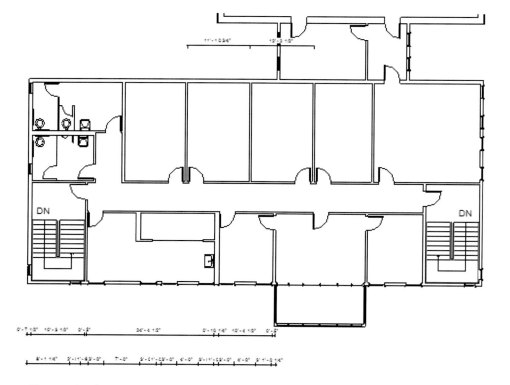

The completed exercise

Completing the Exercise: *To complete the exercise, follow the steps in this book or in the onscreen exercise. In the onscreen list of chapters and exercises, click Chapter 7: Using Dimensions and Constraints. Click Exercise: Work with Dimensions.*

1   Open *i_rac_essentials_dimensions*.rvt or *m_rac_essentials_dimensions*.rvt. The file opens in the
    Main Floor Admin Wing view.
    Note: The illustrations for the metric dataset will be slightly different from those shown here.

2   In the view window, select the interior wall as shown. The temporary dimensions
    are displayed.

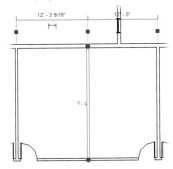

    Note: The temporary dimensions may appear below the wall.

3   Click the dimension symbol to make the dimensions permanent.

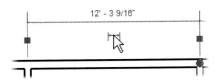

4   Click away from the selected dimension to clear the selection and display the
    permanent dimension.

5   Click the dimension line to select it.

6   To modify the selected dimension:

•   Move the cursor over the dimension line so that it changes to a double arrow.
•   Drag it up away from the wall.

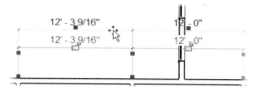

•   Position the dimension line at about the middle of the vertical wall. The exact position is not critical.

7   To shift the position of the left witness line, click the square Move Witness Line control of the left witness line.

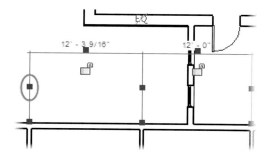

Notice that the left witness line aligns with the right face of the wall. The dimension value also updates.

8   Align the center witness line with the left face of its reference wall as shown. Both the dimensions are updated.

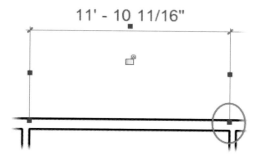

9   Select the interior wall again. Notice that the temporary dimensions display in addition to the permanent dimensions.

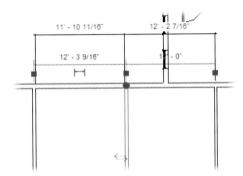

Note: The temporary dimensions may appear below the wall.

10 To move the wall:

- Click the left dimension value of the temporary dimension.
- Enter **8' 0"** (**2400** mm).
- Press ENTER. The wall moves to the left so that the centerlines of the two walls are the specified distance apart.

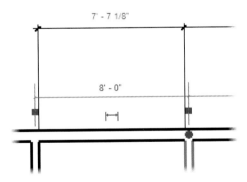

11   To reposition the wall:

- Click the value field of the right temporary dimension to edit it.
- Enter **12' 0"** (**3600** mm).
- Press ENTER. The wall moves to the right.

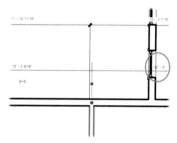

12   To place another wall of the same type, click Modify Walls tab > Create panel > Create Similar.

13   Move the cursor over the hallway wall to the left of the door as shown. Revit displays an alignment line with a perpendicular wall and a listening dimension showing the offset distance from that wall. These dimensions are in bold and you can edit them directly.

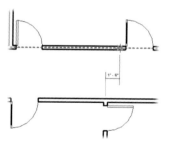

14   Enter **1' 0"** (**300** mm). Press ENTER. The cursor snaps into position at a center-to-center distance of 1' 0" (300 mm) from the referenced wall.

15   To draw a wall:

- Move the cursor upward to connect with the wall above.
- Click to place the wall.

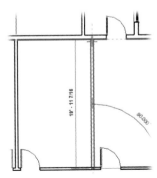

16 You now place dimensions around the exterior of the building to show the locations of the wall and the window. Click Annotate tab > Dimension panel > Aligned.

17 On the Options Bar, verify that Wall Faces is selected in the Place Dimensions list.

18 To place a dimension from the exterior face of the left exterior wall to the interior face of the same wall:

- Zoom in to the lower-left corner of the model.
- Click the exterior face of the vertical wall on the left.
- Click the interior face of the wall.

19 Move from the left to the right to add dimensions for the remaining three walls to the entryway by clicking the wall faces, as shown.

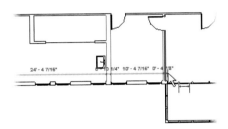

20   When you reach the right face of the interior wall at the left side of the entry, move the cursor to a blank area of the view window below the horizontal wall so that no wall reference is highlighted. Click to place the dimension string.

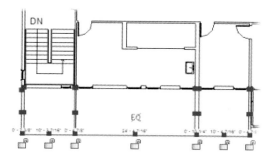

21   You now add dimensions for the windows in the exterior wall. On the Options Bar:
- Select Entire Walls from the Pick list.
- Click Options to specify the dimension options.

22   In the Auto Dimension Options dialog box:
- Select the Openings check box.
- Click Widths.
- Click OK.

23   In the view window, to place dimensions for the openings in the entire wall:
- Select the same horizontal wall for which you placed the dimensions.
- Drag the cursor below the first dimension line and click to place another dimension line.

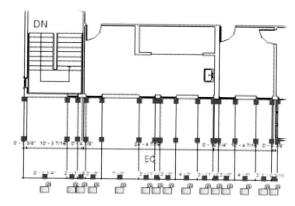

24 The witness lines extend from the dimension strings to the wall. To change the length of the witness lines, open the Type Properties dialog box.

25 In the Type Properties dialog box:
    • Under Graphics, for Witness Line Control, click the value field.
    • Select Fixed to Dimension Line from the list.
    • Click OK.

26 The dimension units show fractional inch (millimeter) values. This is too fine a scale for measuring walls and windows in this overall plan. To change the unit display of the dimensions, open the Type Properties dialog box again.

27 In the Type Properties dialog box, under Text, for Units Format, click the value field.

28 In the Format dialog box:
    • Clear the Use Project Settings check box.
    • For Rounding, select To the Nearest 1/4" (To the Nearest 10) from the list.
    • Click OK.

29 Click OK to close the Type Properties dialog box.

30 Click Modify to exit the Aligned Dimension tool.

31 In the view window, zoom in and verify that all the dimensions have updated.

32 Where dimension values are hard to read, you can select the dimension text field and drag it to a better location, as shown.

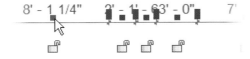

33 Zoom to fit the view in the view window.

34 Clear the selection.

35 Close the file without saving changes.

Lesson 19 | Applying and Removing Constrains

This lesson describes how to apply and remove constraints in a building model. You begin the lesson by learning about constraints and the types of constraints. Then, you learn the steps to apply and remove constraints and some recommended practices for applying constraints. The lesson concludes with an exercise on applying constraints to elements in a building model.

Constraints enable you to lock the position of elements in a building model. Locking elements prevents inadvertent changes to their position. You can lock two elements at a fixed distance and in an alignment. You can also keep a series of elements equally spaced.

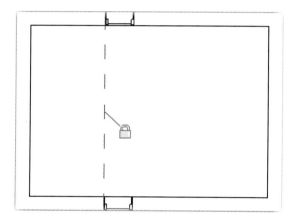

Constraints aligning two windows at the opposite ends of a room

Objectives

After completing this lesson, you will be able to:

- Describe constraints and the types of constraints.

- Apply and remove constraints.

- State the recommended practices for applying constraints.

- Apply constraints to elements in a building model.

About Constraints

You can use constraints to lock the relative or absolute position of one or more elements in a building model. Relational constraints enable you to preserve design intent, such as preserving a line of sight or stacking interior walls on two levels of a building. You can lock dimensions and alignments with constraints while creating the building model. When you lock dimensions, you can either lock the dimension length or placement or set the segments of a dimension chain to the same length.

Definition of Constraints

Constraints are model controls that lock one or more elements in a defined relationship. Constraints can also lock the placement of selected objects. They are displayed in all views in which their references are visible. You often use dimensions to apply constraints to building elements. However, constraints can be made independent of the dimensions.

You make a constraint visible by selecting its references. You can also control the visibility of constraints by turning them on or off on the Annotations tab of the Visibility/Graphics dialog box.

Constraints are of three types:

- Dimension

- Alignment

- Pinning

Dimension Constraints

The two types of dimension constraints are length and equality. You create dimension constraints either by placing and locking dimensions or by locking an alignment. For example, when you place permanent dimensions, you can lock those dimensions so that the length or position of the element does not change. When you lock a dimension, a constraint element represented as a padlock is created.

Length Constraints

When you lock a dimension with a constraint, you prevent that dimension from changing. In the following illustration, the distance between the door and the left wall is constrained. The distance between the door and the right wall is unconstrained. If you move the left wall, the door moves with it, staying at a fixed distance from the wall. However, if you move the right wall, the position of the door does not change because the corresponding dimension is not constrained.

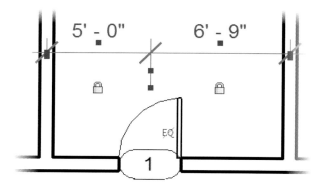

Equality Constraints

An equality constraint locks each segment of a multisegmented dimension to the same length. When you select the dimension line, a blue equal sign (=) is displayed above the entire dimension line to represent the equality constraint.

Alignment Constraints

The alignment between two elements can be locked with an alignment constraint, which is displayed as a padlock next to the dashed line that connects two aligned elements. If you move either of the aligned elements, the other element moves with it, maintaining the alignment as shown.

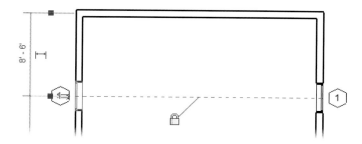

Pinning Constraints

You can select model elements and lock their current position and size by using the Pin tool on the Modify panel of the Modify Walls tab. When you pin an element, it displays a pin icon when it is selected. You can click the icon to unpin the element when you want to move it or change its size. The icon remains with the element as a visible toggle after it is pinned or unpinned.

The following illustrations show a pinning constraint applied to a wall in different views.

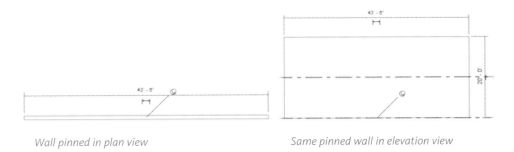

Wall pinned in plan view   *Same pinned wall in elevation view*

The following illustration shows the unpinned wall. Notice that the pin icon remains visible and the size controls are activated.

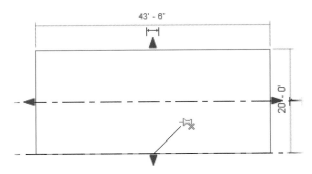

Note: *When you delete pinned objects, a warning message appears.*

Precedence of Constraints

When you set multiple constraints, some constraints take precedence. Alignment constraints override length constraints, and length constraints override equality constraints.

If you set both an alignment constraint and a length constraint on a series of elements and try to move any of the elements, you receive an error message stating that both types of constraints cannot be maintained. When you click Remove Constraints in the error message box, the length constraint is removed and the alignment constraint is maintained, if possible. Similarly, if you set a length and an equality constraint on a series of elements and try to move an element, you receive a warning that both types of constraints cannot be maintained. When you click Remove Constraints in the warning dialog box, the equality constraint is removed and the length constraint is maintained, if possible.

Example of Constraints

Two doors at each end of a long corridor that are locked in alignment are shown.

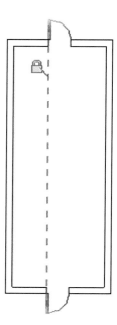

Applying and Removing Constraints

You can constrain dimensions and alignments by placing and locking them. You can also remove constraints by modifying constraint elements. You can modify the constraint elements independently and also when you delete dimensions.

Procedure: Applying a Dimension Constraint

The following steps describe how to apply a dimension constraint to elements in a building model.

1   In the view window:
    - Select the element to which you want to apply the dimension constraint.
    - Click the dimension symbol next to the dimension line to convert the temporary dimension to a permanent dimension.

2   Select the dimension that you want to constrain.

3   Click the open padlock to lock that dimension.

Procedure: Applying an Alignment Constraint

The following steps describe how to apply an alignment constraint to elements in a building model.

1   Click Modify tab > Edit panel > Align.

2   Select the first element to align.

3   Select the other elements to align with the first element.

4   Click the padlock to constrain the alignment.

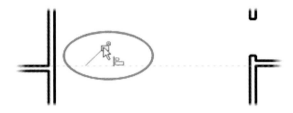

Procedure: Removing a Constraint

The following steps describe how to remove a constraint from an element in a building model.

1   To remove a constraint, select the constrained element and do one of the following:
  - Click the padlock to remove an alignment or dimension constraint.
  - Click the = symbol to remove an equality constraint.
  - Click the pin icon to remove a pinning constraint.

2   You can also select a constrained dimension and press DELETE to remove it.
Note: When you delete the constrained dimension, you see a warning that you are deleting a dimension that has a lock and/or constraint.

3   In the warning dialog box, click Unconstrain to remove the constraint.

Guidelines for Applying Constraints

The following recommended practices help you save time when you use constraints in a building model.

Guidelines

- Place and lock a permanent dimension between two elements. This ensures that an element maintains a specific distance from another element, such as when specifying hallway width, and holds necessary dimensions when you make changes to a plan.

- Use an equality constraint on permanent dimensions between a series of elements to ensure that elements remain equally spaced. For example, with a set of windows across a room, the equal spacing is maintained even if the room changes in size. Calculating placement of elements manually is tedious and error-prone.

- Use the Align tool to place a constraint between two elements to ensure that elements are aligned vertically or horizontally, as with wall faces. This alignment becomes visible when an element is selected.

- Lock alignments carefully to ensure that when you change the entire facade of a building, all walls, floors, rooms, and schedules update automatically.

- Choose one or two most important design rules you want to apply and use constraints to implement them. To ensure flexibility during the modification process, try not to overuse constraints in your designs. This prevents errors and saves your time when unconstraining elements for adjusting a design.

- Pin imported site plans after you start using them to generate toposurfaces or building outlines. Pin grid layouts after they are developed. Pinning plans and grid layouts prevents misplacements that can be difficult to track later in a project.

Example

In the following example, two walls in a building model have been locked using an alignment constraint. The alignment is displayed when you select one of the aligned walls.

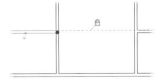

Exercise | Apply Constraints

In this exercise, you apply an alignment and a dimension constraint to elements in a building model. In addition, you temporarily apply a pinning constraint.

You do the following:

You need to align the doors at the ends of a central corridor with each other. You also want to center the front door in the entry lobby and align the side walls of the stairwell at two different levels. In addition, you need to lock the position of an internal wall temporarily.

- Apply an alignment constraint to align doors.

- Apply dimension and equality constraint.

- Apply an alignment constraint to align walls.

- Apply and remove a pinning constraint.

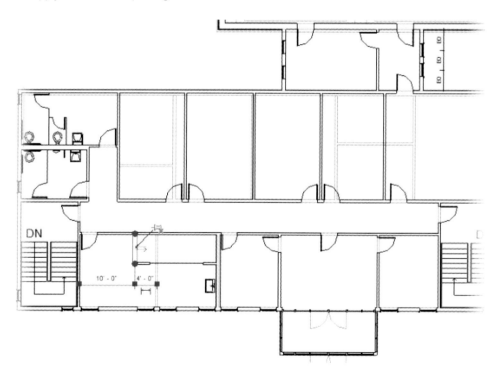

The completed exercise

Apply an Alignment Constraint to Align Doors

1   Open *i_rac_essentials_constraints.rvt* or *m_rac_essentials_constraints.rvt*. The file opens in the Main Floor Admin Wing view.
    Note: The illustrations for the metric dataset will be slightly different from those shown here.

2   Zoom in to the left door at the end of the central corridor.

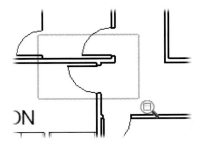

3   You now make this door the alignment control for another door.
    Activate the Align tool.

4   In the view window:

    • Place the cursor on the door to display the centerline as shown.

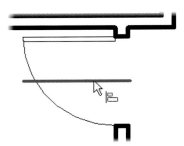

    • Click to select the centerline of the door.

5   Scroll to the right and select the centerline of the door at the opposite end of the corridor. The door aligns.

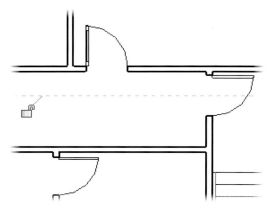

6   Click the padlock to lock the alignment constraint. The padlock symbol changes from unlocked to locked.

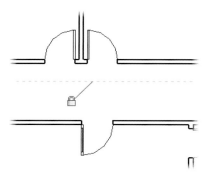

7   Exit the Align tool.

Apply Dimension and Equality Constraints

1   Zoom in to the left door of the corridor again.

2   Click Annotate tab > Dimension panel > Aligned.

3   On the Options Bar:

   • Ensure that Wall Faces is selected from the Place Dimensions list.
   • Ensure that Individual References is selected from the Pick list.

4   In the view window, select the lower face of the corridor wall as shown.

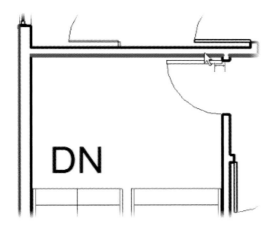

5   Select the wall opening for the door on the swing side as shown.

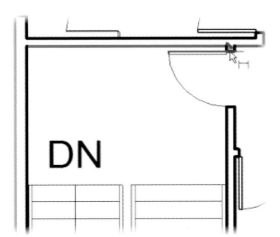

6   Move the cursor to the right of the door and click to place the dimension.

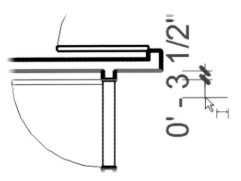

7   Press ESC two times to clear the selection and exit the Aligned tool.

8   In the view window:
- Select the door.
- Click the text field of the dimension you just placed and enter **0' 8"** (**200** mm).
- Press ENTER.

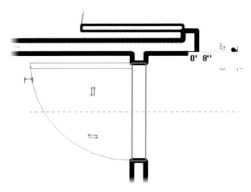

9   Zoom out so that you can see both ends of the corridor. Notice that the right door has also moved.

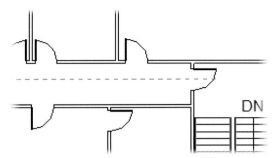

10 In the view window:
    • Select the dimension (not the dimension text) on the left door.
    • Click the open padlock so that it closes to constrain this dimension.
    • Press DELETE to delete the dimension.

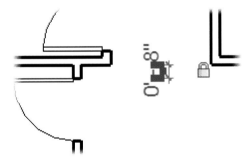

11 In the warning dialog box, click OK to delete the dimension but leave the elements constrained.

12   Select the door to see the constraints.

13   In the view window:
   - Zoom out so that you can view the hallway in the upper part of the plan.
   - Activate the Aligned dimension tool.
   - Click the upper face of the lower wall, the window centerlines, and the lower face of the upper wall, as shown.

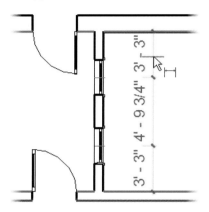

14   In the view window:
   - Click to the right of the wall to place the dimension.
   - Click the EQ symbol to center the windows between the walls.

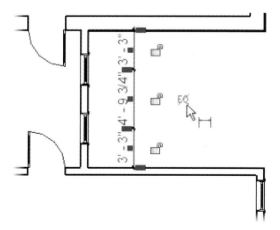

15   Exit the Aligned tool.

Apply an Alignment Constraint to Align Walls

1   You now view another level of the building and align walls in the current view with walls of the other level. Right-click the Main Floor Admin Wing view. Click Properties.

2   In the Instance Properties dialog box:
- Under Graphics, for Underlay, click the value field.
- Select Ground Floor from the list.
- Click OK.
  Note: The walls of the ground floor are displayed in halftone.

3   In the view window, in the upper-left corner of the lower building:
- Select the interior wall to the right of the toilet rooms.
- Drag the interior wall to the right so that the ground floor wall beneath it is displayed.

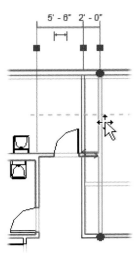

4   Click the Align tool.

5   On the Options Bar, select Wall Centerlines from the Prefer list.

6   In the view window, select the ground floor wall.

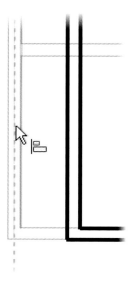

7   Select the main floor wall.

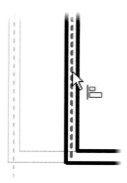

Note: The main floor wall snaps left into position over the ground floor wall.

8   Click the padlock to lock the two walls into alignment.

9   Exit the Align tool.

Chapter 07 | Using Dimensions and Constraints

Apply and Remove a Pinning Constraint

1   Select the short vertical wall as shown. The temporary dimensions of the wall are displayed.

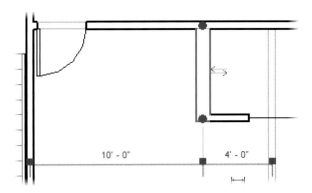

2   Click Modify Walls tab > Modify panel > Pin to constrain the wall. A pin icon appears, and the temporary dimensions disappear.

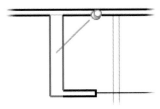

3   On the Modify panel, click Move.

4   In the view window, to move the pinned wall:

   - Click anywhere to establish a start point.
   - Drag the cursor left or right and click anywhere to establish an end point. An error message appears as shown.

5   In the error dialog box, click Cancel.

6   In the view window, to remove the pinning constraint:

   - Select the wall again.
   - Click the pin icon. Notice that a cross is displayed close to the pin, and the temporary dimensions of the wall appear.

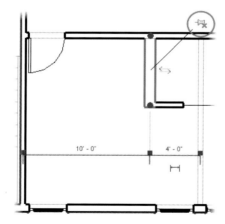

Note: If required, you can now adjust its position, orientation, length, and height.

7   Close the file without saving changes.

Chapter Summary

Now that you have learned how to dimension and constrain objects in your design, you can build intelligence into those designs.

In this chapter, you learned to:

- Work with dimensions in a building model.

- Apply and remove constraints in a building model.

Chapter 8

Developing the Building Model

In this chapter, you learn more about developing your building model by including floors, ceilings, roofs, curtain walls, and stairs and railings in your design.

Objectives

After completing this chapter, you will be able to:

- Create and modify floors.

- Add and modify ceilings in a building model.

- Add and modify the roofs of a building model.

- Add curtain walls in a building model.

- Create stairs, add railings to the stairs, and change the properties of stairs and railings.

Lesson 20 | Creating and Modifying Floors

This lesson describes how to create and modify floors. You begin the lesson by learning about floors and the steps to modify them. Next, you learn some recommended practices for creating and modifying floors. The lesson concludes with exercises on creating and modifying floors.

You can create flat or sloped floors at any level in your model. You can define several types of floors and choose different materials, such as tiles, bricks, wood, steel, concrete, or ceramics, for a floor.

You can use one or more layers of these materials to create a floor that is solid concrete or a carpeted floor over joists. Slabs can be used as a combined floor and foundation system. For example, in a building that has floors on two levels, the slab used as a roof for the first level is the floor for the second level.

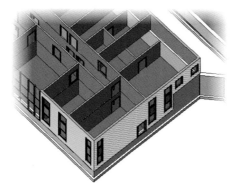

3D view of a building with the ground-level floor visible and the upper-level floor hidden

Objectives

After completing this lesson, you will be able to:

- Describe floors.

- Modify floors.

- State the recommended practices for creating and modifying floors.

- Create and modify floors.

- Create and modify a structural floor.

About Floors

Floors are level-based elements and are essential components of a building model. You can create floors by using the Floor tool. Several predefined floor types are available. You can also create new floor types, such as finish material over plywood sheathing over wood joists, or finish material over concrete over metal deck. In addition, you can edit the required floor types, save, and reuse them within a project. Apart from editing, you can also modify a floor type and the properties of a floor.

Definition of Floors

A floor is a horizontal surface supported by a building structure. All building elements placed on a floor are supported by the floor. To create floors, you need to first sketch their outline. Sketching involves defining the boundaries of a floor either by selecting walls or by sketching lines. You create a floor in the sketch mode by using the Line or Pick Walls tool on the Draw panel of the Create Floor Boundary contextual tab. The Line tool is used to sketch a floor by drawing lines, and the Pick Walls tool is used to select the walls to which a floor is attached. The floor sketch must form a closed loop.

When you add a floor, you specify its vertical position by creating it on a level. The top of a floor is placed by default on the level where it is created, with its thickness projecting downward. In the Instance Properties dialog box, you can specify a height offset of the top surface of the floor from the placement level.

Floors have defined parameters that determine their type and behavior. The type parameters of a floor control the structure and appearance of the floor. The instance parameters of a floor control the vertical placement and phase of the floor.

Creating Sloped Floors

To create a sloped floor, you sketch a floor outline and specify its slope by using a slope arrow. You can modify the slope properties of a sloped floor after sketching it by modifying the properties of the slope arrow.

The following illustration shows the instance properties of a slope arrow.

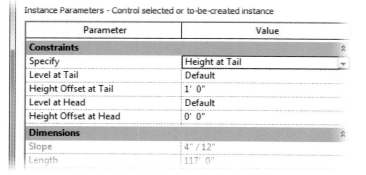

Instance Parameters - Control selected or to-be-created instance

Parameter	Value
Constraints	⫸
Specify	Height at Tail ▼
Level at Tail	Default
Height Offset at Tail	1' 0"
Level at Head	Default
Height Offset at Head	0' 0"
Dimensions	⫸
Slope	4" / 12"
Length	117' 0"

Slope arrow properties always include the level and offset of the tail of the slope arrow. If you select Height at Tail from the Specify list, you need to specify the values for the Level at Head and Height Offset at Head parameters. If you select Slope from the Specify list, you specify the value for the Slope parameter. Height Offset and Slope can be negative values.

Creating Tapered Floors

To create a tapered floor, you can place points or lines on the surface of a floor that are offset vertically. You can place break lines on a floor surface by designating beams, which can be sloped, as supports for the floor. You can edit the position of points or lines that are applied to the floor surface by using shape editing tools. Shape editing tools, such as Add Point and Add Split Line, are available on the Shape Editing panel of the Modify Floors contextual tab that appears when you select a floor. These tools enable you to manipulate the surface of an existing horizontal floor by defining the high and low points for drainage. By specifying the elevation of these points and lines, you can split the surface into subregions that can slope independently. These commands can be used to slope a constant thickness slab or the top surface of a slab with a variable thickness layer.

Structural Floors

A structural floor is a horizontal surface that supports gravity loads and transfers these loads to the supporting structure. For a structural floor, you can specify the maximum or minimum loads. Structural floors created in Autodesk Revit Architecture are not purely structural because you cannot specify load properties for them. You specify the composition and internal structure of floors based on the loads placed on the floors.

You place structural floors to ensure that the depth of the floor support is sufficient for the span, based on standard codes and tables.

You create structural floors by selecting the Structural Floor option from the Floor drop-down on the Build panel of the Home tab.

The following illustration shows the Structural Floor option.

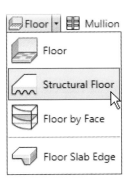

Floors and structural floors created in Revit Architecture are identical elements, and they have the same properties, whether you create them by using the Floor option or the Structural Floor option. Structural floors, such as slabs created in Revit Structure, have structural properties that can be modified in Revit Structure but are read-only in Revit Architecture.

Example of Floors

The following illustrations show different types of floors.

Horizontal floor   *Sloped floor*   *Tapered floor*

Modifying Floors

You can change the structure or shape of a floor after creating it. Often, a floor has an opening for a staircase to another level. You create the opening by editing the floor sketch. You can also place an opening object separate from the floor but hosted by it. In addition, you can modify a floor to create a sloped or a tapered floor.

Floor with an opening for a staircase

Procedure: Creating an Opening in a Floor Sketch

The following steps describe how to create an opening in a floor by editing the floor sketch.

1   Select a floor.

2   Click Modify Floors tab > Edit panel > Edit Boundary.

3   On the Draw panel, click Boundary Line > Line or Pick Walls.

4   Pick or draw lines to indicate the opening boundary.

5   In the view window, drag or trim any boundary lines that overlap or extend beyond another line so that they join and form a single closed boundary loop.
    Note: The boundary loops must be closed. Also, these loops cannot overlap or cross any other floor boundary. This is required because gaps or intersecting lines produce error messages.

6   On the Floor panel, click Finish Floor to complete the opening.

Procedure: Creating a Sloped Floor

The following steps describe how to create a sloped floor by using a slope arrow.

1   Select a floor.

2   Click Modify Floors tab > Edit panel > Edit Boundary.

3   On the Draw panel, click Slope Arrow > Line or Pick Lines.

4   Place a slope arrow in the floor sketch so that it is parallel to the slope with its tail at one defining point and its head at the other.

5   On the Draw panel, click Properties.

6   In the Instance Properties dialog box, specify values for the Height Offset at Tail and either Height Offset at Head or Slope.

7   On the Floor panel, click Finish Floor to include the slope in the floor.

Procedure: Attaching a Floor to Sloped and Nonparallel Supports

The following steps describe how to attach a floor to sloped and nonparallel supports.

1   Select the floor.

2   Click Modify Floors tab > Shape Editing panel > Pick Supports.

3   Select existing beams to define supports for the floor. The floor warps or splits based on the elevations of the beams.

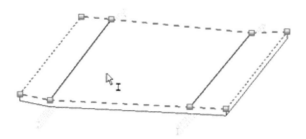

4   On the Quick Access toolbar, click Modify to restore the floor appearance.

Procedure: Creating a Variable Thickness Floor

1   Select a floor.

2   Click Modify Floors tab > Shape Editing panel > Add Point.

3   On the Options Bar, set an offset distance for the point.

4   In the view window, click to place the point.

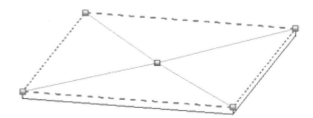

5   On the Quick Access toolbar, click Modify to restore the floor appearance.

6   Open a section view through the altered floor.

7   In the view window, select the floor to create a variable layer in a tapered floor.

8   Open the Type Properties dialog box.

9   In the Type Properties dialog box, for Structure, click Edit.

10 In the Edit Assembly dialog box:
    - Select the layer that you want to make variable in thickness.
    - Select the Variable check box for the selected layer.
    - Click OK.

Guidelines for Creating and Modifying Floors

The following are the recommended practices for creating and modifying floors.

Guidelines

- Offset a floor either up or down from the level on which it is created to ensure flexibility in floor creation. Examples of floors being offset include a mezzanine, a split-level floor plan, and a multilevel deck. You can also create levels specifically for holding partial floors without creating separate views for those floors until the views are required. These practices keep the Project Browser organization simple.

- Combine partial floor views with main floor views by using the Plan Region tool to assign different depth properties to a portion of a plan view. This tool can be accessed from the Plan Views drop-down on the Create panel of the View tab. Combining plan views in this way keeps the Project Browser organization simple.

- Create openings for pipes or ductwork in a floor by creating the basic shape of the floor and then adding openings at required locations. This is advisable because it is easier to place separate openings and modify them than to edit the main floor sketch repeatedly.

- Place floors and openings at an early stage in the design process by using generic floor types as place holders. During design development, you can examine various floor construction methods by changing the floor type and checking the results in section views. This saves time and improves accuracy as you do not need to edit the floor outline sketch.

- Create a sloping floor under the toposurface, and attach the railing or the fence to the floor to show a fence or a railing on sloping topographic site objects. You can hide the floor in elevations, sections, and 3D views to improve the accuracy of those views.

- Use the Add Split Line shape editing tool if you need to specify the exact location of floor tapers or set-downs while creating a tapered floor. This ensures that the tapered floor does not warp in unexpected ways.

- Check the variable thickness property of appropriate layers in the floor structure when you taper the surface of a floor. This ensures that the taper is displayed correctly in section views.

- Pay careful attention to the floor structure, including the insulation. Create floor surface shaping carefully for proper drainage. Exterior patios and decks can become part of rain harvesting measures in dry climates, and floor insulation is important for energy efficiency in cold climates. Whether or not you have access to green design analysis, paying attention to details such as floor structure can raise the sustainability score of your building designs. Floor construction can be an important part of sustainable design efforts for both cold climate and hot climate construction.

Exercise | Create and Modify Floors

In this exercise, you create two floors at two levels in a building model.

You create a concrete floor at the first level of a building that connects with the foundation walls. Next, you create a wood truss floor at the second level that joins with and is supported by the exterior wall structure.

You do the following:

- Create a concrete floor inside the exterior walls.

- Create a wood truss floor that joins exterior walls.

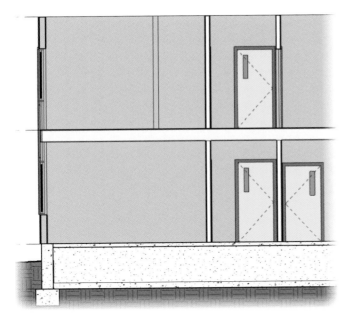

The completed exercise

Completing the Exercise:	*To complete the exercise, follow the steps in this book or in the onscreen exercise. In the onscreen list of chapters and exercises, click Chapter 8: Developing the Building Model. Click Exercise: Create and Modify Floors.*

Create a Concrete Floor Inside the Exterior Walls

1 Open *i_rac_essentials_floors.rvt* or *m_rac_essentials_floors.rvt*. The file opens in the Ground Floor view.
   Note: The illustrations for the metric dataset will be slightly different from those shown here.

2 Open the Section 1 view. Note the height of the concrete exterior walls and the interior partition walls at the ground floor level.

3 Return to the Ground Floor view.

4 To create a floor at the Ground Floor level, click Home tab > Build panel > Floor drop-down > Floor.

5 Ensure that on the Create Floor Boundary tab> Draw panel > Boundary Line > Pick Walls is selected.

6 On the Options Bar, clear the Extend into Wall (to core) check box.

7 To select the inside surface of the exterior walls of the building, in the view window:
   - Move the cursor over the inner side of the north wall to highlight it.
   - Press TAB to highlight all four exterior walls.
   - Click the north wall to select the inner side of the exterior walls.

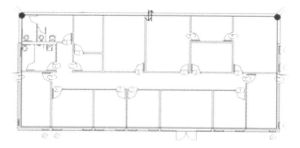

   Tip: You can use the flip control arrows to change the selection to the inner faces of the walls in case you select the outer faces. You can try cycling the arrows but ensure that you return to the inner faces of the walls.

8 On the Element panel, click Floor Properties.

9   In the Instance Properties dialog box:

- Select LW Concrete on Metal Deck from the Type list.
- Click OK.

10 On the Floor panel, click Finish Floor to exit the sketch mode and create the floor.
Note: If prompted to attach walls to the bottom of the floor, click No. If prompted to join the geometry, click No.

11 Open the Section 1 view to view the new floor. Place the cursor on the floor and view the tooltip and the status bar that identify the floor by its type.

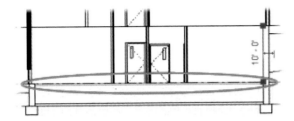

Create a Wood Truss Floor that Joins Exterior Walls

1   Click Home tab > Build panel > Floor.
Note: A floor cannot be placed in a section view. Revit opens the Go To View dialog box and presents options for view selection.

2   In the Go To View dialog box:

- Select Floor Plan: Main Floor from the list.
- Click Open View.

3   Ensure Pick Walls is selected on the Draw panel.

4   On the Options Bar, ensure that the Extend into Wall (to core) check box is selected. This floor will intersect the exterior walls.

5   Select the outside faces of the exterior walls of the building.
Tip: Use the flip control, if necessary, to keep the sketch lines on the external face.

6   If required, use the Trim tool to trim the sketch lines and make four corners as shown.

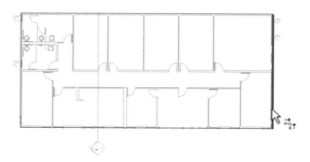

7   You now make two openings in the floor sketch. Zoom in to the room in the lower-right corner.

8   Ensure Pick Walls is selected. Select the right face of the rightmost vertical interior wall.

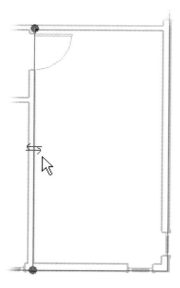

Note: We want to provide for an interior stairwell and a two-story atrium.

9   On the Draw panel, click Line.

10 Sketch a horizontal line from the top of the line you selected to the east exterior wall as shown.

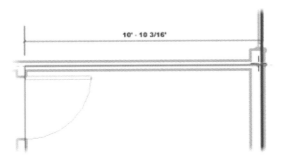

10' - 10 3/16'

11 Click Trim.

12 To create a corner, in the view window:
- Click the horizontal line that you sketched.
- Click the vertical line on the exterior wall above the horizontal line to create a corner.

13   Similarly, trim the lower line as shown.

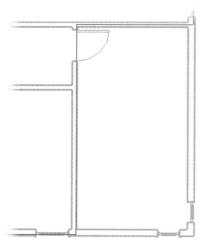

14   Zoom in to the lower-left room on the floor plan and repeat the process to create the stairwell or atrium as shown.

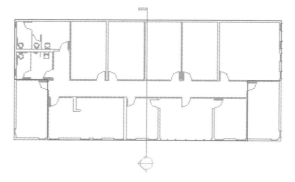

15   Click Floor Properties.

16   In the Instance Properties dialog box:

- Change the floor type to Wood Truss Joist 12" - Carpet Finish (Wood Truss Joist 300mm - Carpet Finish) from the Type list.
- Click OK.

17 Click Finish Floor to complete the floor sketch and exit the sketch mode.
Note: When prompted to attach walls to the bottom of the floor, click Yes. If prompted to join the geometry, click Yes.

18 Open the Section 1 view and zoom in. Notice the two new floors and how they intersect the walls.

19 On the View Control Bar, click Model Graphics Style > Shading with Edges.

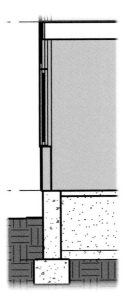

20 In the view window, notice how the interior floors that previously extended to the Main Floor level have attached to the underside of the floor.

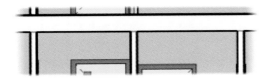

21 Close the file without saving changes.

Exercise | Create and Modify a Structural Floor

In this exercise, you create and modify a structural floor.

You need to place a floor in the equipment bay of the garage floor. On the floor, you want to place a thickened edge under the slab, an opening for a ladder, and slope the floor to the two floor drain points.

You do the following:

- Place a floor.

- Add a thickened edge.

- Split the surface and add lowered points for drain locations.

- Add an opening.

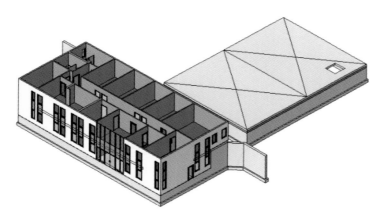

The completed exercise

Completing the Exercise:
To complete the exercise, follow the steps in this book or in the onscreen exercise. In the onscreen list of chapters and exercises, click Chapter 8: Developing the Building Model. Click Exercise: Create and Modify a Structural Floor.

Place a Floor

1   Open *i_rac_essentials_garage_floor.rvt* or *m_rac_essentials_garage_floor.rvt*. The file opens in
    the Garage Floor view.
    Note: The illustrations for the metric dataset will be slightly different from those shown here.

2   You modify the view so that you can see elements of the foundation before creating the
    garage floor. Right-click anywhere in the view window. Click View Properties.

3   In the Instance Properties dialog box, under Graphics:

    • For Underlay, click the value field.
    • Select Ground Floor from the list.
    • Ensure that Underlay Orientation is set to Plan.
    • Click OK. This displays another level of the building. Foundation walls and footings
      appear in halftone.

4   On the Build panel, select Structural Floor from the Floor drop-down.

5   On the Options Bar, ensure that the Extend into Wall (to core) check box is selected.

6   Use Pick Walls, the TAB key, and the flip control arrows to select the exterior walls as shown.
    Note: Use the tooltip or the status bar to identify and select the foundation walls, not
    the footing.

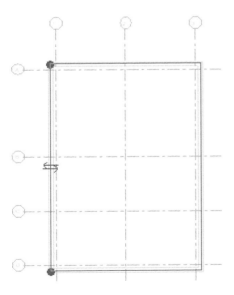

7   Click Floor Properties.

8   In the Instance Properties dialog box, change the floor type to Concrete - 12" (Concrete - 300mm).

9   Finish creating the floor.

10   Open the Instance Properties dialog box for the view.

11   In the Instance Properties dialog box, turn off Underlay.

Add a Thickened Edge

1   You now add a thickened edge to the floor. This is a separate object hosted by the floor. Click Home tab > Build panel > Floor drop-down > Floor Slab Edge. Notice the slab edge type in the Type Selector drop-down.

2   To create a slab edge, in the view window:
     • Place the cursor over an edge of the new floor, as shown.

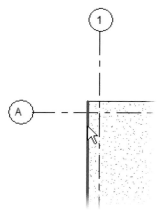

     • Press TAB to highlight all four edges of the floor.
     • Click the edge of the new floor to place the sketch of the slab edge.

3   In the warning message box, read the warning and click OK.

4   Click Place Slab Edge tab > Profile panel > Finish Current to finish creating the edge.

5   To view and adjust the new slab edge, in the view window, create a section as shown.

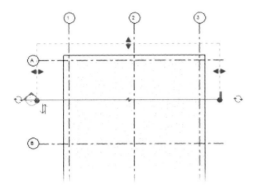

6   Open the Section 2 view.

7   To select the new slab edge:

•   Position the cursor over the slab edge that you created. The thickened slab edge highlights.

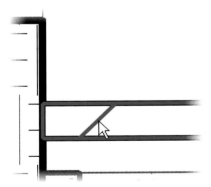

•   Click to select the slab edge.

8   Open the Instance Properties dialog box.

9   In the Instance Properties dialog box:

- Under Constraints, for Vertical Profile Offset, enter **-1** (**-300**). This places the thickened edge below the floor.
- Click OK. The slab edge adjusts in position.

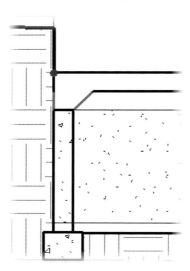

Split the Surface and Add Lowered Points for Drain Locations

1   You now locate drain points and an opening in the floor. Return to the Garage Floor view.

2   In the view window:

- Clear the selection.
- Select the floor.

3   You first add a split line to control surface deflections. Click Modify Floors tab > Shape Editing panel > Add Split Line. Notice that the appearance of the floor outline changes.

4   Place the cursor over the midpoint of the left edge of the floor outline.
Tip: If you have trouble finding the midpoint, you can enter **SM** to force a snap to the midpoint.

5 Click the midpoint to draw a line across the floor to the right edge as shown.

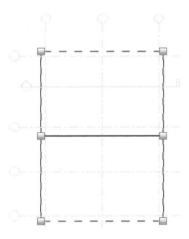

6 To create low points in the floor surface, click Shape Editing panel > Add Point.

7 On the Options Bar, for Elevation, enter **-2"** (**-50** mm).

8 Place a point above and a point below the split line you created along grid line 2, in the middle of the two floor sections. The exact location of the points is not critical.

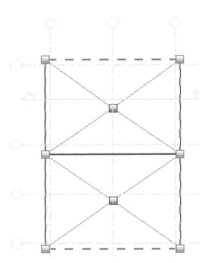

9 On the Quick Access Toolbar, click Modify to exit the floor shape editing tool.

Add an Opening

1   You now place an opening in the floor to provide access to the crawl space below. This will be a separate, hosted object.
    Click Modify tab > Edit Geometry panel > Openings drop-down > Vertical Opening.

2   In the view window, select the floor.

3   Click Create Opening Boundary tab > Draw panel > Rectangle.

4   Place an opening 6' 0" x 6' 0" (1800 mm x 1800 mm), as shown. The exact location of the opening is not critical.

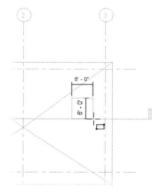

5   On the Opening by Face panel, click Finish Opening.

6   You need to adjust the floor properties so that the floor appears correct in the section because now you have deflected the upper surface. In the view window:

    • Select the section line.
    • Drag the section line so that it passes through the opening you created as shown.

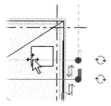

    • Clear the selection.

7   Open the section view for the new section created.

8   In the view window, examine the floor and notice that it appears bent.

9   Select the floor.

10   Open the Type Properties dialog box.

11   In the Type Properties dialog box, under Construction, for Structure, click Edit.

12   In the Edit Assembly dialog box, under Layers, select the Variable check box for the Structure [1] function.

13   Click OK to close all dialog boxes.

14   In the view window, notice that the floor has adjusted its shape to a flat bottom side and variable shape for the floor surface.

15   Press ESC to end the currently active command.

16   Open the default 3D view. Notice that the floor has a thickened edge, a ridge line, drain points, and the opening that you created.
       Note: You can try selecting the opening that you created and dragging it to a new location on the floor.

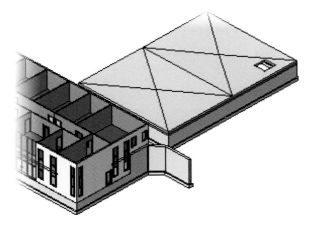

17   Close the file without saving changes.

Lesson 21 | Working with Ceilings

This lesson describes how to work with ceilings in a building model. You begin the lesson by learning about ceilings and the steps to create and modify them. Next, you learn about some recommended practices for working with ceilings. The lesson concludes with an exercise on creating and modifying ceilings and ceiling components.

You use ceilings to host components such as lights and electrical equipment, smoke detectors, and emergency lighting. Depending on the design requirements, you can create different types of ceilings, such as grid and metal rail.

Grid ceiling

Objectives

After completing this lesson, you will be able to:

- Describe ceilings.

- Identify the steps to modify ceilings.

- State the recommended practices for working with ceilings.

- Create and modify ceilings and ceiling components.

About Ceilings

You add ceilings to a building model to specify the placement of ceiling components, such as lights, plumbing fixtures, and ventilating components. You can view ceilings and their contents in ceiling plan views.

Definition of Ceilings

Ceilings are level-based elements that you can create in a building model. Ceilings are automatically offset from a level. You can change the offset value of a ceiling, if required. You can create sloped ceilings and ceilings containing complex structures.

Ceiling Creation Methods

You can create ceilings automatically or manually. You create ceilings automatically by selecting Ceiling on the Build panel of the Home tab, and choosing a predefined ceiling type. You specify the ceiling type while creating a ceiling. You can also modify the ceiling type any time during the design development process. You manually create a ceiling that is specific to your design requirements by sketching the ceiling boundaries specifying the walls to which the ceiling is to be attached.

You need to open the plan view to create a ceiling. Ceiling plan views are specifically used for creating and viewing ceilings. However, you can view a ceiling in other views, such as the section and 3D views.

Examples of Ceilings

The following illustration shows the top view of a stud frame and gypsum board ceiling with a square opening on the left. This ceiling contains round lights and a ceiling-mounted fan. The ceiling on the right uses an acoustic tile grid with lights, air supply registers, and air return registers.

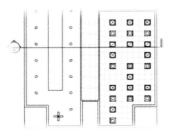

The following illustration shows a section view of two ceilings. The ceiling on the left contains a grid.

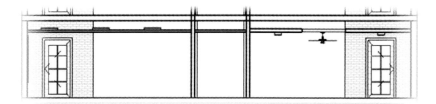

The following illustration shows a 3D view of a gypsum board ceiling.

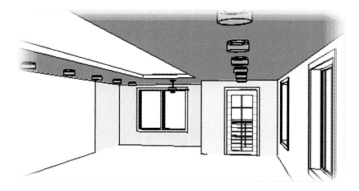

Modifying Ceilings

You can modify ceilings by editing their properties. A design change may specify a 4 x 2 grid after you have placed a 2 x 2 ceiling. In such a situation, you modify the ceiling properties instead of replacing the ceiling.

Ceiling Properties

You can modify ceiling properties before or after you place a ceiling in a drawing by using the Instance Properties or Type Properties dialog box. The following illustration shows the instance properties of a ceiling.

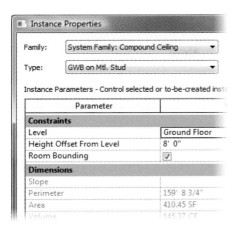

The following illustration shows the type properties of a ceiling. Ceilings can have complex structures similar to floors and roofs, and you can edit the structure by modifying the type properties.

Family:	System Family: Compound Ceiling
Type:	GWB on Mtl. Stud

Type Parameters

Parameter	
Construction	
Structure	
Thickness	0' 4 1/4"
Graphics	
Coarse Scale Fill Pattern	
Coarse Scale Fill Color	■ Black
Identity Data	

Family:	Compound Ceiling
Type:	GWB on Mtl. Stud
Total thickness:	0' 4 1/4"

Layers

	Function	Material	
1	**Core Boundary**	**Layers Above Wr**	0'
2	Structure [1]	Metal - Stud La	0'
3	**Core Boundary**	**Layers Below Wr**	0'
4	Finish 2 [5]	Finishes - Interi	0'

The Type Properties dialog box of a compound ceiling

The Edit Assembly dialog box of a compound ceiling

Procedure: Modifying a Ceiling

The following steps describe how to modify the instance properties or boundary sketch of a ceiling.

1   Select the ceiling to modify.

2   Open the Instance Properties dialog box and change the properties, as required.

3   Draw lines or pick walls to modify the boundary outline sketch.

4   On the Ceiling panel, click Finish Ceiling.

Procedure: Modifying a Ceiling Type Before Creating a Ceiling

The following steps describe how to modify a ceiling type before creating a ceiling.

1   Click Home tab > Build panel > Ceiling.

2   Open the Type Properties dialog box and change the properties, as required.

3   Place or sketch the ceiling.

Guidelines for Creating and Modifying Ceilings

While creating and modifying ceilings, you should follow certain recommended practices to enhance your design accuracy and save time.

Guidelines

- Ensure that you open the ceiling plan view for the level in which you want to place a ceiling. You can create ceilings in a floor plan view; however, when you do this, the software displays a warning message. Checking the current view before adding a ceiling saves time.

- Use the Underlay property of a ceiling plan view to display windows, doors, and furniture while placing components, such as lights and fixtures, in a ceiling. You need to do this because the view range properties of ceiling plan views are different from floor plan views. Therefore, ceiling plans do not display windows, doors, and furniture. Using the Underlay property increases accuracy in placing ceiling components.

- Place components in a ceiling grid and then align them to gridlines so that they move with the grid, if required. You need to do this because ceiling components do not snap to gridlines. Aligning ceiling components to gridlines increases design accuracy.

Exercise | Create and Modify Ceilings and Ceiling Components

In this exercise, you create ceilings of various types in a building model and modify ceiling properties. You create a compound grid ceiling and modify the horizontal and vertical alignment of the ceiling grid. In addition, you sketch a new ceiling. Finally, you place components in the ceiling and attach a wall to the ceiling.

You need to place ceilings in a wing of a building model. According to the design requirements, you need to place ceilings of different types and will specify their height. Finally, you place light fixtures in the ceiling.

You do the following:

- Create a ceiling and modify ceiling properties.
- Edit ceiling grids.
- Sketch a ceiling.
- Place components in a ceiling.
- Attach a wall to a ceiling.

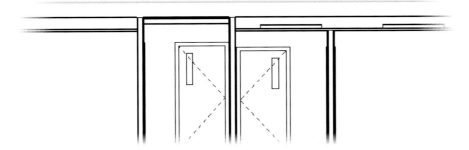

The completed exercise

Completing the Exercise:	*To complete the exercise, follow the steps in this book or in the onscreen exercise. In the onscreen list of chapters and exercises, click Chapter 8:Developing the Building Model. Click Exercise: Create and Modify Ceilings and Ceiling Components.*

Create a Ceiling and Modify Ceiling Properties

1   Open *i_rac_essentials_ceilings.rvt* or *m_rac_essentials_ceilings.rvt*. The file opens in the Ground Floor view.
    Note: The illustrations for the metric dataset will be slightly different from those shown here. The completed exercise illustration may also vary.

2   Open the Ground Floor Ceiling Plan view to place ceilings.

3   Click Home tab > Build panel > Ceiling.

4   Ensure that Compound Ceiling : GWB on Mtl. Stud is selected from the Type Selector drop-down.

5   Open the Instance Properties dialog box to specify the height before you place the ceiling.

6   In the Instance Properties dialog box:
    - For Height Offset From Level, enter **8' 6"** (**2550** mm).
    - Click OK.

7   In the view window, click the main corridor to add the ceiling.

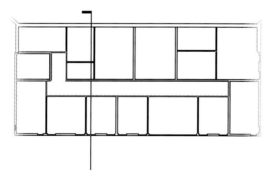

The ceiling is not visible in the current view because the selected ceiling type does not have a surface pattern.

8   In the Instance Properties dialog box:

  • Select 2' x 2' ACT System (600 x 600mm Grid) from the Type list.
  • Set the value of Height Offset From Level to **8' 0"** (**2400** mm).
  • Click OK.

9   In the view window, place the ceiling as shown.

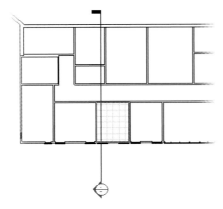

Edit Ceiling Grids

1   The new ceiling grid is centered in the room on a tile. To change its placement, first zoom in as necessary.

2   Exit the Ceiling placement tool.

3   To align the horizontal grid, in the view window:

  • Place the cursor over one of the horizontal gridlines to highlight it.
  • Drag the gridline toward the top until it snaps to the bottom face of the main corridor wall.

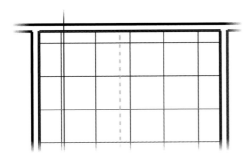

4   Align the vertical grid to the wall face.

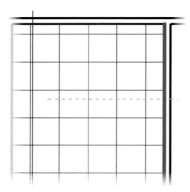

Sketch a Ceiling

1   To begin placing another ceiling by sketching its outline, click Home tab > Build panel > Ceiling.

2   Select Compound Ceiling : 2' x 4' ACT System (Compound Ceiling : 600 x 1200mm Grid) from the Type Selector drop-down.

3   On the Ceiling panel, click Sketch Ceiling.

4   On the Draw panel, click Pick Walls.

5   Zoom in to the northwest corner of the building.

6   Select the interior edges of the four walls of the highlighted room. Use the flip arrows as necessary to select the interior edges of the walls.

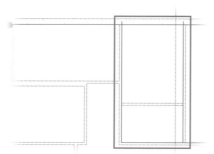

7   Trim the boundary outline as shown.

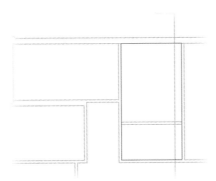

Tip: You can use the Trim tool without switching to another tab.

8   Click Create Ceiling Boundary tab > Ceiling panel > Finish Ceiling to exit the sketch mode and
     view the ceiling grid.

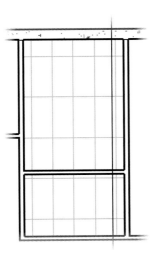

Place Components in a Ceiling

1   To place and align the lighting components, click Home tab > Build panel > Component drop-down > Place a Component.

2   Select Troffer - 2x4 Parabolic : 2 Lamps (M_Troffer - 600 x 600 Parabolic : 2 Lamps) from the Type Selector drop-down.

3   In the view window, click to place the lamp. The exact placement of the lamp is not critical.

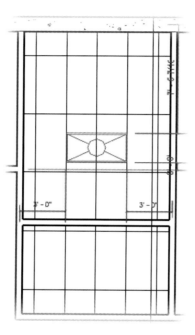

4   Exit the currently active tool.

5   In the view window, select the lamp.

6   Press SPACEBAR one time to rotate the component by 90 degrees.

7   Click Modify tab > Edit panel > Align.

8   To align the fixture with the vertical grids, in the view window:
   - Select a vertical gridline.
   - Click the left side of the light fixture to align it with the gridline.

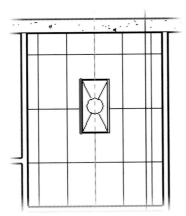

9   Align the fixture with the horizontal grids.

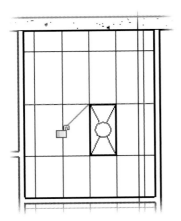

10   Exit the Align tool.

11   To copy the light fixture to another room, in the view window:
   - Select the lamp.
   - Click Modify Lighting Fixtures tab > Modify panel > Copy.

12 To place another light fixture in the ceiling grid:
- Click a grid intersection.
- Place the second light fixture two gridlines down.

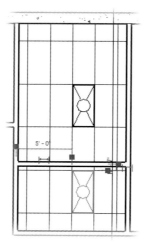

Attach a Wall to a Ceiling

1 Open the Section 1 view to ensure that walls and ceilings are properly configured.

2 In the view window, notice the three ceilings you have placed in separate rooms at different height. You need to adjust a wall that currently extends through a ceiling. This wall will be a room partition that terminates at the ceiling. Select the wall that is passing through the ceiling between the lights.

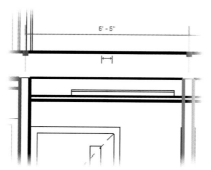

Note: The wall and ceiling appear slightly different in the metric dataset.

3 Click Modify Walls tab > Modify Wall panel > Attach.

4 Select the ceiling. The wall attaches to the ceiling.

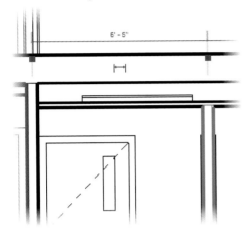

5 Select one of the light fixtures and explore its type properties.

6 Close the file without saving changes.

Lesson 22 | Adding and Modifying Roofs

This lesson describes how to add and modify the roofs of a building model. You begin the lesson by learning about roofs and the process of sketching them. Next, you learn some recommended practices for adding and modifying roofs. The lesson concludes with an exercise on adding and modifying roofs.

In Revit, there are three different ways to create roofs: you can create flat, sloped, or curved roofs. You can also combine simple roof shapes to create complex roof designs. You can place roofs in plan, elevation, and 3D views.

The following illustration shows roofs attached to walls and other roofs.

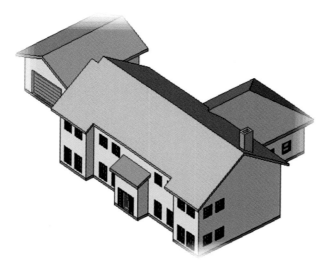

Objectives

After completing this lesson, you will be able to:

- Describe roofs.

- Identify the steps in the process of sketching roofs.

- State the recommended practices for adding and modifying roofs.

- Add and modify roofs.

About Roofs

Roofs are building elements, just like walls and floors. You can design any type of roof for a building model using Revit.

Definition of Roofs

Roofs are building components that represent different types of roofs that you can create when designing building models. You create roofs by sketching footprint outlines or extrusion edges or by picking faces. You can modify roof properties such as outline, structural composition, and slope.

Roof by Footprint

A roof footprint is a 2D sketch of the perimeter of a roof. You draw a footprint by sketching lines or by selecting walls to define the roof perimeter. In both cases, you specify a value to control the offset of the roof from the walls. You create a footprint roof at the level of the plan view where the perimeter is sketched. A sketch of a footprint must be a closed loop that represents the exterior of the roof. A sketch can also contain other closed loops inside the perimeter that define openings in the roof. You define the slopes of a roof by specifying the lines in a footprint as edges of sloping roof planes. You use the Roof by Footprint tool to create the most common roofs such as hip roofs, shed roofs, gable roofs, and flat roofs.

Roof by Extrusion

You create a roof by extrusion by sketching the profile of the top of a roof in an elevation or section view and then extruding the roof. You use the Roof by Extrusion tool to create more complex organic roof designs than the ones created using footprint outlines. You set the start and end points of a roof extrusion to determine the horizontal depth of the roof. You can use a combination of straight lines and arcs to create the roof profile. The location of the profile in the elevation view determines the height of the roof. The sketch of a roof should be a series of connected lines or arcs that are not closed in a loop. Revit applies the roof structure according to the type of roof.

> **Note**: *Only footprint and extrusion methods are covered in this lesson. The third method, roof by face, is part of massing, which is covered in the Advanced course.*

Extrusion Direction of Roofs

The direction in which a roof profile extrudes is known as the extrusion direction. When extruding a roof in an elevation or a section view, you need to determine a perpendicular work plane, such as a wall. You can extend the extrusion toward or away from the view. Extrusion directions that are upward or toward the view are positive, and extrusion directions that are downward or away from the view are negative.

Properties of Roofs

You can modify the instance and type properties of roofs. The instance properties you can modify include outline, slope defining edges, slope angle, and base level. When you modify the type properties of a roof, such as structure, the change affects all instances of the roof type. You can select a roof or a roof sketch to edit its properties.

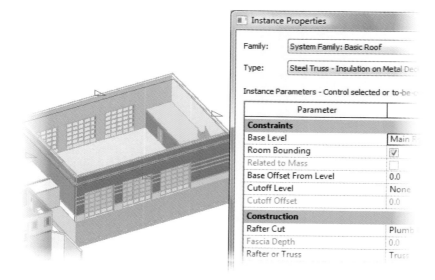

Roof sketch and instance properties

Example of Roofs

The following illustration shows a building model with different roof types.

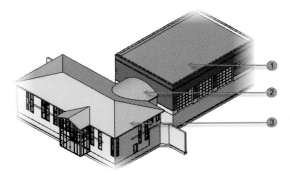

① Flat footprint

② Curved extruded

③ Sloped footprint

Process of Sketching Roofs

You can sketch roofs using footprint, extrusion, and roof by face methods.

Process: Sketching Roofs by Footprint

The following illustration shows the process of sketching roofs by footprint.

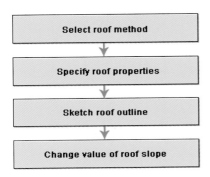

The following steps describe the process of sketching roofs by footprint.

1   **Select roof method.**
    Select Roof by Footprint from the Roof drop-down on the Build panel of the Home tab.

2   **Specify roof properties.**
    Specify the roof instance properties in the Instance Properties dialog box. For Base Offset From Level, you can specify a height value to vertically offset the roof deck from the level at which it is drawn. You can select a generic or a complex roof type from the Type list or create a new type.

3   **Sketch roof outline.**
    Sketch the roof area in the view window using faces of walls or drawing lines.

4   **Change value of roof slope.**
    Change the value of the roof slope for individual edges using the angle symbol displayed below each sketch line.

Process: Sketching Roofs by Extrusion

The following illustration shows the process of sketching roofs by extrusion.

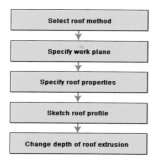

The following steps describe the process of sketching roofs by extrusion.

1   **Select roof method.**
    Select Roof by Extrusion from the Roof drop-down on the Build panel of the Home tab.

2   **Specify work plane.**
    Specify a work plane for the roof in a section or elevation view. You do this using a grid, a previously created reference plane, or a wall face.

3 **Specify roof properties**.
Specify the roof properties. You can specify Instance Properties such as Base Offset From Level for setting a height value to vertically offset the roof deck from the level at which it is drawn. You can select a generic or complex roof type from the Type list or create a new type.

4 **Sketch roof profile**.
Sketch the profile of the top edge of the roof in the view window by drawing lines.

5 **Change depth of roof extrusion**.
Change the depth of the roof by specifying the start and end of the extrusion.

Guidelines for Adding and Modifying Roofs

The following recommended practices help you save time and prevent inaccuracies while adding and modifying roofs.

Guidelines

- Be careful about the level of the plan view in which you are working when you create a footprint roof. You should be careful because while creating a roof on the level above or below the view, you might not view the roof when it is finished. This could lead to mistakes and inaccuracies in the design.

- Pay attention to the View Range properties of the view you use to create a footprint roof. The view range provides better control over the display of roofs in a design.

- Plan each extruded roof ahead of time, study the requirements of the roof, create views that point in the correct direction, and create reference planes, where appropriate. This saves time and enhances accuracy.

- Use the Join/Union Roof tool to create complex roof assemblies. Make multiple roofs and join them to create the conditions that you require. Do not try to model a very complicated footprint roof to match the exterior walls of an elaborate building outline, particularly if the walls are of different heights. This saves time and improves accuracy.

- Specify insulation as part of a roof structure and view sun/shadow performance in the elevation or 3D view. Also, use external applications for energy analysis to calculate the airflow for roofing. Roofs with proper shading or exposure of windows, insulation, and ventilation can significantly reduce the energy costs of a building during its lifetime.

Exercise | Add and Modify Roofs

In this exercise, you add a flat roof, a sloped roof, and an extruded roof to a building model. You then modify the properties of a roof, attach walls to the roof, and add roof details.

You need to place roofs on two connected buildings and the corridor that connects both the buildings in a design project. You need to add flat, sloped, and extruded roofs. You also need to add fascia and gutters to the pitched roof.

You do the following:

- Add a flat roof by footprint.

- Add a sloped roof by footprint.

- Modify roof properties.

- Add an extruded roof.

- Attach walls to a roof.

- Add fascia and gutters.

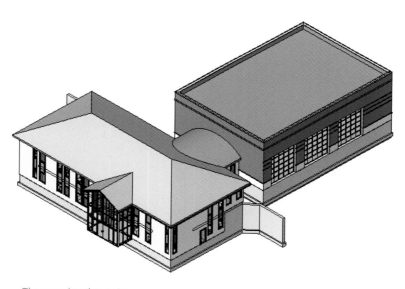

The completed exercise

Add a Flat Roof by Footprint

1   Open *i_rac_essentials_roofs*.rvt or *m_rac_essentials_roofs*.rvt. Ensure that the Main Roof view is displayed.
    Note: The illustrations for the metric dataset will be slightly different from those shown here.

2   Click Home tab > Build panel > Roof drop-down > Roof By Footprint to add a flat roof.

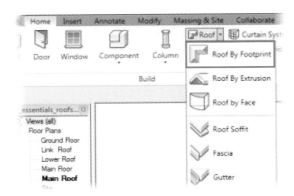

Notice that on the Create Roof Footprint tab, Draw panel, Pick Walls is selected.

3   On the Options Bar:

   • Clear the Defines Slope check box.
   • For Overhang, enter **0**.
   • Select the Extend to Wall Core check box.

4   In the view window:

- Place the cursor over one of the exterior walls of the apparatus bay.
- Press TAB to highlight the exterior walls.
- Click to select all the four walls.

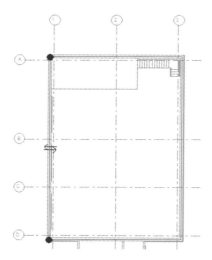

Note: If necessary, click the blue flip control arrows so that the sketch line appears inside, not on the interior faces of walls.

5   On the Element panel, click Roof Properties.

6   In the Instance Properties dialog box:

- Select Steel Truss - Insulation on Metal Deck - EPDM from the Type list.
- Click OK.

7   On the Roof panel, click Finish Roof.

8   Click Yes in the Revit dialog box for joining geometry to add the roof.

9   Open the Section 1 view. Notice the new main roof at the Main Roof level.

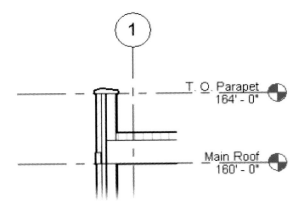

10   Open the default 3D view to examine the new roof.

Add a Sloped Roof by Footprint

1   To begin placing a roof on the other wing of the building, open the Lower Roof view.

2   Zoom to fit in the view.

3   Activate the Roof By Footprint tool.

4   On the Options Bar:
      - Select the Defines Slope check box.
      - For Overhang, enter **2' 0"** (**600** mm).
      - Ensure that the Extend to Wall Core check box is clear.

5   In the view window, select the outer wall segments as shown.
        The side of the wall you pick determines the position of the sketch line. Place the sketch lines on each outer wall.

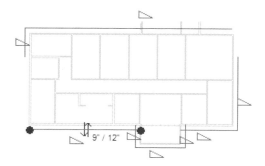

        Note: The left and right walls have two segments; you do not need to click both segments. You will trim corners in the next step.

6   Activate the Trim tool.

7   Trim all the loop segments.

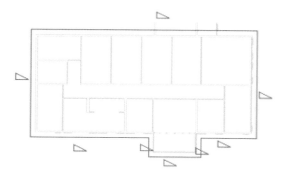

8   To specify the roof properties, open the Instance Properties dialog box.

9   In the Instance Properties dialog box:

- Select Wood Rafter 8" - Asphalt Shingle - Insulated (Wood Rafter 184 mm - Asphalt Shingles- - Insulated) from the Type list.
- Click OK.

10   Finish sketching the roof.

11   Click Yes in the Revit dialog box to attach the highlighted walls to the roof. The new roof is partially displayed in the view. The reason you see a partial view is that most plan views have a default View Range Cut Plane set at 3'-0" (900 mm).

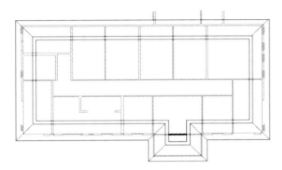

Note: Pitched roofs are not completely displayed in the view.

12   To change the properties of the view for displaying the entire roof, open the Instance Properties dialog box for the floor plan.

13   In the Instance Properties dialog box:
   • Under Graphics, for Underlay, select None from the Value list.
   • Under Extents, for View Range, click Edit.

14   In the View Range dialog box:
   • For Top, select Unlimited from the List.
   • For Cut Plane Offset, enter **20'** (**7000** mm).

15   Close all open dialog boxes.

16   Open the 3D view. Notice the new pitched roof.

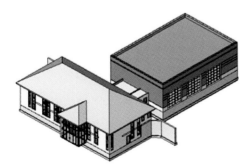

Modify Roof Properties

1   To change the roof over the entrance to a gable, select the pitched roof.

2   Click Modify Roofs tab > Edit panel > Edit Footprint.

3   In the view window, select the sketch line at the entrance.

4   On the Options Bar, clear the Defines Slope check box. Notice that the slope angle symbol disappears.

5   Finish editing the roof. The roof over the curtain wall changes to a gable.

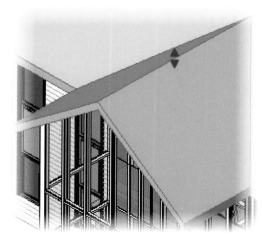

To change the pitch of all the sloping faces of the roof, open the Instance Properties dialog box.

6   In the Instance Properties dialog box:

- Under Dimensions, for Slope, enter **6** (**20**).

Construction	
Rafter Cut	Plumb Cut
Fascia Depth	0' 0"
Rafter or Truss	Truss
Maximum Ridge Height	166' 2 13/32"
Dimensions	
Slope	6" / 12"
Thickness	0' 8 3/8"
Volume	3702.66 CF

Note: The Slope value in the imperial dataset automatically adjusts to 6" / 12". You enter the metric value in degrees.

- Click OK.
  The roof slope adjusts.

7   Clear the selection.

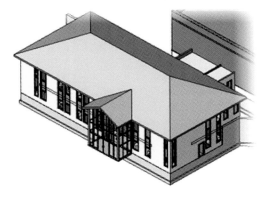

Add an Extruded Roof

1   Open the Link Roof view to add a modern arched roof to the hallway connecting both the buildings.
Note: This simple plan view was created by duplicating the main floor plan, renaming it, and adjusting the crop region in the view properties for the view.

2   Zoom to fit, if necessary.

3   To place a drawing aid called a reference plane that will provide a named work plane for making an extruded roof, click Home tab > Work Plane panel > Ref Plane drop-down > Draw Reference Plane.
    Note: Extruded roofs are created based on a sketch of the roof profile.

4   In the view window, sketch a reference plane horizontally across the corridor. The exact location of the reference plane is not critical, provided the plane is horizontal and above the section line.

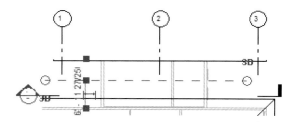

5   Activate the Roof By Extrusion tool.

6   In the Work Plane dialog box:
    • Under Specify a New Work Plane, ensure that Pick a Plane is selected.
    • Click OK.

7   In the view window, click the reference plane you just created.

8   To open a view where you can draw the roof profile, in the Go To View dialog box:
    • Select Section: Section 2.
    • Click Open View. The view changes to Section 2 and the Roof Reference Level and Offset dialog box is displayed.
      Note: The Roof Reference Level and Offset dialog box does not physically locate the roof.

9   In the Roof Reference Level and Offset dialog box:
    • Select Lower Roof from the Level list.
    • Click OK.

10   In the view window, notice the other reference planes that are placed for sketching
      assistance.

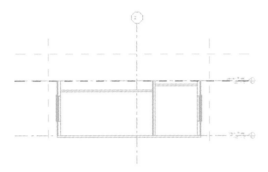

11   Click Create Extrusion Roof Profile tab > Draw panel > Start-End-Radius Arc.

12   Sketch the top edge of the roof, as shown. To do this, moving from left to right, click the
      intersections of the left and right vertical reference planes and the Lower Roof level for the
      start and end points, and the horizontal reference plane as the top of the arc.

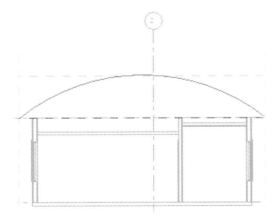

13   Exit the Start-End-Radius Arc tool.

14 To specify the roof properties, open the Instance Properties dialog box.

15 In the Instance Properties dialog box:
- Select Steel Truss - Insulation on Metal Deck - EPDM Thin from the Type list.
- Under Instance Parameters, Constraints, for Extrusion End, enter **3' (900** mm) to set the depth of the roof from the reference plane you created. You will adjust the depth in the subsequent steps to finalize the roof.
- Click OK.

16 Click Finish Roof to complete creating the roof.

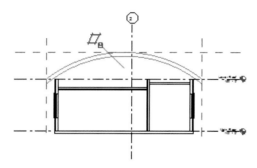

17 To connect the new roof with the building wings, open the 3D view.

18 Zoom in to clearly view the new short 3' (900 mm) curved roof. Notice that the curved roof does not join the garage wall or the roof over the administration wing.

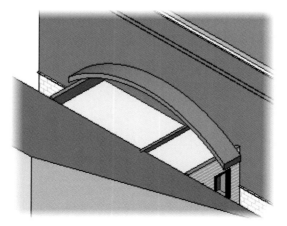

19 To join the curved roof with the garage wall, click Modify tab > Edit Geometry panel > Join/Unjoin Roof.

20 In the view window, select the right edge of the extruded roof.

21 Select the brick wall to the right of the roof to join the extruded roof to the wall face.

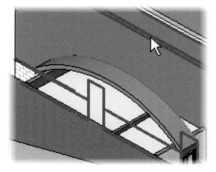

22 To join the curved roof with the roof over the administration wing, activate the Join/Unjoin Roof tool.

23 In the view window, select the left edge of the extruded roof.

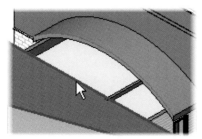

24   Select the right face of the sloped roof.

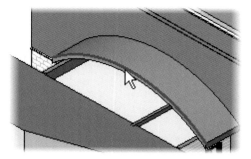

25   Verify that the extruded roof joins the roof of the administration building.

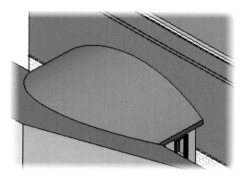

Attach Walls to a Roof

1   Open the Section 2 view to check the walls under the new roof. Notice that the walls are not attached to the new roof.

2   CTRL+select the two exterior walls.

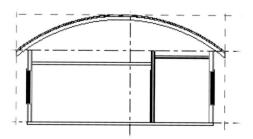

3   Click Modify Walls tab > Modify Wall panel > Attach. Notice that Top is selected by default on the Options Bar.

4   In the view window, select the roof. The walls join to the roof.

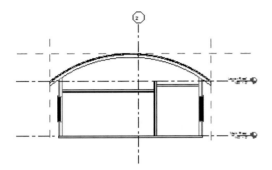

5   Open the default 3D view.

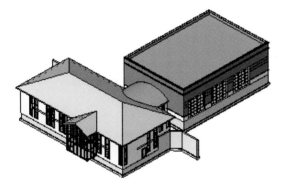

Add Fascia and Gutters

1   To place fascia boards on some of the roof edges of the large pitched roof, zoom in so that you can clearly see the gable roof over the entrance.

2   Click Home tab > Build panel > Roof drop-down > Fascia.

3   Click the upper edge of the left and right sides of the gable roof.

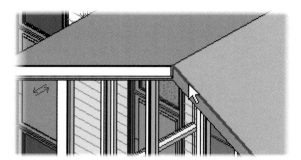

Note: You can use TAB+select connected roof edges to add segments to a connected series of edges.

4   Verify that Fascia boards get added.

5   On the Profile panel, click Finish Current.

6   To place gutter segments, click Roof drop-down > Gutter.

7   Click the lower edge of the roof that is to the right of the new fascia boards.
     Note: As with fascias, you can use TAB+select connected roof edges to put segments on an entire roof outline.

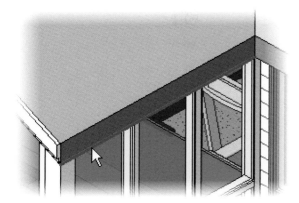

8   Click the next two roof edges to the right to place connected gutter segments.

9   Finish placing the gutter. The gutter is added to the model.

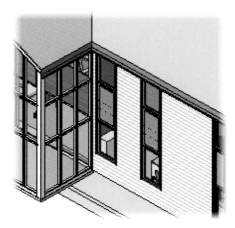

10 Close the file without saving changes.

Lesson 23 | Creating Curtain Walls

This lesson describes how to create curtain walls in a building model. You begin the lesson by learning about curtain walls, curtain grids, and mullions. Next, you learn the steps to create curtain walls and modify curtain grids. You also learn some recommended practices for creating curtain walls, curtain grids, and mullions. The lesson concludes with an exercise on creating curtain walls, curtain grids, and mullions.

In Revit, curtain walls are non-load bearing walls laid out in a grid pattern. You can add curtain walls to a project where the design specifications require. You can create curtain walls with panels of materials other than glass and with non-rectilinear grids. Curtain walls have material properties and can be analyzed for energy calculations.

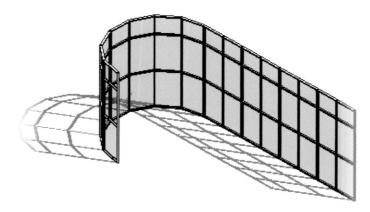

Curtain wall with glass panels

Objectives

After completing this lesson, you will be able to:

- Describe curtain walls.

- Describe curtain grids and mullions.

- Identify the steps to create curtain walls and modify curtain grids.

- State the recommended practices for creating curtain walls, curtain grids, and mullions.

- Create curtain walls, curtain grids, and mullions.

About Curtain Walls

Curtain walls consist of panels separated by horizontal and vertical grid lines on which you can place mullions of different shapes and materials. You can place doors and windows in curtain walls. You can also embed curtain walls in standard walls and host standard walls in curtain walls.

The following illustration shows a curtain wall placed within a standard wall.

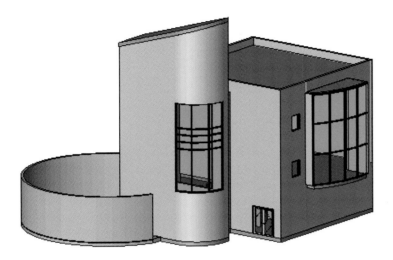

Definition of Curtain Walls

Curtain walls are placed by using the Wall tool to select a curtain wall type from the Type Selector drop-down. Curtain walls are different from basic walls because they have panels and basic walls have structural layers. A curtain wall consists of a panel that is divided by horizontal and vertical grids into multiple panels. You can place grids individually on panels. You can also provide layout rules for the grids that allow you to specify certain layout patterns numerically rather than graphically.

You place mullions on grids in a curtain wall to provide solid dividing elements that hold the panels in place.

Elements in Curtain Walls

If you convert a basic wall to a curtain wall, Revit automatically removes the standard doors and windows from the wall because curtain walls cannot hold standard doors and windows. However, you can place door and window panels specific to a curtain wall. Curtain wall doors and windows are stored in the same folders as regular doors and windows. You create doors and windows in a curtain wall by specifying a panel in a curtain wall as a door or window. Curtain doors and windows fit to the panel they are designated in and resize when the curtain wall panel is resized.

Curtain Panels in Curtain Walls

Curtain walls can comprise one or more curtain panels. You can change a curtain panel in a curtain wall to a basic or a stacked wall by changing the wall type in the Type Selector drop-down or the Instance and Type Properties dialog boxes. You can load additional panel families into a project using the Load From Library option.

When you change the size of a curtain wall, the curtain panels are resized accordingly. Changing the location line of a curtain panel changes the position of the curtain panel in the curtain wall.

Constraint properties of a curtain wall, such as Base Constraint, Base Offset, Geometry, and Unconnected Height have read-only values for a curtain panel. The values of these properties depend on the height and location of a curtain wall.

Example of Curtain Walls

The following illustration shows a curtain wall that is divided into panels of different materials with different transparencies.

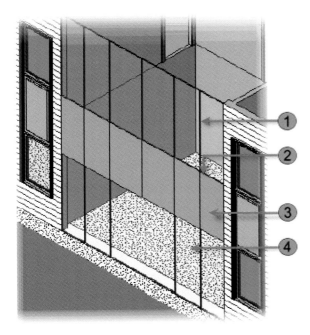

1. Vertical grid line

2. Horizontal grid line

3. Solid panel

4. Glass curtain panel

About Curtain Grids and Mullions

Curtain grids and mullions are elements of a curtain wall. These elements allow you to demarcate grids and panels in a curtain wall.

Definition of Curtain Grids and Mullions

A curtain grid consists of grid lines that divide a curtain wall into panels. Curtain grids are of two types, automatic and manual.

You add mullions to grid lines to provide the structural frame on the grid lines. Mullions define the edges between different panels of a grid and have editable dimensions. You can specify different sizes, shapes, and materials for mullions.

Automatic Curtain Grids

You can set the type parameters of a curtain wall type to automatically create a curtain grid whenever a curtain wall is created. A curtain grid created this way is known as an automatic curtain grid.

The position of automatic curtain grids remains fixed if you resize the curtain wall or change the grid layout with the type properties of the curtain wall. The horizontal and vertical grid lines in an automatic curtain grid are placed independent of each other.

You use the pattern parameters of vertical and horizontal grids to divide a curtain wall with a set number of grid lines, place grid lines at a fixed distance from each other, or use maximum spacing between grid lines. With maximum spacing, curtain grids are placed evenly along the face of a curtain wall at a distance specified for the grid spacing.

 Note: *You cannot move automatic curtain grids after drawing a curtain wall unless you make curtain grids independent.*

Manual Curtain Grids

You use the Curtain Grid tool on the Build panel of the Home tab to manually create grids in a curtain wall. Each new grid created this way makes a panel of the type that you specify while sketching the curtain wall.

Placing Curtain Grids

When you place grids on curtain panels, a preview image of the curtain grid is displayed on the panels.

You can control the placement of a new grid using any the following grid segment options.

Option	Description
All Segments	Places a curtain grid on all panels, either horizontally or vertically.
One Segment	Places a curtain grid on one panel.
All Except Picked	Places a curtain grid on all panels horizontally or vertically, except the panels you select.

Adding Mullions

When you add a mullion to a grid line in a curtain wall, the mullion is center aligned with the curtain grid. If you add a mullion to a grid line on the perimeter of a curtain wall, the mullion aligns with the border of the wall. When you add multiple mullions, each mullion splits automatically at an intersection with another mullion.

You can use one of the following options to add mullions.

Option	Description
Grid Line Segment	Adds a mullion only on the grid line segment in the selected panel.
Grid Line	Adds a mullion on the entire grid line.
All Grid Lines	Adds a mullion on all empty segments by combining them.

Properties of Mullions

You can specify the following properties for mullions while adding them to a project.

Property	Description
Angle	Rotates a mullion by an angle that ranges between -90 degrees and 90 degrees.
Offset	Moves a mullion away from the location line of the wall by the specified distance.
Position	Positions a mullion either perpendicular to the face of a curtain panel or parallel to the ground plane. For sloping curtain panels, this property is set to parallel.
Profile	Modifies the shape of a mullion by allowing you to either load custom profiles or use the profiles available in the library folders.

 Note: *The Position, Angle, and Profile properties of mullions do not apply to mullions that are added to the corners of a curtain wall.*

Example of Curtain Grids and Mullions

The following illustrations show curtain grids and mullions.

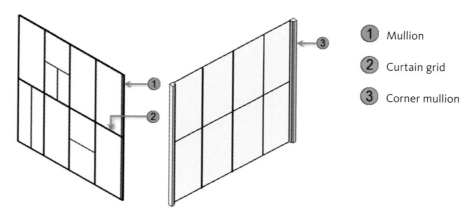

1. Mullion
2. Curtain grid
3. Corner mullion

Creating Curtain Walls and Modifying Curtain Grids

You can place curtain walls with straight or curved segments. Curved segments divide according to the vertical grid layout. You can attach the top or base of curtain walls to other elements such as walls, floors, roofs, and ceilings. In addition, you can edit the elevation profile of a curtain wall.

Curtain wall grids are always straight lines. You can create curtain walls with rectangular or nonrectangular grid patterns to address the design requirements in a building model. After you create a curtain wall, you can place or remove curtain grids from panels. You can also modify an automatic curtain grid.

Procedure: Creating Automatic Rectangular Grid Pattern Curtain Walls

The following steps describe how to create a curtain wall with a specific preset rectangular grid pattern.

1   Click Home tab > Build panel > Wall drop-down > Wall.

2   Select a curtain wall type from the Type Selector drop-down.

3   Click Element panel > Element Properties drop-down > Type Properties.

4   In the Type Properties dialog box:
    - Set the Layout parameter for the grid patterns to insert horizontal and vertical curtain grids automatically.
    - Specify the spacing if you want to keep it fixed or at a minimum or maximum value.

5   In the Instance Properties dialog box, specify an instance parameter if you selected the Fixed Number option in the Type Properties dialog box.

6   In the view window, place the curtain wall using Draw tools such as Pick Lines or Pick Faces.

Procedure: Creating Nonrectangular Curtain Walls

The following steps describe how to create a curtain wall with a nonrectangular grid pattern.

1   Click Home tab > Build panel > Wall drop-down > Wall.

2   Select Curtain Wall : Curtain Wall 1 from the Type Selector drop-down.

3   In the view window, place the curtain wall using Draw tools such as Pick Lines or Pick Faces.

4   Select the curtain wall in an elevation view.

5   Use the Instance Properties dialog box or the Configure Grid Layout control to change the angle and distance offset for the horizontal and vertical grid lines.

Procedure: Placing and Removing Grids on Curtain Panels

The following steps describe how to place and remove grids on curtain panels.

1   In an elevation view, click Home tab > Build panel > Curtain Grid to place individual grid lines on a curtain wall.

2   Select an appropriate placement option on the Placement panel of the Place Curtain Grid contextual tab.

3   In the view window:
- Place the cursor on a curtain wall so that a preview of the grid line is displayed.
- Click to place the grid line.

4   On the Placement panel, ensure that All Except Picked is selected.

5   In the view window, click segments of the grid line to exclude them from curtain panels and display as dashed lines.

6   On the Placement panel, click Finish Current to place another grid.

7   In the view window, select an existing grid line to remove the grid line segment.

8   Click Modify Curtain Wall Grids tab > Curtain Grid panel > Add/Remove Segments.

9   In the view window:
   - Click the selected grid segments to remove them and display them as dashed lines.
   - Click away from the wall to finish.

Procedure: Modifying Automatic Curtain Grids

The following steps describe how to modify an automatic curtain grid.

1   In the view window, select the curtain grid that you want to modify.

2   Click the pushpin to unlock the grid.

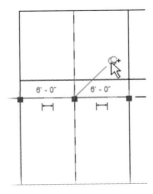

3   Move the grid to the desired position. If you click the pushpin with the cross, the grid returns to its original, automatically set position.

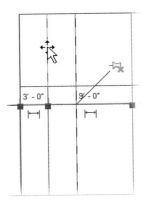

Guidelines for Creating Curtain Walls, Grids, and Mullions

The following recommended practices help you create curtain walls, curtain grids, and mullions effectively.

Guidelines

- If your organization uses standard curtain wall systems across many projects, you should create curtain wall types that define grid layouts and mullions that can be used in any project. These curtain wall types can be modified and used in project templates to save time during design development.

- If you are creating a curtain wall to fit a custom condition, such as an arc, you should first place a single curtain panel and then subdivide it using vertical grids at regular spacing. An arc curtain wall fits to its location line depending on the number of curtain panels in the wall. Creating a wall this way gives you complete control over the shape of the wall.

- You should not model complicated mullion joins and corners unless absolutely necessary. Detail and drafting views are more effective and less time-consuming for specifying complex mullion conditions.

Example

The following illustrations show standard curtain wall parameters and grid lines being placed to define an arc curtain wall.

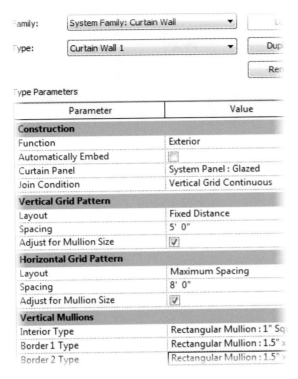

Parameter	Value
Construction	
Function	Exterior
Automatically Embed	☐
Curtain Panel	System Panel : Glazed
Join Condition	Vertical Grid Continuous
Vertical Grid Pattern	
Layout	Fixed Distance
Spacing	5' 0"
Adjust for Mullion Size	☑
Horizontal Grid Pattern	
Layout	Maximum Spacing
Spacing	8' 0"
Adjust for Mullion Size	☑
Vertical Mullions	
Interior Type	Rectangular Mullion : 1" Sq
Border 1 Type	Rectangular Mullion : 1.5" x
Border 2 Type	Rectangular Mullion : 1.5" x

Standard curtain wall parameters such as vertical and horizontal grid patterns and mullions

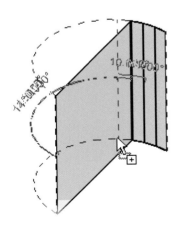

Vertical grid lines being placed to define an arc curtain wall

Exercise | Create Curtain Walls, Curtain Grids, and Mullions

In this exercise, you create a curtain wall and a curtain grid. You also add a door and mullions to the curtain wall. Finally, you change the material of a curtain panel to suit your design requirements.

You plan to make a design change to the front entrance of the fire station by removing a section of the exterior wall and replacing it with a curtain wall. To do this, you split the section of the exterior wall, change the wall type, and add additional sections to the curtain wall. You also add curtain grids, curtain panels, and mullions to the curtain wall.

You do the following:

- Create a curtain wall and curtain grid.

- Change the material of curtain panels.

- Add a door and mullions to a curtain wall.

The completed exercise

Create a Curtain Wall and Curtain Grid

1   Open *i_rac_essentials_curtainwalls.rvt* or *m_rac_essentials_curtainwalls.rvt*. The file opens in the Ground Floor view.
Note: The illustrations for the metric dataset will be slightly different from those shown here.

2   Zoom in to the area around the main entrance of the building as shown.

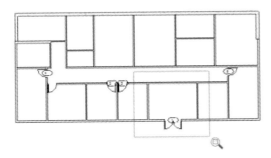

Notice that the wall type is a basic exterior wall; however, you need a curtain wall at the building entrance.

3   Click Modify tab > Edit panel > Split.

4   On the Options Bar, ensure that the Delete Inner Segment check box is cleared.

5   In the view window, split the wall with the double door by clicking just next to the left vertical wall as shown. The exact location is not critical.

6   In the view window:

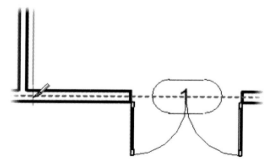

- Click the temporary dimension and enter **6"** (**150** mm).
- Press ENTER to update the dimension.

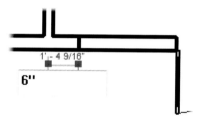

7   Split the wall on the right of the double door as shown.

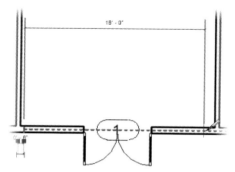

Note: When you split the wall the second time, the first split is not visible but the wall is split and you can view this in the subsequent steps.

8   When the temporary dimension for the split appears, use the Move Witness Line control to drag the left witness line from the left wall to the center of the vertical wall on the right of the double door, until the dashed centerline appears.

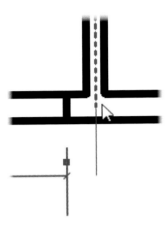

9   Click the temporary dimension and enter **6"** (**150** mm). Press ENTER to update the dimension.

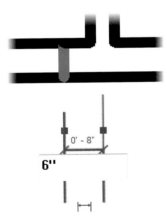

10   Press ESC two times to end the dimension selection and exit the Split tool.

11   In the view window, select the wall segment with the double glass door.

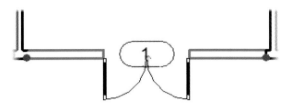

12   Select Curtain Wall : Curtain Wall 1 from the Type Selector drop-down to change the type of the selected wall segment. Notice that when changing the basic wall to a curtain wall, the door inserted in the wall is deleted.

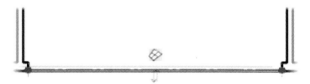

13   Close the warning message that is displayed. The curtain wall consisting of one panel is created.

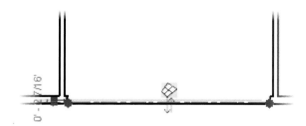

14   Create the grid layout. Click Home tab > Build panel > Curtain Grid.

15 In the view window:

- Place the cursor on the left end of the curtain wall and move it to the right.
- When the cursor is 2' 4" (700 mm) from the left end of the wall, click to split the curtain wall into two panels.

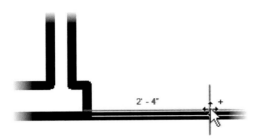

Tip: The snap distance increment for placing grid lines depends on the current zoom level. Scroll in and out until the snaps fall in place.

16 Place another panel of 2' 8" (800 mm) to the right of the first panel.

17 Place two additional panels of 2' 4" (700 mm) and 2' 8" (800 mm) from the right wall. Zoom in if required. This creates a large panel in the middle as shown.

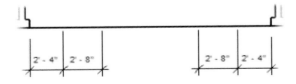

Note: The dimensions do not actually appear. They are shown here only for reference.

18 Press ESC two times to clear the selection and exit the Curtain Grid tool.

19 Open the South elevation view. The curtain wall that you just created is visible with four vertical grid lines.

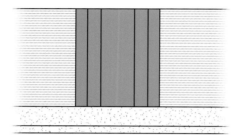

20 Click Curtain Grid.

21 In the view window:
- Place the cursor adjacent to the left vertical edge of the curtain wall so that it snaps to approximately one-third of the height of the curtain wall.
- Click to place the first horizontal curtain grid. The exact position of the grid is not critical.

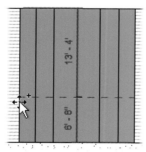

22 Add another curtain grid above the first. The exact position of the grid is not critical.

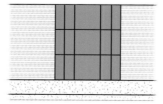

23 Press ESC two times to clear the selection and exit the Curtain Grid tool.

24 In the view window:
    - Select the lower horizontal curtain grid.
    - Click the dimension and change the height to **7' 3"** (**2175** mm) above the floor surface.
    - Press ENTER.

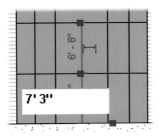

25 In the view window:
    - Select the upper horizontal curtain grid.
    - Click the dimension and change its position to **7' 6"** (**2250** mm) from the top of the curtain wall. Press ENTER.

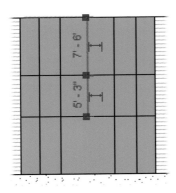

26 Click Curtain Grid.

27   Click Place Curtain Grid tab > Placement panel > All Except Picked.

28   In the view window:
   • Place the cursor in the center of the top edge of the curtain wall.

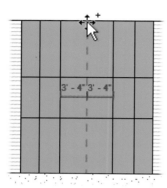

   • When the temporary dimensions indicate the center of the large panel, click to place
     the grid.

29   In the view window:
   • Move the cursor to the bottom of the grid.
   • Click the lower segment of the grid that you just created. The segment is displayed
     with a dashed line, indicating that the lower panel does not have a grid line.

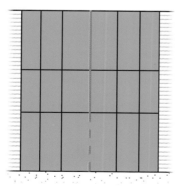

30 On the Placement panel, click Finish Current to complete creating the grid.

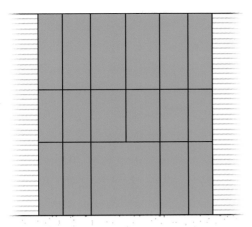

31 Exit the current tool.

Change the Material of Curtain Panels

1   You create and apply custom material to a part of this curtain wall. Click Manage tab > Project Settings panel > Materials.

2   In the left pane of the Materials dialog box:
    • Select Glazing - Curtain Wall Glazing from the list.
    • In the lower corner, click Duplicate.

3   In the Duplicate Revit Material dialog box:
    • For Name, enter **Glazing - Curtain Wall Spandrel**.
    • Click OK.

4   In the right pane of the Materials dialog box, on the Render Appearance tab, under Render Appearance Based On, click Replace.

5   In the Render Appearance Library dialog box:
    • Select Glass from the Class list.
    • Select Glazing Dark Bronze Reflective.

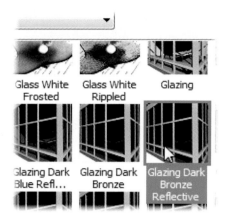

    • Click OK.
6   In the right pane of the Materials dialog box, on the Graphics tab:
    • Under Shading, for Transparency, enter **5%**.

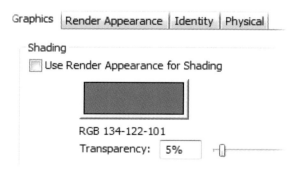

    • Click OK.

You have just created a custom material for the curtain wall. Next, you apply this material to the panels.

7 In the view window, CTRL+select the walls to the left and right of the curtain wall.

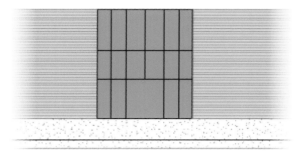

8 On the View Control Bar, select Temporary Hide/Isolate > Hide Element to simplify the view.

9 Draw a selection window from the left to the right around the middle panels in the curtain wall as shown. You will apply the tinted glass material to these panels.

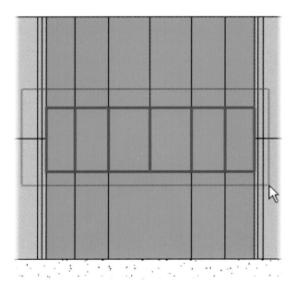

10 Click Multi-Select tab > Filter panel > Filter.

11 In the Filter dialog box:
- Clear the Curtain Wall Grids check box.
- Click OK.

12 Open the Type Properties dialog box.

13 In the Type Properties dialog box, click Duplicate.

14 In the Name dialog box:
- For Name, enter **Spandrel Panel** .
- Click OK.

15 In the Type Properties dialog box:
- Under Materials and Finishes, for Material, click the value field.
- Click [...].

16 In the left pane of the Materials dialog box, select from the list Glazing - Curtain Wall Spandrel you created earlier.

17 Click OK to close the dialog boxes.

18 In the view window, clear the selection.

19 On the View Control Bar, select Temporary Hide/Isolate > Reset Temporary Hide/Isolate.

20 Open the default 3D view. Zoom in to the curtain walls to view the changes.

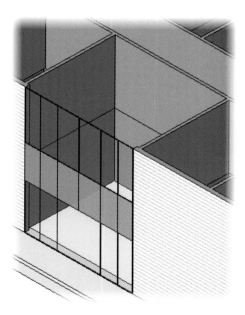

Add a Door and Mullions to a Curtain Wall

1   You now finish creating the curtain wall by placing a door panel and adding mullions. Return to the South elevation view.

2   In the view window, drag a selection box around the large panel where you place the door.

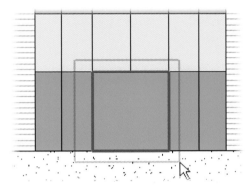

3   Select Curtain Wall Dbl Glass : Curtain Wall Dbl Glass (M_Curtain Wall Dbl Glass : M_Curtain Wall Dbl Glass) from the Type Selector drop-down. The panel updates to create a door.

4   Click Home tab > Build panel > Mullion.

5   Ensure that Rectangular Mullion : 2.5" x 5" rectangular (Rectangular Mullion : 50mm x 150mm) is selected in the Type Selector drop-down.

6   Ensure that Grid Line is selected on the Placement panel.

7   In the view window:
   • Place the cursor on a vertical grid line.
   • Click to place the mullion.

8 Continue to add mullions on the remaining six vertical grid lines, including the left and right edges of the curtain wall.

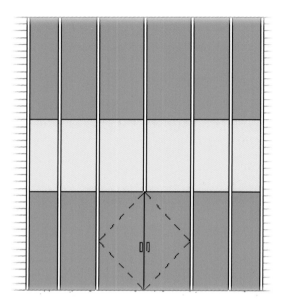

9 You now create a new mullion type. Open the Type Properties dialog box.

10 In the Type Properties dialog box, click Duplicate.

11 In the Name dialog box:
- For Name, enter **5" x 5" rectangular (150mm x 150mm rectangular**).
- Click OK.

12 In the Type Properties dialog box, under Dimensions:
- For Width on Side 2, enter **2 1/2"** (**75** mm). Press ENTER.
- For Width on Side 1, enter **2 1/2"** (**75** mm). Press ENTER.
- Click OK.

13 On the Placement panel, click Grid Line Segment. Notice the mullion type selected in the Type Selector drop-down.

14 In the view window:

- On the lower edge of the curtain wall, place the cursor to the left of the door.
- Click to place a mullion.

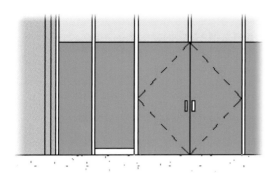

15 Continue to add three more mullions on both the sides of the door on the bottom edge of the wall.

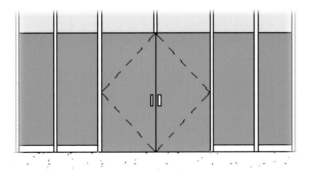

16 On the Placement panel, click Grid Line.

17 Select Rectangular Mullion : 2.5" x 5" rectangular (Rectangular Mullion : 50mm x 150mm) from the Type Selector drop-down.

18 Click the horizontal grid lines above the door and on the top edge of the curtain wall to add mullions to them as shown.

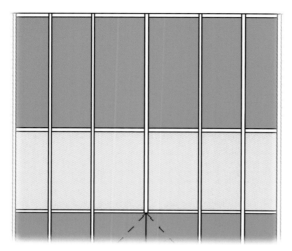

19 Exit the Mullion tool.

20 To edit the mullion intersections:
- Zoom in to the mullion intersection above the door.
- Select the vertical mullion that intersects with the door.
- Click Toggle Mullion Join, which appears as a plus sign in the mullion, as shown, to update the mullion intersection.

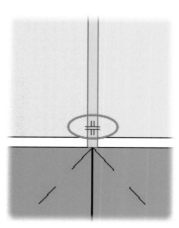

21 Clear the mullion selection.

22 Zoom out to view the curtain wall.

23 Open the default 3D view.

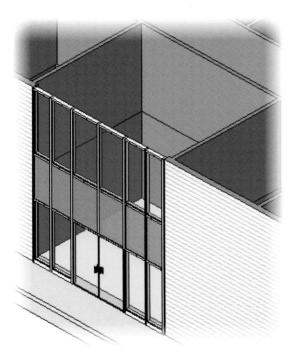

24 Close the file without saving changes.

Lesson 24 | Adding Stairs and Railings

This lesson describes how to add stairs and railings in a building model and change the properties of stairs and railings. You begin the lesson by learning about stairs and railings. Then, you learn the steps and some recommended practices for creating stairs and railings. The lesson concludes with an exercise on creating and modifying stairs and railings.

In a few simple steps, you can create straight, curved, spiral, and almost any other conceivable configuration of stairs for a building design. Railings are freestanding elements that you add to floors or staircases.

U-shaped straight stairs with a rectangular landing and attached railings

Objectives

After completing this lesson, you will be able to:

- Describe stairs and railings.

- Identify the steps to create stairs and railings.

- State the recommended practices for creating stairs and railings.

- Create and modify stairs and railings.

About Stairs and Railings

Stairs and railings are parametric elements in Revit. These elements are easily created to suit any design requirement and can be complemented with various railings.

Definition of Stairs and Railings

Stairs and railings are building elements. You can attach railings to stairs, ramps, and floors as required.

Stairs and railings are system families. You can modify existing stair and railing types to suit your needs and save stair and railing types in project templates.

Properties of Stairs

You create stairs by specifying a stair run or by sketching riser lines and boundary lines. When you select the starting point of the stairs in the plan view, you can calculate the number of treads based on the distance between the floors. You can also define the maximum riser height in the stair properties.

You can specify the dimensions of stairs, such as width, number of risers, and tread depth, in the Type Properties dialog box. You can specify the Base Level, Top Level, Base Offset, and Top Offset properties in the Instance Properties dialog box.

Spiral Stairs

You define a spiral staircase using Center-ends Arc on the Draw panel of the Create Stairs Sketch contextual tab. When you draw spiral stairs, the spiral is limited to less than 360 degrees without an overlap in the spiral stair runs. To create spiral stair landings, you need to sketch arc runs with the same center and radius.

Multistory Stairs

You can set stairs to repeat vertically in a multistory building by using the Multistory Top Level property. For multistory stairs to be accurate, all stories of a multistory building must have the same height between the levels.

The following illustration shows single story and multistory stairs.

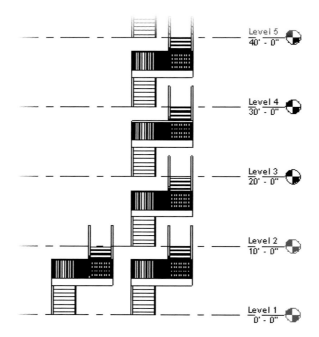

Railing Types

While sketching new stairs, you can specify the railing type to be used using Railing Type on the Tools panel. You select the railing type from the list of available types in the Railings Type list. You can select None if you do not need a railing for the stair or Default to use the default railing and then modify it later. Railing Type is available only while sketching new stairs.

Structure of Railings

Railings consist of rails and balusters. Rails run horizontally, and the top rail height is usually fixed by code. You can place additional rails below the top rail. You can modify the rails by editing rail properties and arrangement in the Edit Rails dialog box.

Balusters are the vertical members in a railing that support the rails between the handrails and stair treads. You arrange baluster families in a repeating pattern and add posts to create balusters. When creating balusters, you define baluster properties and characteristics in the Edit Baluster Placement dialog box. You can access the Edit Rails and Edit Baluster Placement dialog boxes from within the Type Properties dialog box for a selected railing.

You do not add balusters or posts when the railings are wall mounted.

Example of Stairs and Railings

The following illustrations show stairs and railings.

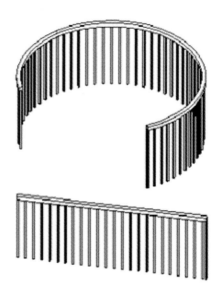

Spiral staircase with single-rail square railing   *Arced and straight railings*

Creating Stairs and Railings

You can create a staircase by sketching run outlines or by sketching boundary lines and risers for the staircase. You can define the type of railings for stairs and modify the railing properties, if required.

Procedure: Creating Stairs by Sketching Boundary Lines and Risers

The following steps describe how to create stairs by sketching boundary lines and risers.

1 Click Home tab > Circulation panel > Stairs.

2 Click Create Stairs Sketch tab > Draw panel > Boundary. Select any draw option.

3 Sketch the side boundaries, which can be single lines or multisegment combinations of straight lines and arcs.

0 RISERS CREATED, 18 REMAINING

> **Note**: The boundaries do not have to be parallel. Do not connect the left and right boundary lines.

4 On the Draw panel, click Riser.

5 Sketch risers between the boundary lines. The number of risers currently created and the number of risers expected, based on the stair parameters, are displayed. This counter updates as you place risers. Riser lines do not have to be parallel.

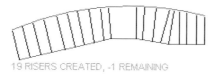

19 RISERS CREATED, -1 REMAINING

> **Note**: Building codes require that flights of stairs (between landings) have equidistant treads, and there are strict limits on the variation in treads between stair flights. It is possible to design illegal or dangerous stairs by sketching risers.

6   To create a landing:

- Provide a space in the sketch with no risers.
- After you sketch the stairs, on the Edit panel, click Split.
- Split the boundary lines where they define the landing.

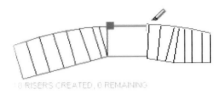

7   On the Stairs panel, click Finish Stairs.

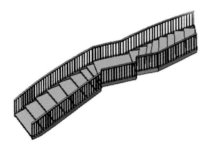

Procedure: Specifying the Railing Type While Creating Stairs

The following steps describe how to specify the type of railings while creating stairs.

1   Activate the Stairs tool.

2   Click Create Stairs Sketch tab > Tools panel > Railing Type.

3   In the Railings Type box, select a railing type. If the railing type you need is not available on the list:

- Quit the stairs.
- Create the new railing type.
- Restart the stairs creation process.
  Note: You can also create stairs using one railing type and change the railings later.

4   Finish sketching the stairs.

Guidelines for Adding Stairs and Railings

You can add various types of stairs and railings in your designs. The following recommended practices help you work efficiently while adding stairs and railings.

Guidelines

- You create stairs going up from the level on which you draw the sketch. To change the direction of stairs, finish sketching the stairs, then select the stairs and click the blue flip control arrow to switch the orientation of the stairs. This eliminates the need to re-create stairs if you inadvertently create them in the wrong direction.

- After creating a set of stairs, you can select the stairs and edit their boundary at any time using Edit Sketch on the Edit panel of the Modify Stairs contextual tab. This saves time while making changes to the stairs.

- You can create reference planes to represent the centerline of the stairs when the stairs plan is being designed. This improves planning during the design phase. In addition, the knowledge of the desired width of the stairs saves time and enhances accuracy when you create U-shaped stairs to fit inside stairwell walls.

- Railings and stairs are system families, and therefore cannot be loaded from library files. Fences are constructed as railings. There are extensive stair, railing, and fence types contained in sample project files in the System Family Files folder in the Metric Library. You will save time if you open these files and copy/paste stairs, railings, and fences into a project and modify them as needed.

- You use the Ramp tool to create a ramp. The process of creating a ramp is similar to that of creating stairs. You can design ramps as big as those for automobile parking lanes or as small as those for pedestrian access with complete control over their thickness and structure.

Example

The following illustration shows reference planes in a stairwell and the flip control arrow.

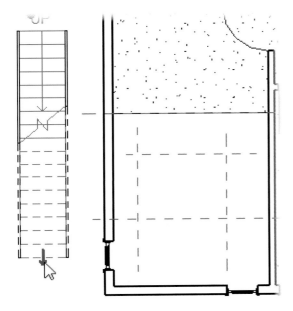

Exercise | Create and Modify Stairs and Railings

In this exercise, you create L-shaped stairs and modify the railings of the stairs. You then add railings on the main floor of the building model.

You need to create an L-shaped stairway from one floor to another in a building model. You also need to add handrails and railings to the stairs and on the landing.

You do the following:

- Create and modify an L-shaped staircase.

- Add railings to stairs and landing.

- Modify railing properties.

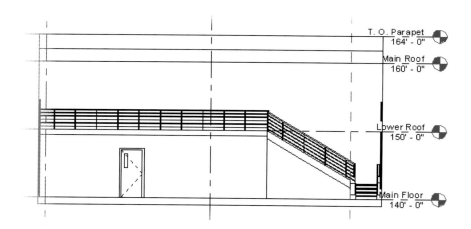

The completed exercise

Completing the Exercise: *To complete the exercise, follow the steps in this book or in the onscreen exercise. In the onscreen list of chapters and exercises, click Chapter 8: Developing the Building Model. Click Exercise: Create and Modify Stairs and Railings.*

Create and Modify an L-Shaped Staircase

1   Open *i_rac_essentials_stairs.rvt* or *m_rac_essentials_stairs.rvt*. The file opens in the Garage
    Floor plan view.
    Note: The metric dataset may appear different at certain steps.

2   In the view window, zoom in to the upper-right corner of the apparatus bay. Reference planes
    have been placed in this area to aid in sketching stairs in this exercise.
    Note: Reference planes are useful in creating stair layouts.

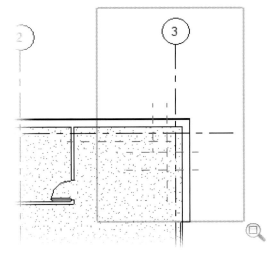

3   In the view window:
    - Select a grid line.
    - Press **VH** to hide grid lines by category in the view.
      Note: This is a shortcut for hiding grid lines. You can also hide them using the
      Visibility/Graphic Overrides dialog box.

4   Click Home tab > Circulation panel > Stairs.

5 In the view window:

- Click the intersection of the lowest horizontal reference plane and the right vertical reference plane.
- Draw a vertical line to the middle horizontal reference intersection.
- Click the intersection to snap the first run of stairs.

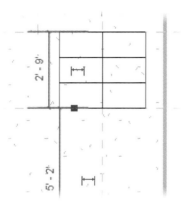

Note: Make the length of the staircase 2' 9" (1650 mm) in case it is different. The number of stairs and their representation will be different for the metric dataset.

6 In the view window:

- Click the intersection of the left vertical reference plane and the upper horizontal reference plane. Zoom in to highlight the intersection, as required.
- Click the intersection of the wall and the horizontal reference plane to snap the second run of stairs.

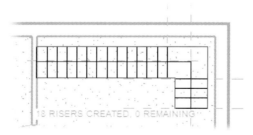

Note: The metric dataset will show 23 risers.

7   Click Create Stairs Sketch tab > Stairs panel > Finish Stairs. The stairs with default railings are updated in the view.

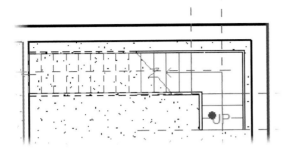

8   You now need to create a new elevation view to check the design of new stairs. To create this elevation, click View tab > Create panel > Elevation. The cursor displays the elevation symbol.

9   In the view window:
  • Move the cursor so that the triangle of the elevation symbol points toward the wall and the stairs.
  • Click to place the symbol.

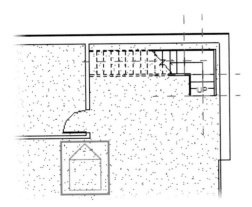

10 Exit the Elevation tool.

11 In the view window:

- Double-click the triangle on the elevation symbol to open the elevation view.
- Zoom in to the stairs.
- Select the stair. Do not select the railing.

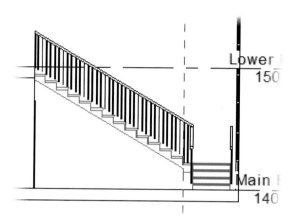

12 To modify the structure of the stairs, open the Type Properties dialog box.

13 In the Type Properties dialog box, under Stringers:

- Set the Right Stringer and Left Stringer to Closed.
- Change the Stringer Thickness value to **9"** (**225** mm).

Riser to Tread Connection	Extend Riser B
Stringers	
Trim Stringers at Top	Do not trim
Right Stringer	Closed
Left Stringer	Closed
Middle Stringers	0
Stringer Thickness	0' 9"
Stringer Height	1' 0"
Open Stringer Offset	0' 0"
Stringer Carriage Height	0' 2 1/2"
Landing Carriage Height	0' 7"
Identity Data	

- Click OK.

14   Click Modify. Notice that the stair treads are enclosed by stringers.

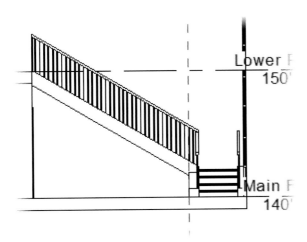

Add Railings to Stairs and Landing

1   To add railings to a floor edge, return to the Garage Floor view.

2   In the view window, CTRL+select both the railings of the staircase.

3   Select Railing : Handrail - Pipe from the Type Selector drop-down to change the railing type.

4   Open the Mezzanine Floor view.

5   To sketch the railing, click Home tab > Circulation panel > Railing.

6   Click Create Railing Path tab > Tools panel > Set Railing Host to associate the railing to a host element such as a floor.

7   Click the mezzanine floor.
     Note: Steps 6 and 7 need not be performed for this model because the floor is flat. The steps have been included to demonstrate its use if the floor is sloped.

8   Open the Instance Properties dialog box to modify the railing properties.

9   In the Instance Properties dialog box:

- Select Handrail - Pipe from the Type list.
- Click OK.

10   On the Options Bar, ensure that the Chain check box is selected.

11   In the view window, sketch along the two exposed edges of the floor to create the railings.

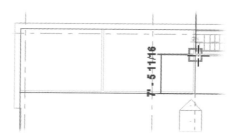

12   Finish sketching the railing.

13   Clear all selections.

14   Open the Elevation 1 - a view that you created. The new railings appear on the mezzanine floor.

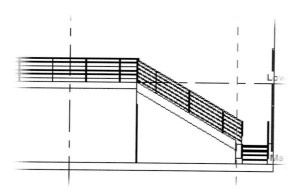

Modify Railing Properties

1   To change the railing properties to suit your design requirements, select a railing.

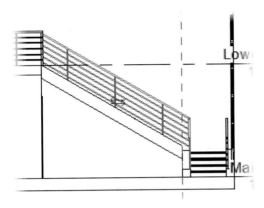

2   Open the Type Properties dialog box.

3   In the Type Properties dialog box, under Construction, for Rail Structure, click Edit to modify the railing properties.

4   In the Edit Rails dialog box:
   - For Rail 1, select Default from the Profile list.
   - For Rail 1, Offset, enter -**0' 3"** (-**75** mm).
   - Click OK.

5   In the Type Properties dialog box, under Construction, for Baluster Placement, click Edit to modify the baluster placement.

6   In the Edit Baluster Placement dialog box:
   - In the Main Pattern section, for row 2, Regular Baluster, set Dist. from Previous to **1' 0"** (**300** mm).
   - Click OK.

7   Click OK to close all the dialog boxes. Notice the change in the railings. The top rail is now bigger than the lower rails and sits outside the stairs, and the posts are closer together.

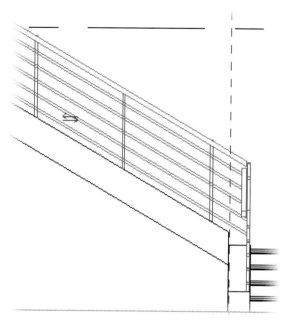

8   Close the file without saving changes.

Chapter Summary

Now you have learned how to include floors, ceilings, roofs, curtain walls, and stairs and railings in your designs, and you can create complete building models.

In this chapter, you learned to:

- Create and modify floors.
- Add and modify ceilings in a building model.
- Add and modify the roofs of a building model.
- Add curtain walls in a building model.
- Create stairs, add railings to the stairs, and change the properties of stairs and railings.

Chapter 09
Detailing and Drafting

In this chapter, you learn about callouts and callout views. You learn how to annotate a model with text and tags, and how to provide information to builders and contractors on how a design should be built using detail views. You also learn how to create and use drafting views to provide specific information that clarifies a model.

Objectives

After completing this chapter, you will be able to:

- Create callout views.

- Work with text and tags.

- Create and use detail views for displaying the construction details of a building model.

- Work with drafting views.

Lesson 25 | Creating Callout Views

This lesson describes how to create callout views. You begin the lesson by learning about callout views and the steps to create reference callouts. Next, you learn some recommended practices for creating callouts. The lesson concludes with an exercise on creating a callout view of a section.

A callout view defines a portion of a view as a separate view at a different scale. Using callout views, you provide an orderly progression of labeled views at increasing levels of detail.

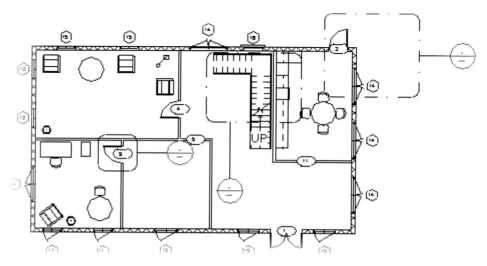

Callout views in a plan

Objectives

After completing this lesson, you will be able to:

- Describe callouts.

- Create reference callouts.

- State the recommended practices for creating callouts.

- Create a callout view of a section.

About Callouts

Callouts are tools for making coherent document sets. They are designed to enable a user to easily navigate from a detail on one page to a detail on another page.

Callout views are used to generate separate views of parts of existing views. You use the callout tag and clip planes to resize callout views. Reference callouts enable you to create callout views that refer to existing views, instead of creating new views.

Definition of Callouts

A callout is a view that you place in a plan, section, detail, or elevation view to create a detailed view of a part of the parent view.

The area enclosed within the callout boundary is the callout bubble. A callout bubble is connected to a symbol called the callout head, which shows the detail number and sheet number when the callout is placed on a sheet. A callout bubble and callout head are connected by a leader line. The callout bubble, callout head, and leader line are together referred to as a callout tag.

Callout Views

When you create a callout, a new view called a callout view is created. A callout view is a separate, large-scaled view of a defined area in a parent view. If the parent view is deleted, the callout view is also deleted.

The following table describes the two types of callout views.

Callout View Type	Description
Callout in parent view	If you want a callout to share the properties of the parent view, you create the callout view using the same view type as the parent. For example, if you create a callout in a floor plan view using a Floor Plan view type, the callout view is displayed under Floor Plans in the Project Browser.
Callout in detail view	If you create a callout in any plan, section, or elevation view using the Detail View type, the callout view is displayed under Detail Views in the Project Browser. Detail views have the properties of being hidden in the parent view at certain scales and can be made visible in intersecting views.

The following illustrations show the two types of callout views in the Project Browser.

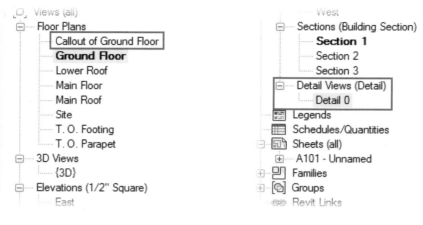

Parent view callout view   Detail view callout view

Callout Tags

Callout tags are annotation objects that mark the location of callouts. You set the callout head and corner radius parameters for callout tags to define the appearance of the callout tags.

Callout tags in both parent view and detail view callout views appear similar; however, they have distinct properties that determine how and when they are displayed.

Clip Planes

The boundaries of the callout bubble define clip planes for the extents of the callout view. You can resize the clip planes to resize the view by selecting the callout bubble and dragging the control dots. Resizing the callout view crop region resizes the callout bubble in the parent view.

Reference Callouts

Reference callouts reference an existing view and do not create a new view. You can place reference callouts in plan, elevation, section, callout, and drafting views. You need to consider the following points when creating reference callouts:

- Reference callouts in section, plan, elevation, or callout views can reference cropped views of the same type as the view in which the reference callout is placed. For example, if you place a callout in Level 2 floor plan and Level 3 floor plan is cropped to show an area that provides the required information, you choose Level 3 floor plan as a reference for the callout.

- Reference callouts in drafting views can reference any plan, section, elevation, or callout view if the crop region is turned on in these views.

There is no parametric relationship between the reference callout and the referenced view, so modifications or resizing performed in a reference callout do not affect the original reference view. For example, resizing the clip planes of a reference callout does not affect the crop region of the original referenced view.

Example of Callouts

The following illustration shows a callout in a plan view.

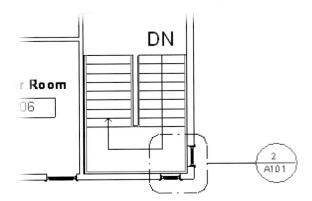

Creating Reference Callouts

You can create a reference callout to point the callout view to an existing view.

Procedure: Creating Reference Callouts

The following steps describe how to create a reference callout.

1   Click View tab > Create panel > Callout.

2   Select the callout type you want to create from the Type Selector drop-down.
    Note: If you want the new callout to appear in the Detail Views area of the Project Browser, select Detail View Detail.

3   On the Options Bar, select the Reference Other View check box.

4   Select the view name that you want to reference from the Reference Other View list. Revit creates a new drafting view if there are no existing views to reference.
    Note: If a view in the Reference Other View list is on a drawing sheet, the detail number and sheet number are displayed next to the view.

5   To place one corner of a callout, click the area of the view where you want to place the callout. Drag the cursor and click again to create a callout bubble.

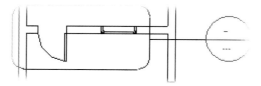

6   Double-click the callout head to make the referenced view the active view, if desired.
    Note: The reference callout head includes a label. To change the label text, you edit the Reference Label type parameter of the callout view.

Guidelines for Creating Callouts

The following recommended practices help you work efficiently while creating callouts.

Guidelines

- You should plan the use of views and callouts to provide a logical sequence that directs the users from views that provide little detail to views with greater levels of detail.

- You can place callouts on the same sheet as the parent view, or place details on sheets by category, such as roof eaves or window sill details. Either way, the sequence should direct the user through the sheet set easily, preferably in one direction. This makes the documents easy to read and avoids requests for additional information about the created document sets.

- You can use standard details in drafting views as references for multiple callouts that detail the same condition. This saves time and enables you to leverage previously drafted document sets.

- You can set the callout head and corner radius parameters for callout tags by using Callout Tags from the Settings drop-down on the Project Settings panel of the Manage tab. If your company practice is to use round callouts, set the radius to a large value. This enables you to quickly standardize the appearance of callouts.

Example

The following example shows a round callout used in a drawing with the radius set to a large value.

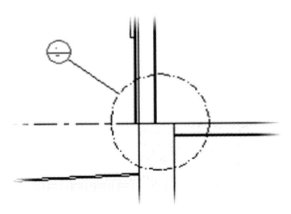

Exercise | Create a Callout View of a Section

In this exercise, you create a callout view of a section to display more detail.

You want to create a callout view to show the intersection of a roof, fascia, soffit, and wall head in more detail than the building section shows.

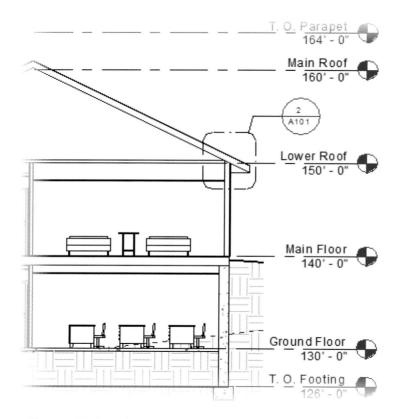

T. O. Parapet
164' - 0"

Main Roof
160' - 0"

2
A101

Lower Roof
150' - 0"

Main Floor
140' - 0"

Ground Floor
130' - 0"

T. O. Footing
126' - 0"

The completed exercise

Completing the Exercise:

To complete the exercise, follow the steps in this book or in the onscreen exercise. In the onscreen list of chapters and exercises, click Chapter 9: Detailing and Drafting. Click Exercise: Create a Callout View of a Section.

1   Open *i_rac_essentials_callouts.rvt* or *m_rac_essentials_callouts.rvt*. The file opens in the default
     3D view.
     Note: The illustrations may look slightly different in the metric dataset.

2   Open the Section 1 view to check a section of the main building and identify the parts of the
     view that need more detailing.

3   The roof-wall intersection needs to be detailed. For this, you need to create a separate view
     for the details and add this view in its own area in the Project Browser. To begin creating the
     callout view, click the View tab > Create panel > Callout.

4   Select Detail View : Detail from the Type Selector drop-down.
     This creates a detail view callout.

5   On the Options Bar, ensure that 3/4" = 1'-0" (1 : 50) is selected from the Scale list.

6   On the right side of the view area where the exterior wall connects to the roof:
     • Click to place the upper-left corner of the callout.
     • Drag the cursor diagonally down to the right of the view.
     • Click to place the lower-right corner of the callout, as shown.

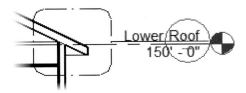

     Notice that in the Project Browser, under Detail Views (Detail), a new Detail view is created
     and numbered.

7   To adjust the graphics for clarity, click the callout boundary to select the callout.

8   Drag the Move Clip Plane control dots of the callout inward to decrease the size of
     the callout.

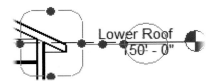

9   Drag the Drag Head control dot up to move the callout head above the level line.

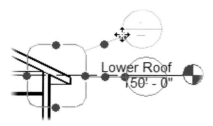

10   Drag the Drag control dot to modify the position of the leader.

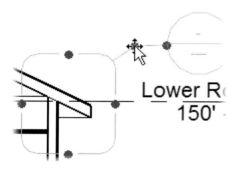

11   Right-click the callout head. Click Go to View to open the callout view showing a view of the roof and wall connection at the specified scale and the medium detail level. This view can now be renamed and is ready for detailing.

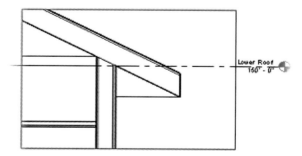

12   Open the A101 - Unnamed sheet.
     Notice that the new callout appears in the section view on the sheet. You will learn about sheets later.

13   In the Project Browser:

- Select and drag Detail o onto the sheet.
- Click to place the detail view. The placement of the new viewport on the sheet is not critical.
  Note: It is easy to create sheets for construction sets.

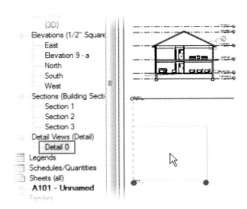

14   Zoom in to examine the building section on the sheet. Notice that the callout tag is updated to show the detail number and the sheet number.

15   Open the Section 1 view.

16   In the view window, notice that the callout tag is updated.

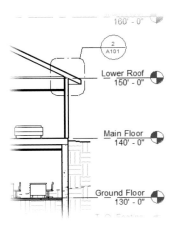

17   Close the file without saving changes.

Lesson 26 | Working with Text and Tags

This lesson describes how to work with text and tags. You begin the lesson by learning about text and tags. Then, you learn some recommended practices for working with text and tags. The lesson concludes with an exercise on working with text and tags.

Annotations, such as text and tags, are an important part of construction documents. Annotations provide specific instructions that are necessary for fabricators and constructors to understand a building design. You use text to provide descriptive information about building elements. Tags are used to label building elements.

The following illustration shows a plan view with wall tags and a text note.

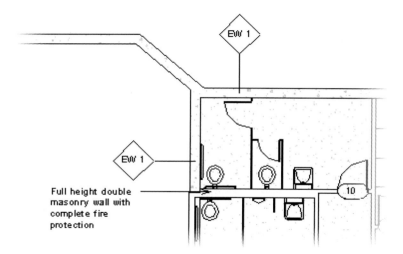

Objectives

After completing this lesson, you will be able to:

- Describe text.

- Describe tags.

- State the recommended practices for working with text and tags.

- Work with text and tags.

About Text

A building design goes through various stages before being implemented. At each stage, different people are involved who may want to add explanations and instructions to the design using text annotations. Text can be added to views or sheets in your project to make the building design easy to understand for the people next in the cycle.

Definition of Text

Text is the information that is added to a drawing to label the building elements or provide some description about them. It is a view-specific component and therefore automatically changes size with the view scale.

You can use the default text types or create custom text types based on font or size, as required. Text can have leaders that point to specific elements, areas, or conditions in a view.

You add text to a drawing as a text note using the Text tool. When you add text, the text and the leaders automatically snap into alignment with other text and leaders in the view. After adding text, you can format it for various parameters, such as size, font, justification, width, underlining, lineweight, background, and color. To keep the view graphics clear and readable, you can move text to different positions. You can also edit and wrap text. In addition, you can copy or paste text from other applications, such as Microsoft Word. You can add or remove leaders of a text note at any time, if required.

Model Text

For special instances, such as putting a representation of signage on a building, you can add model text. Model text is a model component and therefore visible in all relevant model views. It does not change when the view scale is changed.

Example of Text

The following illustration shows a section view with text notes.

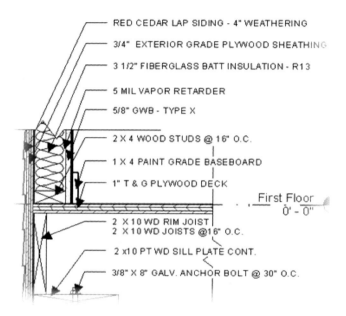

About Tags

You use tags to label building elements. Tags use unique symbols to represent each building element. Unlike text, the values displayed in tags are updated automatically when the building model is updated.

Definition of Tags

Tags are annotations that display parametric information about the elements with which they are associated. Tags are view-specific and therefore scale with the view. When you place tags, they automatically align with other tags in the view.

Revit provides predefined tag families for all building elements. Some of these tags, such as the door, window, wall, room, and area tags are preloaded into the default project templates. These preloaded tags are automatically placed in the view when you add the corresponding building element. For the building elements that do not have the corresponding preloaded tags, you need to load the tags from the software library.

You can create custom tags by editing the predefined tag family files according to your graphic standards. Tags can be placed with or without leaders, and have horizontal or vertical orientation. You can modify tags by changing their position in a view, turning their leaders on or off, and changing their orientation.

Note: *You can tag a building element with more than one tag if you have multiple tag types loaded for that element.*

Types of Tags

The following table describes various types of predefined and preloaded tags.

Type	Description
Door	Displays the Mark property of a door, which is a number that increments automatically whenever a door is placed in a project. Doors are numbered and scheduled individually.
Window	Displays the Type Mark property of windows. Windows are numbered and scheduled by type, not individually.
Room	Displays the name and number of rooms by default.
Area	Displays the name and area of areas by default.
Wall	Displays the Type Mark property for a wall. Wall tags are listed and scheduled by type.

Tag Tools

You can place tags in a view using the tag tools available on the Tag panel of the Annotate tab. The Tag panel provides four tools: Tag by Category, Multi-Category, Material, and View Reference.

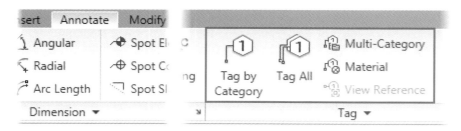

Tag tools on the Tag panel of the Annotate tab.

The following table describes the various tag tools available on the Tag panel.

Option	Description
Tag by Category	Identifies building elements, such as furniture, site components, and plumbing supplies, in a drawing. When you tag building elements by category, Revit recognizes the element type and provides an appropriate tag type. You can place tags by category on all or selected building elements in a view using the Tag All tool.
Multi-Category	Identifies building elements across element categories based on predefined filters.
Material	Identifies materials, such as studs and drywall in walls, as specified in a building model.
View Reference	Indicates the sheet number and detail number of a view that has been split with a matchline. This tool is active only in views with dependency relationships.

Example of Tags

The following illustrations show the tags associated with different building elements.

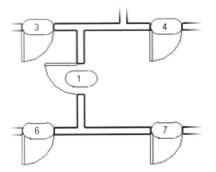

Door tags

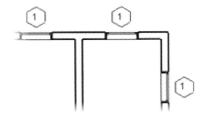

Window tags

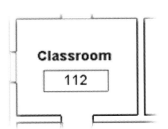

Room tag

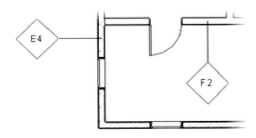

Wall tags

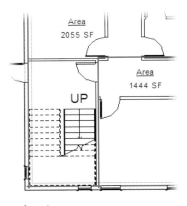

Area tags

Guidelines for Working with Text and Tags

The following recommended practices help you work efficiently with text and tags.

Guidelines

- Place text and tags after a view has been created and made ready for annotations in case you anticipate changes to the view scale. This helps you save the time spent in coordinating the views when you print them.

- Create copies of the main model views and name them appropriately so that you can quickly place text and tags to create specific views. For example, a floor plan view can be duplicated repeatedly to set up the room plan, electrical plan, furniture plan, and flooring plan. Each duplicate plan view can hold the required text and tags. If you repeatedly work on the same model, you can save these plan views in your project template to save the setup time and make the documentation phase faster.

- Plan ahead and crop your documentation views to make placing text notes easier and more efficient.

- Ensure that text notes and their associated leaders do not obscure the graphic display of building elements. Also, check that notes are aligned. These measures will enable users to read text notes easily.

- Create different types of text by adding leaders with different end symbols, such as dot and large arrow. You can then use different text symbols for specific situations or conditions.

- Load more than one tag type for building elements when you want to tag a component for different purposes across views. This gives flexibility to the views and improves the quality of your documents.

- Use the spelling checker available on the Text panel of the Annotate tab to avoid any spelling errors in text and tags.

Exercise | Work with Text and Tags

In this exercise, you place text in a drafting view to illustrate a standard roofing detail. Then, you place tags and text in a plan view to label doors, windows, rooms, and walls. You also modify the wall tags.

You are documenting a building project. To complete a drafted detail, you add text notes. You prepare a plan view by adding tags to identify the building elements.

You do the following:

- Add text to a detail view.

- Add tags and text to a model view.

- Modify tags.

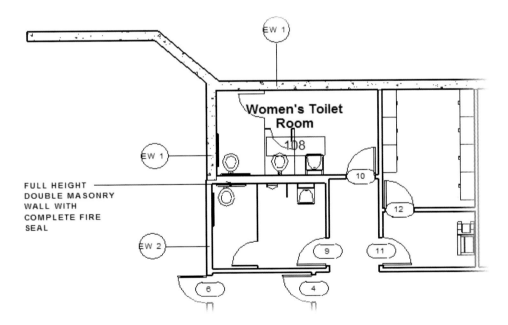

The completed exercise

Completing the Exercise: *To complete the exercise, follow the steps in this book or in the onscreen exercise. In the onscreen list of chapters and exercises, click Chapter 9: Detailing and Drafting. Click Exercise: Work with Text and Tags.*

Add Text to a Detail View

1   Open *i_rac_essentials_text_and_tags.rvt* or *m_rac_essentials_text_and_tags.rvt*. The file opens in the Roof and Drain (Roof and Overflow Drain) drafting view. This 2D view contains detail components, filled regions, detail lines, and dimensions. The 2D views work very well for details. Details such as the roof drain seen in the drawing could be an imported DWG™ detail from your existing library. You will learn more about drafting views later.
Note: The illustrations for the metric dataset will be slightly different from those shown here.

2   Click Annotate tab > Text panel > Text to label the drawing components.

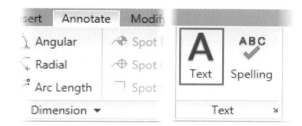

The Place Text tab is displayed.

3   Verify that Text : 3/32" Arial (Text : 2.0 mm Arial) is selected from the Type Selector drop- down.

4   On the Place Text tab:
   • Click Alignment panel > Center to place the text as centrally aligned.
   • Click Leader panel > Two Segments to create a leader with two segments.

5   To place a leader, in the view window:

- Click the left drain cover to start a leader for the text.
- Move the cursor to the position, as shown.

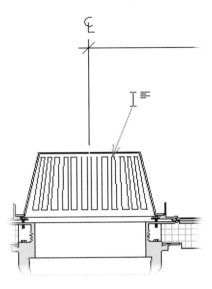

- Click to place the leader elbow.

6   To label the drain dome:

- Move the leader to the right such that it is placed at the center of the two drains.
- Click to start placing the text.
- In the text box, enter **CAST IRON DOME**.

7   Exit the Text tool.

8   Select the new text you just added.

9   Click Modify Text Notes tab > Leader panel > Right Straight.

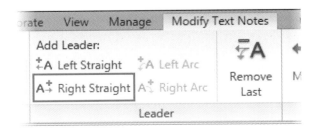

10   In the view window, use the drag controls to adjust the leaders and the text box position.

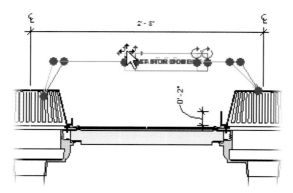

11   Activate the Text tool.

12   Add three more text boxes with text and the left and right leaders.

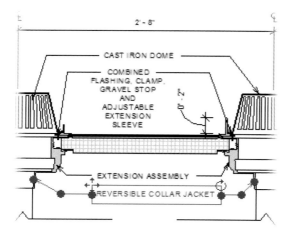

13   Exit the Text tool.

14   To see the complete detail view, zoom to fit in the view window.

Add Tags and Text to a Model View

1   Open the Ground Floor view to add text and tags to this view.

2   Zoom in to the upper-left toilet room.

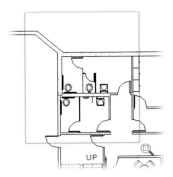

3   Click Annotate tab > Tag panel > Tag by Category.

4   On the Options Bar, verify that the Leader check box is selected.

5   In the view widow:
    • Place the cursor over the upper wall.

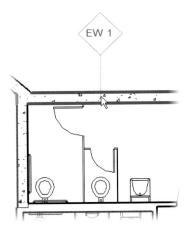

    • Click to place a tag.
      Note: You can have more than one type of tag in a project file for a given type of
      building component.

6   Place two wall tags on the left exterior wall.

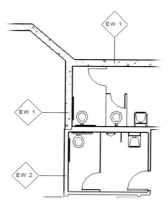

7   On the Tag panel, click Tag All.

8   To place tags on all doors and windows, in the Tag All Not Tagged dialog box:
- CTRL+select Door Tags and Window Tags fields.
- Under Leader, verify that the Create check box is clear.
- Click OK. Doors and windows now show tags.

9   To tag rooms, click Home tab > Room & Area panel > Tag drop-down > Tag Room. All rooms in the view are highlighted in blue.

10   In the view window:
- Position the cursor in the upper-left toilet room.

- Click to place the room tag.
  This is the only room tag you place for this exercise.

11   To place a text note, activate the Text tool.

12   On the Place Text tab:
- Click Alignment panel > Left to place the text aligned to the left.
- Click Leader panel > One Segment to create a leader with one segment.

13   In the view window:
- Click the wall between the two toilet rooms.
- Move the cursor outside the left exterior wall and click to place a text box.
- Enter **FULL HEIGHT DOUBLE MASONRY WALL WITH COMPLETE FIRE SEAL**.
- Click anywhere outside the text box.

14   Exit the Text tool.

15   To adjust the text box position:
- Select the text.
- Click the left drag control of the text box and move it to the right to wrap the text.

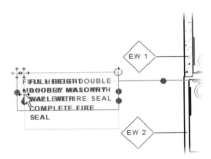

- Click anywhere in the view window to clear the text selection.

Modify Tags

1   To change tags from one loaded type to another:
- Select any one of the wall tags.
- Right-click the selected tag. Click Select All Instances to select all the wall tags.

2   Select Wall Tag Round : 1/2" (M_Wall Tag Round : 12mm) from the Type Selector drop-down. All the tags update.

3   Clear the selection.

4   Close the file without saving changes.

Lesson 27 | Working with Detail Views

This lesson describes how to create and use detail views for displaying the construction details of a building model. You begin the lesson by learning about detail views and the steps to create them. Then, you learn about the process and some recommended practices for saving and reusing detail views. The lesson concludes with an exercise on adding construction details to a detail view.

Construction details provide specific information to builders, fabricators, or installers on how to construct a building design. You display this information in detail views.

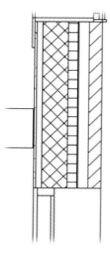

Section detail view of floor/wall join and window head/sill

Objectives

After completing this lesson, you will be able to:

- Describe detail views.

- Create detail views.

- Identify the steps in the process of saving and reusing a detail view.

- State the recommended practices for saving and reusing a detail view.

- Add construction details to a detail view.

About Detail Views

You create detail views to provide information on how a building should be constructed. A detail view represents a building model with finer details in terms of construction and fabrication than large-scale views. Using the detail view, you can add more information to your building model in the form of annotations and 2D lines on specific parts of the model.

Definition of Detail Views

A detail view is a view of all or a specific portion of a plan, elevation, or section view. This view provides a greater level of detail at a different scale from its parent view.

You can create detail views and access them from Detail Views in the Project Browser. You can create a detail view quickly by using the Callout tool. You can also duplicate a view, crop it, and change the scale to make a detail view. Detail View types are available for sections and callouts in the default templates.

The following illustration shows a callout of a plan view listed as a detail view in the Project Browser.

Detail Levels

You can view a building model in three levels of detail: Coarse, Medium, and Fine. These detail levels are available on the View Control Bar.

Changing the detail level affects the display of the elements in your building model. Consider the following illustration as an example. The wall on the left is at coarse detail level and shows only the outlines. The wall on the right is at medium detail level and shows the interior structure.

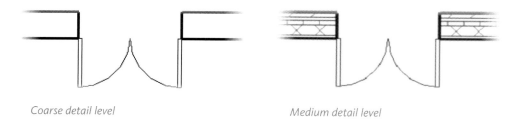

Coarse detail level   Medium detail level

Detail Level Option

To set the detail level based on the view scale for new views that you create, you use the View Scale-to-Detail Level Correspondence dialog box. You can access this dialog box by selecting Detail Level from the Settings drop-down on the Project Settings panel of the Manage tab.

Additionally, depending on a view, you can override the detail level by setting the Detail Level parameter in the View Properties dialog box.

Detailing Tools

You can use the detail view of a part of a building model as background to specify additional information. This process of adding more information is known as detailing. For example, consider a section of a building model where the floor meets a wall. In this section, you can perform detailing by adding information such as text notes, dimensions, and symbols.

You use 2D detailing tools for detailing. These tools are available on the Annotate and View tabs. The following table describes the detailing tools.

Tool	Description
Callouts	Creates a callout to display a close-up view of a plan, section, or elevation view. Details are added to the callout view.
Detail Lines	Places 2D lines in the detail view. These lines can trace over model components or add lines that are not shown in the model.

Tool	Description
Dimensions	Applies specific dimensions to the detail for specifying exact distances or placement instructions.
Text	Specifies construction methods and materials.
Detail Components	Creates and loads custom detail components to place the details. Detail components may be actual construction components, such as structural steel, jambs, and metal studs.
Symbol	Places a symbol such as a direction arrow or a break mark to indicate omitted information.
Filled Regions	Creates detail regions and gives them a fill pattern to represent surfaces such as concrete or compacted earth.
Insulation	Places a detail component to represent insulation. You do this in a section detail that shows the structure of a roof or a wall.
Detail Groups	Places pre-existing groups or combines detail elements into groups that you can reuse within a project or in other projects.

You frequently use some detailing tools, such as Detail Lines, Detail Components, and Filled Regions.

Detail Lines

The Detail Lines tool used for creating 2D detail lines has the same drawing options as the Lines tool used when creating walls, floors, or roofs, except that detail lines are specific to a view. You use detail lines in drafting views, which have no reference to the building model.

Detail Components

You use the Detail Component tool to place 2D detail components, such as fasteners and connections, in a detail view. Detail components are similar to annotation elements and are visible only in the view in which you place them.

You load the detail components into a file from the Detail Component libraries that are installed with Revit. These detail components are stored according to the CSI MasterFormat.

You can use these detail components and create custom detail components when you fill details for construction documents.

The following illustrations show the 2D detail component family of an engineered wood joist.

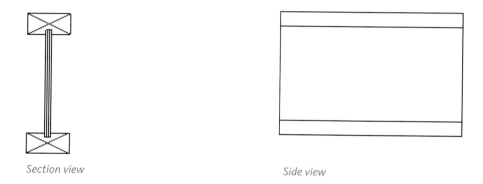

Section view   *Side view*

Filled Regions

Filled regions are detail elements that consist of repeated line patterns within a border. You place a filled region by sketching its border and specifying a pattern. Filled regions can be opaque or transparent. Opaque regions hide the surface on which they are placed.

White and opaque filled regions are known as masking regions. You can set the edge lines of filled and masking regions to invisible linetype, which hides the edge lines.

Hidden Line

The graphics display mode that Revit most commonly uses is known as Hidden Line. This mode shows only surfaces and edges, and objects behind other objects are hidden. You can show the edges of hidden objects in a detail view. To do this, you either add detail lines or override the display of edges by using the Linework tool on the Edit Linework panel of the Modify tab.

Standard drafting convention in plans and sections includes linework that indicates when a line representing an object edge is hidden. At times, when you want to indicate that an item is not really visible, you use the dashed linetype known as Hidden. Revit also provides a linetype named Hidden Line with a slightly different pattern and green color.

The following illustrations show a hidden line view model and the hidden linetype in a section view of a model.

Hidden line view of the model

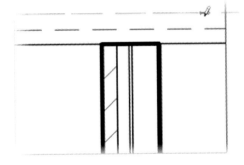

Detail lines using the hidden linetype in a section view of a model

Draw Order of Elements

The draw order of elements in a detail or drafting view determines which 2D elements, such as filled regions, hide other elements. You can set the draw order for detail items in a detail view. By default, elements that are added later hide those placed earlier.

Detail Groups

You can assemble detail objects, such as detail lines, filled regions, and text to create detail groups. You can group model and detail elements and combinations of both. Creating detail groups minimizes repetition of elements. You can place detail groups in many views, save them as library files, and access them from the Project Browser.

Draw Order of Detail Groups

The draw order of a detail group is the sequence in which you group the detail elements. A detail group's draw order does not change when the group is moved, copied, or inserted.

You can change the draw order of individual group members. To do this, you need to edit the group. After you edit the draw order of the members of a detail group, all instances of that detail group are updated with the new draw order.

Sorting Detail Element Display Depth

You sort the display depth of selected detail elements in a view using Bring to Front and Send to Back on the Arrange panel of the Modify Detail Items contextual tab. These options are available when you place or select detail elements in the view.

The following table describes the display depth sorting options.

Option	Description
Bring to Front	Places the detail element in front of all detail elements in the view.
Send to Back	Places the detail element behind all detail elements in the view.
Bring Forward	Moves the detail element incrementally closer to the front of all detail elements in the view.
Send Backward	Moves the detail element incrementally closer to the back of all other detail elements in the view.

Example of Detail Views

The following illustration shows a section detail view before any detailing.

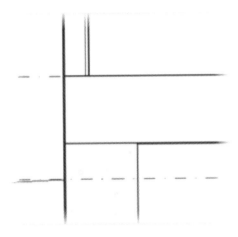

The following illustration shows a section detail view with drafted and model components. The floor and walls are the model components to which text notes have been added. The insulation, siding, baseboard, plywood, joist, sill, wall plate, and anchor bolt are all detail lines or components that have been placed in the view.

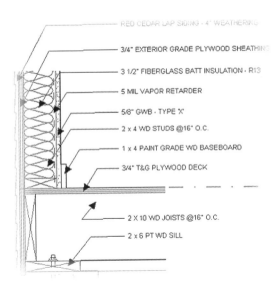

RED CEDAR LAP SIDING - 4" WEATHERING

3/4" EXTERIOR GRADE PLYWOOD SHEATHING

3 1/2" FIBERGLASS BATT INSULATION - R13

5 MIL VAPOR RETARDER

5/8" GWB - TYPE 'X'

2 x 4 WD STUDS @16" O.C.

1 x 4 PAINT GRADE WD BASEBOARD

3/4" T&G PLYWOOD DECK

2 X 10 WD JOISTS @16" O.C.

2 x 6 PT WD SILL

The following illustration shows the detail view with filled region, detail lines, and detail components without text.

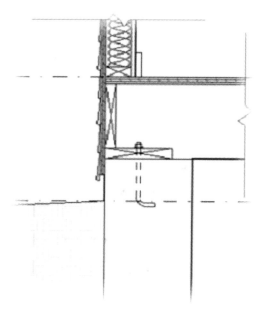

Creating Detail Views

You can change the type of an existing section or callout view or create a new detail view.

Procedure: Creating a Detail View from an Existing View

The following steps describe the procedure to create a detail view from an existing view.

1   Open a section or callout view that you wish to detail.

2   Open the Instance Properties dialog box.

3   In the Instance Properties dialog box:
    • Select Detail from the Type list.
    • Under Graphics, select a view scale from the View Scale list.

4   Resize the crop region, if required.

5   In the Project Browser, rename the new detail view.

> **Note**: *You can change any section view that has not been created with a Detail View type to a detail view. The view will then move to the appropriate Detail View category in the Project Browser. You can also change the view type of callouts placed in section views. You cannot change the view type of callouts placed in plan views.*

Procedure: Creating a New Detail View

The following steps describe the procedure to create a new detail view.

1   Open an existing plan, section, or elevation view.

2   Activate the Callout tool.

3   Select Detail View : Detail from the Type Selector drop-down.

4   On the Options Bar, select a scale view from the Scale list.

5   Click at the starting point of the new detail view and drag it through the building model. Click when you reach the end point of the detail.

6   Exit the Callout tool.

7   Select the callout view.

8   Drag the blue controls to resize the crop region if required. The depth of the detail view changes accordingly.

9   In the Project Browser, rename the new detail view.

Process of Saving and Reusing a Detail View

Saving a detail view increases its usability across projects. You can save views with view-specific elements, such as text, dimensions, detail lines, and detail components, as library content and reuse them in different projects.

Process: Saving and Reusing a Detail View

The following illustration shows the process of saving and reusing a detail view.

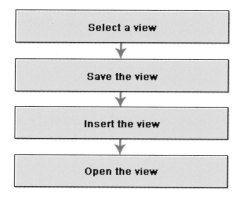

The following steps describe the process of saving and reusing a detail view.

1   **Select a view**.
    Select a view in the Project Browser that you want to save to a separate file. Select Save to
    New File from the shortcut menu.

2   **Save the view**.
    Save the view as an RVT file in a selected library folder.

3   **Insert the view**.
    Insert the view in another project, as required. You can insert schedules, drafting views,
    reports, sheets, or 2D content from one project to another using Insert from File on the
    Import panel of the Insert tab.

4   **Open the view**.
    Open the inserted view to reuse it. You need to ensure that when you open a view for reuse,
    its properties are also transferred to your project. You can also select a view scale for the
    view that you want to reuse.

Guidelines for Saving and Reusing a Detail View

Depending on the requirement of your building model, you should identify the views that you can save in a project to reuse later. The following recommended practices help you save and reuse detail views.

Guidelines

- When you export a sheet, the placement of views on the sheet is maintained. This enables you to create and reuse standard detail sheets. When you import a sheet, the titleblock on the sheet is updated with project information and the sheet name is incremented according to your sheet naming convention.

- To import 2D elements from a saved model detail view, you must activate a drafting view. This results in a successful import of the 2D elements. Model elements are not imported.

- When you import a drafting view, a new drafting view is automatically created to retain the imported view. This enables you to quickly create detail sheets that reuse standard details but vary in layout.

- You can use detailing in Revit to make good use of predrawn detail components. After you create details, particularly standard details that do not reference a specific model, save them to build a library of detail components in the Revit format.

Exercise | Add Construction Details to a Detail View

In this exercise, you add construction details to a detail view.

You want to show the construction details of a wall in a building model. You need to add detail components, repeating details, and detail lines to show your design intent.

You do the following:

- Create a detail view.

- Add detail components and repeating details to the detail view.

- Add detail lines to the detail view.

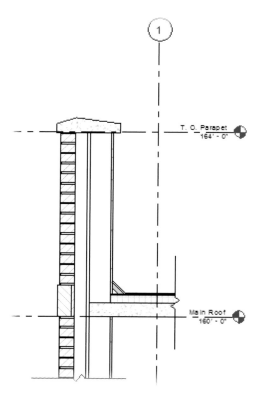

The completed exercise

Create a Detail View

1. Open *i_rac_essentials_detailing.rvt* or *m_rac_essentials_detailing.rvt*. The file opens in an exterior wall section view.
   Note: The illustrations for the metric dataset will be slightly different from those shown here. The completed exercise illustration may also vary.

2. To create a view that shows the wall-roof intersection in detail, activate the Callout tool.

3. Select Detail View : Detail View 1 (Detail View : Detail) from the Type Selector drop-down.

4. On the Options Bar, set the Scale to 1" = 1'-0" (1 : 10).

5. In the view window:
   - Create a detail view of the parapet-roof.
   - Select the callout.

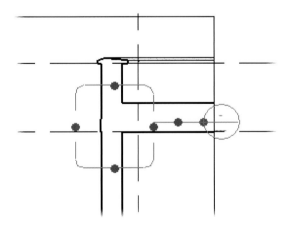

6. Drag the head of the callout to the left for a clear view.

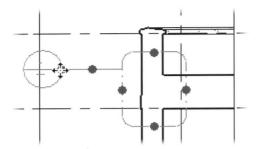

7   In the Project Browser:
   • Expand Detail Views and notice the new view.
   • Rename the detail view to **Parapet – Roof**.

8   Open the Parapet – Roof view.

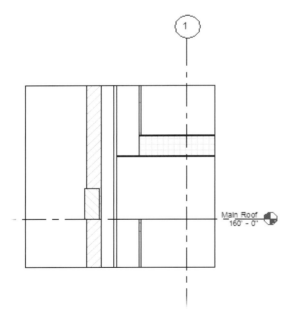

9   Open the Exterior Wall at Grid 1 (Wall Section at Grid 1) view. This is the parent view of the detail section you just created.

10 Zoom in to the callout bubble.

11 In the view window:

- Select the callout.
- Move the clip plane by dragging the control at the top of the bubble up so that the callout includes the top of the parapet wall.

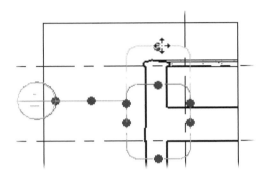

12 Right-click the selected callout bubble. Click Go to View to return to the detail section view.

13 Zoom to fit the view in the view window. Notice that the crop boundary has updated to display the top of the parapet wall.

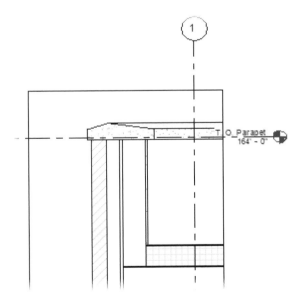

Note: You can also adjust the crop boundary directly in the detail view.

14   Click View tab > Graphics panel > View Properties.

15   In the Instance Properties dialog box, under Extents:
- Select Independent from the Far Clip Settings list.
- Set the Far Clip Offset value to **6'** (**1800** mm).
- Click OK.

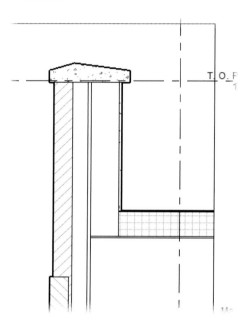

The far wall is no longer visible in the view.

16   Select the roof.

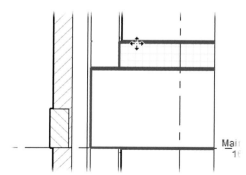

17 Select Basic Roof : Concrete - Insulated from the Type Selector drop-down. The roof changes to the new type and changes its appearance.

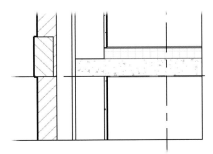

Note: You may need to adjust the crop boundary to view the roof changes.

Add Detail Components and Repeating Details to the Detail View

1 To add detailing to the view, click Annotate tab > Detail panel > Component drop-down > Detail Component.

2 Ensure that Mortar Joint : Brick Joint (m_Mortar Joint : m_Mortar Joint) is selected in the Type Selector drop-down.

3 In the view window:
- Zoom in to the sweep in the left face of the wall. This is a soldier brick course.
- Position the cursor to place the mortar joint below the sweep.

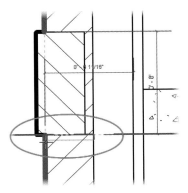

- Click to place the joint. It snaps to the wall face.

4   Exit the Detail Component tool.

5   In the view window, select the mortar joint that you placed.
Note: If the detail component is placed incorrectly, you can move it using the arrow keys.

6   To make copies of the joint indicating a brick wall in a section, click Array.

7   On the Options Bar:
- Ensure that the Group And Associate check box is selected.
- For Move To, ensure that 2nd is selected.
- Select the Constrain check box.
- For Number, enter **7**.

8   Click the mortar joint to select the start point.

9   Move the cursor down the wall.

10   When the cursor is 0' 2 5/8" (75 mm) below the first mortar joint, click to place the joint.
Tip: Alternatively, you can enter the dimension **2 5/8"** (**75** mm).

11   Notice that the mortar joints are added.
Note: If required, drag the crop region down to view all the mortar joints.

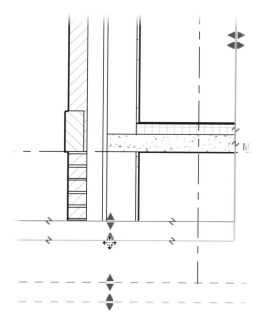

12   Exit the Array tool.

13   To place copies of the mortar joint component by drawing a placement line, click Annotate tab > Detail panel > Component drop-down > Repeating Detail.

14   Open the Type Properties dialog box.

15   In the Type Properties dialog box, click Duplicate.

16   In the Name dialog box:
      - Enter Mortar Joint.
      - Click OK.

17   In the Type Properties dialog box, Type Parameters section, under Pattern:
      - Select Mortar Joint : Brick Joint (m_Mortar Joint) from the Detail list.
      - Select Fixed Distance from the Layout list.
      - Select the Inside check box.
      - For Spacing, enter **2 5/8" (75** mm).

18   Click OK to close the Type Properties dialog box.

19   In the view window:
      - Place the cursor over the top of the sweep at the wall face.

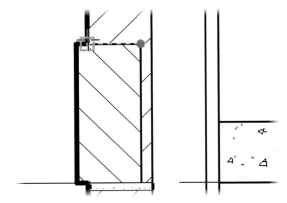

      - Click to start placement of the repeating detail.

20   Drag the cursor up to the parapet cap. Click at the intersection of the wall and cap to place the repeating detail.

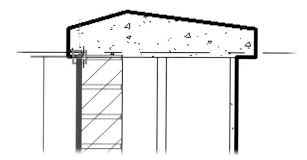

21 Exit the Repeating Detail tool.
Note: You used two different methods to place copies of the detail component. Using the Array tool, you specified the number and spacing, and using the Repeating Detail tool, you specified the overall distance and spacing.

22 Zoom in to the roof and wall connection.

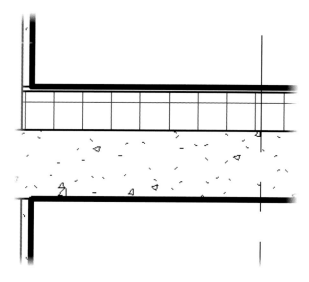

23 To place a component to indicate waterproofing, activate the Detail Component tool.

24 Select Cant Strip : 3" x 3" (m_Cant Strip : 75mm x 75mm) from the Type Selector drop-down.

25 Place the Cant Strip as shown. It snaps weakly to the face of the wall and roof.

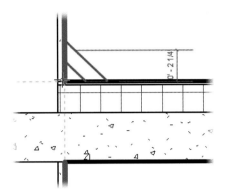

Add Detail Lines to the Detail View

1 To draft lines in the view, click Annotate tab > Detail panel > Detail Line.

2 Select Medium Lines from the Line Style drop-down.

3 On the Options Bar:
- Ensure that the Chain check box is selected.
- For Offset, enter **0' 1/4"** (**6** mm).

4 Place the cursor over the upper corner of the Cant Strip and click when the endpoint snap icon displays.

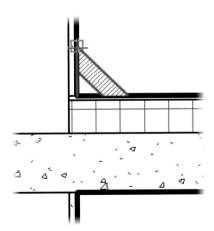

5   Click the lower-right corner of the Cant Strip to draw an offset line.

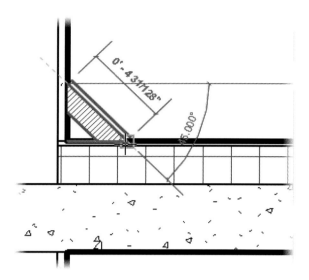

6   Draw a second line segment to the right, past the grid line. The exact length is not critical. This places lines that indicate a roof covering membrane.

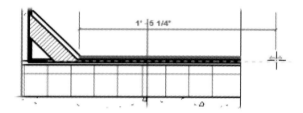

7   To clean up a drafted element, click Modify tab > Edit panel > Extend drop-down > Trim/Extend Single Element.

8   In the view window:

   • Click the right face of the wall.

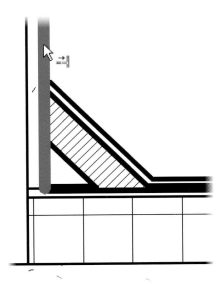

- Click the first line segment you drew so that it extends to meet the wall face.

9   To prepare the view to be inserted on a sheet, in the view window, zoom to fit.

10 On the View Control Bar, click Hide Crop Region.

11 Activate the Detail Component tool.

12 Select Break Line : Break Line from the Type Selector drop-down.

13 In the view window:
- Place the cursor over the lower part of the wall.

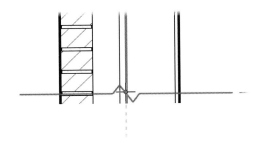

- Click to place the break line component.
  Note: A break line consists of a standard symbol and a masking region.

14 Exit the Detail Component tool.

15 Select the break line component. Press SPACEBAR to flip the component so that the masking region hides the lower part of the wall edge.

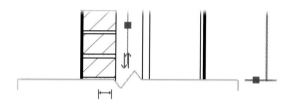

Note: You can move the break line by dragging or using the arrow keys, and you can drag the various shape handles to change the shape.

16 To add another break line to the right of the roof, activate the Detail Component tool.

17 In the view window:
   - Place the cursor over the roof to the right of grid line 1.
   - Press SPACEBAR to rotate the break line component by 90 degrees with each press.

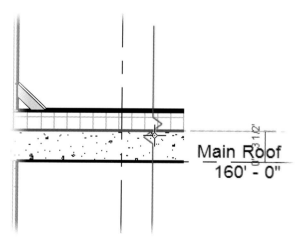

   - When the temporary dimensions appear on the side away from the wall, click to place the break line.

18 Exit the Detail Component tool. This view is now ready for text notes and other annotations. Changes to the design may require adjustments to the placement of the detail component and other 2D components or annotations in the detail view.
Note: You can turn off the grid line if you want to simplify the view and make it a standard detail view.

19 Close the file without saving changes.

Lesson 28 | Working with Drafting Views

This lesson describes how to work with drafting views. You begin the lesson by learning about drafting views. Next, you learn the steps in the process of reusing them. The lesson concludes with exercises on creating drafting views and importing a view and a CAD file in another drafting view.

When you create and document a building model, you may want to create a detail that is not associated with the building model. Instead of creating a model view callout and then detailing it, you can use drafting views to create details entirely in 2D. You can save drafting views and reuse them across projects.

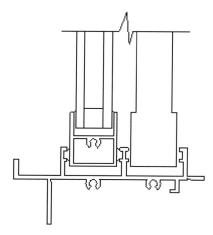

Drafting view of an aluminum sliding door fixed in a jamb section

Objectives

After completing this lesson, you will be able to:

- Describe drafting views.

- Identify the steps in the process of creating and reusing drafting views.

- State the recommended practices for reusing drafting views.

- Create drafting views.

- Import a view and a CAD file.

About Drafting Views

Drafting views provide 2D detail drawings of specific parts of a building without showing the model. You create drafting views when a project contains drafted details.

In model views with 2D detail components, you may need to adjust the detail components if the model changes. However, drafted details do not change when you modify a building model.

You or your firm may already have libraries of 2D details that can be reused for your Revit projects in drafting views.

Definition of Drafting Views

Drafting views include detail lines, detail groups, detail components, insulation, reference planes, dimensions, symbols, and text. Drafting views show details of specific parts of a building; they are drawn, not modeled. For example, a drafting view of the intersection between a floor and a wall does not include the wall and floor elements, but shows only lines that represent the floor and the wall.

In drafting views, you include only those elements that you create with 2D detailing tools or import from your CAD detail library. You can create drafting views at different view scales and detail levels. You can save drafting views and reuse them across projects.

Viewing Drafting Views

You can place a drafting view on a drawing sheet by dragging the view. Drafting views are saved with the project and displayed in the Project Browser under Drafting Views.

Example of Drafting Views

The following illustration shows detail components with dimensions and text notes in a drafting view.

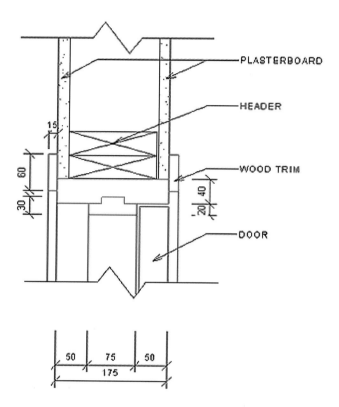

Process of Creating and Reusing Drafting Views

You can save the drafting views that you create in a building project as separate files in your detail drawing library. You can then reuse these drafting views in other projects.

Process: Creating and Reusing Drafting Views

The process of creating and reusing drafting views is shown in the following illustration.

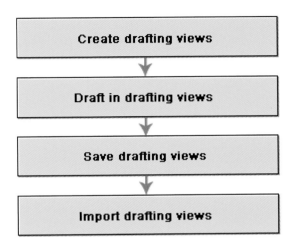

The following steps describe the process of creating and reusing drafting views.

1   **Create drafting views**.
    You create a drafting view using the Drafting View tool on the Create panel of the
    View tab. You can create different types of drafting views to help organize the
    Project Browser.

2   **Draft in drafting views**.
    You can draft in your drafting views using the tools on the Detail panel of the Annotate tab.
    These tools include Detail Lines, Detail Components, Repeating Details, Insulation, Filled
    Regions, Detail Groups, and Symbols.

3   **Save drafting views**.
    To save a drafting view to an external file, right-click the view in the Project Browser. Click
    Save To New File.

4   **Import drafting views**.
    You can reuse an existing drafting view by importing it into the current project. For this, you
    need to click Insert Views from File on the Insert from File drop-down on the Import panel of
    the Insert tab.

Guidelines for Reusing Drafting Views

The following recommended practices help you reuse drafting views effectively.

Guidelines

- Save drafting views so that members of other teams can reuse them. Saving drafting views allows you to build a detail library with Revit files.

- Work with your existing file system so that useful files are visible to others, and the file names are relevant. Working with the existing file system also increases production speed and reduces errors.

- Get your drafting views ready to print before saving them. For this, ensure that you post the revised versions of views, if any details change, in the drafting views. This increases the design production speed and reduces errors.

- Export views to CAD formats and import CAD files to drafting views when other members of your project team are working in CAD. This allows detailers who are proficient in programs other than Revit to participate in a Revit project.

Exercise | Create Drafting Views

In this exercise, you create a drafting view to provide a detailed drawing of the roof drains in the project. You want to provide a detailed drawing of roof drains on the roof in the project. To show these details, you create a drafting view. You can reuse the detailed drawing in future projects.

You do the following:

- Add a drafting view to the drawing.

- Place a detail component representing a roof drain.

- Add filled regions and detail lines.

- Mirror detail components in the view.

- Modify an instance of the roof drain component.

- Add dimensions to the detail components.

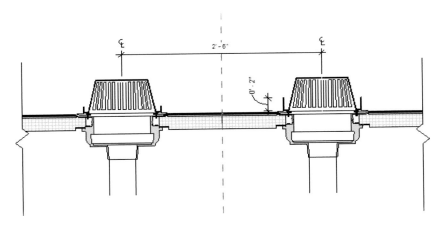

The completed exercise

Completing the Exercise: *To complete the exercise, follow the steps in this book or in the onscreen exercise. In the onscreen list of chapters and exercises, click Chapter 9: Detailing and Drafting. Click Exercise: Create Drafting Views.*

Add a Drafting View to the Drawing

1   Open *i_rac_essentials_draftingviews.rvt* or *m_rac_essentials_draftingviews.rvt*. The file opens in the default 3D view.
    Note: The illustrations for the metric dataset will be slightly different from those shown here.

2   To create a drafting view to hold 2D details of roof drains, click View tab > Create panel > Drafting View.

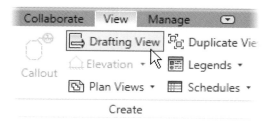

3   In the New Drafting View dialog box:
    - For Name, enter **Roof & Overflow Drain**.
    - Ensure that 1 1/2" = 1'-0" (1 : 10) is selected from the Scale list.
    - Click OK to open a blank drafting view. The drafting view is added to the Project Browser and it becomes the active view.

Place a Detail Component Representing a Roof Drain

1   To place a detail component representing a roof drain, you first need to set up the drawing space. Click Home tab > Work Plane panel > Ref Plane drop-down > Draw Reference Plane.

2   Draw a vertical reference plane in the middle of the view window. You use this reference plane as a construction line in the subsequent steps.

3   Click Annotate tab > Detail panel > Component drop-down > Detail Component.

4   Select Roof Drain : Roof Drain (m_Roof Drain : m_Roof Drain) from the Type Selector drop-down.

5   Place an instance of the roof drain to the left of the reference plane.

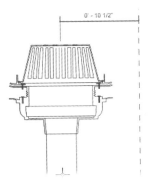

6   Exit the Detail Component tool.

7   To adjust the position of the drain:
- Select the drain.
- Click its temporary dimension.
- Enter **1' 3"** (**380** mm). Press ENTER.

Add Filled Regions and Detail Lines to Represent Roof Construction

1   To begin drafting various parts of the roof construction, click Annotate tab > Detail panel > Region drop-down > Region.

2   In the view window, zoom in to view the roof drain.

3   To draw the roof insulation, in the view window, sketch an outline that is approximately 2" (50 mm) thick. This represents the outline of the rigid insulation layer.

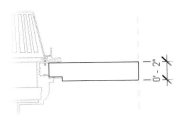

Tip: Do not place the dimension. It is for reference only.

4   Click Modify.

5   Zoom in to the roof insulation to ensure that the roof insulation sketch matches the
     illustration as shown. Adjust lines as required using the Move tool or arrow keys.

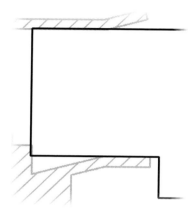

6   In the view window, select the upper horizontal line of the insulation.

7   On the Element panel, select <Invisible Lines> from the Line Style list to make sure that the
     line is invisible when the filled region is completed.

8   Click Region Properties.

9   In the Instance Properties dialog box:
     • Select Ortho Crosshatch - Small from the Type list.
     • Click OK.

10   Click Finish Region to finish sketching the region.

11   To begin drafting the region that represents bedding for the roofing membrane above the
     insulation, activate the Region tool.

12   In the view window:
     • Zoom in to the upper horizontal line that was made invisible.
     • Draw a rectangular chain of thin lines with a thickness of 1/4" (7 mm) above the
       insulation. The rectangle extends from the reference plane to the drain.

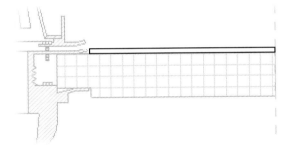

13 Click Modify.

14 In the view window:
   - Select the right vertical line of the rectangle you just sketched.
     Tip: Zoom in to the east end of the roof membrane layer to select the line with ease.
   - Select ‹Invisible Lines› from the Line Style list.

15 Click Region Properties.

16 In the Instance Properties dialog box:
   - Select Sand - Very Dense from the Type list.
   - Click OK.

17 Click Finish Region. Notice that the region updates.

18 To draw the roof membrane surface, click Annotate tab > Detail panel > Detail Line.

19 Select Thin Lines from the Line Style list.

20 In the view window, zoom in toward the flange on the drain.

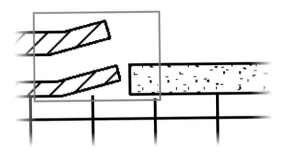

21   Draw the top surface of the roof as two lines starting from within the flange and continuing to the reference plane on the far right.

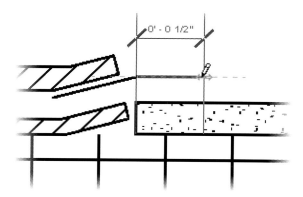

22   Exit the Detail Line tool.

23   In the view window, zoom in and CTRL+select the two new lines.

24   On the Modify panel, click Copy.

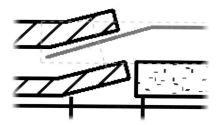

25   Click anywhere in the view window and move the cursor straight down.
     Tip: Selecting away from the existing lines can make your edits easier because snaps are not activated.

26   For the listening dimension of the lines:
     • Enter **1/8"** (**3** mm).

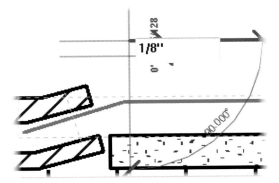

- Press ENTER.

27   Exit the Copy tool and verify that the roof covering is added.

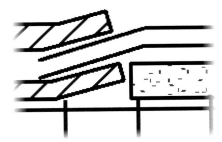

Mirror Detail Components in the View

1   To begin reusing what you have drawn, select the detail lines and filled regions using a selection window.

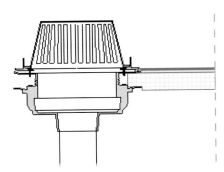

2   Click Multi-Select tab > Modify panel > Mirror drop-down > Pick Mirror Axis.

3   In the view window:
   • Move the cursor over the roof drain to highlight the vertical centerline of the drain.

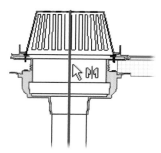

   • Click the vertical centerline of the roof drain as the mirror axis.

4   To finish one side of the drawing, activate the Detail Component tool.

5   Select Break Line : Break Line from the Type Selector drop-down.

6   In the view window:
   • Position the cursor to the left of the roof drain.
   • Press SPACEBAR to rotate the break line 90 degrees.
   • Click to place the break line on the left end of the roof details.

7   Exit the Detail Component tool.

8   To use the reference plane and duplicate the details, in the view window, select all elements except the reference plane.

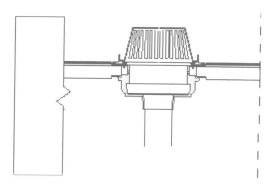

9   Activate the Pick Mirror Axis tool.

10   In the view window, click the reference plane as the mirror axis to place a second drain to the right of the first drain.

11   Exit the Pick Mirror Axis tool.

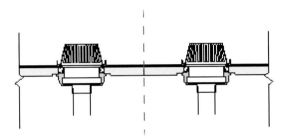

Modify an Instance of the Roof Drain Component

1   Right-click the drain on the right of the reference plane. Click Element Properties. This allows you to take advantage of the parametric properties of library detail components for changing one of the roof drains.

2   To change the ring height, in the Instance Properties dialog box:
- Under Other, for Ring Height, enter **0' 2"** (**50** mm).
- Click OK. The representation of the drain collar updates.

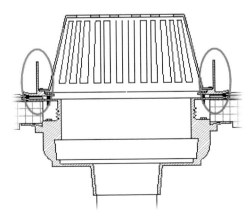

3   Clear the selection.

Add Dimensions to the Detail Components

1   To add a dimension to call out the collar height on the right drain, in the view window, zoom in to the drain on the right of the reference plane to view the whole drain.

2   Place a dimension for the ring element of the right drain. Click Annotate tab > Dimension panel > Aligned.

3   In the view window:
  - Click the horizontal shape handle of the roof drain to begin placing the dimension.
  - Drag the cursor to the top of the ring to highlight the horizontal shape handle.

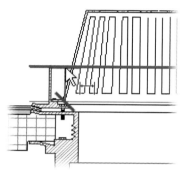

  - Click the horizontal shape handle.

4   Click to the left of the shape handles to finish placing the dimension.

5   Select the Drag Text handle and move the dimension upward for clarity. Notice that the Aligned dimension tool is still active.

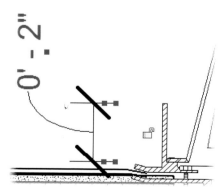

6 To place a horizontal dimension between the two drains, in the view window:

- Select the vertical centerlines of both the drains.
- Click above the drains to place the dimension.

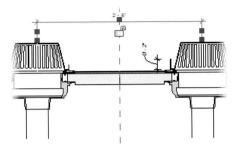

7 Open the Type Properties dialog box.

8 To add centerline graphics to the dimension style, in the Type Properties dialog box:

- Under Graphics, select Centerline (M_Centerline) from the Centerline Symbol list.
- Click OK.

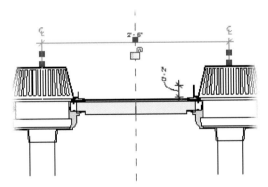

The dimension display updates.

9 Click Modify.

10 In the Project Browser, right-click the Roof & Overflow Drain view. Click Save to New File. Save the drafting view on the desktop.
You have just created the Revit detail for your library that can be reused in other projects in the future.

11 Close the file without saving changes.

Exercise | Import a View and a CAD File

In this exercise, you import a saved view into a drafting view and you import a CAD file into another drafting view.

You are preparing the construction documents for a building project. You know that drafted details from another Revit project and an AutoCAD project are useful in your work. Therefore, you import the drafting details of those projects rather than spend time creating them from scratch.

You do the following:

- Insert a Revit drafting view into the project.

- Import a CAD file into a drafting view.

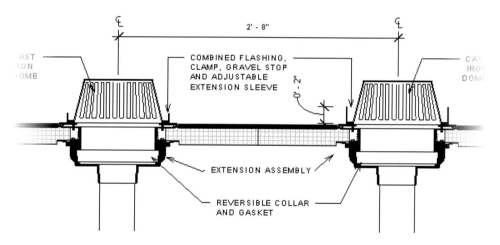

The completed exercise

Completing the Exercise: *To complete the exercise, follow the steps in this book or in the onscreen exercise. In the onscreen list of chapters and exercises, click Chapter 9: Detailing and Drafting. Click Exercise: Import a View and a CAD File.*

Insert a Revit Drafting View into the Project

1   Open *i_rac_essentials_importview.rvt* or *m_rac_essentials_importview.rvt*. The file opens in the
    default 3D view.
    Note: The illustrations for the metric dataset will be slightly different from those shown here.
    The completed exercise illustration may also vary.

2   To import a Revit drafting view to use in this project file, click Insert tab > Import panel >
    Insert from File drop-down > Insert Views from File.

3   In the Open dialog box, navigate to the location where you saved the datasets.

4   In the Open dialog box:
    - Select *i_rac_essentials_view_to_import.rvt* (*m_rac_essentials_view_to_import.rvt*).
    - Click Open.

5   In the Insert Views dialog box:
    - Under the Views list, ensure that the Drafting View: Roof and Drain (Drafting View:
      Roof and Overflow Drain) check box is selected.

    - Click OK.

6   In the Duplicate Types dialog box, click OK.

7   Close the warning box that is displayed. The new drafting view opens and is ready to be used
    in this project.

Import a CAD File into a Drafting View

1 To import a CAD file to use in a drafting view, create a new drafting view with the name **Roof Drain Detail from CAD**.

2 Click Insert tab > Import panel > Import CAD.

3 In the Import CAD Formats dialog box:
   - Navigate to the location where you saved the datasets.
   - Select *Roof and Two Drains Imperial.dwg* (*Roof and Two Drains Metric.dwg*).
   - Select Black and White from the Colors list.
   - Click Open.

4 Zoom to fit the view in the view window. The CAD import is displayed in the drafting view.

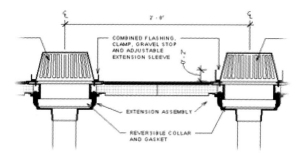

5 Select the CAD import symbol.

6 Notice that the Modify Roof and Two Drains Imperial.dwg (Modify Roof and Two Drains Metric.dwg) tab is displayed on the ribbon.

   You can use the Import Instance panel of this tab to change the appearance of layers in this item or explode it into individual lines and text. You can then edit the lines and text as necessary to make the drawing fit to use as a drafting view in your project.

7 Close all files without saving changes.

Chapter Summary

Now that you have learned how to create and use callouts and callout views, text and tags, detail views, and drafting views, you can supplement your designs with detailed information on how to build your designs.

In this chapter, you learned to:

- Create callout views.
- Work with text and tags.
- Create and use detail views for displaying the construction details of a building model.
- Work with drafting views.

Chapter 10
Construction Documentation

One of the benefits of building information modeling is the ability to automate the creation of schedules. In this chapter, you learn about schedules, how to create basic schedules and room schedules, and how to modify the appearance of schedules and export them. You also learn about creating legends and keynotes.

Objectives

After completing this chapter, you will be able to:

- Create and modify schedules.
- Create rooms and room schedules.
- Create legends and keynotes.

Lesson 29 | Creating and Modifying Schedules

This lesson describes how to create and modify schedules. You begin the lesson by learning about the types, characteristics, and properties of schedules. Next, you learn steps to export schedules and modify the fields in a schedule. Then, you learn some recommended practices for creating and modifying schedules. The lesson concludes with an exercise on creating and modifying schedules.

Schedules provide information about building elements in a project, such as doors and windows that can be exported to other applications for cost lists, estimates, and other quantity tallies. You use schedules to display the properties of selected building elements in a tabular format. In Autodesk Revit Architecture, the schedules update automatically, and therefore eliminate the errors that can occur in a manually compiled list.

Window Schedule			
Mark	Width	Height	Family and Type
1	2' - 0"	4' - 7 3/4"	Window: 24"
2	3' - 0"	4' - 7 3/4"	Window: 36"
3	3' - 0"	4' - 7 3/4"	Window: 36"
5	3' - 0"	4' - 7 3/4"	Window: 36"
7	3' - 0"	4' - 7 3/4"	Window: 36"
9	3' - 0"	4' - 7 3/4"	Window: 36"
10	3' - 0"	4' - 7 3/4"	Window: 36"
11	2' - 0"	4' - 7 3/4"	Window: 24"
12	2' - 0"	4' - 7 3/4"	Window: 24"

Window schedule

Objectives

After completing this lesson, you will be able to:

- Describe the types and characteristics of schedules.

- Describe the properties of schedules.

- Export schedules.

- Modify the fields that appear in schedules.

- State the recommended practices for creating and modifying schedules.

- Create and modify schedules.

About Schedules

You can view a building model in different ways. One way is to create a schedule that displays information about elements in a tabular format. A schedule updates automatically as the building model develops. You can format, view, and export schedules. You can also place them on drawing sheets to be used in documentation sets.

Definition of Schedules

A schedule is a formatted view of a building model based on the criteria you provide. It is a tabular display of information extracted from the properties of elements in a building model. Each property of an element is represented as a field in the schedule. Schedules can list every instance of a particular type of element in different rows or condense information about multiple instances of an element into a single row.

Types of Schedules

You can create three types of schedules using the Schedule/Quantities tool from the Schedules drop-down on the Create panel of the View tab. The three types of schedules are component schedules, multi-category schedules, and key schedules. You can also create specialized schedules from the Schedules drop-down: material takeoffs, drawing lists, note blocks, and view lists.

The following table describes various Schedule/Quantities types.

Schedule/ Quantities Type	Description
Component	Lists the selected component properties in a tabular format. For example, you can create a door schedule that lists the properties of doors, such as dimensions, finish, fire rating, and cost. Component schedules can be instance or type schedules. Instance schedules list each component as a separate line item, whereas type schedules group components of the same type into a single line item
Multi-category	Lists the components that hold shared parameters. Shared parameters span more than one project. The available fields for this type of schedule include the shared parameters.

Schedule/ Quantities Type	Description
Key	Lists the keys that you define for elements that consist of multiple items with the same characteristics. The keys act as a grouping mechanism, like style definitions. Key schedules are automatically populated with information about the element properties in the schedule fields. For example, a room schedule might have fields for floor finish and wall finish. Instead of manually entering the information for each room in the schedule, you can define keys that fill in the information according to a room type. You define key schedules according to project specifications. When you define a key, it becomes part of the instance properties of the scheduled element. If you display the properties of that element, you see the new key name. When you apply a value to the key, the attributes of the key are applied to the element.

Material Takeoffs

A material takeoff is a specific type of component schedule. It lists the subcomponents or materials of any Revit family. Material takeoffs have all the functionality and characteristics of other schedules. They help you display details of the assembly of a component. Any material that is used in an element within Revit can be scheduled.

Drawing Lists

A drawing list is a schedule of all drawing sheets in a project. It functions as a table of contents for the project and is typically placed on the first sheet of a documentation set.

Note Blocks

Note blocks are schedules that list the instances of annotations that you apply by using the Symbol tool on the Detail panel of the Annotate tab. Note blocks are useful for listing notes that are applied to elements in a project. For example, you can provide building descriptions for walls by attaching a note to each wall.

View Lists

A view list is a schedule of all views that show view parameters. You use view parameters for grouping and filtering the Project Browser organization. You can view and modify various view parameters for multiple views at a time.

Keynote Legends

A keynote parameter is available for all model elements, detail components, and materials. Keynote legends group common types of keynotes. Keynote legends can be placed on multiple sheet views. You create keynote legends using the Legends drop-down on the Create panel of the View tab.

Revision Schedules

Revision schedules are included with most Revit titleblocks. After you create a drawing sheet with a default titleblock, you can begin recording revision information on that sheet. You can add a revision schedule to a custom titleblock.

Note: *Revision schedules are part of titleblocks and will be covered in detail in that lesson.*

Schedule Management

After you create a schedule, you can perform various operations on it, such as viewing and updating the schedule.

When you create a schedule, it is added to the Project Browser listing. You can display the schedule in the view window by double-clicking the schedule name. You can also add the schedule to a drawing sheet by dragging the schedule to the drawing sheet in the view window.

A schedule is a view of the model that updates automatically when you make changes to those parts of the project that affect it. For example, if you move a wall, the floor area of the room in the room schedule updates accordingly. Schedules are associated with an entire project, including the building model. Therefore, when you change the properties of building components in a project, the associated schedule is also updated. For example, you can select a door in a project and change its manufacturer property. As a result, the door schedule updates to show this change. You can also edit a property of a building model by selecting the field corresponding to the property in the schedule and entering a new value for the property. Consequently, the schedule and the element type change.

Example of Schedules

The following illustration shows a wall schedule.

Wall Schedule				
Area	Length	Volume	Width	Family
490 SF	27' - 0"	326.89 CF	0' - 8"	Basic Wall
540 SF	27' - 0"	360.00 CF	0' - 8"	Basic Wall
540 SF	27' - 0"	360.00 CF	0' - 8"	Basic Wall
527 SF	27' - 0"	351.11 CF	0' - 8"	Basic Wall

About Schedule Properties

Schedules contain a list of fields that display element properties, such as the areas of rooms or the levels of doors. The properties of a schedule include the fields to be included, the sequence of the fields, and the way the fields are presented.

You define the properties of schedules by using the tabs in the Schedule Properties dialog box. Based on project requirements, you can add, filter, sort, format, and change the appearance of the fields for properties in a schedule.

Definition of Schedule Properties

Schedule properties define the structure and presentation of a schedule. These properties help you modify the information types that you want to include in a schedule and the appearance of that information.

Schedule Properties Tabs

You use the five tabs available in the Schedule Properties dialog box to control the display of schedule views and the content contained in a schedule.

The following illustration shows the Schedule Properties dialog box.

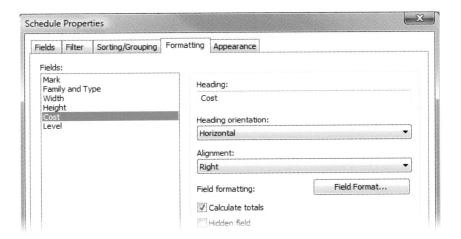

The following table describes the functions of the tabs in the Schedule Properties dialog box.

Tab	Functions
Fields	Places parameters as fields in a schedule and sets the order in which the fields are displayed. You use the Fields tab to add user-input and calculated fields to a schedule. Material, finish, and door mark are examples of user-input fields. Area and cost are examples of calculated fields.
Filter	Controls the display of elements in single and multi-category schedules, view lists, drawing lists, and note blocks.
Sorting/ Grouping	Sorts and groups the rows of a schedule. You can sort a schedule based on a field, for example, sorting by the cost of doors. Use grouping to group rows based on the element type. For example, you can show the total cost of wooden doors and glass doors separately. You can also use this tab to add blank lines between groups and group totals.

Tab	Functions
Formatting	Controls the formatting, such as column headings, text alignment, and orientation, of the schedule view and the way numerical data is displayed. For example, you can specify the number of decimal places in a numerical field.
Appearance	Controls the appearance of a schedule on a drawing sheet. For example, you can modify the appearance of a schedule by changing the font types and sizes and hiding the schedule title and column headers.

Example of Schedule Properties

The following illustration shows a wall schedule displaying the wall type and dimensions.

Wall Schedule				
Family and Type	Width	Area	Volume	Length
Basic Wall: Exterior - Siding	0' - 7 3/8"	868 SF	525.36 CF	86' - 3 1/8"
Basic Wall: Exterior - Siding	0' - 7 3/8"	542 SF	326.63 CF	29' - 9 7/16"
Basic Wall: Exterior - Siding	0' - 7 3/8"	324 SF	197.45 CF	22' - 3 3/4"
Basic Wall: Exterior - Siding	0' - 7 3/8"	83 SF	50.32 CF	10' - 0 9/16"
Basic Wall: Foundation - 12" Concr	1' - 0"	1108 SF	1108.31 CF	85' - 8"
Basic Wall: Foundation - 12" Concr	1' - 0"	120 SF	119.96 CF	29' - 5 7/8"
Basic Wall: Foundation - 12" Concr	1' - 0"	339 SF	338.67 CF	85' - 8"
Basic Wall: Foundation - 12" Concr	1' - 0"	265 SF	265.17 CF	39' - 8"
Basic Wall: Footing	2' - 0"	129 SF	257.00 CF	85' - 8"
Basic Wall: Footing	2' - 0"	60 SF	119.00 CF	39' - 8"
Basic Wall: Footing	2' - 0"	126 SF	251.00 CF	85' - 8"
Basic Wall: Footing	2' - 0"	63 SF	125.00 CF	39' - 8"

Exporting Schedules

You can export a schedule to spreadsheet applications. When you export a schedule, you save it as a delimited text file so that it can be opened in other applications. If you repeatedly export schedule information to the same file location, you can update the spreadsheet as desired while building a project.

Procedure: Exporting Schedules

The following steps describe how to export schedules.

1. In the Project Browser, under Schedules/Quantities, open the schedule.

2. On the application menu, click Export > Reports > Schedule.

3. In the Export Schedule dialog box, specify a name and directory for the schedule and click Save.

4. In the Export Schedule dialog box, under Schedule Appearance, specify the display options for the schedule in a spreadsheet.

5. Under Output options, specify values of the parameters for the text file. The text file can be opened in a spreadsheet application.

Modifying Schedule Fields

You can add new fields to a schedule using the Add Parameter option. You can also modify the existing fields in a schedule. For example, you may need to change a schedule from an instance list to a type list, or calculate totals of the cost information.

Procedure: Modifying Fields in Schedules

The following steps describe how to modify the fields in a schedule.

1. In the Project Browser, under Schedules/Quantities, open the schedule.

2. In the Project Browser, right-click the schedule view. Click Properties.

3. In the Instance Properties dialog box, under Other, for Fields, click Edit.

4. In the Schedule Properties dialog box, on the Fields tab, add fields, create custom fields, calculate a value based on other fields, or change the order of fields.
   Note: You can specify the calculation criteria in the Calculated Value dialog box.

Guidelines for Creating and Modifying Schedules

The following guidelines help you effectively create and modify schedules.

Guidelines

- Create schedules that display only important or critical fields so that the schedules are easy to understand. Use the Hidden Field option on the Formatting tab to hide the fields that you want to keep available but not show in the schedule view.

- Use headers, footers, and blank lines to identify and separate groups of similar information in a schedule to improve readability. You can create these headers, footers, and blank lines using the Sorting/Grouping tab in the Schedule Properties dialog box.

- Click Show repeatedly in the Show Elements in View dialog box to open all the model views that display the element selected in the schedule table. This helps you easily check and modify the selected element in all views.

Exercise | Create and Modify Schedules

In this exercise, you create and modify schedules. You create a component door schedule and a door hardware key schedule and assign hardware to the doors. You also work with the appearance of the schedule and add it to a drawing sheet.

You need to create a door schedule that also shows hardware types. In addition, you want to create a key schedule and assign hardware values to doors to automatically populate the door schedule. Finally, you want to format the appearance of the schedule, limit its view to the ground floor doors in your project, and add it to a drawing sheet.

You do the following:

- Create a door schedule and add values to it.

- Create a door hardware key schedule.

- Assign hardware to doors.

- Add hardware to the door schedule.

- Sort the schedule view by levels and add details.

- Create a duplicate schedule for the ground floor doors.

- Create a new drawing sheet and add a schedule to the sheet.

Ground Floor Door Schedule						
Door Type	Width	Height	Cost	Hardware Type	Lockset	Hi
Single-Flush Vision: 36" x 80"	3' - 0"	6' - 8"	227.58	Locking Office	ANSI F8	BB - BS kn u
Single-Flush Vision: 36" x 80"	3' - 0"	6' - 8"	227.58	Locking Office	ANSI F8	BB - BS kn u
Single-Flush Vision: 36" x 84"	3' - 0"	7' - 0"	240.15			
Single-Flush Vision: 36" x 84"	3' - 0"	7' - 0"	240.15			
Single-Glass 1: 36" x 84"	3' - 0"	7' - 0"	196.00	Egress	Series 22 Ext Devi	BB - BS kn u
Single-Glass 1: 36" x 84"	3' - 0"	7' - 0"	196.00			
Single-Glass 1: 36" x 84"	3' - 0"	7' - 0"	196.00			
Single-Flush: 36" x 80"	3' - 0"	6' - 8"	213.75	Restroom	Push Pull	BB - BS kn u
Single-Flush: 36" x 80"	3' - 0"	6' - 8"	213.75	Restroom	Push Pull	BB - BS kn u
Single-Flush Vision: 36" x 80"	3' - 0"	6' - 8"	227.58			
Single-Flush Vision: 36" x 80"	3' - 0"	6' - 8"	227.58			
Single-Flush Vision: 36" x 80"	3' - 0"	6' - 8"	227.58			
Single-Glass 1: 34" x 80"	2' - 10"	6' - 8"	181.65			
Single-Glass 1: 34" x 80"	2' - 10"	6' - 8"	181.65			
Single-Flush Vision: 36" x 80"	3' - 0"	6' - 8"	227.58			
Single-Flush: 34" x 80"	2' - 10"	6' - 8"	200.52			

The completed exercise

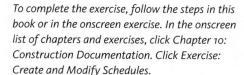

Completing the Exercise: *To complete the exercise, follow the steps in this book or in the onscreen exercise. In the onscreen list of chapters and exercises, click Chapter 10: Construction Documentation. Click Exercise: Create and Modify Schedules.*

Create a Door Schedule and Add Values to it

1 Open *i_rac_essentials_basic_schedules.rvt* or *m_rac_essentials_basic_schedules.rvt*. The file opens in the Ground Floor view.
   Note: The illustrations for the metric dataset will be slightly different from those shown here.

2 You create a schedule for the doors in the model. Click View tab > Create panel > Schedules drop-down > Schedule/Quantities to create a new schedule.

3 In the New Schedule dialog box:
   • Select Doors from the Category list.
   • Verify that Schedule Building Components is selected.
   • Click OK.

4 In the Schedule Properties dialog box, Fields tab:
   • Select Mark from the Available Fields list.
   • Click Add to add the Mark field to the Scheduled Fields (in order) list.

5 Add the following fields to the Scheduled Fields (in order) list:
   • Family and Type
   • Width
   • Height
   • Cost
   • Level

Note: You can double-click a field name to add it quickly. To reorder the Scheduled Fields (in order) list, click Move Up or Move Down.

6   In the Schedule Properties dialog box, Sorting/Grouping tab:
- Select Mark from the Sort By list.
- Click OK to create and open the door schedule.

Mark	Family and Type	Width	Height	Co=
1A	Curtain Wall	6' - 5 1/8"	7' - 1 1/4"	1895.0
1B	Curtain Wall	6' - 5 1/8"	7' - 1 1/4"	1895.0
2	Single-Flush	3' - 0"	6' - 8"	227.58
3	Single-Flush	3' - 0"	6' - 8"	227.58
4	Single-Flush	3' - 0"	7' - 0"	240.1=
5	Single-Flush	3' - 0"	7' - 0"	240.1=
6	Single-Glass	3' - 0"	7' - 0"	196.00
7	Single-Glass	3' - 0"	7' - 0"	196.00
8	Single-Glass	3' - 0"	7' - 0"	196.00
9	Single-Flush:	3' - 0"	6' - 8"	213.7=
10	Single-Flush:	3' - 0"	6' - 8"	213.7=

Door Schedule

Note: The door schedule has been added to the Project Browser. You can expand the field or cell width in the schedule by dragging the vertical lines.

7   You update cost information for a door type. To do so, in the 1A row:
- For Cost of Curtain Wall Dbl Glass: Curtain Wall Dbl Glass (M_ Curtain Wall Dbl Glass: M_ Curtain Wall Dbl Glass), enter **2250**.
- Press ENTER.

8   In the Revit dialog box, click OK to apply the change to all the elements of the Curtain Wall Dbl Glass (M_ Curtain Wall Dbl Glass) type. The Cost field is updated for the rows 1A and 1B.

9   In the view window, for the door schedule:
- Select Mark 3.
- Notice the level of the project where this door is located.

10   Open the Ground Floor view. Notice that door 3 is selected.

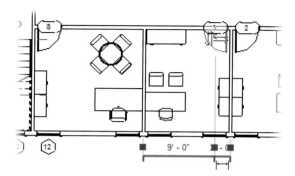

Note: A schedule is a parametric view of the model. If you modify the door in the plan view or the schedule view, it updates in all model views.

Create a Door Hardware Key Schedule

1   You now create a schedule for door hardware. Click View tab > Create panel > Schedules drop-down > Schedule/Quantities to create another schedule.

2   In the New Schedule dialog box:
   • Select Doors from the Category list.
   • For Name, enter **Door Hardware Schedule**.
   • Click Schedule Keys.
   • For Key Name, enter **Door Hardware**.
   • Click OK.

3   You add custom parameters to use in your schedule. In the Schedule Properties dialog box, Fields tab, click Add Parameter.

4   In the Parameter Properties dialog box:
   • For Name, enter **Hardware Type**.
   • Verify that Text is selected from the Type of Parameter list.

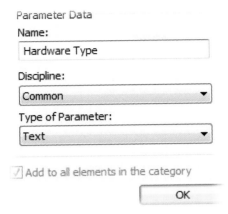

Parameter Data

Name:

Hardware Type

Discipline:

Common

Type of Parameter:

Text

☑ Add to all elements in the category

OK

- Click OK.

5　Add two more text parameters with the names Lockset and Hinges.

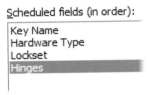

Scheduled fields (in order):

Key Name
Hardware Type
Lockset
Hinges

6　You now add a parameter that is not a text field. Click Add Parameter again.

7　In the Parameter Properties dialog box:
- For Name, enter **Closer**.
- Select Yes/No from the Type of Parameter list.

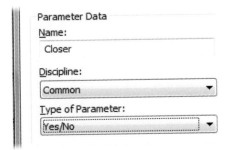

Parameter Data

Name:

Closer

Discipline:

Common

Type of Parameter:

Yes/No

- Click OK.

8   Add parameters with the names Frame Silencer and Kickplate of the Yes/No parameter type.

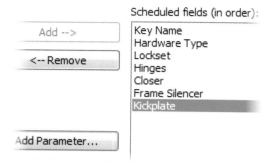

9   Click OK to close the Schedule Properties dialog box. This displays the door hardware schedule in the view window. Notice that the new parameters form the column names, and currently, there are no rows in the schedule.

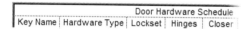

10   Click Modify Schedule/Quantities tab > Schedule panel > Rows: New to add a new row in the schedule.

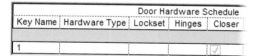

Note: You can widen the columns to display a long field entry clearly.

11   To add values to the schedule fields in the schedule displayed in the view window:
     - For Hardware Type, enter **Passage**.
     - For Lockset, enter **A-Series**.
     - For Hinges, enter **BB 1 1/2 pr - BB 5 knuckle**.
     - Clear the Closer and Kickplate check boxes.
     - Ensure that the Frame Silencer check box is selected.
       Note: You need to click a check box several times to activate the field and then clear or select it as needed.

12   Click Rows: New five times to add five new rows.

13 For the Hardware Type and Lockset fields, enter the values as shown.

Key Name	Hardware Type	Lockset
1	Passage	A-Series
2	Locking Office	ANSI F8
3	Egress	Series 22 Ext D
4	Entry	Series 22 Ext D
5	Restroom	Push Pull
6	Storage	ANSI F86

Note: After you type a field value in a cell, the field value is available in the cell drop-down list. If you need the same value, you can select it from the list.

14 For the Hinges, Closer, Frame Silencer, and Kickplate fields, enter the values as shown.

Hinges	Closer	Frame Sil	Kickp
BB 1 1/2 pr - BB 5 knuckle	☐	☑	☐
BB 1 1/2 pr - BB 5 knuckle	☐	☑	☐
BB 1 1/2 pr - BB 5 knuckle	☑	☑	☑
BB 3 Pr - BB 5 knuckle	☑	☑	☐
BB 1 1/2 pr - BB 5 knuckle	☑	☑	☐
BB 1 1/2 pr - BB 5 knuckle	☐	☐	☐

Assign Hardware to Doors

1 You now assign to doors the hardware values you have just defined. Open the Ground Floor view.

2 In the view window, zoom in to the left side of the building model as shown.

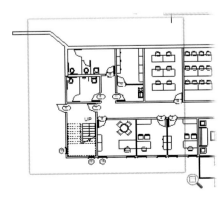

3   CTRL+select doors 9 and 10.
     Note: Tags and doors are different elements. Ensure that you select only the doors.

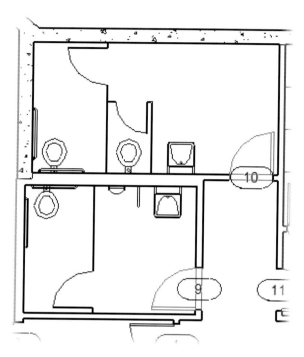

4   Open the Instance Properties dialog box.

5   In the Instance Properties dialog box:
     • Under Other, notice the new door hardware parameters.
     • Under Identity Data, for Door Hardware, enter **5**. All the door hardware parameters are updated.
     • Click OK.

6   In the view window, select door 6.

7   Open the Instance Properties dialog box again.

8   In the Instance Properties dialog box:
     • Assign the Door Hardware type as **3**.
     • Click OK.

Add Hardware to the Door Schedule

1   You now add hardware to the door schedule. In the Project Browser, under Schedules/
    Quantities, right-click Door Schedule. Click Properties.

2   In the Instance Properties dialog box, under Other, for Fields, click Edit.

3   In the Schedule Properties dialog box:
    - Select Door Hardware from the Available Fields list.
    - Click Add to add the Door Hardware to the Scheduled Fields (in order) list.

4   Repeat the process to add the Hardware Type, Lockset, Hinges, Closer, Frame Silencer, and
    Kickplate fields to the Scheduled Fields list.

5   Click OK to close all the dialog boxes.

6   Open the Door Schedule view.

7   In the view window, for the rows 1A, 1B, 2, and 3, specify the Door Hardware field values from
    the list as shown. The other hardware fields are automatically updated.

    Note: This schedule lists the doors for the entire project and can now be exported as is to a
    spreadsheet format using the Export Reports Schedule option on the application menu.

edule

Door Hardwar	Hardware Type	Lockset
3	Egress	Series 22 Ext
3	Egress	Series 22 Ext
2	Locking Office	ANSI F8
2	Locking Office	ANSI F8
(none)		

Sort the Schedule View by Levels and Add Details

1   You now change the schedule so that it reports doors according to the level and also reports cost totals. Right-click anywhere in the view window. Click View Properties.

2   In the Instance Properties dialog box, under Other, for Sorting/Grouping, click Edit.

3   In the Schedule Properties dialog box, Sorting/ Grouping tab:
   • Select Level from the Sort By list to sort the schedule fields.
   • Select the Header check box.
   • Select Mark from the Then By list.
   • Verify that the Header check box below the Then By list is clear.
   • Select the Grand Totals check box to calculate the grand total of the sorted fields.

4   In the Schedule Properties dialog box, Formatting tab:
   • Select Cost from the Fields list to calculate the totals for the Cost field.
   • Select Right from the Alignment list.
   • Select the Calculate Totals check box.

5   On the Formatting tab, to hide the display of the Level field in the schedule:
   • Select Level from the Fields list.
   • Select the Hidden Field check box.

6   To continue formatting the schedule, on the Formatting tab:
   • Select Family and Type from the Fields list.
   • For Heading, enter Door Type.

7   Click OK to close all the dialog boxes. The schedule is sorted by floors. At the bottom, the schedule reports the totals for the number of doors and cost.

38	Overhead–Se	14' - 0"	14' - 4"	12420.00	(non
39	Overhead–Se	14' - 0"	14' - 4"	12420.00	(non
40	Single–Glass	3' - 0"	7' - 0"	196.00	(non
41	Single–Glass	3' - 0"	7' - 0"	196.00	(non
42	Single–Flush	3' - 0"	7' - 0"	240.15	(non
43	Single–Flush	3' - 0"	7' - 0"	240.15	(non
44	Single–Flush	3' - 0"	7' - 0"	240.15	(non
48	Single–Flush	3' - 0"	7' - 0"	240.15	(non
Grand total: 46				87144.07	

Create a Duplicate Schedule for the Ground Floor Doors

1   You make a schedule for doors on only one level. This is useful for construction workers who install doors.

In the Project Browser, duplicate and rename the Door Schedule to Ground Floor Door Schedule. The Ground Floor Door Schedule becomes the active view.

2   Right-click anywhere in the view window. Click View Properties.

3   In the Instance Properties dialog box, under Other, for Sorting/Grouping, click Edit.

4   In the Schedule Properties dialog box, Sorting/Grouping tab, select (none) from the Sort By list.

5   On the Filter tab:
   • Select Level from the Filter By list.
   • Verify that Equals is selected in the list to the right of the Filter By list.
   • Select Ground Floor from the list below the Filter By list.

6   Click OK to close all the dialog boxes. Notice that the Ground Floor Door schedule now displays only the ground floor door details.

Mark	Door Type	Width	Height
2	Single-Flush Vision: 36" x 80	3' - 0"	6' - 8"
3	Single-Flush Vision: 36" x 80	3' - 0"	6' - 8"
4	Single-Flush Vision: 36" x 84	3' - 0"	7' - 0"
5	Single-Flush Vision: 36" x 84	3' - 0"	7' - 0"
6	Single-Glass 1: 36" x 84"	3' - 0"	7' - 0"
7	Single-Glass 1: 36" x 84"	3' - 0"	7' - 0"
8	Single-Glass 1: 36" x 84"	3' - 0"	7' - 0"
9	Single-Flush: 36" x 80"	3' - 0"	6' - 8"
10	Single-Flush: 36" x 80"	3' - 0"	6' - 8"
11	Single-Flush Vision: 36" x 80	3' - 0"	6' - 8"
12	Single-Flush Vision: 36" x 80	3' - 0"	6' - 8"
13	Single-Flush Vision: 36" x 80	3' - 0"	6' - 8"

Create a New Drawing Sheet and Add a Schedule to the Sheet

1   You now place a schedule on a sheet and check the formatting. In the Project Browser, right-click Sheets (All). Click New Sheet.

2   In the Select a Titleblock dialog box, click OK. A new sheet becomes the active view.

3   In the Project Browser, select the Ground Floor Door Schedule view.

4   To add a schedule to the drawing sheet:
   • Drag the selected schedule to the view window.
   • Click to place the schedule.

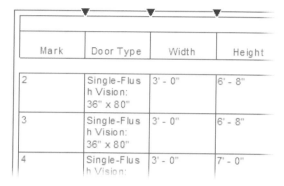

5   In the Project Browser, right-click Ground Floor Door Schedule. Click Properties.

6   In the Instance Properties dialog box, under Other, for Appearance, click Edit.

7   To change the print format, in the Schedule Properties dialog box, Appearance tab:
   • Under Graphics, clear the Blank Row Before Data check box.
   • Under Text, change Header Text from 1/8" (3.1750 mm) to **3/16**" (**5** mm).
   • Select the Bold check box.

8   In the Schedule Properties dialog box, Formatting tab:
   • Verify that Mark is selected in the Fields list.
   • Select the Hidden Field check box.
   • Select Door Hardware from the Fields list.
   • Select the Hidden Field check box.

9   Click OK to close all the dialog boxes.

10 To resize the schedule columns on the drawing sheet, in the view window:
- Select the schedule on the drawing sheet.
- Drag the triangular column grips to resize the required columns so that the text fits in the columns.

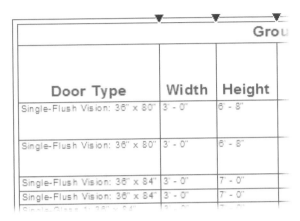

11 Click an area in the drawing sheet outside the schedule to clear the selection.

Note: You can now export the schedule to a spreadsheet format or print the sheet as part of the construction documentation set.

12 Close the file without saving changes.

Lesson 30 | Creating Rooms and Room Schedules

This lesson describes how to create rooms and room schedules. You begin the lesson by learning about rooms and room schedules. Next, you learn the steps to add a room tag and modify room area and volume. Then, you learn about material takeoffs and some recommended practices for creating rooms and room schedules. The lesson concludes with an exercise on creating rooms and a room schedule.

You can create rooms using the Room tool or by placing the rooms from a room schedule. You create room schedules to display the properties of room elements in a tabular format.

You can create and use material takeoffs to display the properties of the materials used in a room element. A material takeoff also provides the cost and quantity estimation of the material used in a building model.

Room Schedule		
Number	Name	Level
101	Lobby	Not Placed
102	Corridor	Not Placed
103	Office	Not Placed
104	Office	Not Placed
105	Office	Not Placed
106	Large Office	Not Placed

Room schedule

Window Material Takeoff		
Material: Nam	Material: Area	Material: Volume
Glass	24 SF	0.64 CF
Glass	41 SF	1.10 CF
Glass	41 SF	1.10 CF
Glass	41 SF	1.10 CF
Glass	41 SF	1.10 CF
Glass	41 SF	1.10 CF
Glass	41 SF	1.10 CF
Glass	24 SF	0.64 CF
Glass	24 SF	0.64 CF

Material takeoff schedule

Objectives

After completing this lesson, you will be able to:

- Describe rooms.

- Describe room schedules.

- Add room tags.

- Modify room area and volume.

- Describe material takeoffs.

- State the recommended practices for creating rooms and room schedules.

- Create rooms and a room schedule.

About Rooms

You add rooms to specify information about user-defined or automatically calculated spaces in a building design. You create rooms using the Room tool on the Room & Area panel of the Home tab. In addition, you can create new rooms or place unallocated rooms using a room schedule.

Definition of Rooms

Rooms are building elements just like walls, doors, and windows. You associate a room element with a bound space in a plan or a reflected ceiling plan view. The space in a room is bounded when the space consists of either three or more walls or three or more separation lines.

Room Bounding Elements

The following elements and their types are specified as bounding elements for room area and volume calculations:

- Curtain, standard, in-place, and face-based walls

- Standard, in-place, and face-based roofs

- Standard, in-place, and face-based floors

- Standard, in-place, and face-based ceilings

- Architectural columns

- Curtain systems

- Room separation lines

Room Bounding Walls

You can specify the walls of a room as bounding or nonbounding by modifying the wall properties. When you specify that a wall is nonbounding, Revit does not use it to calculate the area or volume of the room or any adjacent rooms. For example, you may want to define toilet partitions as nonbounding because they are not usually included in room calculations.

You change a wall to a bounding wall for a room by selecting the Room Bounding Instance parameter check box for the wall. Similarly, you can clear the check box to make a wall nonbounding for a room.

Room Separation Lines

Room separation lines are lines that define the area of rooms in plan, 3D, and camera views. The defined area has all the functionality associated with rooms. For example, you can apply room color or create room schedules with an area designated by separation lines. To define rooms with separation lines, you select Room Separation Line from the Room drop-down on the Room & Area panel of the Home tab.

Example of Rooms

The following illustrations show rooms highlighted in the plan and section views and room tags in a plan view.

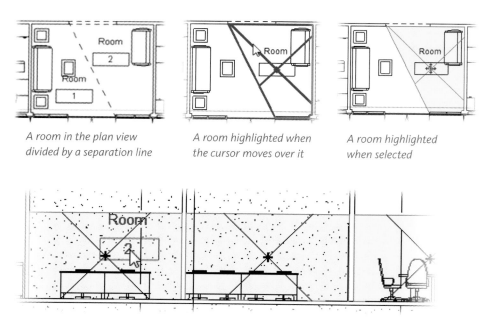

A room in the plan view divided by a separation line

A room highlighted when the cursor moves over it

A room highlighted when selected

Rooms visible after tags are placed in a section view

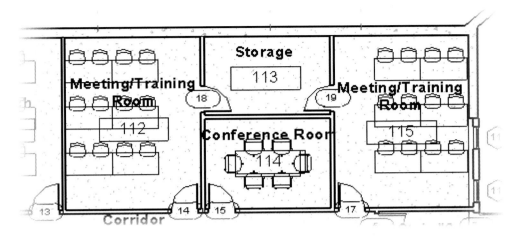

Room tags in a plan view

About Room Schedules

As an aid to the initial design phase, you can add rooms to a schedule before you define walls or place rooms in a plan view. You can then place the predefined rooms from the room schedule at a later stage in the project.

Definition of Room Schedules

A room schedule is a type of component schedule. It is a tabular view that represents the data specific to various room elements used in a building model. You extract building model data from the properties of room elements.

Room schedules and rooms are associated; the fields in a room schedule are properties of the rooms. If you modify field values in a schedule, the corresponding property values are updated for the room.

Room Tags

Room tags are view-specific components that are associated with room elements. You can include tags while placing rooms. You use the Tag Room tool on the Room & Area panel of the Home tab to place tags in existing rooms. You can place and display room tags in floor plan, reflected ceiling plan, and section views. A standard room tag comprises a room name and a number label. You can also display area, volume, and other parameters in a room tag.

The following illustration shows rooms with room tags.

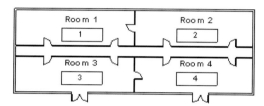

By default, room tags orient horizontally or vertically. You can set the orientation of room tags to Model. This allows you to rotate tags or align them to nonorthogonal walls. You can use the Tag All Not Tagged tool to place room tags in all rooms in a view at once.

The following illustration shows rooms with tags aligned to nonorthogonal walls.

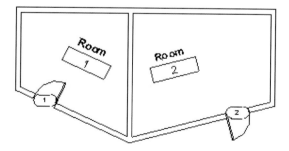

Rooms and Room Tags

A room element can exist without an associated room tag. However, a room tag element must have an associated room. There is a one-to-one relationship between room tags and rooms. If a room tag already exists in a specific area of a view, any new tag in that area is associated with the same room. If you delete a room tag, the associated room is not deleted from the project. The data associated with the room, such as the room area or color continues to exist because the room is still in the project.

Room Schedules and Room Tags

If you delete a room from a room schedule, the corresponding room tag is also deleted. However, when you delete a room tag in a view, the room persists.

When you update values in a room schedule, the corresponding label values of associated room tags are also updated. For example, when you change the room name in a schedule, the room tag name label displays the modified room name.

However, when you move a room element that has been tagged from one bounded space to another, Revit issues the following warning with the option to move the room tag with the room.

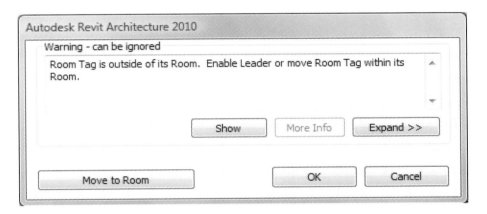

Creating Rooms

You create rooms by creating a new row in a room schedule or by placing a room element in a space with a specific boundary. When you create a new row in a room schedule, the room is created without an associated room tag. You need to place a room tag in a bounded space to populate the fields for the area, perimeter, and level in the room schedule. If the space defined as a room is bounded by walls, the room area is calculated from the inside face of the walls.

The following illustrations show reference lines of a room that identify the rough extent and interior area of a room that is used for area calculations.

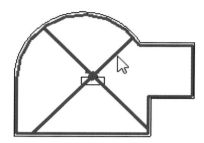

Reference lines

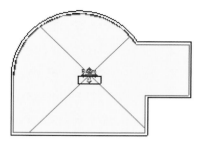

Room area selected

Example of Room Schedules

The following illustration shows a room schedule with room properties.

Room Schedule			
Area	Level	Name	Department
721 SF	Level 1	Room	
1246 SF	Level 1	Room	
1065 SF	Level 1	Room	
902 SF	Level 1	Room	

Adding Room Tags

When you add room tags, you can change their orientation and specify whether they include leader lines.

The following illustration shows a vertical room tag.

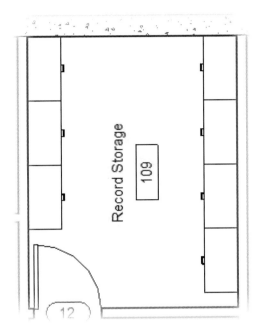

The following illustration shows a room tag with a leader line.

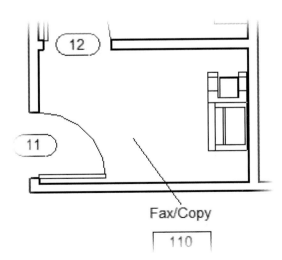

Procedure: Adding Room Tags

The following steps describe how to add a room tag.

1   Open the view in which you want to place the tag.

2   Click Home tab > Room & Area panel > Tag drop-down > Tag Room.
     Note: Untagged rooms become visible if already placed in a view.

3   On the Options Bar:
     • Select the Leader check box to include a leader line with the room tag, if required.
     • Set the orientation to Horizontal, Vertical, or Model.

4   Click in an enclosed area of the view to place the room tag.

5   Press SPACEBAR to orient the tag.

Modifying Room Area and Volume

The area of rooms is calculated by default in Revit. You enable the calculation of room volume by using the Area and Volumes radio button in the Area and Volume Computations dialog box. The dialog box can be accessed by selecting Area and Volume Computations from the Room & Area panel drop-down of the Home tab.

You can modify the area and volume of a room by modifying the room boundary locations and changing the room bounding properties of surrounding walls or columns. You can also specify the upper limit and offset value for a room.

Procedure: Modifying Room Area and Volume

The following steps describe how to modify room area and volume.

1   Open a plan, elevation, or section view of the room you wish to change.

2   Move a room bounding wall or room separation line. This updates the area values of the associated room or rooms.

3   Select a room component.

4   Open the Instance Properties dialog box for the room.

5   In the Instance Properties dialog box, under Constraints Parameters, change the Upper Limit, Upper Limit Offset, or Base Offset values for the room.

The volume value updates if Compute Room Volumes is selected in the Room and Area Settings dialog box.

Note: To make room area or volume values visible, you need to load Room Tags with labels that display the area or volume values.

About Material Takeoffs

Material takeoffs are used to simplify the tracking of material quantities in cost estimates. You can also use material takeoffs to calculate detailed material quantities based on the properties of materials used in different building elements. You can use information about material quantities in sustainable design analysis.

Definition of Material Takeoffs

A material takeoff is a type of a component schedule. It presents a detailed list of material quantities in a table.

All tools and methods that are used for component schedules apply to material takeoffs. You can export a material takeoff to an external database such as a spreadsheet application.

Material Takeoff and Building Elements

A material takeoff updates automatically when you change the material properties of building elements. You can modify building elements after extracting material quantity data from them.

Example of Material Takeoff

The following illustration shows a material takeoff with material name and cost of walls.

Wall Material Takeoff		
Family and Type	Material: Name	Material: Cost $
Basic Wall: Exterior	Wood - Stud Layer	250.00
Basic Wall: Exterior	Wood - Sheathing - plywood	180.00
Basic Wall: Exterior	Finishes - Exterior - Siding / Clapboard	200.00
Basic Wall: Exterior	Air Barrier - Air Infiltration Barrier	250.00
Basic Wall: Exterior	Vapor / Moisture Barriers - Damp-proofing	200.00
Basic Wall: Exterior	Finishes - Interior - Gypsum Wall Board	150.00
Basic Wall: Exterior	Wood - Stud Layer	250.00
Basic Wall: Exterior	Wood - Sheathing - plywood	180.00
Basic Wall: Exterior	Finishes - Exterior - Siding / Clapboard	200.00
Basic Wall: Exterior	Air Barrier - Air Infiltration Barrier	250.00
Basic Wall: Exterior	Vapor / Moisture Barriers - Damp-proofing	200.00
Basic Wall: Exterior	Finishes - Interior - Gypsum Wall Board	150.00

Guidelines for Creating Rooms and Room Schedules

The following recommended practices help you save time and prevent errors while creating rooms and room schedules.

Guidelines

- You can create room schedules based on common room types used by your company and add these schedules to project templates. This saves time while defining rooms and room types because your team members can select room names or designations from a predefined list.

- You can create separate plan views for walls and rooms so that you can place appropriate annotations easily.

- You can place rooms without room tags and then place tags at the start of the annotation phase of the project. This provides better workflow during the design development phase without any loss of information.

- Room objects hold energy requirement and consumption information when processed in Revit MEP, or if your project is submitted to sustainable design analysis. Proper management of rooms will enable you to track and report information that is not readily available any other way.

Exercise | Create a Room and Room Schedule

In this exercise, you create rooms and a room schedule and add room tags in a building model. You also create a material takeoff schedule.

You need to create rooms and schedules for the rooms in a building model. You also want to add room tags in the plan and section views. In addition, you want to create a material takeoff schedule.

You do the following:

- Create rooms and a room schedule.

- Add tags to rooms on the ground floor.

- Add tags to rooms on the main floor.

- Create a material takeoff schedule.

Room Schedule					Ground Floor Door Material Takeoff			
Number	Name	Level	Area	Comments	Material: Name	Material: Area	Material: Volume	Material: Mark
101	Lobby	Ground Floor	241 SF	Public Entrance	Glass	4 SF	0.04 CF	G
102	Corridor	Ground Floor	410 SF		Door - Frame	23 SF	0.70 CF	DF
103	Office	Ground Floor	143 SF		Door - Panel	42 SF	3.19 CF	DP
104	Office	Ground Floor	143 SF		Glass	4 SF	0.04 CF	G
105	Office	Ground Floor	143 SF		Door - Frame	23 SF	0.70 CF	DF
106	Large Office	Ground Floor	183 SF		Door - Panel	42 SF	3.19 CF	DP
107	Men's Toilet	Ground Floor	108 SF		Glass	4 SF	0.04 CF	G
201	Sleeping Qu	Main Floor	230 SF		Door - Frame	23 SF	0.73 CF	DF
202	Sleeping Qu	Main Floor	235 SF		Door - Panel	44 SF	3.36 CF	DP
203	Sleeping Qu	Main Floor	229 SF		Glass	4 SF	0.04 CF	G
204	Sleeping Qu	Main Floor	229 SF		Door - Frame	23 SF	0.73 CF	DF

The completed exercise

Completing the Exercise: *To complete the exercise, follow the steps in this book or in the onscreen exercise. In the onscreen list of chapters and exercises, click Chapter 10: Construction Documentation. Click Exercise: Create a Room and Room Schedule.*

Create Rooms and a Room Schedule

1. Open *i_rac_essentials_room_schedules.rvt* or *m_rac_essentials_room_schedules.rvt*. The file opens in the Ground Floor plan view.
   Note: The illustrations for the metric dataset are slightly different from those shown here.

2. To place rooms in the project so that you can extract information about them, you first create a room schedule that will be used as a list when placing rooms. For this, click View tab > Create panel > Schedules drop-down > Schedule/ Quantities.

3. In the New Schedule dialog box:
   - Select Rooms from the Category list.
   - Notice that Schedule Building Components is selected by default.
   - Click OK.

4. To add Number in the schedule table, in the Schedule Properties dialog box, Fields tab:
   - Under Available Fields, click Number.
   - Click Add.

   Similarly, add the fields Name, Level, Area, and Comments.

5. In the Schedule Properties dialog box, Sorting/Grouping tab, select Number from the Sort By list.

6. On the Formatting tab:
   - Select Area from the Fields list. The Heading field updates to display Area.
   - Select Right from the Alignment list.
   - Select the Calculate Totals check box.

7   Click OK to close the Schedule Properties dialog box. The room schedule is displayed in
the view window. Notice that the schedule is empty because no rooms have been placed in
the model.

In the following steps, you will create room definitions for use when you are adding rooms.

8   On the Schedule panel, click Rows: New to add a new row in the room schedule.

9   In the view window:
   • For Number, enter **101**.
   • For Name, enter **Lobby**.

10   In the view window:
   • Add five more rows. The numbers will increment automatically.
   • Edit the names as shown.
     Tip: As you add room names, they become available on a list. Use the list to
     repeatedly enter the Office room names. Also notice that the rooms show Not Placed
     at this time.

| Room Schedule | | |
Number	Name	Level
101	Lobby	Not Placed
102	Corridor	Not Placed
103	Office	Not Placed
104	Office	Not Placed
105	Office	Not Placed
106	Large Office	Not Placed

Add Tags to Rooms on the Ground Floor

1   Return to the Ground Floor view.

2 In the view window, zoom in to the entrance of the administration building.

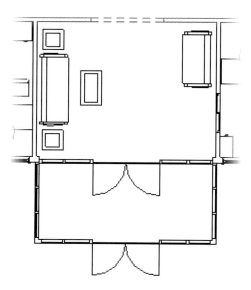

3 Click Home tab > Room & Area panel > Room drop-down > Room.

4 On the Options Bar, select 101 Lobby from the Room list.

5 In the view window:
- Position the cursor on the lobby area of the administration building.
- Click to place the room and room tag.

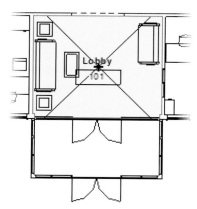

6   Place the other rooms, as shown.

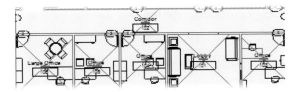

7   Exit the Room tool.

8   In the view window, select the Lobby room component. Do not select the room tag.

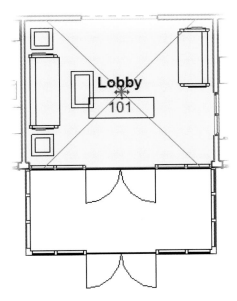

9   Open the Instance Properties dialog box.

10   In the Instance Properties dialog box:
- Under Instance Parameters, Identity Data, Comments, enter **Public Entrance**.
- Click OK.

11 Open the Room Schedule view. Notice that the Comments column for Lobby is updated.

Room Schedule			
Name	Level	Area	Comments
Lobby	Ground Floor	241 SF	Public Entrance
Corridor	Ground Floor	410 SF	
Office	Ground Floor	143 SF	
Office	Ground Floor	143 SF	
Office	Ground Floor	143 SF	
Large Office	Ground Floor	183 SF	

12 Return to the Ground Floor View.

13 Place a new room for the toilet room next to the stairs. The room is numbered automatically and added to the schedule.

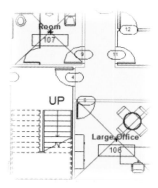

14 Exit the Room tool.

15 In the view window:

- Select the room tag in the new room you just placed.
- Click the name and enter **Men's Toilet**.

- Press ENTER.

Add Tags to Rooms on the Main Floor

1   Open the Main Floor plan view to place rooms.

2   In the view window, create a room adjacent to the toilet room with the number **201** and name **Sleeping Quarters**.

3   Create another room on the right of room 201 and name it **Sleeping Quarters**. Notice Revit increments the room number.

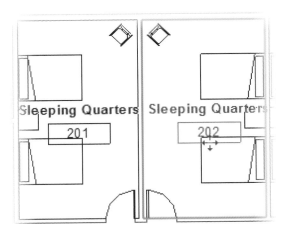

4   To copy rooms and tags to take advantage of their ability to auto-size and auto-number, in the view window, select the component and tag for room 202.

5   Click Multi-Select tab > Modify panel > Copy.

6   On the Options Bar, ensure that the Copy and Multiple check boxes are selected.

7   In the view window:
    • Click anywhere in room 201.
    • Move the cursor to the right and click room 202. A new room with the room tag 203 is created.

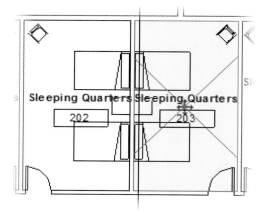

8   Click in room 203 to place another room to its right.

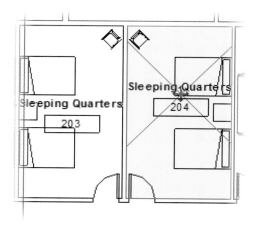

9   Exit the Copy tool.

10   To check the room schedule against the model, open the Room Schedule view.

11   In the room schedule, for Number 101, under Name, select Lobby.

Room Schedule				
Number	Name	Level	Area	
101	Lobby	Ground Floor	241 SF	Pub
102	Corridor	Ground Floor	410 SF	
103	Office	Ground Floor	143 SF	
104	Office	Ground Floor	143 SF	
105	Office	Ground Floor	143 SF	
106	Large Office	Ground Floor	183 SF	
107	Men's Toilet	Ground Floor	108 SF	
201	Sleeping Qu	Main Floor	230 SF	
202	Sleeping Qu	Main Floor	235 SF	
203	Sleeping Qu	Main Floor	229 SF	
204	Sleeping Qu	Main Floor	229 SF	

12   On the Schedule panel, click Highlight in Model.
     Notice that the Lobby room is highlighted in the view window.

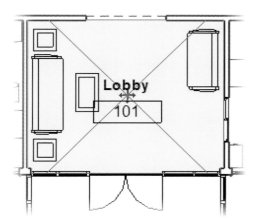

13   In the Show Element(s) In View dialog box, click Close.

14   To begin adding tags to rooms in other views, open the Ground Floor ceiling plan view.

15   Click Home tab > Room & Area panel > Tag drop-down > Tag Room. All the rooms
     become visible.

16   In the view window, click each room to place a tag. The tags display the room name and number.

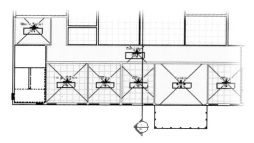

17   Open the Section 1 view.

18   Click Annotate tab > Tag panel > Tag All.

19   In the Tag All Not Tagged dialog box:
      • Under Category, select Room Tags.
      • Click OK.

20   Click Yes in the Revit notification to display the room tags.

Create a Material Takeoff Schedule

1   To create a material takeoff for establishing material quantities for certain elements in the model, click View tab > Create panel > Schedules drop-down > Material Takeoff.

2   In the New Material Takeoff dialog box:
      • Select Doors from the Category list.
      • For Name, enter **Ground Floor Door Material Takeoff**.
      • Click OK.

3   In the Material Takeoff Properties dialog box, Fields tab:

- Add the following fields to the schedule.

Scheduled fields (in order):

Material: Name
Material: Area
Material: Volume
Material: Mark

- Click OK.
  Notice that the Ground Floor Door Material Takeoff schedule is displayed in the view window and added to the Project Browser.

4   Specify the Material: Mark column values of the doors as follows:

- Glass: **G**.
- Door - Frame: **DF**.
- Door - Panel: **DP**.
  Note: You only need to enter the value in the required field for the first row of that type. When you press ENTER, all the fields of that type update.

Ground Floor Door Material Takeoff

erial: Name	Material: Area	Material: Volume	Material: Mark
s	4 SF	0.04 CF	G
- Frame	23 SF	0.70 CF	DF
- Panel	42 SF	3.19 CF	DP
s	4 SF	0.04 CF	G
- Frame	23 SF	0.70 CF	DF
- Panel	42 SF	3.19 CF	DP
s	4 SF	0.04 CF	G
- Frame	23 SF	0.73 CF	DF
- Panel	44 SF	3.36 CF	DP

5   On the application menu, click Export > Reports > Schedule to export the materials takeoff schedule.

6   In the Export Schedule dialog box:

- In the Save In field, navigate to the desktop.
- Click Save.

7   In the Export Schedule dialog box:

- Under Output Options, select comma (,) from the Field Delimiter list.
- Click OK.

A delimited text file is created in the specified folder where you saved the schedule. You can open this file in Notepad or Microsoft Excel.

8   Close the file without saving changes.

Lesson 31 | Creating Legends and Keynotes

This lesson describes how to create legends and keynotes and add them to sheets. You begin the lesson by learning about legends and the steps to control legend visibility. Then, you learn about keynoting, steps to link keynote files and add keynotes, and some recommended practices for creating legends and adding keynotes. The lesson concludes with an exercise on creating legends and keynotes.

You use legends to easily identify the components, annotations, and symbols used in a project and accurately interpret a building design. You use keynotes to streamline the process of manually annotating the construction documents in a project.

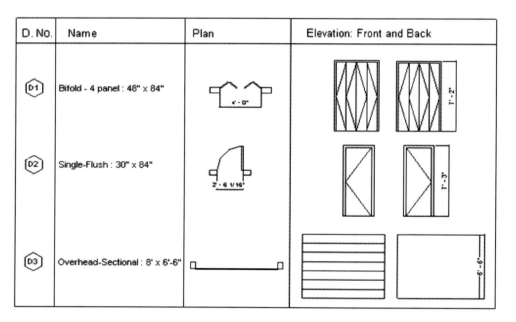

Legend displaying different types of doors and door symbols

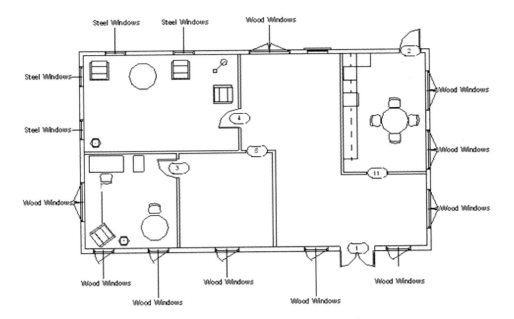

Plan view with text window keynotes

Objectives

After completing this lesson, you will be able to:

- Describe legends.

- Control legend visibility.

- Describe keynoting.

- Link keynote files and add keynotes.

- State the recommended practices for creating legends and adding keynotes.

- Create legends and keynotes.

About Legends

You use legends as references to interpret the graphic displays of building components or annotations.

Definition of Legends

A legend is a view that contains tabular representations of building components or annotations along with information related to the symbols. Any element that can be placed in drafting views, such as detail lines, text, dimensions, tags, symbols, and filled regions, can be placed in a legend.

Adding legends to drawing sheets helps explain the abstract and condensed information that appears on views such as plans or sections in the documentation of a project. You can use the same legend on multiple drawing sheets.

 Note: *A drawing sheet is a view to which you add model views.*

Types of Legends

There are various types of legends that you can create and use.

The following table describes some of the commonly used legends.

Type	Description
Annotation Symbol	Displays symbols for 2D components such as section heads, level heads, spot elevations, and tags. Each symbol has a related text that describes the symbol.
Model Symbol	Displays symbols for 3D components such as electrical fixtures, plumbing fixtures, mechanical equipment, site objects, doors, windows, and ceiling types. Each symbol has related text that describes the symbol.

Type	Description
Line Styles	Displays a view or table of selected line styles along with related text that describes the line styles. Fire rating lines, property lines, setback lines, electric wiring, plumbing, utilities, and center lines are some examples of line styles displayed on legends.
Material	Displays a sample of a cut or surface pattern along with related text that describes the material associated with that pattern.
Phasing	Displays sections of walls shown with selected graphic overrides along with related text.

Legend Components

The various building component symbols that you can add to a legend view are called legend components. Examples of legend components are types of walls, ceilings, doors, floors, and furniture. You can add these components to a legend view by using the Legend Component tool.

Legend Tools

You use annotation tools to add information to the legend components in a legend view. Text and Dimension are two commonly used annotation tools. Using the Text tool, you can specify the name or any other information for a legend component. Using the Dimension tool, you can add dimensions to a legend component to specify its size and the distance between two points within the component.

You cannot add dimensions to system families or to host components such as walls, ceilings, and floors in legends.

Example of Legends

The following illustrations show a casework legend and a door legend added to a drawing sheet.

Casework Legend			
C. No.	Name	Plan	Elevations
C1	Base Cabinet-Corner Unit-Angled		
C2	Base Cabinet-Double Door & 2 Drawer		
C3	Base Cabinet-Single Door & Drawer		
C4	Counter Top		
C5	Counter Top-L Shaped 2		
C6	Counter Top-L Shaped w Sink Hole		

Casework legend

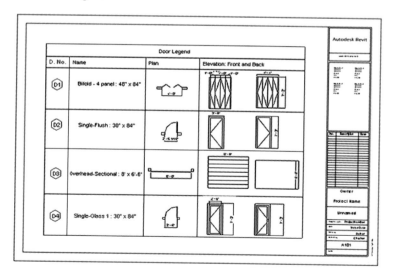

Door legend

Controlling Legend Visibility

You can control the visibility of subcategories of legend components to highlight specific information that may be required in a legend view.

You create a legend view for a specific purpose by controlling the visibility and appearance of the legend components in the view. You control visibility by toggling on or off the visibility of the desired categories of the component in the Visibility/Graphic Overrides dialog box.

You can also modify line weights, line colors, line patterns, and materials of the component symbols by using the Object Styles option in the Visibility/Graphic Overrides dialog box. Changes made using the Object Styles option affect all views.

Example of Controlling Legend Visibility

The following illustration shows the appearance of legend components controlled in a legend view. Notice the change in the appearance of the window components when you turn off the visibility for all the window subcategories except Glass.

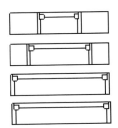

Before turning off visibility of subcategories

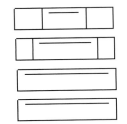

After turning off visibility of subcategories

Procedure: Controlling Legend Visibility

The following steps describe how to control the visibility of legend component subcategories.

1   Open the legend view that you need to modify.

2   Open the Visibility/Graphic Overrides dialog box.

3   In the Visibility/Graphic Overrides dialog box, Model Categories tab, under Visibility, expand the legend component category for which you want to control visibility.
     Tip: Click Expand All to expand all the categories simultaneously.

4   Clear the check boxes corresponding to the subcategories under a category for which you want to turn off visibility.
Tip: To turn off the visibility of all the subcategories under a category, clear the check box corresponding to that category.

About Keynoting

A keynote helps provide extra information or special instructions about a building component. Keynoting helps you save time spent on documenting and coordinating the components used in a building project.

Definition of Keynoting

Keynoting is a method of annotating different types of elements, materials, and user-defined components used in a building project. You add keynotes to model views of a building design. Keynotes are standardized notes that are controlled through an external file.

Types of Keynotes

The following table explains the three types of keynotes.

Type	Description
Element	Annotates building elements. When you add an Element keynote to a model view, it is attached to a building element. The keynote links to an external file that holds element category information coded according to specified industry standards or custom specifications.
Material	Annotates building materials. When you add a Material keynote to a model view, it is attached to a building material. You specify the material designation, which then appears on all keynotes attached to the same material in other components.
User	Annotates user-defined components. When you add a User keynote to a model view, it is attached to the component to which you assign it.

Keynote Legends

You generate a keynote legend to list and explain the keynotes that you add to the plan view of a building. Using a keynote legend, you can easily locate all the instances of a particular keynote in a project. The keynotes in a keynote legend need to be from the same keynote database. This ensures that when you modify a keynote in a project, all other instances of the keynote are updated throughout the project.

Note: *When you add or delete keynotes, you need to manually add or delete the keynote references in the keynote legend or generate a new legend.*

Example of Keynoting

The following illustrations show various instances of keynotes used in a project.

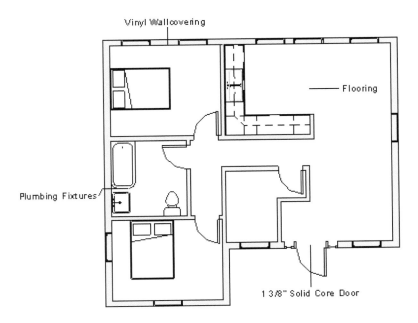

Text keynotes attached to building elements

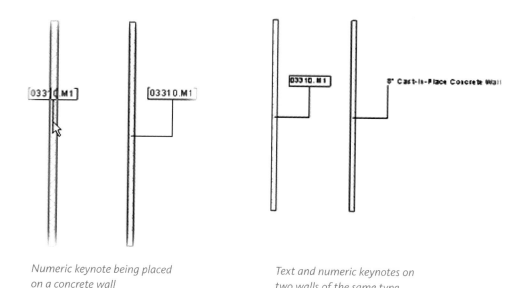

Numeric keynote being placed on a concrete wall

Text and numeric keynotes on two walls of the same type

Linking Keynote Files and Adding Keynotes

Before you can add keynotes to a model view, you need to store the keynoting data in a keynote source file. Using the keynote tools, you link the keynote source file to a project file and then add keynotes to model views. The keynotes that you add are numbered according to one of two keynote numbering methods.

Keynote Source Files

A keynote source file, called a keynote table, stores keynoting data in an external tab delimited text file. You modify the files using a text editor and not from within the software. In Revit, keynote source files are provided in the Imperial or Metric Library folders. You can use these files or create your own.

Note: *A tab delimited text file is a file with text format that uses tab characters as separators between fields.*

You link a keynote table to a project using the Keynoting Settings dialog box. In this dialog box, you specify the path for the keynote table and select the path type. You also specify the required keynote numbering method. You access the dialog box using Keynoting Settings on the Tag panel drop-down of the Annotate tab.

The following illustration shows a keynote source file.

```
keynote_library - Notepad

File   Edit   Format   View   Help

1           ELEMENTS
101         ELEVATOR SHAFT WALL      1
102         ELEVATOR CAB      1
103         FLOOR SYSTEM      1
104         CONCRETE PIT WALL        1
105         WATERPROOF MEMBRANE      1
106         GRAVEL BED        1
107         DRAINAGE PIPE     1
2           MATERIALS
201         COMPACTED CRUSHED STONE 2
202         WASHED DRAINAGE ROCK    2
203         CONCRETE SLAB     2
204         GWB TYPEX Layer 2 of 2   2
205         GWB TYPEX Layer 1 of 2   2
```

Keynote Numbering Methods

You can number keynotes by keynote or by sheet. Numbering by keynote lists keynotes sequentially based on the order in which they are added to a project. Numbering by sheet lists keynotes sequentially based on the order in which they are added to a sheet.

Note: *The attribute to be displayed inside a sheet keynote is determined when you place the view on a sheet, not at the time of insertion.*

Procedure: Adding Keynotes

The following steps describe how to add keynotes to a model view of a building design.

1   Click Annotate tab > Tag panel > Keynote drop-down > Element, Material, or User.

2   Select the appropriate option from the Type Selector drop-down to set the display of the keynote number or the text value.

3   On the Options Bar, set the placement options, such as Leader and Orientation.
Note: You can define the orientation by selecting an option from the drop-down to the left of Loaded Tags on the Options Bar.

4   Select the keynote value from the keynote table, if necessary.

5   In the view window, place the keynote tag.

Guidelines for Creating Legends and Keynotes

You use legends and keynotes to easily understand information related to a building model. The following recommended practices help you in creating legends and keynotes.

Guidelines

- You can use legends for any combination of symbols and text that appear on more than one page of a document set, or on the same page in a document for many projects. For example, boilerplate texts such as abbreviation lists are more efficient when placed on sheets as legends rather than text objects. Using legends saves time and reduces error because all legend instances are automatically updated when you edit a legend.

- If your organization's standard for scheduling windows and doors includes graphic representations, you should place a schedule close to an appropriately designed legend on a sheet. A legend is simpler and easier to edit than creating several elevation views of individual doors or windows and placing them on the sheet next to the schedule.

- The keynote system in the standard keynote table text file supplied with Revit is elaborate and appropriate for large projects. If you use a simpler system, create your own keynote table text file and store it on a shared network drive. The work necessary to make your own keynote reference saves time in project documentation.

- If you use text keynotes, there is no need for a keynote legend. However, if you use numbered keynotes, be sure to create a keynote legend and place it on sheets where appropriate. This makes your documents easy to read and understand.

Exercise | Create Legends and Keynotes

In this exercise, you create a legend by opening a legend view and adding legend components, text, and dimensions to the legend view. You also link a keynote table, add keynotes to a plan view, and add a keynote legend to a sheet.

You are working on a building project that has various window components. Now, you want to create a legend view for the windows used in the design.

To provide information on the elements, materials, and other components used in the building design, you add element, material, and user-defined keynotes to a plan view. Then, you create a legend for the keynotes and add the plan view and the keynote legend to a sheet.

You do the following:

- Open a window legend view and add legend components.

- Add text to the legend view.

- Add dimensions to the legend components.

- Link and load keynote files.

- Add keynotes to a plan view.

- Add a keynote and window legend to a sheet.

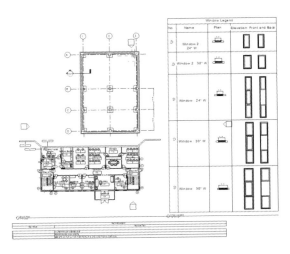

The completed exercise

Open a Window Legend View and Add Legend Components

1   Open *i_rac_essentials_legends.rvt* or *m_rac_essentials_legends.rvt*. The file opens in the Window Legend view. Notice that a six-row table is displayed in the view that was created using the Line tool. You can adjust the lines in the table as necessary. A text title has also been added to the table.
    Note: The illustrations for the metric dataset will be slightly different from those shown here.

2   To fill the window legend that will illustrate windows in the plan and elevation views along with their tag designations, click Annotate tab > Detail panel > Component drop-down > Legend Component.

3   On the Options Bar:
    - Select Windows : Window 2 : 24" W (Windows : M_Window 2 : 610 mm W) from the Family list.
    - Ensure that Floor Plan is selected in the View list.
    - For Host Length, enter **4' 0"** (**1200.0** mm) to set a length for the wall that hosts the window.
    Note: The length of the host should be a little more than the component length so that part of the host is visible with the component.

4   In the view window, click the third cell in the second row of the table to add the plan window symbol.

5   On the Options Bar, select Elevation : Front from the View list.

6   In the view window, click the fourth cell in the second row of the table to add the window symbol.

7   On the Options Bar, select Elevation : Back from the View list.

8   In the view window, place the back elevation to the right of the window symbol you have just added.

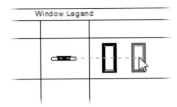

9   Add window symbols in the third, fourth, fifth, and sixth rows of the table, using the following
    family types, respectively.

    - Windows : Window 2 : 30" W (Windows : M_Window 2 : 762 mm W)
    - Windows : Window : 24" W (Windows : m_Window : 610 mm W)
    - Windows : Window : 30" W (Windows : m_Window : 762 mm W)
    - Windows : Window : 36" W (Windows : m_Window : 914 mm W)

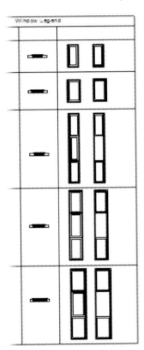

Note: As you place components, you can align them with other components using the
alignment lines.

10 Finish placing window legend components.

Add Text to the Legend View

1. To add text as legend headers, activate the Text tool.

2. Verify that Text : 1/4" Arial (Text : 6 mm Arial) is selected from the Type Selector drop-down.

3. Click Place Text tab > Alignment panel > Center.

4. Click Place Text tab > Leader panel > No Leader.

5. In the view window:
   - Zoom in to the first cell of the first row of the table.
   - Click to place a text box. The exact location of the text box is not critical.
   - In the text box, enter **No**.

6. Exit the Text tool.

7. Select the text object you just placed to display the drag symbol on the left and the rotate symbol on the right of the inserted text.

8. Use the drag symbol or the rotate symbol to position the text in the center of the first cell in the first row of the table.

9. In the second, third, and fourth cells of the first row of the table, place text blocks named **Name**, **Plan**, and **Elevation**: **Front** and **Back** and position the text in the center of the cells, as shown.

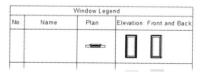

Note: Text snaps to other text for easy alignment.

10 Exit the Text tool.

11 To place Window tag symbols and modify their numerical display, click Annotate tab > Detail panel > Symbol.

12 Select Window Tag : Window Tag (M_Window Tag : M_Window Tag) from the Type Selector drop-down.

13 In the view window, place an instance of the window tag.

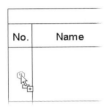

14 Zoom in to the symbol. Notice that it shows the default label text from the Window Tag family, which is not appropriate. You need to cover it with text.

15 Activate the Text tool.

16 Select Text : 3/32" Arial (Text : 2.5 mm Arial) from the Type Selector drop-down.

17 On the Place Text tab, Alignment panel, ensure that Center is selected.

18 In the view window:
   • Click the symbol you just placed.
   • In the text box, enter **17**.
     The text values you add here and in the following steps are the Type Mark values that appear in Window Tags, in model views.

19 Exit the Text tool.

20 In the view window, position the text symbol so that it hides the default tag text.

21   Zoom out of the text symbol. You now need to copy the symbol and text to other rows.

22   Clear the selection.

23   In the view window, CTRL+select the window tag symbol and the text.

24   Activate the Copy tool.

25   On the Options Bar, select the Multiple check box.

26   In the view window, click the left endpoint of the third horizontal line of the table to establish a start point.

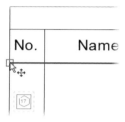

27   Move the cursor down and click to place copies of the symbol and text in all the rows.

28 Exit the Copy tool.

29 In the view window, edit the text of the copied symbols to **18**, **10**, **11**, and **12**, respectively.
Note: TAB+select will let you cycle to find the text objects easily because they are placed on top of the tag symbols.

30 To identify the windows by name, activate the Text tool.

31 Select Text : 1/4" Arial (Text : 6 mm Arial) from the Type Selector drop-down.

32 On the Alignment panel, ensure that Center is selected.

33 In the Name column, enter the name of each type of window you inserted in the table. The exact position of the text is not critical.

Note: You can drag the sides of the text box to adjust text wrapping. You can also press ENTER to create a line break while adding text.

Add Dimensions to the Legend Components

1 To begin adding dimensions in the drawing, click Annotate tab > Dimension panel > Aligned.

2 On the Options Bar, ensure that Individual References is selected from the Pick list.

3 To add a dimension to the plan component, in the view window:
   • Zoom in to the first window legend component in the third column of the table.
   • Click a point of the component on the wall opening to specify the first reference point for dimensioning.

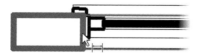

4 Click to place the second reference point.

5 Click at a point above the component symbol so that the dimensioning is clearly visible.

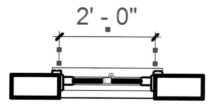

6 Add dimensions to the rest of the plan legend components in the table. Press ESC two times to exit the Dimension tool.

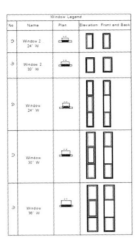

Link and Load Keynote Files

1   To place keynotes in a plan view, open the Ground Floor view.

2   Click Annotate tab > Tag panel drop-down > Keynoting Settings.

3   In the Keynoting Settings dialog box, under Keynote Table, For Full Path, click Browse.

4   In the Browse for Keynote File dialog box:
    • Navigate to the folder where you installed the datasets.
    • Select the *keynote_library.txt* file.
    • Click Open.

5   In the Keynoting Settings dialog box:
    • Under Path Type, ensure that Absolute is selected.
    • Under Numbering Method, select By Sheet.
    • Click OK.

Add Keynotes to a Plan View

1   Zoom in to the left side of the plan view.

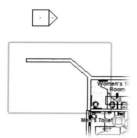

2   Click Annotate tab > Tag panel > Keynote drop-down > Element.

3   Verify that Keynote Tag : Keynote Number - Boxed - Large (M_Keynote Tag : Keynote Number - Boxed) is selected from the Type Selector drop-down.

4   On the Options Bar, verify that Horizontal is selected in the Orientation list.

5   In the view window:
   • Click the outer edge of the horizontal wall on top.
   • Click outside the wall to specify the height of the keynote.

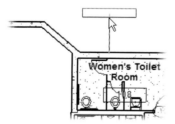

   • Click again outside the wall to place the element keynote tag.

6   In the Keynotes dialog box:
   • Under Key Value, expand 1.
   • Select 105.
   • Click OK.

7   Exit the Element Keynote tool.

8   To place a keynote of another type, click Keynote drop-down > Material.

9   Place the Material keynote tag on the floor of the Women's Toilet room.

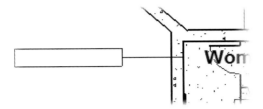

10 In the Keynotes dialog box:
- Under Key Value, expand 2.
- Select 210.
- Click OK.

11 Exit the Material Keynote tool.

12 To place the third type of keynote, click Keynote drop-down > User.

13 In the view window, place the keynote tag on the left horizontal wall.

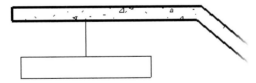

14 In the Keynotes dialog box:
- Under Key Value, expand 3.
- Select 302.
- Click OK.

Add a Keynote and Window Legend to a Sheet

1   To fill in the keynote numbers, you need to place the plan view on a sheet. Click View tab > Sheet Composition panel > New Sheet to add a new sheet.

2   In the Select a Titleblock dialog box:

- Ensure that Titleblock E1 30 x 42 Horizontal : E1 30x42 Horizontal (A0 metric) is selected.
- Click OK.
  A new sheet is added in the Project Browser, under Sheets (All). The sheet is displayed in the view window.

3   From the Project Browser, drag the Ground Floor view to the view window.

4   In the view window, click to place this plan view on the sheet.

5   Zoom in to the area you worked in. The keynote numbers are displayed in the keynote tag boxes.

6   To create a keynote legend for displaying the full values of the keynotes, click View tab > Create panel > Legends drop-down > Keynote Legend.

7   In the New Keynote Legend dialog box, click OK.

8   In the Keynote Legend Properties dialog box:

- Ensure that the Key Value and Keynote Text fields are displayed under Scheduled Fields.
- Click OK.
  The keynote legend is displayed in the view window and is added to the Project Browser, under Legends.

9   Adjust the cell width in the keynote legend.

10   Open the A101 - Unnamed sheet view.

11   In the view window, zoom to fit the view.

12   From the Project Browser, under Legends, drag Keynote Legend to the view window and place it at any convenient location on the sheet.

13   In the view window, drag the legend columns using the triangular grips, as necessary.

14   From the Project Browser, under Legends, drag Window Legend to the view window and place it at a convenient location on the sheet.

15   Click anywhere in the view window to clear selection.

16   Close the file without saving changes.

Chapter Summary

Now that you know how to create and modify the appearance of schedules, you can create unique schedules for the various parts of your building projects. In this chapter, you learned to:

- Create and modify schedules.
- Create rooms and room schedules.
- Create legends and keynotes.

Chapter 11

Presenting the
Building Model

Lesson 32 | Working with Drawing Sheets

This lesson describes how to create and modify drawing sheets. It also describes how to specify options for printing drawing sheets. You begin the lesson by learning about drawing sheets and the process of previewing and printing sheets and views. Next, you learn some recommended practices for working with drawing sheets. The lesson concludes with an exercise on creating, modifying, and specifying print options for drawing sheets.

Drawing sheets are used as construction documents. You can print drawing sheets to paper or electronic files to deliver document sets to clients, collaborators, or government organizations.

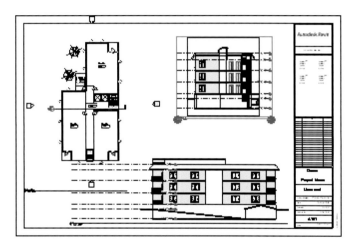

Drawing sheet

Objectives

After completing this lesson, you will be able to:

- Describe drawing sheets.

- Identify the steps in the process of previewing and printing sheets and views.

- State the recommended practices for working with drawing sheets.

- Create, modify, and specify print options for drawing sheets.

About Drawing Sheets

Revit enables you to create drawing sheets to hold model views. You can use these sheets to create document sets that can also be printed. You can place any model view on a drawing sheet, specify the scale of the view, and add annotations to the sheet.

Definition of Drawing Sheets

Drawing sheets are project views on which you place building model views, such as plans, elevations, sections, 3D views, schedules, and legends. Drawing sheet views are listed under Sheets in the Project Browser.

```
⊞ ⸢◻⸣ Views (all)
    ▦ Legends
⊞ ▦ Schedules/Quantities
⊟ ▦ Sheets (all)
    ⊞    A101 - Floor Plans
    ⊞    A102 - Exterior Elevations
    ⊞    A103 - Interior Elevations
    ⊞    A104 - Room Analysis
⊞ ◲ Families
⊞ ◎ Groups
    ◷ Revit Links
```

Drawing sheets in the Project Browser

Views on a drawing sheet are instances of the views in the Project Browser. When you modify a view on a drawing sheet, the changes are automatically applied to the original view.

If a drawing sheet does not exist in the Project Browser, then create a new drawing sheet and drag a view from the Project Browser to the sheet.

Viewport Properties

A viewport is a rectangular boundary around a view placed on a drawing sheet. Each viewport has an identifying title below the rectangular boundary. You can align the view titles when you place the viewport in a drawing sheet by dragging the view titles to an appropriate position. The view titles stay aligned with the viewport when the viewport size changes. You can control the display of viewport titles and create viewport types without titles.

In addition to moving a viewport title, you can set the viewport type properties of the title, such as horizontal line weight, pattern, and color. You can also modify viewport instance properties to change the appearance of a view in a drawing sheet.

The following table describes the viewport instance properties you can modify.

Property	Description
Rotation on Sheet	Rotates a view by 90 degrees either in the clockwise or counterclockwise direction in a drawing sheet.
View Scale	Specifies the scale or appearance of the view in a drawing sheet.
Detail Level	Controls the level of detail in the model view.
Detail Number	Controls the number inside the view title bubble.
Model Graphics Style	Specifies the display style of a view to hidden line, wireframe, shading, or shading with edges.
Underlay	Controls the display of an underlay in a plan view.
View Name	Controls the name of the model view in the Project Browser.
Title on Sheet	Controls the name of the viewport that appears on the viewport title bar.

Activating and Deactivating Viewports

You can activate a viewport placed on a drawing sheet and work on the building model in that view while the drawing sheet is inactive and visible in the background. Activating a viewport is necessary to modify a view directly from the drawing sheet. You can activate a viewport by selecting it and using Activate View on the Sheet Composition panel of the View tab. You can also activate a view from the viewport shortcut menu.

You can activate only one view at a time in a drawing sheet. To deactivate an active view after making the required changes, you can use Deactivate View on the Sheet Composition panel of the View tab. You can also deactivate a view from the viewport shortcut menu.

Example of Drawing Sheets

The following illustrations show drawing sheets.

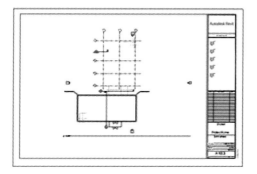

Drawing sheet showing the Ground Floor plan view

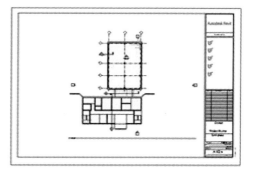

Drawing sheet showing the Reflected Ceiling plan view

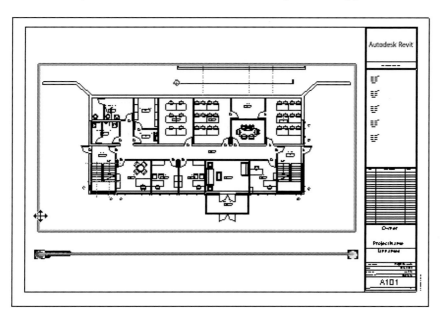

Drawing sheet showing the viewport selected in the plan view

Process of Previewing and Printing Sheets and Views

You can print drawing sheets or model views, if required. For printing a sheet or a view, you need to select a printer and create a print setup. You can preview a drawing sheet or a view before printing it. You can also create a sheet or view list so you can print multiple sheets or views.

Process: Previewing and Printing Sheets and Views

The following illustration shows the process of previewing and printing sheets and views.

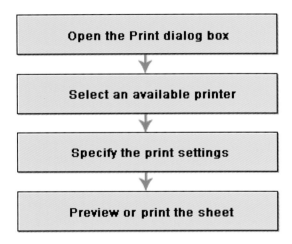

The following steps describe the process of previewing and printing sheets and views.

1   **Open the Print dialog box.**
    To open the Print dialog box, on the application menu, click Print > Print.

2   **Select an available printer.**
    You can select a stand-alone or a networked printer. Specify the properties of the printer, such as paper size, orientation, and print quality. Some electronic output formats are also listed as printers in the printer list.

3   **Specify the print settings.**
    Specify settings, such as zoom and hidden lines, in the Print Setup dialog box. Use these settings to highlight specific aspects of the building model.

4   **Preview or print the sheet.**

Preview the sheet after specifying the print range as the current window or the visible area of the current window. You can also specify a selection of views or sheets to print using the View/Sheet Set dialog box. Then, print the selected sheet or view. You can also save the print setup to be used later in the project.

Guidelines for Working with Drawing Sheets

The following recommended practices help you effectively work with drawing sheets in a project.

Guidelines

- Create and carefully name several copies of views for different design and documentation purposes, for example, Ground Floor Furniture Plan and Ground Floor Electrical Plan. Do this because you can place each view, other than legends, only once in a sheet set. Moreover, a viewport name on a sheet can be different from the view name in the Project Browser. Creating and meaningfully naming views enables your project team members to easily locate design views both on drawing sheets and in the Project Browser.

- Create viewport types that do not display the title or extension line, or use custom linetypes. For example, if you place a 3D view or a rendered image on a sheet as an illustration, the view does not typically need a detail number; therefore, you set that viewport type not to show a title symbol. Controlling the title status enables you to quickly build complex pages.

- Create sheet views without titleblocks by deleting the titleblock after creating the sheet. Titleblocks are standard parts of drawing sheets. They define the sheet size and hold borders, company logo, and other information in the sheet. Titleblocks are created as separate family files and loaded into projects or project templates. Sheet views without titleblocks can hold illustration views for printing or exporting to image formats, which will expand your design output.

- Create drawing sheets in your company project templates and place views on drawing sheets at an early stage in a project. The drawing sheets and viewports update automatically as the model develops, and you can print sheets at any time. Predefined sheet sets in project files save time and promote design accuracy.

- Save multi-page print setups as part of project templates. These setups can be calibrated to different project stages. For example, when a project is in a design development stage, the concept design setup might only print 3D views. Using print setups saves time and reduces waste.

Example

The following illustration shows a sheet view with an untitled viewport; using this viewport enables you to quickly build complex pages.

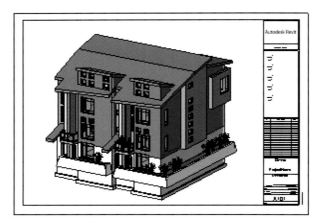

The following illustration shows a sheet view without titleblocks; this sheet view enables you to expand your design output.

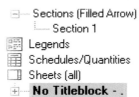

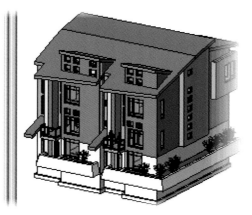

Exercise | Work with Drawing Sheets

In this exercise, you create a drawing sheet and modify its view properties. Then, you place a plan and a section view in a drawing sheet and specify print options for the selected sheets and views.

You do the following:

You need to create a drawing sheet and then place a plan view on it. You also want to modify the view properties of the drawing sheet to display the plan view and a section view of the building model. Finally, you specify various print options for selected sheets and views.

- Create a drawing sheet and modify its properties.

- Place section views in a drawing sheet.

- Specify print options for selected sheets and views.

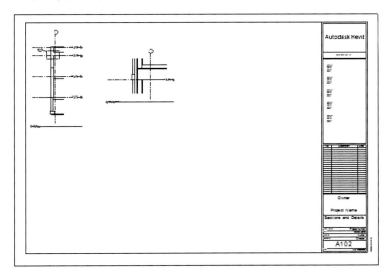

The completed exercise

Completing the Exercise: *To complete the exercise, follow the steps in this book or in the onscreen exercise. In the onscreen list of chapters and exercises, click Chapter 11: Presenting the Building Model. Click Exercise: Work with Drawing Sheets.*

Create a Drawing Sheet and Modify its Properties

1   Open *i_rac_essentials_sheets.rvt* or *m_rac_essentials_sheets.rvt*. The file opens in the Ground Floor view.
    Note: The illustrations may look slightly different in the metric dataset.

2   To add a new sheet, click View tab > Sheet Composition panel > New Sheet.

3   In the Select a Titleblock dialog box:
    • Ensure that E1 30 x 42 Horizontal : E1 30x42 Horizontal (A1 metric) is selected.
    • Click OK. The new drawing sheet is added to the Project Browser and becomes the active view.

4   Create a duplicate Ground Floor plan view with detailing.

5   Right-click the Copy of Ground Floor view. Click Properties to set the properties of the floor plan.

6   In the Instance Properties dialog box, Instance Parameters:
    • Under Identity Data, for the View Name parameter, enter **Administration Building Ground Floor**.
    • Under Extents, select the Crop View and Crop Region Visible check boxes.
    • Click OK.

7   Make the A101 - Unnamed sheet view active.

8   To place a view on the sheet, click View tab > Sheet Composition panel > View.

9   In the Views dialog box:
    • Select Floor Plan: Administration Building Ground Floor.
    • Click Add View to Sheet.

10 In the view window:
    • Position the viewport in the center of the sheet.
    • Click to place the viewport.

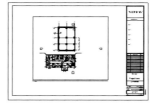

Note: You can also place the view by dragging the view from the Project Browser to the sheet.

11   To make some changes in the model view without closing the active sheet, ensure that the viewport is selected.

12   Click Modify Viewports tab > Viewport panel > Activate View. By activating the view, you can work on the model through the sheet.
      Note: You can also activate the view using the View shortcut menu.

13   Click View tab > Graphics panel > View Properties.

14   In the Instance Properties dialog box:
      • Under Graphics, for View Scale, select 1/4" = 1'-0" (1 : 50).
      • For Visibility/Graphics Overrides, click Edit.

15   In the Visibility/Graphic Overrides dialog box, Annotation Categories tab, clear the Elevations and Grids check boxes.

16   Click OK two times to close the dialog boxes.

17   To avoid a large view size, you need to crop the viewport to fit it on the sheet and at the new scale. Begin cropping the viewport by selecting the border of the viewport in the view window.

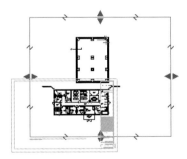

18   Drag the Control grips to include only the lower part of the building in the border of the viewport.

Note: You may need to adjust the view crop so the viewport fits on the sheet.

19   On the View Control Bar, click Hide Crop Region.

20   Right-click the view window. Click Deactivate View.

21   In the view window:
   • Select the viewport.
   • Center the viewport on the sheet.

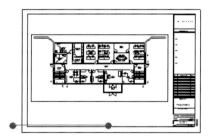

22   In the view window:
   • Clear the selection.
   • Select the view title below the viewport.

23   Drag the view title to the lower-left area of the viewport.

24 In the view window:
- Select the viewport to display the drag dots at the ends of the view title.
- Drag the right dot to ensure that the length of the view title is same as the width of the viewport.

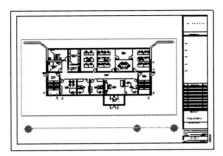

Note: You can open the Administration Building Ground Floor view to see the changes that you made to the sheet and the view. Notice that the elevations and grids are turned off in this view. Similarly, you can open the Ground Floor plan view to see the changes.

Place Section Views in a Drawing Sheet

1 Add a new sheet to place section views.

2 In the Select a Titleblock dialog box:
- Ensure that E1 30 x 42 Horizontal : E1 30x42 Horizontal (A1 metric) is selected.
- Click OK.

3 To rename and number the new sheet, in the Project Browser, right-click the new sheet and click Rename.

4 In the Sheet Title dialog box:
- Ensure that Number is A102.
- For Name, enter **Sections and Details**.
- Click OK.

5   In the view window:

- Drag the Section 2 view onto the drawing sheet.
- Click to place the Section 2 view in the upper-left corner of the sheet.

6   In the view window:

- Drag the Callout of Section 2 view on the drawing sheet.
- Click to place the Callout of Section 2 view.

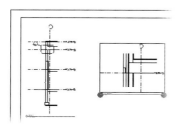

7   Clear the selection.

8   To verify that the callout bubble has updated, zoom into the section view.

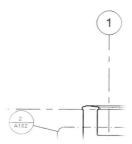

9   To check that section markers are updating properly in model views, activate the Main
    Floor view.

10 Zoom in to the upper-left corner of the building.

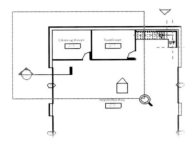

11 Verify that the section head in the apparatus bay is updated to show the detail number and
    sheet number for the added view. View tag reference update is a powerful and time-saving
    feature of Revit.

Specify Print Options for Selected Sheets and Views

1   Open the A102 - Sections and Details view.

2   On the application menu, click Print > Print.

3   In the Print dialog box, under Print Range:
    • Click Selected Views/Sheets.
    • Click Select.

4   In the View/Sheet Set dialog box:
    • Select the 3D View: {3D}; Sheet: A101 - Unnamed; and Sheet: A102 - Sections and
      Details check boxes.
    • Click OK.

5   In the Save Settings dialog box, click No for not saving the settings.

    Note: There are other print options available, such as the Print to file check box. If you have a
    printer, you can check the output for different settings by printing sheets and views.

6   Close the Print dialog box.

7   Close the file without saving changes.

Lesson 33 | Working with Titleblocks

This lesson describes how to add titleblocks to a drawing sheet and update the project information displayed in the titleblock. You begin the lesson by learning about titleblocks. Then, you learn about the steps and some recommended practices for creating and updating titleblocks. The lesson concludes with an exercise on working with titleblocks.

You use titleblocks when you want to place views of a building model on a drawing sheet in a specific format. Titleblocks define the size and appearance of a drawing sheet. Titleblocks can include borders, company logos, and project and sheet information.

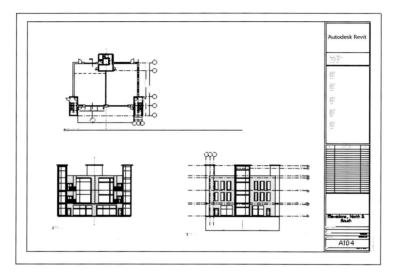

Building model views added to a drawing sheet with the titleblock

Objectives

After completing this lesson, you will be able to:

- Describe titleblocks.

- Create and update titleblocks.

- State the recommended practices for creating and updating titleblocks.

- Add and update titleblocks and edit titleblock families.

About Titleblocks

A titleblock defines a printed page. It holds space for view information that helps you to identify a building model for construction purposes. A titleblock also provides technical information about a project, such as the name and location of the project and the sheet issue date.

Definition of Titleblocks

Titleblocks are templates for drawing sheets. You can load standard titleblocks into a project or create custom titleblocks using the Family Editor and save them on the network. When you load a titleblock, Revit searches for the titleblocks in the *Titleblocks* folder in the default Imperial and Metric libraries. However, you can change this path based on your requirements.

You can create titleblocks by specifying the required sheet size and then adding borders, company logo, and other information on the drawing sheet. You can import JPEG or BMP images in a titleblock. You can also import existing drawing formats from other software packages by exporting a CAD titleblock page in the DXF™ or DWG™ format and then importing the titleblock page to a Revit titleblock file. For instance, you save the titleblock as a family file with a Revit *.rfa* extension.

Elements of Titleblocks

You can create different elements of a titleblock, such as family types, dimensions, lines, and masking regions, by using various tools available as part of the Family Editor. Titleblock elements contain all the information that is to be placed in the drawing sheet.

The following illustration shows the Create tab in the Family Editor.

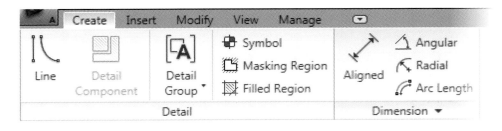

The following table describes basic tools on the Create tab in the Family Editor.

Tool	Icon	Description
Family Types	Types	Allows you to specify and manage predefined properties within a family using the Family Types dialog box. The most common use of titleblock family types is for creating titleblocks of different sizes.
Dimension	Aligned, Angular, Radial, Arc Length, Dimension ▾	Shows and controls distances between borders or lines placed in a titleblock.
Line	Line	Draws borders around titleblocks. You also use the Line tool to draw lines and shapes to divide the drawing sheet into two areas, one that holds views and another that holds project and company information.
Reference Line	Reference Line ▾	Creates a parametric family skeleton. The elements of a titleblock can align with or attach to reference lines. Reference lines are invisible when a titleblock is loaded into a project and do not highlight when a titleblock instance is selected.
Masking Region	Masking Region	Applies a white filled region as a mask to hide a region of a family.
Filled Region	Filled Region	Creates a view-specific, 2D graphic. Filled regions are areas that are parallel to the sketch plane of a view and contain a pattern that can be edited.
Symbol	Symbol	Places 2D annotation drawing symbols, such as a North arrow, into a titleblock.

Tool	Icon	Description
Text	A Text	Adds text to a titleblock. You need to use the Family Editor to add or modify titleblock text. You cannot modify the text in a titleblock directly when it has been loaded into a project because the text is static.
Label	A Label	Places a data field in text format that specifies various parameters when a titleblock is loaded into a project. The standard titleblock label parameters are Project Name, Project Number, Scale, Sheet Name, and Sheet Number. Unlike text, labels change as their parameters change.

Example of Titleblocks

The following illustration shows a titleblock with labels displaying project information:

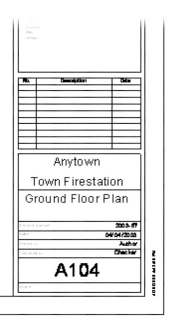

Creating and Updating Titleblocks

You change a view of a model into a construction document by placing the model view on a sheet with a titleblock. To add a titleblock, you create it as a separate file and then save the customized titleblock in your company library. When you load a titleblock in a project, its labels are automatically updated with information, such as the project name and status.

Procedure: Creating Titleblocks

The following steps describe how to create a titleblock.

1   On the application menu, click New > Title Block.

2   In the New Title Block - Select Template File dialog box, specify the sheet size to be used as a template.

3   In the Family Editor, sketch the border and dividing lines.

4   In the titleblock, include labels such as project issue date, project status, and client name.

5   Save the titleblock as an RFA family file.

Procedure: Editing Titleblocks

The following steps describe how to edit a titleblock.

1   In the sheet view, select the titleblock you want to edit.

2   On the Modify Title Blocks tab > Family panel > click Edit Family.
    Tip: If Edit Family is not displayed, you need to reload the titleblock family.

3   In the Revit dialog box, click Yes to open the selected titleblock for editing.

4   In the Family Editor, make the necessary changes to the titleblock.

5   Click Create tab > Family Editor panel > Load into Project to reload the edited titleblock in the project.

6   Save the file to retain the changes in the library copy, if required.
    Note: You cannot edit titleblock families that are created using earlier versions of the software even if the project is updated to a later version in which these titleblock families are present.

Procedure: Replacing Titleblocks on Drawing Sheets

The following steps describe how to replace a titleblock with another on a drawing sheet.

1   Open an existing drawing sheet.

2   Ensure that the titleblock you want to add is loaded.
    Tip: If you need to load a titleblock, click Insert tab > Load from Library panel > Load Family.

3   In the view window, select the titleblock that you want to replace.

4   Select the titleblock that you want as a replacement from the Type Selector drop-down. The new titleblock replaces the original.

Procedure: Specifying Project Information

The following steps describe how to specify project information that appears on labels in a titleblock.

1   Click Manage tab > Project Setting panel > Project Information.

2   In the Instance Properties dialog box, enter values for fields, such as Project Issue Date and Client Name.

3   Create or open a drawing sheet with a titleblock to view the updated information.

Guidelines for Creating and Updating Titleblocks

The following are some recommended practices for working effectively with titleblocks.

Guidelines

- Create a titleblock for each size of paper that your company uses when plotting document sets. For example, you can include a letter-size titleblock for use as a fax page or a quick single-page printout. You can load each titleblock size into your company project template files so that they are readily available. Using preloaded titleblocks saves considerable time for design team members.

- Create titleblock styles that visually represent each phase of the design development process and switch between styles as the project develops. This helps in maintaining better workflow. You should use this guideline if your company differentiates between the phases of a project, such as Schematic Design, Design Development, and Construction Documentation.

- Load an alternate titleblock into a project that is not included in the project template by using the Load Family option. This saves time because you do not need to re-create the titleblock each time.

- Place a titleblock on a sheet by dragging it from the Project Browser. You can also place a view on a sheet in this way. Dragging titleblocks and views onto sheets can speed up the process of creating sheet sets.

- Create custom labels if you know how to set up and use shared parameters. Custom labels make titleblocks more informative and well-organized.

Exercise | Work with Titleblocks

In this exercise, you add a titleblock to a drawing sheet and then update the project information of the titleblock.

You have completed the design development phase of your project and now you want to create a drawing sheet for model views, such as the ground floor plan, sections views, and detail views. In addition, you need to specify the project-related information in the drawing sheet.

You do the following:

- Create a titleblock and place views.

- Edit the titleblock family.

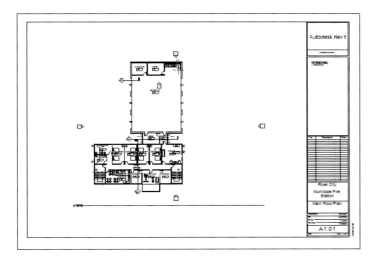

The completed exercise

Completing the Exercise: *To complete the exercise, follow the steps in this book or in the onscreen exercise. In the onscreen list of chapters and exercises, click Chapter 11: Presenting the Building Model. Click Exercise: Work With Titleblocks.*

Create a Titleblock and Place Views

1   Open *i_rac_essentials_titleblocks.rvt* or *m_rac_essentials_titleblocks.rvt*. The file opens in the Ground Floor view.
    Note: The illustrations for the metric dataset will be slightly different from those shown here.

2   To open the sheet and titleblock that has been created for you, open the A101 - Unnamed sheet view.

3   In the view window:
    • Zoom in to the lower-right corner of the sheet.
    • Click the titleblock to select it.
      If you move the cursor over fields, the parameters that you can edit are highlighted.

4   To edit the project and titleblock information, in the view window:
    • Click Unnamed and enter **Ground Floor Plan**. Press ENTER.
    • Click Owner and enter **River City**. Press ENTER.
    • Click Project Name and enter **Municipal Fire Station**. Press ENTER.

5   Open the A102 - Sections & Details sheet view.

6   In the view window, zoom in to the lower-right corner of the sheet. Notice that the owner and project name parameters are now updated. These parameters are a part of project information and appear in all titleblocks.

7   Add a new sheet.

8   In the Select a Titleblock dialog box:
     • Ensure that E1 30 x 42 Horizontal : E1 30x42 Horizontal (A1 Metric) is selected.
     • Click OK.

9   In the view window, zoom in to the lower-right corner of the new sheet. Notice that the owner and project name fields are the same as specified on other sheets.

10   Click Manage tab > Project Settings panel > Project Information to open the Instance Properties dialog box. Under Other, notice that the client name is River City and the project name is Municipal Fire Station.

11   In the Instance Properties dialog box, enter the following values:
     • For Project Issue Date, enter the current date.
     • For Project Status, enter **Client Review**. Press ENTER.
     • For Project Number, enter **2010-67**. Press ENTER.
     • Click OK.

12   In the view window, notice that the Project Number and Date fields have updated. Click the titleblock to select it.

13   Open the Instance Properties dialog box.

14   In the Instance Properties dialog box:
- For Sheet Name, enter **Main Floor Plan**.
- For Sheet Number, enter **A1.01.**
- Click OK.

15   In the view window:
- Notice that the fields have updated.

- Enter **ZF** to zoom out.

16   In the view window:
- Drag the Main Floor view to the titleblock sheet.
- Click to place Main Floor on the titleblock sheet.
- Select the titleblock.

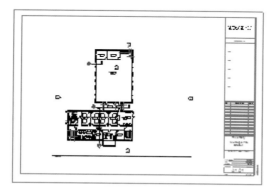

Edit the Titleblock Family

1 To edit the titleblock family so that one change will appear on all pages, click Modify Title Blocks tab > Family panel > Edit Family.

2 In the Revit dialog box, click Yes to open the titleblock for editing.

3 In the view window:

- Zoom in to the upper-right corner of the titleblock.
- Double-click the first consultant address block to highlight it. This is a text block you can edit.
- For the first text note, enter **Upright Steel Engineering, 123 Main Street, River City, LA, 1-800-123-4567**.
- Resize the text block using the Drag dot on the right side of the text block.
  Note: You can also substitute other addresses.

4 In the Family Editor, select and delete the remaining consultant address text blocks.

5 On the Family Editor panel, click Load into Project.
   Note: If you have opened multiple projects in the software, the Load into Projects dialog box is displayed. In the Load into Projects dialog box, select the titleblocks project and click OK.

6 In the Family Already Exists dialog box, click Overwrite the Existing Version. The titleblock updates on every sheet.

7 Open the sheets to verify the changes.

8 Close all files without saving changes.

Lesson 34 | Managing Revisions

This lesson describes how to create revisions and then update the information in a revision table. You begin the lesson by learning about revision tracking and how to create revision clouds. Then, you learn about the process of creating and linking Drawing Web Format (DWF™) files and some recommended practices for managing revisions. The lesson concludes with an exercise on revising a drawing and publishing a DWF file.

When you work on building projects, you need to make changes in the project to meet client or regulatory requirements. You need to track these changes for future reference. To track the changes, you might need to refer to the revision history for identifying why the changes were made, the date of the revision, and who authorized the change.

The following illustration shows a partial view of a sheet in a plan view with revision clouds, revision tags, and a revision schedule in the titleblock.

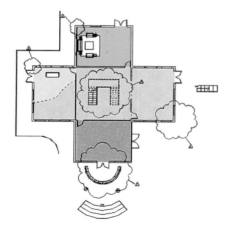

Objectives

After completing this lesson, you will be able to:

- Describe revision tracking.

- Create revision clouds.

- Identify the steps in the process of creating and linking DWF files.

- State the recommended practices for managing revisions.

- Revise a drawing and publish a DWF file.

About Revision Tracking

You make revisions to a building project to meet the changed requirements from a client or an onsite inspector. You display and track revisions using revision clouds, revision tags, revision tables, and revision schedules.

Definition of Revision Tracking

Revision tracking is the process of tracking every change made to the building project after you present the design on sheets.

Sheet Issues/Revisions Dialog Box

You create revisions and set their properties in the Sheet Issues/Revisions dialog box. You access this dialog box by selecting Sheet Issues/Revisions from the Settings drop-down on the Project Settings panel of the Manage tab. The rows and columns in the Sheet Issues/Revisions dialog box appear as entries in the revision table for the titleblock.

This dialog box also displays the Issued check box for each row. After you make changes to a building design and revise the sheet views, you use the Issued check box to lock a revision by issuing it. This ensures that you have a record of the revision and no further changes can be made to it. You then publish the revised construction documents to make the revision available to your team members.

Sheet Issues/Revisions							
Sequence	Numbering	Date	Description	Issued	Issued to	Issued by
1	Numeric	06/06	Changes to storage	☑	Client	JJG
2	Numeric	08/08	Changes to entrance	☐		

Sheet Issues/Revisions dialog box

Revision Clouds

Revision clouds are members of an annotation family that graphically indicates changes to the construction documents. You place a revision cloud by drawing its outline. You can sketch revision clouds in all views except the 3D view. You can view a revision cloud only in the view in which it is sketched. After you place the revision cloud, you can place a tag to identify the cloud.

You can also create a copy of a view by duplicating the revision clouds of the original view in the copy. You can edit the clouds in each view separately.

The following illustration shows a revision cloud placed in a plan view.

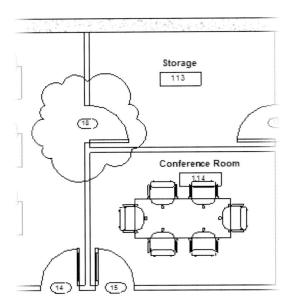

You use revision tables to manage revision clouds and set revision properties, such as numbering method and description. You can draw multiple revision clouds for every revision in the revision table. A revision cloud has certain read-only properties. You can change other properties, such as revision, comment, and mark, for each revision cloud.

The following table displays the read-only properties of a revision cloud.

Property	Description
Revision Number	Specifies the revision tag number.
Revision Date	Specifies the date of release of a revision.

Property	Description
Issued To	Provides details about the entity to which the building model is being issued, such as the builder or the client. When a revision is issued, the construction documents are officially updated to include the changes that the revision specifies. When a revision is issued, further revision clouds cannot be added for that revision, and you must create a new revision in the revision table. **Note**: To edit an issued revision, you need to unlock it by clearing the Issued check box. However, unlocking an issued revision is not advisable.
Issued By	Provides details about the issuer of the revision, such as the designer or the reviewing architect.

Revision Tags

You tag revision clouds to provide graphic identification of the cloud; the tag details are also displayed in the revision table and schedule. To tag revision clouds, you must load the revision tag family. When you tag a revision cloud, the tags are numbered on the basis of the numbering method that you specified while creating the revision table. You can tag a revision cloud even if the revision has been issued.

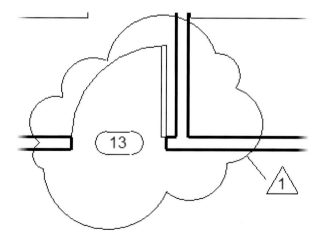

A tagged revision cloud

Revision Schedule

A revision schedule displays information derived from revision clouds. It is a part of a titleblock that can be viewed only in the sheet view. Most titleblocks that Revit provides include revision schedules. You can place revision schedules in custom titleblocks. As you add views with revision clouds to a sheet, the revision information is automatically displayed in the revision schedule in a titleblock. The schedule tracks only the revision numbers and not the actual changes in the building design. You can edit a revision schedule in the titleblock family to modify the columns or headings of the schedule.

The following illustration shows a revision schedule in a titleblock.

No.	Description	Date
1	Changes to storage	06/06
2	Changes to entrance	08/08

Example of Revision Tracking

The following illustrations show a revision cloud with a tag, a revision table, and a revision schedule.

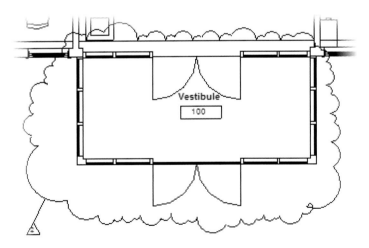

Revision cloud placed and tagged

Sequence	Numbering	Date	Description	Issued
1	Numeric	06/06	Changes to storage	☑
2	Numeric	08/08	Changes to entrance	☐

Revision table that assigns revision tag numbers

No.	Description	Date
1	Eliminated window at entry	11/3/06
2	Added support column	3/15/07
3	Widened Kitchen	4/8/07

Revision schedule displaying the revision table information

Creating Revision Clouds

You create revision clouds by sketching them and assigning them to revisions.

Procedure: Creating Revision Clouds

The following steps describe how to create a revision cloud and assign it to a revision.

1   Click Annotate tab > Detail panel > Revision Cloud.

2   Click Create Revision Cloud Sketch tab > Tools panel > Draw Lines.

3   In the view window:
   • Click near the elements you have changed to start creating a revision cloud.
   • Move the cursor in a clockwise direction and click to create a segment of the cloud.
   • Repeat until all the segments of the cloud are drawn and the ends of the clouds
     are connected.

4   Click Create Revision Cloud Sketch tab > Element panel > Revision Cloud Properties.

5   In the Instance Properties dialog box, under Identity Data, for Revision, select a revision number from the Value list.

6   Click Create Revision Cloud Sketch tab > Revision Cloud panel > Finish Cloud to exit the sketch mode.

After finishing a cloud, you can select a finished revision cloud and choose a revision from the Revision list on the Options Bar.

Process of Creating and Linking DWF Files

At times, you need to send an electronic copy of a drawing for review to a client, a consultant, or any regulatory agency. To do this, you can use a DWF file, which is created using the DWF tool. DWF files are small in size and can be easily transferred over the Internet. You can send these file to the recipients in a format in which they can read and insert comments or markup, but not edit. To enter markups in a DWF file and return it, the recipient should have the necessary DWF markup software, such as Autodesk® Design Review.

After you receive DWF markups, you link these into Revit so that you can make the necessary changes to the building model.

Process: Creating and Linking DWF Files

The process of creating and linking DWF files is shown in the following illustration.

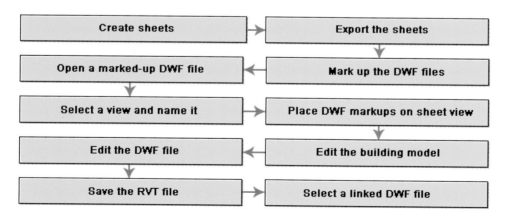

The following steps describe the process of creating and linking DWF files.

1 **Create sheets**.
Create sheets in your project and add the desired view types.

2 **Export the sheets**.
Export the desired sheets to DWF and send the DWF file to the client or the consultant who will review and mark it up.
Note: You can export model views to DWF and mark them up, but they will not be part of a linked markup set.

3 **Mark up the DWF files**.
When you receive a DWF file, mark it up in a program such as Autodesk Design Review. When you mark up the DWF file, you mark on top of the plotted views, which is similar to using a red marker on a printout. You need to mark up the DWF file to link it back into the original project. This is followed by sending the DWF file to the client or the consultant who reviews it and makes the changes to the model.

4 **Open a marked-up DWF file.**
Open the marked-up DWF file that you have received from the client or the consultant using the options in the Import/Link DWF File dialog box. You access this dialog box using DWF Markup on the Link panel of the Insert tab.

5 **Select a view and name it.**
Select a Revit view, such as a sheet view, in the Link Markup Page to Revit Sheets dialog box. You select a sheet view if the Revit View value is set to Not Linked. You can also select the sheet view if you have several other sheet views in the project file and want to apply the markups to one of the other sheet views. However, to do this, the other sheet view titleblocks should be of the same size as the original.

You select a name in the Link Markup Page to Revit Sheets dialog box to name the Revit view. If the sheet name from the DWF file is the same as the sheet name from the file in the software, the Revit sheet name is automatically inserted in the Revit View column.

6 **Place DWF markups on sheet view**.
Place the DWF markups on a sheet view as an import symbol. The markups are pinned. You cannot modify, copy, rotate, mirror, delete, or group markups.
Note: If the markups are created in Autodesk Design Review using its markup tools, you can modify some instance properties, such as Status and Notes, in Revit.

7 **Edit the building model.**
Make changes in the RVT file based on the markups.

8 **Edit the DWF file**.
Select DWF markup items and change their properties to reflect their new status. You can set the markup status as <None>(the default), Question, For Review, or Done. Further, you can place notes in the DWF.

9 **Save the RVT file**.
Save the RVT file. The changes are then saved to the linked DWF file. You can view the changes in the DWF file by selecting the corresponding markup item.
Note: The RVT file and the DWF file remain in synchronization with the markups. For example, if you include notes with the markups, save the markups and link them to the DWF file. The project architect can read the notes in a DWF viewer.

10 **Select a linked DWF file**.
Select a linked DWF file in the Manage Links dialog box and save the changes that you made to mark up objects. The changes to the markup objects are visible in the DWF file the next time you open it.

Guidelines for Managing Revisions

The following recommended practices help you manage revisions effectively.

Guidelines

- Use the built-in revision system in Revit that associates revision clouds with the revision table. This will enable you to identify revisions and the revision schedule that automatically appears on sheet titleblocks. Revisions in Revit are more reliable than manually drafted clouds.

- Change the appearance of the revision schedule components available in titleblock templates to suit your company standards when you create custom company titleblocks. This saves time later in the design process, when you can use the parametric revision annotations in Revit.

- Show or hide issued revisions. In a project with many revisions, you might want to print and save versions of your sheet files as revisions are issued and then turn off the visibility of issued revisions to reduce visual clutter. You can turn on issued revisions later if you need to print them.

- Export DWF files regularly, regardless of whether you and other collaborators go through markups electronically. This gives you lightweight files that can be viewed in the DWF viewer. These files can be sent with email messages or posted on Web pages for secure viewing. The email messages and Web pages can have links for automatic download and installation of the viewer.

Exercise | Revise a Drawing and Publish a DWF File

In this exercise, you create a revision cloud and then add information in a revision table. You also export a sheet, including revisions to a DWF file.

You have a completed building model and a document set. You add a wall and change a door in the building model. You then create revision clouds around the wall and the door to specify that you have made changes in the building design. You also edit the revision table for the revision cloud to update the revision schedule on a sheet.

You do the following:

- Modify a project model.

- Create a revision cloud.

- Add information in a revision table.

- Publish a sheet to a DWF file.

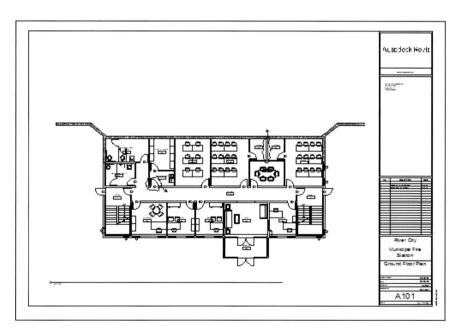

The completed exercise

Modify a Project Model

1   Open *i_rac_essentials_revisions.rvt* or *m_rac_essentials_revisions.rvt*. The file opens in the Administration Building Ground Floor plan view.
    Note: The illustrations for the metric dataset will be slightly different from those shown here.

2   To modify a project model, begin by zooming in to the upper-right quadrant of the building model.

3   Select the wall between Conference Room 114 and Storage 113.

4   Click Modify Walls tab > Create panel > Create Similar.

5   In the view window, place a wall from the midpoint of the selected wall to the external wall.

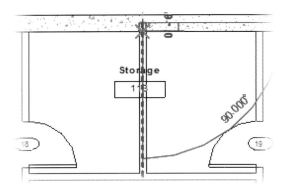

6   Exit the Create Similar tool.

7   For imperial users, drag the Room tag for room 113 to the left of the new wall.
    For metric users, drag the Room tag for room 113 to the right of the new wall.

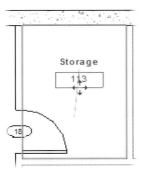

8   To place a new room in the undefined space, click Home tab > Room & Area panel > Room drop-down > Room.

9   For imperial users, in the view window, click to the right of the new wall to place a room. For metric users, in the view window, click to the left of the new wall to place a room.

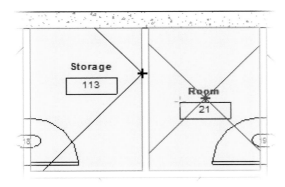

10   Exit the Room tool.

11   Select the new Room tag.

12   Rename the Room tag to Storage and rename the tag to **120**.

13   To relocate a door, begin by zooming in to Fax/ Copy Room.
     For metric users, zoom in to Room 110. In the subsequent steps, use Room 110 whenever there is a reference to Fax/Copy Room.

14   Select door 11.

15 Click Modify Doors tab > Clipboard panel > Cut.
Notice that the door disappears.

16 To place a new door with the same tag, click Modify tab > Clipboard panel > Paste.

17 Press SPACEBAR to shift the hinge to the left.

18 Place the door on the wall between Fax/Copy Room and Corridor.

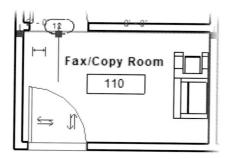

19 To add a door tag:

- Click Annotate tab > Tag panel > Tag by Category.
- On the Options Bar, clear the Leader check box.
- Click the new door to place a tag.
Notice that the door tag displays the same tag as before.

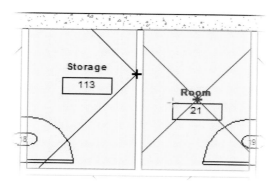

Create a Revision Cloud

1   To mark your changes with revision clouds, click Annotate tab > Detail panel > Revision Cloud.

2   In the view window, sketch a revision cloud clockwise around the door you moved.

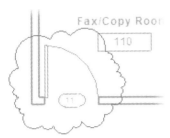

Note: The cloud closes when you return to the origin.

3   When you complete sketching the revision cloud, click Create Revision Cloud Sketch tab > Revision Cloud panel > Finish Cloud.

4   Create a revision cloud around the wall between Storage rooms 113 and 120.

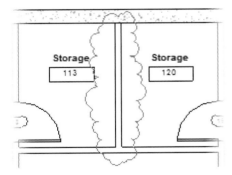

5   To tag the revisions:
   • Activate the Tag by Category tool.
   • On the Options Bar, ensure that the Leader check box is selected.

6   In the view window, place a tag on the revision cloud for the wall.

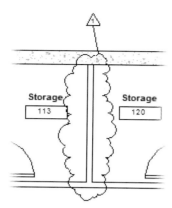

7   Similarly, place a tag on the revision cloud for the door.

8   Press ESC to exit the Tag by Category tool.

9   To modify the appearance of the revision clouds for greater emphasis, click Manage tab >
     Project Settings panel > Settings drop-down > Object Styles.

10   In the Object Styles dialog box, Annotation Objects tab, for Revision Clouds:
     • Change Line Weight to 4.
     • Click Black in the Line Color field.

11   In the Color dialog box, under Custom Colors, select red.

12   Click OK in both the dialog boxes.

Add Information in a Revision Table

1   Open the A101 - Ground Floor Plan sheet view.

2   Zoom in to the revision schedule in the titleblock to view the default information.

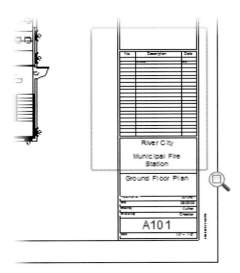

3   To create descriptions for the two changes you made, click Manage tab > Project Settings panel > Settings drop-down > Sheet Issues/Revisions.

4   In the Sheet Issues/Revisions dialog box, click Add to create a second row.

5   To specify details for Sequence 1:
     • For Date, enter the current date.
     • For Description, enter **Added wall in Storage room**.
     • For Issued To, enter **Commercial Builders**.

6   For Sequence 2:
     • For Date, enter the current date.
     • For Description, enter **Moved Door to Fax Room**.
     • For Issued To, enter **Commercial Builders**.

7   Click OK to apply the changes. Notice that only the entry for adding the wall in the storage room is listed in the revision schedule in the titleblock.

8   To modify the revision clouds and update the schedule, activate the view for the viewport of the A101 - Ground Floor Plan view.

9   Select the revision cloud for the door of Fax/Copy Room.

10   Open the Instance Properties dialog box.

11   In the Instance Properties dialog box:
      - Select Seq. 2 Moved Door to Fax Room from the Revision list.
      - Click OK.

12   To view the changes, deactivate the view for the viewport.

13   Zoom to fit the view. Notice the new entry in the revision schedule on the titleblock for moving the door to the fax room.

14   Open the Sheet Issues/Revisions dialog box.

15   Select the Issued check boxes for both Sequence 1 and Sequence 2.

16   Click OK to apply the changes.

17   Open the Administration Building Ground Floor plan view.

18   Activate the Revision Cloud tool. An error message indicates that the current revision has been issued and no new revision cloud can be created.
      Note: You can add new Revision Sequences in the Sheet Issues/Revisions dialog box, if required.

19   Click Cancel to close the error message.

Publish a Sheet to a DWF File

1   Open the A101 - Ground Floor Plan view.

2   On the application menu, click Export > DWF.

3   In the DWF Export Settings dialog box:
     - On the View/Sheet Set tab, ensure that <Current View/Sheet Only> is selected in the Export list.
     - On the DWF Properties tab, click Print Setup.

4   In the Print Setup dialog box:
   - Under Paper, select ANSI E : 34 x 44 in (ISO: A1 594 x 841 mm) from the Size list.
   - Under Zoom, click Fit to Page.
   - Click OK.

   Note: If Revit prompts, you can save the settings and use them later.

5   In the DWF Export Settings dialog box, click Export.

6   In the Export DWF dialog box:
   - Specify desktop as the location for saving the DWF file.
   - Click Export to export the sheet.

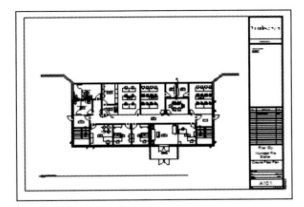

7   Browse to where the export file is saved. If Autodesk DWF Viewer or Autodesk Design Review are installed on your computer, double-click the file to open it.
   Note: If the Autodesk Design Review Information dialog box appears, click Close.

8   Close Autodesk DWF Viewer or Design Review.

9   Close the file without saving changes.

Lesson 35 | Creating Renderings

This lesson describes how to create renderings for building models. You begin the lesson by learning about renderings and the settings for creating renderings. Then, you learn some recommended practices for creating renderings. The lesson concludes with an exercise on creating a rendering.

Renderings simulate the real-life view of a building model by generating photorealistic images of its interior and exterior areas. You can use these photorealistic images for marketing and making presentations to clients.

The following illustration shows a rendered 3D view of a building model.

Objectives

After completing this lesson, you will be able to:

- Describe renderings.

- Identify the settings for creating renderings.

- State the recommended practices for creating renderings.

- Create a rendering.

About Renderings

Renderings help you visualize the true perspective and beauty of a building model. They create a lighting environment that reflects the location, materials, and conditions of a building model in realistic colors and textures. To render a building model, you first need to create a 3D view. Then, you can set up the 3D view by placing the camera and target, setting the resolution, or changing the crop region size.

Definition of Rendering

Rendering is the process of generating a real-life image of a building model. Rendering uses the raytracing technique in which the rendering engine in the software analyzes the effect of lights and shadows on a building model and creates a pixel-by-pixel display of the complete or partial building model.

Rendering helps you create realistic images by adding effects such as artificial and natural lighting, skies with clouds, and plants and people to the rendered image. You can create low-resolution or high-resolution renderings, as required. The time taken by the rendering process depends on the complexity, size, and resolution of the image.

Lighting

Lighting shows the physical features of a building design and helps convey the design intent. In the absence of lighting, rendering generates a black image. Lighting effects, such as skylight, light reflected from the ground, and light reflected off surfaces, vary between the exterior and interior areas of a building.

While rendering a building model, you can use interior lighting, exterior lighting, or both to illuminate the building. For interior lighting, you can add and group lighting fixtures, turn on or off individual lighting fixtures or light groups, and adjust their intensity, as required. You need to specify the location, date, and time of the day for exterior lighting to achieve a realistic representation of sunlight on the building.

You can use overhead lighting when you want to show strong shadows in the rendered image. You can use sideways lighting to give the building model a more dramatic look by enhancing its textures and colors. For example, you can show the difference in the appearance of a house at noon in natural light and at dusk with illuminating floodlights.

The following table describes the types of lighting.

Type of Lighting	Description
Default lights or headlights	Provide illumination for shaded views to prevent a building model from appearing completely black. You cannot move or see headlights because they appear only in the form of rays of light. Headlights do not affect rendering.
Sunlight	Provides illumination to create the exterior rendering of a building model. Sunlight can be used to create the daylight exterior renderings easily.
Artificial lights	Provide more lighting effects than those using only sunlight. Artificial lights take time to set up and render. You can use artificial lights in combination with sunlight to create indoor renderings of a building model.

Raytracing

Raytracing is the process of tracing the light rays backward from the eye of the viewer to the source of light and determining how the rays are affected as they travel from the source to the eye. This information is used to calculate rendering properties, such as brightness, transparency, and reflectivity of each building model component. You can also calculate the properties for each pixel, objects in the view, and the light sources from the eye of the viewer. Raytracing determines the color and intensity of the pixels that create an image on the screen. Therefore, when an image is raytraced, you can accurately and clearly see the effect of lighting on the building model.

Rendering Process Time

The rendering process may take several minutes or even hours to complete. The following table describes the factors that affect rendering.

Factor	Description
Model complexity	A large and complex building model with complicated surfaces and reflective materials takes longer to render than a simple model. For example, an exterior view of a multitower glass skyscraper takes longer than an exterior view of a small brick house.

Factor	Description
Image size	A large image takes longer to render. For example, if a camera view is set to 1,024 x 768 pixels, an image will take longer to render than an image of 640 x 480 pixels.
Image resolution	A high value of dots per inch (DPI) results in longer rendering process time. For example, if you use Medium or High options from the Settings list, the image takes longer to render.
Lights	The rendering process time decreases if you turn on only the lights required for a view. For example, for daytime exterior renderings, you can render only with the sun turned on and all artificial lights turned off.

Example of Rendering

The following illustrations show rendered images of the exterior and interior areas of a building model.

An exterior scene in which the time of the day is set for low-angle shadows. Landscaping and entourage components cast shadows on the facade. Sky and clouds form the background behind other landscaping elements, and the toposurface divides into concrete and grass.

An interior scene lit by suspended ceiling light fixtures and wall sconces. Notice that the glass looks transparent, shiny surfaces reflect, and solid objects cast shadows.

Settings for Creating Renderings

You can specify various settings when you render a building model. The values of the settings determine the final appearance and quality of the rendered image. You can specify quality, output, lighting, background, image, display, and sun and shadow settings for a rendering. You can also specify materials or texture settings for the model elements. To specify these settings, you use the Rendering and Materials dialog boxes.

Rendering Settings

You specify rendering settings using the Rendering dialog box. The Rendering dialog box contains various controls for rendering 3D views. It provides customized values that help you generate high-quality rendered images easily without having an in-depth understanding of the rendering process. You access the Rendering dialog box by selecting the Show Rendering Dialog on the View Control Bar. The Show Rendering Dialog option is present only in 3D views.

Rendering dialog box

The following table describes various settings that you can specify in the Rendering dialog box.

Setting	Description
Render	Starts the raytracing process to generate the rendered image. You can specify a render region to generate a partial rendering of the building model by selecting the Region check box. Partial rendering helps you check colors and materials prior to the final rendering.
Quality	Determines the time taken by the rendering process. You can use the Draft or Low options from the Settings list to quickly generate rendered images without many details. The Medium or High options generate images with more details but take longer than the fast-speed options.
Output Settings	Specifies the output medium, such as screen or printer. You can specify resolution settings to control the output by selecting the Printer option.
Lighting	Specifies interior or exterior lighting or a combination of natural and artificial light. You can specify sun settings for specific angles or by global location. You can also group interior lights to control lighting efficiently.
Background	Specifies a sky background with varying amounts of cloud or a single color. You can also specify haze effects.
Image	Adjusts the image exposure or brightness after the rendering is created. You can also specify settings to save the rendered image as a view inside a project or export it to an external file.
Display	Shows or hides the rendering so that you can adjust the model or view.

Sun and Shadows Settings

The Sun and Shadows Settings dialog box helps you control the sun angle for renderings and solar studies. You access this dialog box from the Rendering dialog box. You can create different sun and shadow settings by varying the values for place, time, and date. You can also rename or delete these settings, as required.

Materials Dialog Box

You can control the appearance of building components in rendered views by setting the properties of the materials in the Materials dialog box. A large number of render textures are available in the software library that you can assign to materials. The render textures help you generate a realistic image.

You access the Materials dialog box from the Project Settings panel of the Manage tab.

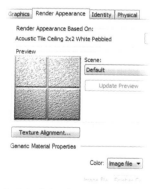

Materials dialog box

The Render Appearance tab in the Materials dialog box lets you set the render appearance of any material in a project file. You can adjust the reflectivity and transparency of materials using the Materials dialog box. The Replace option opens the Render Appearance Library dialog box in which you assign render textures to the materials from the render appearance library.

Guidelines for Creating Renderings

The following recommended practices help you create rendered images successfully.

Guidelines

- Use the Region option to test materials, lighting, and exposure settings when you first set up a rendered view. You can use the Region option to check the rendering for a region before you render the complete image.

- Use the Draft setting for the first few renderings of a 3D view to save time. Once the 3D view is set up, you can use a slow-speed, high-quality option.

- Adjust the final position and orientation of rendering components, such as the camera location, clouds, materials, humans, landscaping, and entourage, as you start the rendering process. When you are satisfied with the composition of your image and the effects such as shadows and reflections, you can pin items in place for the final rendering.

Example

The following illustration is an example of how a region of a building model is rendered to test materials, lighting, and exposure settings before you render the complete building.

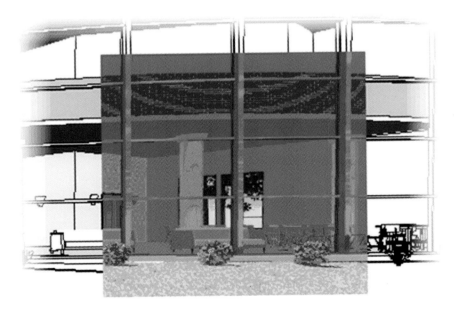

Exercise | Create a Rendering

In this exercise, you create a rendering for a building project.

You are preparing a presentation for the client and need a realistic image depicting your building project as it will be when completed. To do this, you create a rendering of a 3D perspective view of the building project.

The completed exercise

Completing the Exercise: *To complete the exercise, follow the steps in this book or in the onscreen exercise. In the onscreen list of chapters and exercises, click Chapter 11: Presenting the Building Model. Click Exercise: Create a Rendering.*

1   Open *i_rac_essentials_rendering.rvt* or *m_rac_essentials_rendering.rvt*. The file opens in 3D View 1.

   Note: The illustrations for the metric dataset will be slightly different from those shown here.

2   On the View Control Bar, click Show Rendering Dialog to specify the settings for rendering.

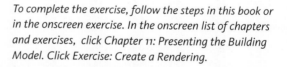

3   In the Rendering dialog box, under Lighting, select Edit/New from the Sun list to specify the sun and shadow settings for the building model.

4   In the Sun and Shadows Settings dialog box:
   • Under Name, Still tab, verify that Sun and Shadow Settings is selected.
   • Under Settings, click By Date, Time and Place.
   • Click [...] next to the Place field to specify a city.

5   In the Manage Place and Locations dialog box:
   • Select Boston, MA from the City list.
   • Select the Automatically Adjust Clock for Daylight Savings Changes check box.
   • Click OK.
     Note: You can specify your own location. This will change the effect of sunlight and shadows.

6   In the Sun and Shadows Settings dialog box:
   • Under Settings, specify the current date and time in the Date and Time fields.
   • Click OK.
     Tip: The time specified should be daytime because a night rendering will show a black image.

7   In the Rendering dialog box, under Background:
   • Verify that Color is selected from the Style list.
   • Click the Change the Haziness color panel.

8   In the Color dialog box:
   • Notice the color selected by default.
   • Click Cancel.

9   In the Rendering dialog box:
   • Under Background, select Sky: Few Clouds from the Style list to set a background with sky and clouds.
   • Select the Region check box at the top of the dialog box. A render region is displayed in the view window.

10 In the view window:
   • Select the render region.
   • Drag the Adjust Render Region controls to select some sky region above the building in the region to render.

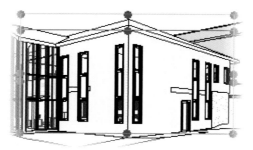

11   In the Rendering dialog box:

- Under Quality, verify that Draft is selected from the Setting list to quickly generate a
  partial rendering.
- Click Render. The rendering process takes a few minutes. A partial rendering is
  displayed when the process is complete.

Note: The shadows depend on the location and time settings you specify.

12   In the Rendering dialog box, under Image, click Adjust Exposure.

13   In the Exposure Control dialog box:

- For Exposure Value, enter **13** to specify the image clarity.
- Click OK.

14   In the Rendering dialog box:

- Under Display, click Show the Model.
- Clear the Region check box to hide the render region.

15   In the view window, click the crop region.

16   Click Modify Cameras tab > Crop panel > Size Crop.

17   In the Crop Region Size dialog box:

- Under Model Crop Size, for Width, enter **6"** (**150** mm).
- Under Change, click Scale (Locked Proportions).
- Click OK. The crop region size changes.

18   In the Rendering dialog box:

- Under Quality, select Medium from the Setting list to generate a complete rendering with enough details.
- Under Background, verify that Sky: Few Clouds is selected from the Style list.
- Click Render. The rendering process takes a few minutes.
- Under Image, click Save to Project to add the rendered image to the project.

19   In the Save To Project dialog box:

- For Name, enter **Front Entrance**.
- Click OK.

Note: The rendered images are saved under Renderings in the Project Browser. You can also export the image to an external file.

20   Close the Rendering dialog box.

21   Close the file without saving changes.

Lesson 36 | Using Walkthroughs

This lesson describes how to create and export a walkthrough of a building model. You begin the lesson by learning about walkthroughs. Then, you learn about some recommended practices for using walkthroughs. The lesson concludes with an exercise on creating and exporting a walkthrough.

Walkthroughs allow you to show your building model to clients or regulators in an animated form that can be played in any media player. You create a walkthrough to view the interior or exterior of a building model as a movie.

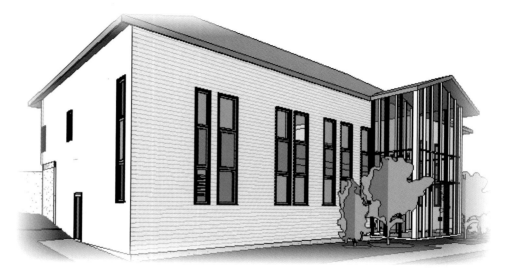

Walkthrough image

Objectives

After completing this lesson, you will be able to:

- Describe walkthroughs.

- State the recommended practices for using walkthroughs.

- Create and export a walkthrough.

About Walkthroughs

You use a walkthrough to view your building model by means of a camera placed at strategic angles in and around the building model. You create a walkthrough by placing the camera on a path that forms an animated sequence of views of a building model.

Definition of Walkthroughs

A walkthrough is a collection of camera views or frames placed in a sequence. You create a walkthrough in your project by placing keyframes to generate a camera path in a plan view. You then adjust view properties, such as position, direction, and field of the camera, for different keyframes, as required. You can adjust the properties of all the keyframes that are a part of the walkthrough in the Instance Properties dialog box.

Keyframes

A keyframe is a modifiable frame in a walkthrough. You can manage the direction and position of the camera at a keyframe. The properties of all the frames between two keyframes are linked. Therefore, you do not have to adjust the camera at frames in between the keyframes, Revit does this automatically.

If you adjust the camera differently at two keyframes, the software minimizes the difference between the keyframes. This ensures smooth transition between keyframes in the walkthrough.

You can open the camera view at any frame and play the walkthrough in the project file.

Camera and Path

You create a walkthrough by placing the keyframes of a camera along a path in a plan view. Revit uses a spline to connect the keyframes that you place while drawing the path. Once you have finished drawing a path, you can edit it by moving, adding, or deleting keyframes.

When you place a camera at a keyframe, you can set the camera to perspective view or orthographic view. You can also set the level and height offset for the camera location. By default, the camera is set to average eye height above the given level.

You can change the camera angle and depth of field of a view after the walkthrough path is defined. To do this, you open the view for a keyframe in a walkthrough and change the field of a view. Use Steering Wheels to alter the camera placement and direction.

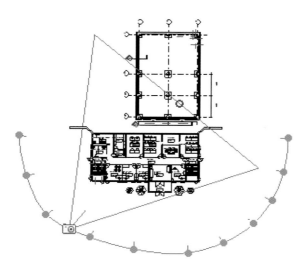

Walkthrough path and the field of view for a camera

Example of Walkthroughs

The following illustrations show a walkthrough in the plan and camera views. In the plan view, the triangle represents the field of a camera view and the red dots represent the keyframes on the walkthrough path. The camera view shows a keyframe of the walkthrough.

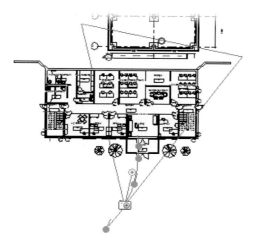

Walkthrough in a plan view

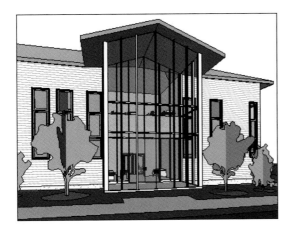

Walkthrough in a camera view

Guidelines for Using Walkthroughs

Walkthroughs present the building model in the form of a movie that can be played without using Revit. The following recommended practices help you use walkthroughs effectively.

Guidelines

- Create a walkthrough that examines or illustrates a particular area of the building model from more than one point of view. You can use such a walkthrough to describe the problem areas of the building model in more detail instead of using a walkthrough that examines the building model from a single point of view covering interior hallways.

- Minimize side-to-side movement of the camera while creating a walkthrough. For example, if you swing the camera from left to right quickly, the viewer will not be able to see what you are trying to illustrate. Also, jerky camera movements can make some viewers uncomfortable.

- Place a circular walkthrough with the camera focusing inward in your project template file if a certain size is specified for a building project. This way, as soon as you create the building model, you can study its exterior in the walkthrough and send the walkthrough to your client for review. This reduces the time taken in the review cycle.

- Place the walkthrough camera away from the model rather than close. This results in more realistic perspective angles in the camera view.

- Adjust the depth of the field control to ensure that all the important parts of the building model, such as walls in the background of a view, are visible. This saves time on adjustments later in the design process.

- Experiment with camera placement and angle. For example, if you place keyframes together, the movement of keyframes along the path slows down and you can adjust the camera angle to look up and down a facade. This makes the walkthrough an effective analysis and display tool.

- Adjust the playing speed of the walkthrough. Playing speed refers to the number of frames per second. Adjusting the playing speed controls the display quality when you create the export file.

- Use the Hidden Line display while setting up the walkthrough and change to Shading with Edges or Rendering for the final export. Shaded or rendered files take longer to generate. Therefore, plan your workflow accordingly. You can save time by not using time-consuming procedures until views and settings are correct.

Example

The following illustration shows a circular walkthrough with the camera focusing inward. Using this walkthrough, you can study the building exterior and send the walkthrough to your client for review, reducing the review cycle.

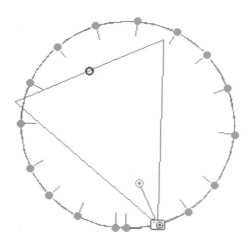

Exercise | Create and Export a Walkthrough

In this exercise, you create a walkthrough for a building model. Then, you export the walkthrough to an AVI file.

You want to create a walkthrough showing the exterior of a building model to a client who does not have Revit. You need to create and edit a walkthrough. Then, you need to export the walkthrough to an AVI file so that the client can view the walkthrough in any media player without using Revit. After exporting, you play the AVI file in a media player to check its functionality.

You do the following:

- Create a walkthrough.

- Edit a walkthrough.

- Export and play the walkthrough.

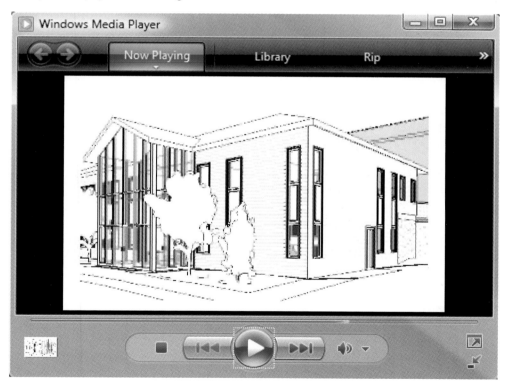

The completed exercise

Create a Walkthrough

1   Open *i_rac_essentials_walkthrough.rvt* or *m_rac_essentials_walkthrough.rvt*. The file opens in 3D View 1, a camera view of the administration wing of the building project.
    Note: The illustrations for the metric dataset will be slightly different from those shown here. The completed exercise illustration may also vary.

2   To create a video animation for showing the client the three public sides of the administration wing, open the Ground Floor plan view.

3   In the view window:

    • Zoom to fit the view.
    • Zoom out (2x) to ensure space in the view around the building.

4   Click View tab > Create panel > 3D View drop- down > Walkthrough.

5   In the view window:

    • Place the cursor on the west side of the administration wing.

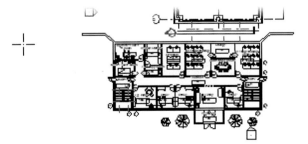

    • Click on the west side of the administration wing to place a keyframe.

6   In the view window, move the cursor down to the right and click to place three or four keyframes in a rough quarter circle, as shown. The exact position of the keyframes is not critical.

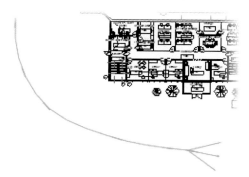

7   Click below the main entrance to place another keyframe.

8   Continue placing keyframes upward and to the right until you have 10 to 12 frames.

     This creates a rough half circle around the administration building. The path you create may look different.

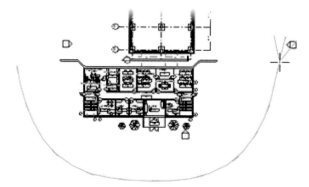

9   When you finish creating the path, click Walkthrough tab > Walkthrough panel > Finish Walkthrough.

Edit a Walkthrough

1   Ensure the cameras point at the building. To begin, click Modify Cameras tab > Walkthrough panel > Edit Walkthrough.

2   On the Options Bar:
- Verify that Active Camera is selected in the Controls list.
- Verify that Frame is set to 300.0 of 300.

3   In the view window, to set the camera orientation, drag the Walkthrough : Move Target Point control, which is the magenta circle at the end of the camera direction indicator, toward the building model such that the camera field outline points at the building model, as shown.

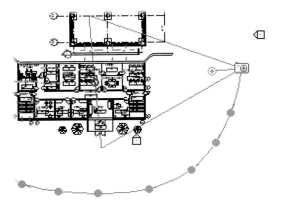

4   To activate the camera field for the previous camera, on the Walkthrough panel, click Previous Key Frame.
Note: Do not click Previous Frame because it will activate the camera field for the previous frame and not the previous keyframe.

5   Reset the camera orientation towards the building model by dragging the Walkthrough : Move Target Point control so that the camera field outline points at the building model.

6   Reset the camera orientation for all keyframes. The path displays camera direction indicators for each keyframe.

7   Drag the depth of field control, the blue circle, to the middle of the far side of the field of view triangle so as to ensure the camera view covers the entire depth of the model.

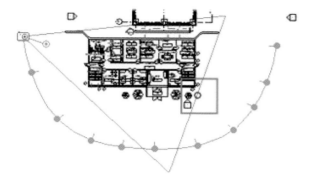

8   To open the walkthrough camera view, on the Walkthrough panel, click Open Walkthrough.

9   Adjust the crop region so that you can see the complete building exterior within the keyframe without focusing on the sky or grass. This adjustment controls the crop region size for all frames.

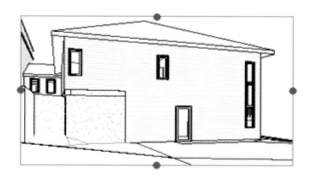

Note: If a Revit dialog box appears with a message to confirm quitting editing, click No. This dialog box appears whenever you click in open space when editing a walkthrough.

10 To open the crop area for the next keyframe, on the Walkthrough panel, click Next Key Frame.

11 Adjust the crop region to view the complete building model, if necessary.

12 Check and adjust the crop region in all the keyframes.

13 To return to the first frame, on the Options Bar, Frame field, enter **1**.

14 On the Walkthrough panel, click Play to start viewing the frames.
    Note: You can experiment with different model graphics style options while in frame views. If you change the model graphics style, you have to select the view frame and click Edit Walkthrough to display all the options.

15 Open the Ground Floor plan view.

16 In the Project Browser:
    • Under Views (All), expand Walkthroughs.
    • Right-click Walkthrough 1. Select Show Camera.

17 On the Walkthrough panel, click Edit Walkthrough.

18 On the Options Bar, select Path from the Controls list.

19 In the view window, drag the keyframes, as required, to adjust the path if any camera locations are too close or too far from the building.
    Note: If you relocate keyframes, you may have to reorient the camera.

Export and Play the Walkthrough

1 To create an animation from the walkthrough, on the Walkthrough panel, click Open Walkthrough.

2 On the application menu, click Export > Images and Animations > Walkthrough.

3 In the Length/Format dialog box:
   • Under Format, ensure that <Hidden Line> is selected from the Model Graphics Style list.
   • Click OK.
     Note: In the Length/Format dialog box, you can select all the frames or a frame range and specify dimensions, the image size, the speed, and the zoom factor.

4 In the Export Walkthrough dialog box:
   • Specify the desktop as the location to save the walkthrough.
   • Specify a file name for the walkthrough.
   • Click Save.

5   In the Video Compression dialog box:

    • Select Microsoft Video 1 from the Compressor list.
    • Click OK. The software generates the AVI file. This may take a few minutes.

6   Browse to the desktop.

7   On the desktop, right-click the AVI file. Click Open With.
     Note: You can directly open the file if the shortcut menu displays the Play with Windows
     Media Player option.

8   In the Open With dialog box:

    • Under Programs, select Windows Media Player from the list.
    • Click OK to play the AVI file.
       Note: You can also use a different media player installed on your computer. When the
       player opens, you can pause, stop, fast-forward, or rewind the file.

9   Close Windows Media Player.
     Note: You can burn the AVI file to a disc or post the file online to share with clients or
     collaborators without sharing the original project file. You can also use various video
     processing applications to create lightweight formats from AVI.

10   Close the file without saving changes.

Lesson 37 | Using Sun and Shadow Settings

This lesson describes how to use sun and shadow settings in a building model. You begin the lesson by learning about sun and shadow settings and some recommended practices for using these settings. The lesson concludes with an exercise on using sun and shadow settings to create shadows of a building model.

Sun and shadow settings help you analyze sun positions and solar effects on a building model. You can use the analysis to plan the placement of a building model and its surrounding components, such as playgrounds and lighting fixtures.

The following illustration shows a building model in a plan view with sun and shadow settings applied at two different angles. Notice that southeast is appropriate for a winter morning in the northern hemisphere.

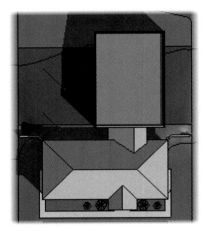

Sun from the southeast direction

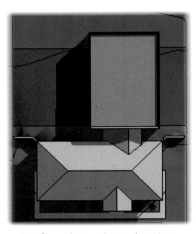

Sun from the northeast direction

Objectives

After completing this lesson, you will be able to:

- Describe sun and shadow settings.

- State the recommended practices for using sun and shadow settings.

- Use sun and shadow settings to create shadows of a building model.

Sun and Shadow Settings

The application of sun and shadow settings to the building model helps in the presentation and evaluation of a building design. You can view the effects of sun and shadows for a building model and its components in plan, elevation, section, and 3D views as a solar study in the form of frames. You can also export the solar study as snapshots in the form of an AVI file.

You apply sun and shadow settings by using the Graphic Display Options and the Sun and Shadows Settings dialog boxes. In the Graphic Display Options dialog box, you specify the direction of the sun, the intensity of sunlight and shadows, and a line style for silhouette edges. When you use the Sun and Shadows Settings dialog box, you can either use the default sun and shadow settings or create custom settings for a building model.

Using both the dialog boxes, you can apply sun and shadow settings to a view in any model graphics style except Wireframe. If there is no site object visible in a view, you can specify a ground plane on which the shadow will display.

The following illustration shows the direction of the sun and the resultant shadow cast by a building model in a 3D view.

Silhouette Edges

A silhouette style determines the display of the silhouette edges of walls and wall components, such as doors and windows. You use the Silhouette Style list in the Graphic Display Options dialog box to set a line style for silhouette edges. This dialog box can be accessed by selecting Graphic Display Options from the Shadows On/Off list on the View Control Bar. You can override a silhouette style to highlight the building edges even if shadows are applied to the entire building model.

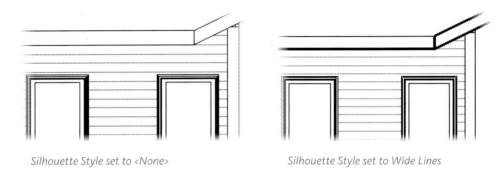

Silhouette Style set to <None>   *Silhouette Style set to Wide Lines*

Sun and Shadows Settings Dialog Box

You access the Sun and Shadows Settings dialog box by clicking [...] in the Graphic Display Options dialog box.

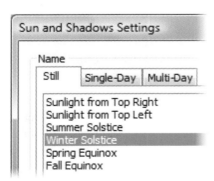

The following table describes the tabs in the Sun and Shadows Settings dialog box.

Tab	Description
Still	Specifies the effects of the sun and shadows on a building model for a particular date, time, and place. You can also specify the effects of the sun and shadows for a particular azimuth and altitude of the sun.
Single-Day	Specifies the effects of the sun and shadows on a building model for one complete day between specified time intervals.
Multi-Day	Specifies the effects of the sun and shadows on a building model between specified dates and time intervals.

Guidelines for Using Sun and Shadow Settings

The following recommended practices help you to use sun and shadow settings effectively.

Guidelines

- Create multiple sun and shadow settings that show shadows at equinox and solstice days or at morning, noon, and late afternoon. This helps you create a ready reference for sun and shadow settings that can be loaded into a project template. These settings are valuable in designing window locations and roof overhangs, which can have a significant impact on building energy profiles.

- Avoid using views for late afternoons and early mornings for presentations because during these times of the day, the sun casts dramatic and long shadows, which can completely darken a building facade. To represent long shadows, set the shadow intensity to a low value.

- Create an in-place family to represent trees for shadow studies because in Revit, landscaping objects and plantings do not cast shadows in plan views. Creating an in-place family is helpful when the shadows cast by large trees are an important factor in the design of a building.

Example

The following illustrations show how shadows are cast on a building model when custom settings are specified in the Sun and Shadows Settings dialog box. This setting enables you to avoid the darkening of a building facade.

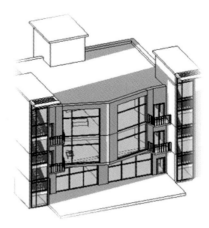

Sun and Shadows Settings dialog box with Building model with long shadows at low intensity custom settings

Exercise | Use Sun and Shadow Settings

In this exercise, you use sun and shadow settings to create shadows for different views and create a presentation sheet for the views.

You do the following:

You need to study the effect of sunlight on a building model at different times in a day and on different days in various months. You create a presentation sheet consisting of the views of the building model with sun and shadow settings applied to the building model.

- Create still shadows in the plan view.

- Create still shadows in elevation and 3D views.

- Create shadows for a single day.

- Create shadows for multiple days.

- Create a presentation sheet consisting of views.

The completed exercise

Create Still Shadows in the Plan View

1   Open *i_rac_essentials_sun_settings.rvt* or *m_rac_essentials_sun_settings.rvt*. The file opens in the Site view.
    Note: The illustrations for the metric dataset will be slightly different from those shown here. The completed exercise illustration may also vary.

2   Begin preparing a view to show sunlight penetration through windows on the south face of the building. Open the Ground Floor Shadow Study view.

3   On the View Control Bar, click Shadows Off > Graphic Display Options.

4   To specify the shadow settings, in the Graphic Display Options dialog box, under Sun and Shadows:

    • Select the Cast Shadows check box.
    • For Sun, enter **80**.
    • For Shadows, enter **50**.

    Note: You can also set the values for Sun and Shadows using the sliders.

5   Click [...] to the right of the Sun Position list.

6   To create a sun and shadow setting with a specific date, time, and place, in the Sun and Shadows Settings dialog box, under Name, Still tab:

    • Select Sun and Shadow Settings.
    • Click Duplicate.

7   In the Name dialog box:

    • For Name, enter **Ottawa PM**.
    • Click OK.

8   In the Sun and Shadows Settings dialog box:

    • Under Settings, click By Date, Time and Place.
    • Click [...] to the right of the Place field.

9   In the Manage Place and Locations dialog box:

- Select Ottawa, ON Canada from the City list.
- Select the Automatically Adjust Clock for Daylight Savings Changes check box.
- Click OK.

Note: Shadows are affected by the place that you select from the City list. For example, If you select a location in the southern hemisphere, the shadows will appear different from the illustrations.

10 In the Sun and Shadows Settings dialog box:

- For Date and Time, select today's date from the Date list. This setting affects the angle of shadows.
- For Date and Time, select 2:00 PM from the Time list. This setting affects the angle and length of shadows.
- Select the Ground Plane at Level check box.
- Select Ground Floor from the list below the Ground Plane at Level check box.

Note: The shadows are affected by the date and the time selected. Therefore, the shadows may appear different from the illustrations.

11 Click OK to close all open dialog boxes. In the resulting view, shadows are displayed. The length and angle of shadows varies with the location, date, and time.

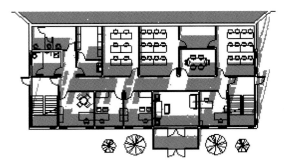

Note: The steps to specify the date, time, and place can be repeated for different months, dates, and times.

12 To adjust the view to change the shadow display, right-click in the view window. Click View Properties.

13 Move the Instance Properties dialog box to a side so that you can see the view window.

14   In the Instance Properties dialog box, under Extents, for View Range, click Edit to modify the cut plane of the view.

15   In the View Range dialog box, under Primary Range, for Cut Plane Offset, enter **7' 0"** (**2100** mm).

16   Click Apply to update the view window.

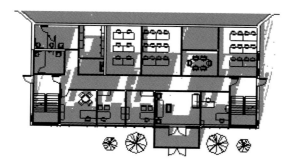

17   Click OK to close all open dialog boxes.
      Notice that in the plan view, shadows in the rooms at the top of the view are not accurate. This is because Revit shows shadows cast by the walls, with no ceiling or roof to obstruct sunlight.

Create Still Shadows in Elevation and 3D Views

1   Open the South elevation view.

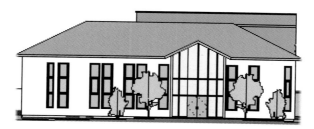

2   To apply sun and shadow settings to the South elevation view, click View tab > Graphics panel > dialog launcher to open the Graphic Display Options dialog box.

3   In the Graphic Display Options dialog box, under Sun and Shadows:
     • Select the Cast Shadows check box.
     • For Sun, enter **80**.
     • Verify that Shadows is set to **50**.

4   Open the Sun and Shadows Settings dialog box.

5   To make Ottawa PM the active sun and shadow setting, in the Sun and Shadows Settings
     dialog box:
     • Under Name, Still tab, select Ottawa PM.
     • Click OK.

6   Click OK to close the Graphic Display Options dialog box. Notice that shadows are displayed
     in the view.

7   Open the Front Perspective 3D view.

8   Apply the Ottawa PM sun and shadow settings to the 3D view.

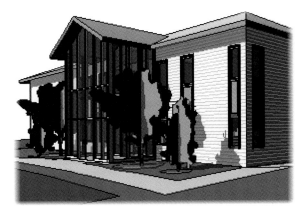

Create Shadows for a Single Day

1   To begin checking shadows over a period, open the South elevation view.

2   On the View Control Bar, click Shadows On > Graphic Display Options.

3   Open the Sun and Shadows Settings dialog box.

4   In the Sun and Shadows Settings dialog box:
   • Under Name, click the Single-Day tab.
   • Under Settings, click [...] to the right of the Place field.

5   In the Manage Place and Locations dialog box:
   • Verify that Ottawa, ON Canada is selected from the City list.
   • Click OK.

6   In the Sun and Shadows Settings dialog box, under Settings:
   • Select today's date from the Date list.
   • Verify that the Sunrise to Sunset check box is selected.
   • Select 30 Minutes from the Time Interval list.
   • Verify that the Ground Plane at Level check box is selected.
   • Select Ground Floor from the list below the Ground Plane at Level check box.

7   Click OK to close all open dialog boxes.

8   On the View Control Bar, click Shadows On > Preview Solar Study. The Options Bar displays controls to step through or play an animated sequence of frames for a whole day from dawn to dusk.

9   On the Options Bar, click Play. The view shows a series of shadow placements, one for each frame defined in the solar study.

Note: You can also export this solar study to an AVI file, by clicking application menu > Export > Animated Solar Study. This solar study is used for giving presentations to clients and/or government agencies.

Create Shadows for Multiple Days

1   Open the Graphic Display Options dialog box.

2   Open the Sun and Shadows Settings dialog box.

3   Under Name, click the Multi-Day tab.

4   Open the Manage Place and Locations dialog box.

5   In the Manage Place and Locations dialog box:
   - Verify that Ottawa, ON Canada is selected from the City list.
   - Click OK.

6   In the Sun and Shadows Settings dialog box, under Settings:
   - Select September 21, 2010 from the Date list on the right.
   - Select March 21, 2010 from the Date list on the left.
   - Select 2:00 PM from the Time box.
   - Select One Month from the Time Interval list. This generates 6 frames.
   - Select Ground Floor from the list below the Ground Plane at Level check box.

7   Click OK to close all open dialog boxes.

8   Click Preview Solar Study.

9   On the Options Bar, click Play to start the animated sequence of frames.

10   On the Options Bar, click Previous Frame two times to go to frame 4. The date will read June 21, 2010. This is the longest day of the year in the northern hemisphere. The sun is at its highest angle. Notice the shadows on the upper windows. The roof overhang protects them from unwanted solar gain.

11   On the Options Bar, click Next Frame two times to go to frame 6. The date will read August 21, 2008.

     This is late summer in the northern hemisphere, and even in a northern city such as Ottawa, unwanted solar gain can make rooms uncomfortably hot without air conditioning. Notice that the upper windows are no longer protected by the overhang. The lower floor windows are also exposed.

Create a Presentation Sheet Consisting of Views

1   Create a new sheet view.

2   In the Select a Titleblock dialog box:
   - Verify that Landscape Presentation is selected.
   - Click OK. A blank sheet opens in the view window.

3   In the view window:

- Drag the Ground Floor Shadow Study view on the sheet.
- Click to place the plan view in the upper-left corner of the sheet.

4   Place the South elevation and Front Perspective views on the presentation sheet. Arrange them from left to right, as shown.

Tip: Add the views one by one to the sheet.

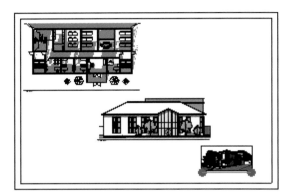

5   Close the file without saving changes.

Chapter Summary

Now that you have learned about sheets, titleblocks, revisions, renderings, sun and shadow settings, and walkthroughs, you can present your designs in many unique and creative ways.

In this chapter, you learned to:

- Create, modify, and specify print options for drawing sheets.
- Add and update titleblocks and edit titleblock families.
- Create revisions and then update the information in a revision table.
- Create renderings for building models.
- Create and export a walkthrough of a building model.
- Use sun and shadow settings in a building model.

Additional Resources

A variety of resources are available to help you get the most from your Autodesk® software. Whether you prefer instructor-led, self-paced, or online training, Autodesk has you covered.

For additional information, please refer to the files you downloaded that accompany this training guide.

- Learning Tools from Autodesk

- Autodesk Certification

- Autodesk Authorized Training Centers (ATC®)

- Autodesk Subscription

- Autodesk Communities

Learning Tools from Autodesk

Use your Autodesk software to its full potential. Whether you are a novice or an advanced user, Autodesk offers a robust portfolio of learning tools to help you perform ahead of the curve.

- Get hands-on experience with job-related exercises based on industry scenarios from Autodesk Official Training Guides, e-books, self-paced learning, and training videos.

- All materials are developed by Autodesk subject matter experts.

- Get exactly the training you need with learning tools designed to fit a wide range of skill levels and subject matter—from basic essentials to specialized, in-depth training on the capabilities of the latest Autodesk products.

- Access the most comprehensive set of Autodesk learning tools available anywhere: from your authorized partner, online, or at your local bookstore.

- To find out more, visit *http://www.autodesk.com/learningtools*.

Autodesk Certification

Demonstrate your experience with Autodesk software. Autodesk certifications are a reliable validation of your skills and knowledge. Demonstrate your software skills to prospective employers, accelerate your professional development, and enhance your reputation in your field.

Certification Benefits

- Rapid diagnostic feedback to assess your strengths and identify areas for improvement.

- An electronic certificate with a unique serial number.

- The right to use an official Autodesk Certification logo.

- The option to display your certification status in the Autodesk Certified Professionals database.

For more information:

Visit *www.autodesk.com/certification* to learn more and to take the next steps to get certified.

Autodesk Authorized Training Centers

Enhance your productivity and learn how to realize your ideas faster with Autodesk software. Get trained at an Autodesk Authorized Training Center (ATC) with hands-on, instructor-led classes to help you get the most from your Autodesk products. Autodesk has a global network of Authorized Training Centers that are carefully selected and monitored to ensure you receive high-quality, results- oriented learning. ATCs provide the best way for beginners and experts alike to get up to speed. The training helps you get the greatest return on your investment, faster, by building your knowledge in the areas you need the most. Many organizations provide training on our software, but only the educational institutions and private training providers recognized as ATC sites have met Autodesk's rigorous standards of excellence.

Find an Authorized Training Center

With over 2,000 ATCs in more than 90 countries around the world, there is probably one close to you. Visit the ATC locator at *www.autodesk.com/atc* to find an Autodesk Authorized Training Center near you. Look for ATC courses offered at *www.autodesk.com/atcevents*.

Many ATCs also offer end-user Certification testing. Locate a testing center near you at *www. autodesk.starttest.com.*

Autodesk Subscription

Autodesk® Subscription is a maintenance and support program that helps you minimize costs, increase productivity, and make the most of your Autodesk software investment. For an attractive annual fee, you receive any upgrades released during your Subscription term, as well as early access to product enhancements. Subscription also gives you flexible license terms, so you can run both current and previous versions (under certain conditions) and use the software on both home and office computers. In addition, Subscription gives you access to a variety of tools and information that save time and increase productivity, including web support direct from Autodesk, self-paced learning, and online license management.

- Autodesk Subscription offers a way to make software costs predictable. Whether a customer opts for a one-year subscription or a multiyear contract, the costs are known for the entire term of the contract.

- A complete library of interactive learning tools and high-quality, self-paced lessons help users increase their productivity and master new skills. These short lessons are available on demand and complement more in-depth training provided through Autodesk Authorized Training Centers.

- Autodesk Subscription makes managing software licenses easier. Customers have added flexibility to allow their employees to use their Subscription software—in the office or at home. Better yet, designers are entitled to run previous versions of the software concurrently with the latest release under certain conditions.

- Get what you need to stay productive. With web support, Autodesk support technicians provide answers to your installation, configuration, and troubleshooting questions. Web and email communications deliver support straight to your desktop.

- For more information, visit *www.autodesk.com/subscription.*

Autodesk User Communities

Autodesk customers can take advantage of free Autodesk software, self-paced tutorials, worldwide discussion groups and forums, job postings, and more. Become a member of an Autodesk Community today!

Note: *Free products are subject to the terms and conditions of the end-user license agreement that accompanies download of the software.*

Feedback

Autodesk understands the importance of offering you the best learning experience possible. If you have comments, suggestions, or general inquiries about Autodesk Learning, please contact us at *learningtools@autodesk.com.*

As a result of the feedback we receive from you, we hope to validate and append to our current research on how to create a better learning experience for our customers.

Useful Links

Learning Tools
www.autodesk.com/learningtools

Certification
www.autodesk.com/certification

Find an Authorized Training Center
www.autodesk.com/atc

Find an Authorized Training Center Course
www.autodesk.com/atcevents

Autodesk Store
www.store.autodesk.com

Communities
www.autodesk.com/community

Student Community
www.students.autodesk.com

Blogs
www.autodesk.com/blogs

Discussion Groups
www.discussion.autodesk.com

Index